Comparative Perspectives on the Rise of the Brazilian Novel

COMPARATIVE LITERATURE AND CULTURE

Series Editors
TIMOTHY MATHEWS AND FLORIAN MUSSGNUG

Comparative Literature and Culture explores new creative and critical perspectives on literature, art and culture. Contributions offer a comparative, cross-cultural and interdisciplinary focus, showcasing exploratory research in literary and cultural theory and history, material and visual cultures, and reception studies. The series is also interested in language-based research, particularly the changing role of national and minority languages and cultures, and includes within its publications the annual proceedings of the 'Hermes Consortium for Literary and Cultural Studies'.

Timothy Mathews is Emeritus Professor of French and Comparative Criticism, UCL.

Florian Mussgnug is Reader in Italian and Comparative Literature, UCL.

Comparative Perspectives on the Rise of the Brazilian Novel

Edited by Ana Cláudia Suriani da Silva
and Sandra Guardini Vasconcelos

UCLPRESS

First published in 2020 by
UCL Press
University College London
Gower Street
London WC1E 6BT

Available to download free: www.uclpress.co.uk

A CIP catalogue record for this book is available from The British Library.

ISBN: 978-1-78735-473-9 (Hbk)
ISBN: 978-1-78735-472-2 (Pbk)
ISBN: 978-1-78735-471-5 (PDF)
ISBN: 978-1-78735-474-6 (epub)
ISBN: 978-1-78735-475-3 (mobi)
DOI: https://doi.org/10.14324/111.9781787354715

Contents

List of Contributors vii

Introduction: A Novel Approach to the Rise of the Brazilian Novel 1
Sandra Guardini Vasconcelos and Ana Cláudia Suriani da Silva

1. *Misterios del Plata*: (Dis)Figuring History to Forge a Space for a Woman's Agency 26
   Rita Terezinha Schmidt
2. The Historical Significance of *Memórias de um sargento de milícias* 45
   Edu Teruki Otsuka
3. *A providência, recordação dos tempos coloniais* and the Novel in Brazil 63
   Marcus Vinicius Nogueira Soares
4. Maria Firmina dos Reis and the First Afro-Brazilian Novel 84
   Eduardo de Assis Duarte
5. 'A suspicious sound interrupted the gentle harmony': *Iracema* by José de Alencar 107
   Thiago Rhys Bezerra Cass
6. Displaced Experience and Magic Compromise 127
   Jorge de Almeida
7. Brazilian Landscape: A Study of *Inocência* 141
   Eduardo Vieira Martins
8. Silences and Voices of Slavery: *A escrava Isaura* and *Incidents in the Life of a Slave Girl* 161
   Heloisa Toller Gomes

9. The Construction of Pseudo-Modern Individuals in *Senhora* by José de Alencar 180
Maria Eulália Ramicelli

10. Maria Benedita Câmara Bormann's *Lésbia*: The Creation of the Woman Writer in Brazil 203
Margaret Anne Clarke

11. *O Ateneu:* A Singular Masterpiece about the Nineteenth-Century Civilizational Crisis 226
André Luiz Barros da Silva

12. *O aborto* and the Rise of Erotic Popular Print in Late Nineteenth-Century Brazil 239
Leonardo Mendes

13. Machado de Assis and the Novel 257
Sandra Guardini Vasconcelos

14. Capitu against the Elegiac Narrator 277
Ana Cláudia Suriani da Silva

15. On Moral and Financial Bankruptcy: Adultery and Financial Speculation in *A falência* by Júlia Lopes de Almeida 297
Cintia Kozonoi Vezzani

Index 317

List of Contributors

Jorge de Almeida holds a degree (1992) and a PhD (2000) in philosophy from the University of São Paulo (USP). He is an associate professor in the Department of Literary Theory and Comparative Literature at the same institution. He was a visiting professor at Freie Universität Berlin and Université Paris VIII. He has translated Theodor Adorno's works into Portuguese, is one of the editors of the collection *Pensamento alemão no século XX* (2013) and is the author of *Crítica dialética em Theodor Adorno: música e verdade nos anos vinte* (2007). At present, he is undertaking the research project 'Critical Theory and Literature: The Crisis of the Novel in the 1920s'.

Thiago Rhys Bezerra Cass is an assistant professor of English literature at the Federal University of Rio de Janeiro (UFRJ). A member of the International Association for the Study of Scottish Literatures since 2014, he is the author of two book-length studies on James Macpherson's *Ossian*: *Sombras no paraíso: dos* Poemas de Ossian *à prosa indianista de José de Alencar* (2013) and *Ossian: entre a epopeia e o romance* (forthcoming).

Margaret Anne Clarke graduated from the University of Liverpool with a PhD in twentieth-century Brazilian literature, which focused on the modernist and Catholic poet Jorge de Lima. Her research interests include comparative studies of lusophone literatures, specializing in two areas: revisionist studies of late nineteenth-century and twentieth-century novelists and poetry, and contemporary Brazilian digital culture and writing. She has published articles and book chapters in all these areas. She has worked at universities in the UK and in Brazil, including as visiting lecturer in comparative literature at the Federal University of Rio de Janeiro and most recently as senior lecturer in Portuguese at the University of Portsmouth.

Eduardo de Assis Duarte holds a PhD in literary theory and comparative literature (USP, 1991) and is a member of the Graduate Program in Literary Studies at the Federal University of Minas Gerais (UFMG) and of the Group of Interdisciplinary Studies of Alterity (Núcleo de Estudos Indisciplinares da Alteridade – NEIA). He is the author of *Jorge Amado: romance em tempo de utopia* (1996) and *Literatura, política, identidades* (2005) and editor of *Machado de Assis afrodescendente* (3rd edn, 2020). As coordinator of the collective research project 'Afro-descendants: Race/Ethnicity in Brazilian Culture', he has edited *Literatura e afrodescendência no Brasil: antologia crítica* (2nd edn, 2014, 4 volumes), *Literatura afro-brasileira: 100 autores do século XVIII ao XXI* (2nd edn, 2019), *Literatura afro-brasileira: abordagens na sala de aula* (2nd edn, 2019). He is also responsible for **literafro:** *The Portal for Afro-Brazilian Literature* (http://www.letras.ufmg.br/literafro).

Heloisa Toller Gomes received her PhD from the Pontifical Catholic University of Rio de Janeiro (PUC-RJ) in 1989 and was a Fulbright/LASPAU scholar at Howard University and Yale University. She taught literature at PUC-RJ and Rio de Janeiro State University (UERJ) and maintains a research affiliation with the Programa Avançado de Cultura Contemporânea (PACC–UFRJ), where she developed two postdoctoral projects: 'Postcolonialism, Ethnicity and Cultural Formations' and 'A Cartography of Coloniality: The African-Brazilian Case in Perspective'. Her most recent book is *As marcas da escravidão* (2009, 2nd edn). She has translated into Portuguese W. E. B. Du Bois' *The Souls of Black Folk*. Her publications include 'A problemática do arquivo nas Américas: espaços de tensão, pontos de encontro' (*Modos de arquivo*, 2018), 'Brasil e Estados Unidos: considerações sobre o tratamento discursivo da etnicidade, ontem e hoje' (*Literatura e voz subalterna*, 2016), 'Africanidade e território na inscrição (da escrita literária) brasileira' (*Africanidades e brasilidades*, 2014) and 'The Uniqueness of the Brazilian Case: A Challenge for Postcolonial Studies' (*Journal of Postcolonial Writing*, 2011). She is a member of the International Advisory Board of the *Journal of Postcolonial Writing* and participates in the GT/ANPOLL 'Relações Literárias Interamericanas'.

Eduardo Vieira Martins is an associate professor in the Department of Literary Theory and Comparative Literature at the University of São Paulo. In his PhD, published later as *A fonte subterrânea*, he discussed the critical texts of the Brazilian novelist José de Alencar, relating them to the handbooks of rhetoric and poetics that circulated in Brazil in the nineteenth century. His most recent research centres on the construction of the imagery of the *sertão* in nineteenth-century narratives. He was a visiting professor at Université Paris 8 and is an associate researcher at the Biblioteca Brasiliana Mindlin (BBM-USP). He was a member of the Editorial Board of *Literatura e Sociedade* (2016–17) and is a referee for several peer-reviewed journals.

Leonardo Mendes obtained his PhD in literary theory at the University of Texas at Austin. He is an associate professor at the State University of Rio de Janeiro (UERJ). He specializes in nineteenth-century Brazilian fiction, literary naturalism and pornographic literature. He has published *O retrato do imperador: negociação, sexualidade e romance naturalista no Brasil* (2000).

Edu Teruki Otsuka is an assistant professor in literary theory and comparative literature at the University of São Paulo. He is the author of *Marcas da catástrofe: experiência urbana e indústria cultural em Rubem Fonseca, João Gilberto Noll e Chico Buarque* (2001) and *Era no tempo do rei: atualidade das Memórias de um sargento de milícias* (2016).

Maria Eulália Ramicelli teaches British and American literature at the Federal University of São Paulo (UNIFESP). Her main research interests are the circulation of British fiction in nineteenth-century Brazil and the relationships between British and Brazilian fiction. She has published on various aspects of these research topics in Brazil and abroad.

Ana Cláudia Suriani da Silva is an associate professor in Brazilian studies at University College London (UCL). She works on Brazilian literature, book and press history with a focus on the works of Machado de Assis, prose fiction, the nineteenth-century press and fashion history. She has published articles and book chapters on the works of Machado de Assis, Artur Azevedo and Joseph Conrad and on the relationship between fashion, literature and the press. She is the author of *Machado de Assis's Philosopher or Dog? From Serial to Book Form* (2010). She has produced a genetic and critical edition of Machado de Assis's short story 'Linha reta e linha curva' (2003), a bilingual edition of *Queda que as mulheres têm para o tolos* (2008) and a hypertext edition of the serial version of *Quincas Borba* (with John Gledson, 2015) and co-edited multi-author volumes such as *The Foreign Political Press in Nineteenth-Century London: Politics from a Distance* (2017).

André Luiz Barros da Silva is an assistant professor of Brazilian literature at UNIFESP. He holds a post-doctorate in modern literatures from the University of São Paulo (USP) and a PhD from the State University of Rio de Janeiro (UERJ). He specializes in nineteenth-century Brazilian literature and eighteenth-century French literature (Rousseau, Diderot, Sade). He is the author of *Sensibilidade, coquetismo e libertinagem – a* Pamela *inglesa, as* Pamelas *francesas e as transformações éticas e estéticas no século* (2019) and the translator of *Novelas trágicas* (2018), an anthology of short stories from Sade's *Les crimes de l'amour* (1799).

His published articles include 'Estética e reconciliação em Machado de Assis e Raul Pompeia' (*Revista Tempo Brasileiro*, 2015), '*Jacques le fataliste*: dialogismo, antifinalismo, espinozismo e o desejo moderno' (*Lettres Françaises*, 2017), 'Literatura na margem: pensando o par centro/periferia entre literatura e estética' (*O Eixo e a Roda*, 2017) and 'Ecos de Luciano e dos romances antigos: certa recepção na França dos séculos XVII e XVIII' (*Caletroscópio*, 2018).

Rita Terezinha Schmidt has an MA and a PhD in literature from the University of Pittsburgh. She has taught at the Graduate Faculty of Literary and Linguistic Studies at the Federal University of Rio Grande do Sul, Brazil, and has been a researcher of the National Council of Research (CNPq) since 1992. She is a founding member of the task force 'Women in Literature' created in 1988 in a forum of the National Association of Graduate Studies and Research in Literature and Linguistics in Brazil and an elected member of the Gender Committee of the International Comparative Literature Association (ICLA). She has co-edited seven books on comparative literature, including the ebook *Sustainability: What Literature Can Do* (2015), in addition to several critical new editions of volumes of fiction and poetry by Brazilian women writers of the nineteenth century. She has contributed a chapter to the books *Episodes from a History of Undoing: The Heritage of Female Subversiveness* edited by Reghina Dascal (2012), *The Cambridge History of Latin American Women's Literature* edited by Eleana Rodríguez and Monica Szurmuck (2015), *Tropical Gothic in Literature and Culture: The Americas* edited by Justin Edwards and Sandra Guardini Vasconcelos (2016) and *Brazilian Literature as World Literature* edited by Eduardo Coutinho (2018). She is also the author of many articles published in Brazilian and international peer-reviewed journals, and of the monograph *Descentramentos/convergências: ensaios de crítica feminista* (2017).

Marcus Vinicius Nogueira Soares has a PhD in comparative literature from the State University of Rio de Janeiro (UERJ) and is an associate professor of Brazilian literature in the same institution. He is a member of the CNPq group 'The Belle Époque Culture and Literary Studies' (LABELLE), the author of *A crônica brasileira do século XIX: uma breve história* (2014) and co-author of '500 anos de ficção' in *Brasiliana da Biblioteca Nacional* (2002). Among other articles, he has published 'João do Rio e a nova esfera da crônica no século XX' (*Belle Époque*, 2016), 'A unidade romântica como crítica ao realismo oitocentista em *A pata da gazela*, de José de Alencar' (*José de Alencar*, 2015) and 'Literatura e música: o romance e a ópera no Brasil oitocentista' (*Atualidade da ópera*, 2012).

Sandra Guardini Vasconcelos is full professor of English and comparative literature at the University of São Paulo (USP). She has authored articles and chapters both in Brazil and abroad and has recently edited *Books and Periodicals in Brazil 1768–1930: A Transatlantic Perspective* with Ana Cláudia Suriani da Silva (2014) and *Tropical Gothic in Literature and Culture: The Americas* with Justin D. Edwards (2016). She is the curator of the João Guimarães Rosa Archive at the Institute for Brazilian Studies (University of São Paulo) and holds a CNPq research grant.

Cintia Kozonoi Vezzani is a PhD student at Northwestern University working on a dissertation entitled 'Shared Secrets, Public Lies: The Crisis of Marriage in Turn-of-the-Century Brazilian Literature', in which she is investigating the epistolary history of female adultery. From a comparative perspective, she is examining the circulation of epistolary and adultery novels between France, Portugal and Brazil in order to situate Brazilian literary production within a global dialogue about female sexuality. She is part of the inaugural group of Northwestern University students participating in the Dissertation Proposal Development (DPD) programme organized by the Social Science Research Council (SSRC) in collaboration with other American universities. With generous support from the Andrew W. Mellon Foundation and the Graduate School at Northwestern University, Vezzani has conducted research in Portugal, France, Germany and Brazil. She holds a BA from the University of São Paulo (USP) in French, Portuguese and Brazilian literature (2012), has been an exchange student at the Université Lumière Lyon 2 (2010–11) and was a member of the Northwestern Paris Program in Critical Theory (2018–19) in partnership with the Université Sorbonne Nouvelle – Paris 3.

Introduction: A Novel Approach to the Rise of the Brazilian Novel

Sandra Guardini Vasconcelos and Ana Cláudia Suriani da Silva

This volume explores the rise of the Brazilian novel in the nineteenth century from a comparative viewpoint, by bringing the emergence of the new genre in the spatiotemporal context of the formation of the new nation into conversation with European and North American models and traditions. It builds on research into comparative, postcolonial, world and national literatures, book history, gender studies, archival and editorial work on women writers and periodicals conducted in the last 40 years, and on the long history of scholarship on the formation of Brazilian literature, to present a comparative framework based on a systematic and empirical approach to the study of the novel. It applies that framework to the analysis of key nineteenth-century Brazilian novels, canonical and less well known, published during the period in which the forms and procedures of the novel were acclimatized as the genre was established and consolidated in Brazil.

The distinctive feature of this book is that it is conceived as an introduction to the nineteenth-century Brazilian novel from a comparative perspective, differing therefore from literary histories and monographs on specific authors or works. The selection of novels here, not intended to be comprehensive, includes a good number of non-canonical texts that have not yet been translated into English. Translation practices have perpetuated a Brazilian literary identity based exclusively on elite canonical works and publishers. José de Alencar's *Iracema* (1865, Chapter 5) and Visconde de Taunay's *Inocência* [*Innocencia*] (1872, Chapter 7) were already available to anglophone readers by the end of the nineteenth century.[1] Machado de Assis's novels (Chapters 13 and 14) now each have at least one translation into English and can be easily acquired in the United Kingdom and the United States. The absence of women's novels in English translation is remarkable but not surprising.[2]

Women's underrepresentation in Brazilian literary histories is the main reason why there is no English translation, so far as we could find out, of any nineteenth-century Brazilian novel by a woman, including the four examined in this book:[3] Juana Manso's *Misterios del Plata* [*Mysteries of the Plate River*] (1852, Chapter 1), Maria Firmina dos Reis's *Úrsula* (1859, Chapter 4), Maria Benedita Câmara Bormann's *Lésbia* (1884, Chapter 10) and Júlia Lopes de Almeida's *A falência* [*The Bankruptcy*] (1901, Chapter 15).[4]

The digitization of periodicals and rare editions by, for example, the Brazilian National Library, the Brasiliana José and Guita Mindlin Library and the Digital Library of Portuguese[5] has had a great impact on research not only of nineteenth-century Brazilian women's literary production but also of serial and sensational novels by male writers, such as Antônio Gonçalves Teixeira e Sousa's *A providência, recordação dos tempos coloniais* [*Providence, Remembrances of Colonial Times*] (1854, Chapter 3) and Alberto Figueiredo Pimentel's *O aborto* [*The Abortion*] (1893, Chapter 12). As Leonardo Mendes discusses in Chapter 12, traditional historiography disregarded smaller publishers and works that, though bestsellers at the time, fell outside canonical definitions of literature. In consequence, *A providência* and *O aborto* have had the same fate as the above-mentioned women's novels: virtually no reception until very recently, since they were not re-edited in the twentieth century and have not been translated into English.[6]

Much of the bibliography available in English which deals with Brazilian literature from a comparative perspective retains the focus on a very small number of nineteenth-century canonical novels, leaving works by the first Brazilian women and popular writers largely unexplored. *Cosmopolitan Desires: Global Modernity and World Literature in Latin America* by Mariano Siskind is concerned with the contemporary production and reproduction of discourses on globalization and the ways in which those discourses determine the imaginaries and their forms in late nineteenth-century novels, magical realism, above all, and modernism.[7] There are now a number of groundbreaking studies that undertake a comparison of the literatures and cultures of North, Central and South America, constituting the fairly new field of, as Earl Fitz calls it, 'Latin (and inter) American comparatism'.[8] These include Stephanie Merrim's *Logos and the Word: The Novel of Language and Linguistic Motivation in Grande Sertao: Veredas and Tres Tristes Tigres* and Judith Payne and Earl Fitz's *Ambiguity and Gender in the New Novel of Brazil and Spanish America: A Comparative Assessment*.[9] Both books focus on key narrative works that belong nevertheless to twentieth-century Latin American literatures. José de Alencar's *Sonhos d'ouro* [*Golden Wildflowers*] (1872), Machado de Assis's *Memórias póstumas de Brás Cubas* [*The Posthumous Memoirs of Brás Cubas*] (1881) and Aluísio Azevedo's *O coruja* [*The Owl*] (1885) have been examined in depth by Zephyr Frank in *Reading Rio de Janeiro: Literature and Society in the Nineteenth Century*.[10] His study explores the intersection between history and literature and engages closely with Roberto Schwarz's critical ideas, in order to show through these three novels how the *Bildungsroman* became acclimatized in Brazil.

What makes the present collection unique is the fact that its 15 chapters explore the links between themes, narrative paradigms, and techniques of nineteenth-century Brazilian, European and North American novels and the development of the Brazilian novel, covering a wide range of literary traditions and periods. They are in conversation with the different trends that characterized the rise of the novel in Brazil.

(Dis)placing and (De)centring Novels

This book examines how individual Brazilian novels negotiate their place in this process of the dissemination of the genre. This aim raises a few questions, which are worth addressing. How could a literary form arising in a specific historical context – that of the emergence of the European bourgeoisie and capitalism – travel and take root in other territories? How did it accommodate to its new cultural environment? How did it translate a new reality and different contents across linguistic boundaries? How and to what extent did it change in the face of new uses, new situations, in a new place and time? In order to answer these questions the notions of centre and periphery, (dis)placement and (de)centring, and the recent redefinition of 'comparative literature' deserve comment.

A field of investigation instituted in the nineteenth century, traditionally Eurocentric, comparative literature has been confronted with the need to redefine its principles and practices and to reinvent itself in view of the new challenges posed by the historical, political and cultural transformations that could be felt especially from the 1990s onwards. One of the first signposts of this reaction could be detected in a collection of essays organized by Charles Bernheimer and published in 1995. The editor identified a kind of unrest that seemed to lurk among the comparatists, whose field is by nature 'unstable, shifting, insecure, and self-critical'.[11] The crisis was not recent. Since at least 1958 René Wellek had diagnosed the precarious situation of this discipline that 'had not been able to establish a distinct subject matter and a specific methodology'.[12]

In the ensuing years, without forfeiting its emphasis on national and linguistic identities, the discipline strived to expand its horizons and embraced multiculturalism and identity politics in an effort to overcome some of its impasses. Some decades after Wellek's conclusions, the field still seemed to be grappling with dilemmas of definition. The perception of the gains and losses resulting from the diverse paths trodden in those days, as well as awareness of the urgent call to offer responses to the contemporary state of affairs, led Bernheimer to espouse 'a global broadening of perspective', a 'quality of dispossession', and to question 'centralizing authority', steps he believed to be essential to foster collaborative work among specialists in specific languages and literatures and to facilitate interface with complementary areas like anthropology, history and sociology, among others. According to him, they would be demands to meet in order to devise 'new disciplinary configurations with a multicultural comparative outlook'.[13]

This position challenged some of the postulates on which comparative literature was erected, and posited a displacement of some of its axes, calling for a reconceptualization of the foundations sustaining the critical practice of comparatists – our understanding of what is literature, the meaning of the aesthetic, the concept of national, the very nature of the discipline and of the field of study. Concurrently, it interrogated the well-known dichotomy between centre and periphery, suggesting that centres are multiple, circumstantial and mobile and, therefore, inviting a re-examination of the relations that comparative literature has established among cultures and literatures and reconsideration of the categories that have guided our work.

Taking the notions of displacement and decentring, this book explores the possibilities opened by understanding the novel as a transnational genre, that is, as a genre that, though rooted in specific contexts, has from its origins spread across national borders. We ponder the role the novel played in this process of blurring territorial limits from its emergence in England in the early eighteenth century to the first decades of the twentieth. These temporal demarcations frame the long period of its formation and consolidation as the nineteenth century's hegemonic literary form, the form that accompanied the formation of the nation-state and the expansion of capitalism, until the novel experienced its first significant crisis with the avant-garde and modernism, when it came to incorporate the crisis of realism into its very form.

To retrace this trajectory, it seems useful to remark that 'centre', as a matter of common sense, is a spatial and eminently relational concept, which entails its opposite, that which is not the centre or is not at the centre; or that which can only be defined in contraposition to what is not the centre. Therefore, this is a concept that depends on a standpoint, on a place or situation from which relations are defined. The provisional relational nature of this political, economic, cultural and symbolic space can be illustrated by referring to a capital that could be qualified as 'ex-centric' or 'margino-centric'. A small colonial village since its foundation, Rio de Janeiro was elevated to the status of seat of the Portuguese Empire between 1808 and 1821, before becoming the capital of independent Brazil, without losing its double condition of centre in relation to the Brazilian provinces and of periphery in relation to the European metropolises. This reversibility and provisionality introduce, thus, another dimension, now temporal and historical, to the spatiality that the notion of centre suggests and entails.

Centre, centres, therefore. The recognition of the plural nature of this concept has brought about in the contemporary debate about comparative literature the need to confront what was deemed to be the Eurocentric bent of the discipline and has led some theorists and critics, mainly over the last decade, to retrieve the concept of *Weltliteratur*. Initially proposed by Goethe in 1827, this concept has been interpreted differently over time, but always as some kind of counterpoint to national literatures. Discussion of it was rekindled with the publication in 2000 of 'Conjectures on World Literature' in the *New Left Review*: Franco Moretti retrieved Goethe's concept as emblem of the yearning for a world in which the encounter of writers and their works might be possible, and as a category that would supersede those of nations and civilizations. According to Moretti, a return to the old ambition of *Weltliteratur* was a possible response to the awareness that 'the literature around us is now unmistakably a planetary system'.[14] The problem, for him, resided less in *what* should be done than in *how* to undertake this task, in the face of the expansion of the field of investigation and the impossibility of dealing with the superabundance of texts, authors, languages and cultures that literary production and the very horizon of comparative literature demand us to engage with. Provocatively, Moretti took issue with many of the critical positions and interpretative schemes that predominated in the American academy, brandishing arguments against close reading (that legacy of New Criticism), against the limited dimensions of the canon and against the permanence of national borders in comparative studies. The following are just a few of the ideas central to his argumentation. Firstly, there is a questioning of the very possibility of renewal of the concept of world literature, which would only be justifiable if it worked as 'a thorn in the side, a permanent intellectual challenge to national literatures – especially the local literature'.[15] In Moretti's assessment, the project of comparative literature has not met the expectations it has raised, owing to its intellectual modesty and circumscription to Western Europe.

Moretti's second principle lies in the observation that 'world literature is not an object, it's a *problem*, and a problem that asks for a new critical method'.[16] In an openly disparaging manner, he calls 'close reading' into question as a way of reading par excellence of 'an extremely small canon', and as such incapable of dealing with a much broader and renewed literary history. Instead, Moretti argues for 'distant reading', based on a methodology deriving from the controversial import of the quantitative methods of the social and biological sciences, to produce 'graphs, maps, and trees [that] place the literary field literally in front of our eyes'.[17] 'Distance', believes Moretti, 'is a *condition of knowledge*: it allows you to focus on units that are much smaller or much larger than the text: devices, themes, tropes – or genres and systems.'[18]

The responses to Moretti were not late in coming. This is not the place to reproduce the heated debate that ensued, took up several issues of *New Left Review* and extended to other publications, developing into a polemics that foregrounded conflicting interpretations of the meaning and scope of terms such as 'literature' and 'world', disparate visions about the objects and modalities of reading, and contestations of the centrality of the novel, the genre privileged by Moretti.[19] David Damrosch, for instance, suggested the expansion of comparative literature beyond its European foundations so that the world would become its foster home. He thought it necessary to understand world literature not as a predetermined canon, but as a mode of circulating and reading texts, which would return the work of the comparatist to the confines of the possible. In his words:

> I take world literature to encompass all literary works that circulate beyond their culture of origin, either in translation or in their original language … a work only has an effective life as world literature whenever, and wherever, it is actively present within a literary system beyond that of its original culture.[20]

Damrosch also voiced another disagreement with Moretti, in his defence of intensive reading, more or less along the lines of Auerbach, as a means to reinscribe the works of world literature in an elliptic space to be created between the source culture and the receiving culture:

> The receiving culture can use the foreign material in all sorts of ways: as a positive model for the future development of its own tradition; as a negative case of a primitive, or decadent, strand that must be avoided or rooted out at home; or, more neutrally, as an image of radical otherness against which the home tradition can more clearly be defined.[21]

The responses to Moretti also included accusations against his 'Anglo-globalism', a phrase coined by Jonathan Arac to refer to what he considered to be a stiffening of the core and periphery categories, the privileging of the English language as mediator ('the crucial enabling medium', 'the global language of exchange and information') and Moretti's neglect of the need to master other languages ('criticism deals concretely with the language of texts') in order to understand local narrative voices and to study the world evolution of the novel.[22] If much of this criticism of an essay and argument rife with traps of various orders is well founded, at least two merits cannot be denied to Moretti. Aware that world literature is a *problem*, as he puts it, Moretti suggests that collaborative work may be a way out of this critical bind. On the other hand, the reminder that the literary world system is one and unequal should continue to make us reflect on the impasses and limitations of the concept of world literature, which replicates, at the level of literary forms and in the study of the relations between different literatures, the inequalities that characterize one's place in the real world. The World Republic of Letters, to use the phrase Pascale Casanova has put back in circulation,[23] is also characterized by power relations and depends, as she demonstrates, on instances of consecration that were or are still situated in the metropolitan centres – be they London, Paris or New York.

The tensions that have always pervaded the field of comparative literature are still active, maybe in new configurations, and have resurfaced in the present context of globalization: ways of reading, the relations between core and periphery, national literatures and world literature, local and universal,[24] Claudio Guillén's 'lo uno y lo diverso' [the one and the many].[25]

Fredric Jameson's contribution to the debate has offered a very lucid treatment of this issue, or cluster of issues, which entails confronting the asymmetries produced by the combined and uneven development of the global order. Jameson has often dealt with the topic of world literature in the context of globalization by means of a dialectic reading of problems that are simultaneously literary and historical, or political. On the one hand, he does not overlook the fact that the communicational dimension of the concept of globalization allows the celebration of cultural difference, once 'suddenly all cultures around the world are placed in tolerant contact with each other in a kind of immense cultural pluralism which it would be very difficult not to welcome'.[26] He notes the emergence of 'a whole immense range of groups, races, genders, ethnicities, into the speech of the public sphere; a falling away of those structures that condemned whole segments of the population to silence and to subalternity'.[27] On the other hand, he remarks, from an economic perspective there is very little to celebrate, since globalization has produced 'pictures of standardization on an unparalleled new scale; of forced integration as well, into a world-system'. As the cultural and the economic spheres are not autonomous, they need to be dialectically related; with the projection of the economic axis on to the cultural, what we shall witness is the 'worldwide Americanization or standardization of culture, the destruction of local differences, the massification of all the peoples on the planet'.[28]

The spirit of the new times, as Tariq Ali denounces elsewhere, enables us to enjoy the same junk food, the same junk culture and the same junk novels from New York to Beijing, via Moscow and Vladivostok.[29] Out of this picture there emerges, thus, 'a kind of global culture', whose successful productions often supplant local ones and end up erasing the differences between core and margins. In this hypothetically free market, there seem to be no barriers to circulation, be that of goods, people or literary texts. Under this purported freedom, globalization conceals what it truly is – 'a structure of inequalities' – in the apt description of Aijaz Ahmad.[30] These critiques are very helpful as necessary antidotes against the pitfalls of globalization and the danger of forgetting that power relations remain actively and forcefully at work in a world only apparently multicultural and globalized.

In a lecture given at Duke University in 2008, on the occasion of Norway's awarding him the Holberg International Memorial Prize, Jameson drew attention to the tensions that pervade world literature by bringing back on the agenda the issue of the nations and the relation of national literatures to each other as an inescapable dimension of the problem. Intertwining world literature, nation, national culture and literary value in an exposition that tried to address the contradictions inherent in each of these controversial concepts, Jameson makes a fruitful contribution to help us think about the contemporary cultural situation, as well as the impasses that yet prevail in the field of comparative literature. He reminds us that nation-states have not disappeared in times of globalization and are one of its essential components;[31] in his words, the national is pre-eminently the place of the dialectical union of opposites: it is the space of xenophobia, of fanaticism, of the most abominable forms of ethnic cleansing, yet it is also a collective space, of communal spirit and of solidarity. It is the ideological argument used to justify the most unjustifiable actions, but it is also one of the dimensions of our existential experience.

To address this dialectical ambivalence, as well as the controversial problem of terms like 'nation', 'national' and 'nationalism' as synonymous with collectivity, Jameson proposes the notion of *national situation*, which, he argues, makes Goethe's concept of world literature more coherent and useful, once the latter refers not to a collection of works and canonical, universal authors but to the emergence of institutions of cultural communication (such as the famous nineteenth-century periodicals) that enable foreigners to approach the national situation of one country, including its literary and intellectual situation, the current debates, concepts, literary forms, all of which confront the dilemmas and contradictions of that particular national situation. We should then be engaged no longer with a classic or a universal literature, but with the 'complex contact between histories and concrete historical situations'.[32] According to Jameson, there emerge out of this contact the radical singularity and the concrete difference of each of these situations, rather than a vision of a teleological pathway to modernity which defines some situations as more advanced and others as less so. Each situation is unique and specific, that is, uniquely national. Rather than taking world literature to be a realm in which works share the same universal values, he prefers to posit it as 'a space and site of struggle, of competition and opposition'.[33] This struggle may take the form, for example, of the literary struggle between big-power languages and small-power languages, or of the control of institutions of translation and transmission that regulate this struggle.

From a dialectical perspective, he finally argues, world literature should be understood in terms of the relations between different national productions and, therefore, in terms of both difference and identity, of both universality and particularity. Local, singular and universal are reversible categories, which need to be treated dialectically; the same is true of the disjunction between domestic and foreign, or between individual and collective, without collapsing one into the other. Jameson concludes, thus, that world literature is not an already existing pantheon, or an imaginary museum to which new masterpieces are added every day. It is, rather, a concept that must include the operation not only of radical difference and opposition, but also of dialectical ambivalence, of unevenness and canonical inequality. It is, above all, an ongoing problem that calls for displacement and raises questions that cannot yet be answered, such as: 'how do differences relate, how can nationality be universal, how can global multiplicity be imagined without a center?'[34]

Generally speaking, this is the operation the novel genre performed in the nineteenth century. Though an important instrument in the different processes of nation- and identity-building, from its origins the novel challenged real and imaginary borders and, through transmigration and transculturation, questioned what was national and what was foreign, what was local and what was universal. Any opposition between the national and the global is, therefore, a false problem, since it only makes sense to think of the novel – and literature – with regard to those networks and relations we participate in always from a national situation, to retrieve Jameson's idea. As part of the world system, countries – or national situations – do not occupy equal positions in this larger totality.[35] By the same token, their systems of social relations – a subject matter of great relevance to novels – can hardly be described as equal either. The same could be said about literary traditions or systems.

The Novel as an Inter/transnational Genre

Bearing in mind, then, the precariousness and state of permanent crisis that seem to characterize comparative literature[36] and the impasses entailed in the concept and in the practice of world literature, it would appear to be appropriate to go on to examine some aspects of the theory and history of the novel, a subject that lends itself to problematizing many of the issues brought up so far.

A brief theoretical digression will, hopefully, justify the centrality of the novel in this debate. Open, contingent and multiform, without crystallized conventions, the novel has always shown an exceptional capacity to work with the materials at its disposal, which has over time enabled it to be reinvented in the face of each new challenge, each new historical situation. Since its rise in the eighteenth century, the modern novel has shaped in its form the historical experience of the problematic relationship between individual and society, has established a close relation with reality and has focused on the socio-historical processes, emphases and subject matter that have enabled it, in the words of Michael McKeon, to 'display both the continuity of an integral entity and, within that continuity, the discontinuity that confirms its existence over time and space, its capacity to change without changing into something else'.[37]

The novel's relation to spatiality is intrinsic to the genre. In it space has constituted the concrete ground wherein the succession of human events is rooted, with a decisive bearing on the characters' fate and the development of the plot. Robinson Crusoe's island in Daniel Defoe, the estates and manors in Jane Austen's novels, Honoré de Balzac's Paris, Joseph Conrad's sea, James Joyce's Dublin, the pampas in Juana Manso (Chapter 1), the backlands in Visconde de Taunay (Chapter 7), and Rio de Janeiro in the works of Manuel Antônio de Almeida (Chapter 2) and Machado de Assis (Chapters 13 and 14) – these and other places in different novels acquire very precise contours and define individual trajectories as they assume a considerable concreteness and play a central role in the plotline and in the set-up and development of the personal and social relations thematized in the narrative. Hence the relevance of place to the genre, the displacement and mobility of characters across different spaces enacting specific historical experiences – exclusion, borders, colonialism, otherness, nationalism. Fictional space, geographical space and historical space intersect, overlap and establish internal relations that the genre incorporates as a compositional element inherent to its form.

The appropriation of the novel by different national projects, which justified Franco Moretti's description of the novel 'as the symbolic form of the nation-state',[38] and Doris Sommer's reading the nineteenth-century Latin-American novels as foundational fictions – an intersection of romance and the allegorical construction of the nation[39] – should not conceal the international vocation of the genre, one that has never been constrained by borders and has acclimatized in very diverse parts of the world, benefiting from its formal and often unconventional freedom, and from its formation and consolidation in the wake of the world expansion of trade and capitalism.

Even if, in art, genres correspond to universals, the system of conventions and minimal rules that regulate the novel has arisen from a long historical process and has never worked as a straitjacket that has inhibited its renewal or prevented ruptures or formal innovation. Its potential, its incompleteness, a form always in the making, as Bakhtin puts it,[40] have enabled the novel to be transplanted to very diverse literary traditions as beneficiary of an unprecedented process of dissemination promoted by the democratization of reading, the spread of libraries and circulating libraries and the expansion of the international book trade. Thus, the eighteenth- and nineteenth-century novel enjoyed a very significant circulation and development as a result of the exchanges, translations, imitations and reverberations that characterized its diffusion on the European continent. Although the pace of the development and affirmation of the genre was uneven, themes, narrative paradigms and ideas, as well as formal procedures, travelled and took root in different European countries and further afield.

Since its inception, the novel has crossed borders and travelled to different corners of the globe. The pace of the development of the genre in different countries was uneven, but themes and technical devices made their way across boundaries, found fertile soil and germinated in local works, in a movement of cross-fertilization unprecedented in the history of literature. The novel feeds the novel, argues Alain Montandon,[41] explaining the to and fro and the ramifications of different narrative forms on European soil – sea fiction and adventures, the picaresque, the epistolary novel, the *Bildungsroman* and novel of education, the sentimental novel – and their huge popularity in France, Britain, Germany and elsewhere.

The paths were multiple and the novelistic net stretched its mesh in several directions, acclimatizing to the particularities of each country, in an incessant search for and discovery of new forms, themes and narrative modes. Characters journeyed around the world; plots and models were transformed by geographical displacements and by their appropriation by different literary traditions. The novel's itinerancy was not merely thematic – as in the roams of a Quixote or a Robinson Crusoe – for as a form it flaunts a 'poetic story', that is, 'one of cross-cultural and supranational transit, translation, and appropriation'.[42] Through transmigration and transculturation, the novel has challenged what constitutes a polity or nation and what is internal or foreign to these boundaries. The most symptomatic evidence of this porousness are certainly the intersections, the mutual appropriations and interactions, that have always characterized the genre – as hybrid, mixed, mimetic and cosmopolitan par excellence.

If the association between novel, capitalism, and nation made it possible for the genre to be taken as a vehicle for projects of nation-building, its international circulation enabled Franco Moretti to formulate the proposal of a literary geography – the study not of space in literature, but of literature in space. The last essay in his *Atlas of the European Novel* – entitled 'Narrative Markets' – is an investigation of the novel as a migratory form, which had Great Britain and France – the two narrative superpowers of the nineteenth century – as the centres of production and export of fiction to the rest of Europe. With that move, he tried to erase national frontiers and to reinscribe the novel in space – no longer that demarcated by borders, but one that is transnational in nature.[43] 'This most European of forms',[44] which resulted from the constant and very effective literary and cultural exchanges across the English Channel during the eighteenth and nineteenth centuries, was forged by the two countries that exercised the central political and economic role in the 'transformation of the world between 1789 and 1848'.[45] The novel may have been an 'inter-national invention'[46] initially, but its transnational calling did not take long to transpire.

With these central tenets, we take genre to be not a constraint but a frame against which to measure the solutions Brazilian novelists came up with to tackle the problems that were presented to them, while also challenging the notion of a purely nationally based literary formation. Contrary to views current even today, one needs to complicate the idea that in the nineteenth century there was mere adaptation of 'imported European ideas and artistic practices' to the new environment, as Eduardo Coutinho would have it, in his introduction to *Brazilian Literature as World Literature*.[47] There was never a mere accommodation of foreign models; instead novelists wrestled with the local matter they had on their hands in order to try to shape it, while looking to those models and to the context around them. So, when one moves the focus from the geography of Europe, with its internal asymmetries – we are thinking here of Moretti's literary geography and the imbalances he points to in his *Atlas* – one needs to consider other disparities pertaining to the specific situation of Brazil and the Brazilian novel in relation to the more global historical and literary context, which Moretti describes as 'one and unequal'.[48]

The Brazilian Case

Compared with its metropolitan counterpart, the novel was a latecomer in a country that only became independent in 1822 and where censorship had prevented unimpeded and uncontrolled access to printed matter in general until not long before.

In the course of their dissemination around the world, novels reached Rio de Janeiro harbour in the early nineteenth century, carrying within them the accumulation of their already long history. Filling the stacks of the newly opened bookshops and circulating libraries, they became part of the cultural landscape of the capital of the new empire.[49] Thus, not only were they made available to the common reader, as countless newspaper advertisements attest, but they came to be an important staple for the writers engaged in creating a national literature. Thus, the statement that 'the novel had existed in Brazil before there were any Brazilian novelists'[50] should come as no surprise. Novels had been circulating on Brazilian territory long before the first Brazilian novel was published, in 1843 (*O filho do pescador*, by Teixeira e Sousa).[51]

From 1808 on, a passer-by who walked the streets of Rio de Janeiro, or a reader whose eyes were caught by the adverts in the newspapers starting to circulate in that town, would have a direct experience of the consequences of the hegemony just referred to. European novels, mostly French and British, became increasingly available in Rio from the first decades of the nineteenth century, especially after the suspension of censorship in 1821, and soon spread to other provinces of the Empire. For rental or sale in the apothecaries and bookshops, or on loan in the circulating libraries of the capital, were French, British and Portuguese novels, by writers famous and anonymous; a medley of eighteenth- and nineteenth-century works, feuilletons, historical, gothic, sentimental novels, novels of adventure – in sum, a little bit of everything that had been produced in Europe over the previous century and a half. The adverts and catalogues give evidence of what Brazilian critic Marlyse Meyer has described as a 'seaquake of novels that overflowed from the English Channel', a true 'Internationale Romancière'.[52] So, rather than a reduced canon, we find a great assortment of titles and authors, from the very well known to the minor or forgotten. The coexistence in the same cultural space of works from different literary traditions and periods produces a very interesting phenomenon, one we could explain as a kind of temporal compression, through bringing together novels produced in Europe over a long stretch of time. This almost simultaneous presence in the same space of such variety challenges the proverbial laggardness of Brazilian culture, since it enabled the circulation of a remarkable repertoire of themes, forms, techniques and procedures that became available to any apprentice Brazilian novelist. In other words, these came to be integrated into a literary system still in the making, as part of the amalgam of European models that Brazilian writers could negotiate, incorporate, renew, recreate, translate or refute.

As a form that is known to be, alongside the essay, 'the only genre to have emerged under the conditions of epistemological and historiographic self-consciousness that characterize the modern period',[53] the novel has been identified with modernity itself.[54] This modernity entered the Brazilian ports and was gradually assimilated into Brazilians' imagination. This movement in space also entailed a temporal displacement, which confronted two uneven and combined temporalities – the developed centre, already bourgeois and industrialized (notwithstanding its internal asymmetries), and the peripheral country, newly out of colonial rule and facing its construction as a nation. In this process, what Machado de Assis described as 'external influx'[55] was integral to the constitution of Brazilian literature, which a critic has characterized as the 'permanent admixture of European tradition and the discoveries about Brazil'.[56]

When asked once what the Argentinian tradition might be, Jorge Luis Borges answered that 'our tradition is the whole of Western culture', a claim that came with the suggestion that one can and should get hold of all the European themes, use them fearlessly and irreverently, and the results will be fruitful.[57] The European repertoire should be meddled with and transformed upon entering a new literary landscape. In the relationship between two or more literary traditions, what matters is to examine how a writer uses and explores texts and techniques that have become part of a shared archive, which is then drawn upon to produce new meanings in the new environment, and not mere imitation or reproduction of the so-called original. One's models need to be submitted to a critical check whereby dominant traditions are evaluated against one's own historical experience: in the case of Brazil a uniqueness that 'lay in its formation as part of the world system of capital, its *historical specificity* as a slave-owning economy structurally integrated with the liberal order of international trade'.[58] The Brazilian novel relativizes the forms and concepts of the European tradition in light of the Brazilian milieu and imposes on them the inflections of a particular history. This specificity the Brazilian critic Antonio Candido described thus in an interview:

> If one of our [Latin American] literatures claimed it wants to be European, it would be lost. The movement should state it has nothing to do with Europe: I am a Brazilian writer, I sing the Indian. And in fact he sings him in Italian stanzas, or imitating Chateaubriand's poetic prose. What I would like to show is that the literary process, in a world ruled by the interdependency of all peoples, encompasses both the cosmopolitan point of view and the local one. … I believe we need to perceive a dialectical movement, which occurs in our history, between the local and the universal.[59]

This volume is an attempt to reread and reconceptualize the rise of the novel in Brazil, in both a literary and a social sense, from a comparative perspective. If on one hand Antonio Candido has posited that the novel was 'a true instrument of exploration and discovery of the country',[60] he has also claimed that 'to study Brazilian literature is to study comparative literature'.[61] He has described Brazilian literature as 'a synthesis of particularistic and universalist trends',[62] as the essays in this collection demonstrate. They explore how Brazilian novels and novelists both inhabited and challenged the literary space embodied in the concept of 'world literature', and how forms were 'brought into being (and often into collision, with other, pre-existing forms)'.[63] Their purpose is to investigate the 'transformations that aesthetic forms undergo when they cross cultural boundaries'.[64] The assemblage of these essays intends to underscore the participation of local forms in the international culture of the novel.

The Chapters

The chapters that follow cover a long period in the history of the novel in Brazil, from its rise in the 1830s and 1840s to its fully fledged formation in the first decades of the twentieth century. The variety of themes, formal features and solutions novelists mobilized and the conversations they engaged in with their foreign counterparts are evinced in each one of them. They show how the consolidation of the genre in the country was the result of the novelists' exploration of all the possibilities afforded to them by a form that had a long history in Europe, and of their transformation of the novelistic paradigms they had access to. Focusing on the urban milieu or probing the further regions of the country, covering a wide range of topics, Brazilian novelists deployed the resources of the gothic, the historical novel, melodrama, autobiography, romance, and borrowed from the repertoire of a number of different literary traditions, in order to tell stories about national identity, slavery, the predicaments and plights of women, the indigenous population, in their endeavour to configure the tensions and contradictions that pervaded Brazilian society. The social dynamic, interpersonal relationships, issues of individual experience and subjectivity, love and marriage, and money are all submitted to critical evaluation against the background of a slaveholding nation where liberal ideas find no correspondence with everyday experience. In its own way, each novel under scrutiny has made a significant contribution to the understanding of Brazil's place in world literature.

The sequence of chapters follows the chronological order of publication in serial or book form of the works discussed. We have chosen this more traditional organization, rather than trying to group chapters according to common themes, because the intersections between the novels are multiple. Moreover, this arrangement highlights, even with this small sample of novels, the need to reassess Brazilian literary historiography in the light of the several works by less-known authors, both male and female, only recently (re)discovered.

The first chapter centres on the understudied historical novel *Misterios del Plata*, published in instalments by the Rio-based Argentinian writer Juana Manso in the women's periodical *O Jornal das Senhoras* in 1852. The events narrated are not strictly speaking part of Brazilian history. Yet, the novel was published in Portuguese in Rio de Janeiro's local press, which allows us to claim it as part of the Brazilian literary system. Rita Terezinha Schmidt argues that, although the prologue makes reference to the founder of the historical novel, Walter Scott, as well as to Eugène Sue's *Les mystères de Paris* [*The Mysteries of Paris*] (1842–3), Manso refuses subservience to any European literary model. *Misterios del Plata* deviates from the staple romantic love plot, traditionally attributed to women's writing, by rewriting the relationship of woman and nation in a drama of nation-building.

The two other works traditionally defined as historical novels which are examined here are Antônio Gonçalves Teixeira e Sousa's *A providência, recordação dos tempos coloniais* [*The Providence, Remembrances of Colonial Times*] and José de Alencar's *Iracema*. Originally published in the newspaper *Correio Mercantil* in 1854, *A providência* is Teixeira e Sousa's fourth work of historical fiction and his sixth and last novel. In Chapter 3, Marcus Vinicius Nogueira Soares argues that *A providência* is in fact a blend of different fictional traditions. Besides its connection with the historical novel, it also employs a theological diction, associated with the sermon, as may be noticed in the articulation between the epigraphs and the chapters they introduce. According to Thiago Rhys Bezerra Cass, *Iracema* (1865), examined in Chapter 5, also deviates from the historical novel. Alencar's work has been consistently read as an allegory of racial and/or cultural conciliation, following the model of Alencar's first Indigenist novel, *O guarani* [*The Guarany*] (1857), and overcoming the themes of interdiction and sterility that had previously defined novelistic renderings of interracial love in the New World, such as René de Chateaubriand's *Atala* (1801) and James Fenimore Cooper's *The Last of the Mohicans* (1826). Cass argues that, by presenting *Iracema* as a piece of primitive poetry, reminiscent of *Ossian*, Alencar produced a novel whose monologism ceases to demarcate the difference between European and Indian voices. Its overarching cadences and tropes efface the conflict occasioned by the colonial encounter.

The abolitionist novel is represented in this book by Maria Firmina dos Reis's *Úrsula* (1859) and Bernardo Guimarães's *A escrava Isaura*

[*Isaura the Slave Girl*] (1875), in Chapters 4 and 8, respectively. *Úrsula* has until very recently been largely ignored by Brazilian literary historiography, although it is the first novel by an Afro-descendant writer in Brazilian literature and the first abolitionist novel written in Brazil. *A escrava Isaura* is a much more well-known work and has for long been part of the Brazilian literary canon. Read together, the books expose two contrasting points of view on enslavement as well as the ambiguous, blurred lines that separate fiction and non-fiction. Both novels are here compared to slave narratives of other contemporary traditions: *Úrsula* to Mahomah Gardo Baquaqua's autobiography (1854) and Harriet E. Wilson's autobiographical novel *Our Nig* (1859); *A escrava Isaura* to Linda Brent's *Incidents in the Life of a Slave Girl* (1861).

The romanticization of the landscape and human types of the interior of Brazil is discussed in Eduardo Vieira Martins' chapter on *Inocência* (1872) by Alfredo d'Escragnolle Taunay. Written at a time when romantic aesthetics were beginning to decline and trust in the powers of the creative imagination were yielding to the cult of observation, Taunay sought to fictionalize the interior of Brazil through established tropes of the nineteenth-century novel. In Chapter 7, Martins examines the role of quotations from works of the Western tradition, particularly Bernardin de Saint-Pierre's *Paul et Virginie* [*Paul and Virginia*] (1787) in the construction of a rural idyll amid the American scenery, articulating the tragic fate of this idyll's protagonists with a tale of unhappy love much appreciated by readers at the time.

Chapters 2, 6, 9, 10 and 11 deal with the problematic development of the depiction of experience in Brazilian literature. Edu Teruki Otsuka's chapter on Manuel Antônio de Almeida's *Memórias de um sargento de milícias* [*Memoirs of a Militia Sergeant*] (1852–3) departs from Antonio Candido's classic essay, 'Dialect of Malandroism', to examine the disparity between the individualistic and liberal values of the European novel and the asymmetrical relations between the free lower classes and those representing the judicial and police systems.[65] The acclimatization of European forms transforms the Spanish *pícaro* into the Brazilian *malandro*, giving birth to a genuinely Brazilian literary type. The reader follows the adventures and misfortunes of Leonardo from toddler to young ruffian and idler. Through humour Almeida is able to apprehend the social and political landscape of Rio de Janeiro more effectively than previous literary attempts to combine imported forms with the local environment.

In Chapter 6, Jorge de Almeida discusses how Ian Watt's emphasis on the relationship between the rise of the novel and the socio-historical conditions functions as a 'negative' parameter for the analysis of the rise of the novel in nineteenth-century Brazil.[66] Almeida argues that 'autonomous individual', 'public sphere', 'experience' and new conceptions of 'time' and 'space' acquire different meanings in Joaquim Manuel de Macedo's *A luneta mágica* [*The Magic Eyeglass*] (1869) and that it is only through magic that this contradictory reality could be grasped in literary form. The formal contradictions of *A luneta mágica*, a moral fable in a slaveholding society, provide a good opportunity to discuss how the models and assumptions of European novels were acclimatized in imperial Brazil.

The narrative incongruities of another canonical Brazilian novel is the subject of Chapter 9. Following from Robert Schwarz's critical approach, Maria Eulália Ramicelli discusses the problematic nature of the romantic couple in José de Alencar's *Senhora: perfil de mulher* [*Senhora: Profile of a Woman*] (1875). Ramicelli argues that Alencar took important steps towards the literary representation of individual subjectivity through the use of internal focalization. Yet, he built characters whose inner ideas and feelings do not correspond to modern progressive individualized thinking. The reader is encouraged to pay close attention to the underlying archaic patron–client relationship in the love story presented in the novel. Because of Brazil's socio-cultural particularities, its protagonists represent incomplete modern subjectivities.

With Chapters 10 and 11 we move on to two stories of self-development published at the end of the nineteenth century. Margaret Anne Clarke proposes a reading of Maria Benedita Câmara Bormann's *Lésbia* (1884) as a *Künstlerroman*. Clarke argues that the novel is the first of its genre to be published by a female writer in Brazil, and examines it against the backdrop of the reading public of women's writing and the publishing culture in the times of the Empire and the First Republic. She provides an overview of the novel's themes, the eclectic range of influences and affiliations that inform these themes, and the fundamental ways in which the subversion of these influences differs from adaptations of the European literary canon by Bormann's male contemporaries. Chapter 11 analyses the long and arduous process of a boarding-school boy's coming to maturity in Raul Pompeia's *O Ateneu* [*The Athenaeum*] (1888). André Luiz Barros da Silva reads Pompeia's only novel as a *Bildungsroman* that blends psychological analysis, a bleak description of the educational institution as a disciplinary system (with both objective and internalized consequences) and an ultra-pessimistic view of aggression and competition between individuals (as seen in the philosophies of Schopenhauer and Nietzsche, influential in that period). The density of the novel's language, in striking contrast to the 'realistic' tone of the times, recalls ancient classical rhetoric.

Chapter 12 complements Clarke's overview of the reading public and publishing practices in Brazil by exploring the dynamic market of popular erotic literature at the end of the nineteenth century. According to Leonardo Mendes, the appropriation of naturalist fiction as erotic literature was a widespread reading practice at the time. Mendes argues that naturalist novels such as Figueiredo Pimentel's *O aborto* (1893) are better understood if we see them not as 'experimental novels' but as major titles in a late-century trend of erotic publications – or, in other words, as pornographic literature.

Two canonical authors are examined in more than one chapter. Chapters 5 and 9 centre on José de Alencar's *Iracema* and *Senhora*, respectively. Machado de Assis's novels as a whole and *Dom Casmurro* in particular are the subjects of Chapters 13 and 14. Sandra Guardini Vasconcelos discusses the whole oeuvre of novels by Machado de Assis in the light of the history of the genre since its emergence in eighteenth-century Europe. She argues that the nine novels published between 1872 and 1908 constitute a true summary of the literary form, which had become hegemonic in Europe by the time Machado adopted it. Each of his novels engages in a conversation with different European narrative paradigms, which he borrows from critically, since they needed to be acclimatized in order for him to address the specific Brazilian experience of living in a slave-owning society. Novelistic procedures and conventions are put in the service of probing and exposing the habits and idiosyncrasies of an elite reluctant to let go of its privileges. In Chapter 14, Ana Cláudia Suriani da Silva investigates to what extent we can consider *Dom Casmurro* (1900) to be an elegiac romance. She presents the main characteristics of the elegiac romance and compares *Dom Casmurro* with *Lord Jim* (1900) in order to highlight what makes the relationship between narrator and hero(es) in *Dom Casmurro* unique. *Dom Casmurro* can be considered a double elegy: the bitter and mournful laments for the death of Capitu and Escobar are intertwined in the self-reflexive narrative, shedding light on the changing sexual, gender and social relations at the end of the nineteenth century.

The last chapter of this book is devoted to one of the few fin-de-siècle novels of adultery and financial speculation written by a Brazilian woman, Júlia Lopes de Almeida's *A falência* (1901). Cintia Kozonoi Vezzani argues that Almeida's work, on the one hand, prefigures the interventions of contemporary feminist economists who have expounded the contribution of unpaid female labour to the rise of the modern capitalist economy and, on the other, recalls Gustave Flaubert's triangulation, in his classic work *Madame Bovary*, between adultery, illusions and credit. Vezzani demonstrates how an emphasis on female solidarity distinguishes *A falência* from the conventions of adultery novels predominantly written by men.

Although far from comprehensive, this collection demonstrates to what extent the rise of the Brazilian novel involved not 'imitation' or 'mechanic reproduction', but rather 'participation in resources that became common property'.[67] This foreign contribution was undeniable in the constitution of literature in Brazil, a country 'characterized by the intense intersection of cultures'.[68]

Notes

1. Alencar 1886; Taunay 1889.
2. On the underrepresentation of nineteenth-century women's writers in Brazilian literary histories, see Schmidt 2016; Muzart 1999.
3. See Melo 2019; Barbosa 1994; Treece and Keenoy 2001; Treece and Keenoy 1995; Fitz 2005, 152–76.
4. Juana Manso's *Misterios del Plata* was published in Portuguese as a feuilleton in *O Jornal das Senhoras* (Rio de Janeiro, 1852). The first book edition of the Portuguese version of the novel was published by Editora Mulheres in 2014. Maria Firmina dos Reis's *Úrsula: romance original brasileiro* was first published in São Luís by Tipografia do Progresso in 1859. The second edition is a facsimile edition (Reis 1975). Maria Benedita Câmara Bormann's *Lésbia* was first published as a feuilleton in *O Paiz* in 1884. The first edition in book format is from 1890 and the first re-edition was organized by Norma Telles and published by Editora Mulheres in 1998. Júlia Lopes de Almeida's *A falência* was originally published in 1901 by Officinas de Obras d'A Tribuna. Two editions were released in 1901. Its third edition came out in 1978.
5. Digital Library of Portuguese-Language Literature, https://www.literaturabrasileira.ufsc.br/?locale=en; Digital Library of the Brazilian National Library, http://bndigital.bn.gov.br/; Brasiliana José and Guita Mindlin Library, https://www.bbm.usp.br/
6. Antônio Gonçalves Teixeira e Sousa's *A providência* was published as a feuilleton in *Correio Mercantil* in 1854. Its only edition in book format appeared in 1854. Alberto Figueiredo Pimentel's *O aborto* was published as a feuilleton in *Província do Rio* in 1889. It has had two editions in book format (Pimentel 1893; Pimentel 2015).
7. Siskind 2014.
8. Fitz 2004, 12.
9. Merrim 1983; Payne and Fitz 1993.
10. Alencar 1997; Assis 1998; Azevedo 2008; Frank 2016.
11. Bernheimer 1995, 2.
12. Wellek 1963, 282. 'An artificial demarcation of subject-matter and methodology, a mechanistic concept of sources and influences, a motivation by cultural nationalism, however generous – these seem to me the symptoms of the long-drawn-out crisis of comparative literature' (Wellek 1963, 290). According to him that was what had to be faced and dealt with.
13. Bernheimer 1995, 12–14.
14. Moretti 2000. Reprinted in Prendergast 2004, 148–62.
15. Moretti 2000, 68.
16. Moretti 2000, 55.
17. Moretti 2007, 2. See also Moretti 2013.
18. Moretti 2000, 57, original emphasis.
19. See, for example, Prendergast 2001.
20. Damrosch 2003, 4.

21. Damrosch 2003, 283.
22. Arac 2002, 35–45.
23. Casanova 2002; Casanova 2004.
24. 'Universality in fact results from the hegemonic universalization of the cultural particularity of European modernity and its values and institutions' (Siskind 2014, 25).
25. Guillén 1985; Guillén 1993.
26. Jameson 1998, 61. Jameson retrieves some meanings of the concept and asserts his preference for taking globalization to be an 'intrinsic feature' of a 'new or third, multinational stage of capitalism' (1998, 54).
27. Jameson 1998, 61.
28. Jameson 1998, 61. This is a drastic summary of Jameson's sophisticated argument. It is evident that he also makes the reverse movement, projecting the cultural axis on to the economic one, to show how 'the rhetoricians of the market pop up and feverishly reassure us as to the richness and excitement of the new free market all over the world' (1998, 62). But this aspect of the problem has less relevance to the purposes of this introduction.
29. Ali 1993, 140.
30. Ahmad unpublished.
31. Jameson 2008.
32. Jameson 2008.
33. Jameson 2008.
34. Jameson 2008.
35. Different countries, Trotsky observed, developed to a large extent *independently* from each other, in ways that were *quantitatively* unequal (e.g., the local rate and scope of economic growth and population growth) and *qualitatively* different (e.g., nationally specific cultures and geographical features). In other words, countries had their own specific national history with national peculiarities. At the same time, the different countries did not exist in complete isolation from each other; they were also interdependent parts of a world society, a larger totality, in which they all coexisted, shared many characteristics and influenced each other through processes of cultural diffusion, trade, political relations and various spillover effects from one country to another. See Trotsky 1967.
36. Wellek 1963, 282.
37. McKeon 2000a, xiv.
38. Moretti 1997, 20.
39. See Sommer 1991.
40. Bakhtin 1986, 3–40.
41. Montandon 1999, 275.
42. Cohen 2003, 481.
43. See Moretti 1997, 141–97.
44. Moretti 1997, 186.
45. Hobsbawm 1996, ix.
46. Cohen and Dever 2002.
47. Coutinho 2018, 1–19.
48. Moretti 2000, 55.
49. On the circulation of novels between Brazil and Europe, see Silva and Vasconcelos 2014; Silva and Abreu 2016; Abreu 2017.
50. Schwarz 1992, 41
51. Teixeira e Sousa 1977.
52. Meyer 2007.
53. McKeon 2000b, 254.
54. Magris 2015, 96.
55. Assis 1992, 813.
56. Antonio Candido n.d., Vol. 1, 28.
57. Borges 1999, 290 and 291, respectively.
58. Mulhern 2012, xi–xii, original emphasis.
59. Antonio Candido 1980, 8.
60. Antonio Candido n.d., Vol. 2, 110.
61. Antonio Candido 1993b, 211.
62. Antonio Candido n.d., Vol. 1, 23.

63. Warwick Research Collective (WReC) 2015, 50–1.
64. Siskind 2014, 15.
65. Antonio Candido 1993a, 19–54; Antonio Candido 1995.
66. Watt 1957.
67. Antonio Candido 1987, 19.
68. Antonio Candido 1993b, 215.

Bibliography

Abreu, Márcia (ed.). *The Transatlantic Circulation of Novels between Europe and Brazil, 1789–1914*. London: Palgrave, 2017.

Ahmad, Aijaz Ahmad. 'World Literature in a World Globalized and Unequal'. Unpublished.

Alencar, José Martiniano de Alencar. *Iracema, the Honey-Lips, a Legend of Brazil*, translated by Isabel Burton. London: Bickers, 1886.

Alencar, José de. *Sonhos d'ouro*. São Paulo: Rideel, 1997.

Ali, Tariq. 'Literature and Market Realism', *New Left Review* 199 (1993): 140–5.

Almeida, Júlia Lopes de. *A falência*. Rio de Janeiro: Officinas de Obras d'A Tribuna, 1901.

Almeida, Júlia Lopes de. *A falência*. São Paulo: Editora HUCITEC, 1978.

Antonio Candido. 'Para uma crítica latino-americana', *Punto de Vista* 3, no. 8 (1980): 5–9.

Antonio Candido. 'Literatura e subdesenvolvimento'. In *A educação pela noite e outros ensaios*, 140–162. São Paulo: Ática, 1987.

Antonio Candido. 'Dialética da malandragem'. In *O discurso e a cidade*, 19–54. São Paulo: Duas Cidades, 1993a.

Antonio Candido. 'Literatura comparada'. In *Recortes*, 211–15. São Paulo: Companhia das Letras, 1993b.

Antonio Candido. 'Dialectic of Malandroism'. In *On Literature and Society*, ed. Howard S. Becker, 79–103. Princeton, NJ: Princeton University Press, 1995.

Antonio Candido. *Formação da literatura brasileira (momentos decisivos)*. São Paulo: Livraria Martins Editora, n.d.

Arac, Jonathan. 'Anglo-Globalism?', *New Left Review* 16 (2002): 35–45.

Assis, Machado de. 'A nova geração'. In *Obra completa*, Vol. 3, 809–36. Rio de Janeiro: Nova Aguilar, 1992.

Assis, Machado de. *The Posthumous Memoirs of Brás Cubas*, translated by Gregory Rabassa. Oxford: Oxford University Press, 1998.

Azevedo, Aluísio Azevedo. *O coruja*. São Paulo: Editora Global, 2008.

Bakhtin, Mikhail. 'Epic and Novel'. In *The Dialogic Imagination*, edited by Michael Holquist, 3–40. Austin: University of Texas Press, 1986.

Barbosa, Heloisa Gonçalves. 'The Visual Image: Brazilian Literature in English Translation'. PhD dissertation, University of Warwick, 1994. http://wrap.warwick.ac.uk/56829/1/WRAP_thesis_Barbosa%2C%20Heloisa%20Goncalves.pdf

Bernheimer, Charles. 'The Anxieties of Comparison'. In *Comparative Literature in the Age of Multiculturalism*, edited by Charles Bernheimer, 1–17. Baltimore, MD: Johns Hopkins University Press, 1995.

Borges, Jorge Luis. 'O escritor argentino e a tradição'. In *Obras completas*, Vol. 1, 288–96. Rio de Janeiro: Editora Globo, 1999.

Bormann [Délia], Maria Benedita Câmara. *Lésbia*. Rio de Janeiro: Typografia Central de Evaristo Rodrigues da Costa, 1890.

Bormann, Maria Benedita [Délia]. *Lésbia*, edited by Norma Telles. Florianópolis, Santa Catarina: Editora Mulheres, 1998.

Casanova, Pascale. *A república mundial das letras*, translated by Marina Appenzeller. São Paulo: Estação Liberdade, 2002.

Casanova, Pascale. *The World Republic of Letters*, translated by Malcolm B. DeBevoise. Cambridge, MA: Harvard University Press, 2004.

Cohen, Margaret. 'Traveling Genres', *New Literary History* 34, no. 3 (2003): 481–99.

Cohen, Margaret, and Carolyn Dever (eds). *The Literary Channel. The Inter-national Invention of the Novel*. Princeton, NJ: Princeton University Press, 2002.

Coutinho, Eduardo (ed.). *Brazilian Literature as World Literature*. London: Bloomsbury, 2018.
Damrosch, David. *What is World Literature?* Princeton, NJ: Princeton University Press, 2003.
Fitz, Earl E. 'Spanish American and Brazilian Literature in an Inter-American Perspective: The Comparative Approach'. In *Comparative Cultural Studies and Latin America*, edited by Sophia A. McClennen and Earl E. Fitz, 69–88. West Lafayette, IN: Purdue University Press, 2004.
Fitz, Earl E. *Brazilian Narrative Traditions in a Comparative Context*. New York: Modern Language Association of America, 2005.
Frank, Zephyr L. *Reading Rio de Janeiro: Literature and Society in the Nineteenth Century*. Stanford, CA: Stanford University Press, 2016.
Guillén, Claudio. *Entre lo uno y lo diverso. Introducción a la literatura comparada*. Barcelona: Editorial Crítica, 1985.
Guillén, Claudio. 'The One and the Many'. In *The Challenge of Comparative Literature*, translated by Cola Franzen, 13–23. Cambridge, MA: Harvard University Press, 1993.
Hobsbawm, Eric J. *The Age of Revolution, Europe 1789–1848*. New York: Vintage Books, 1996.
Jameson, Fredric. 'Notes on Globalization as a Philosophical Question'. In *The Cultures of Globalization*, edited by Fredric Jameson and Masao Miyoshi, 54–77. Durham, NC: Duke University Press, 1998.
Jameson, Fredric. 'World Literature'. Lecture presented at the John Hope Franklin Center at Duke University, 4 December 2008. http://www.youtube.com/watch?v=EUtV4kCzvnU
Magris, Claudio. 'A Cryptogram of Its Age', *New Left Review* 95 (2015): 95–107.
Manso, Juana. *Misterios del Plata*. Ilha de Santa Catarina: Editora Mulheres, 2014.
McKeon, Michael. 'Introduction'. In *Theory of the Novel: A Historical Approach*, edited by Michael McKeon, xiii–xviii. Baltimore, MD: Johns Hopkins University Press, 2000a.
McKeon, Michael. 'Watt's *Rise of the Novel* within the Tradition of the Rise of the Novel', *Eighteenth-Century Fiction* 12, nos 2–3 (2000b): 253–76.
Melo, Cimara Valim de. 'Mapping Brazilian Literature Translated into English', *Modern Languages Open*. Last modified 15 July 2019. https://www.modernlanguagesopen.org/articles/10.3828/mlo.v0i0.124/
Merrim, Stephanie Merrim. *Logos and the Word: The Novel of Language and Linguistic Motivation in Grande Sertao: Veredas and Tres Tristes Tigres*. Berne: Perter Lang, 1983.
Meyer, Marlyse. 'Book Flap'. In Sandra Guardini Vasconcelos, *A formação do romance inglês. Ensaios teóricos*. São Paulo: Editora HUCITEC/FAPESP, 2007.
Montandon, Alain. *Le roman au XVIIIe siécle en Europe*. Paris: PUF, 1999.
Moretti, Franco. *Atlas of the European Novel 1800–1900*. London: Verso, 1997.
Moretti, Franco. 'Conjectures on World Literature', *New Left Review* 1 (2000): 54–68.
Moretti, Franco. *Graphs, Maps, Trees*. London: Verso, 2007.
Moretti, Franco. *Distant Reading*. London: Verso, 2013.
Mulhern, Francis. 'Introduction'. In Roberto Schwarz, *Two Girls and Other Essays*, edited by Francis Mulhern, ix–xviii. London: Verso, 2012.
Muzart, Zahidé L. (ed.). *Escritoras brasileiras do século XIX: antologia*. Florianópolis: Editora Mulheres; Santa Cruz do Sul: EDUNISC, 1999.
Payne, Judith, and Earl E. Fitz. *Ambiguity and Gender in the New Novel of Brazil and Spanish America: A Comparative Assessment*. Iowa City: University of Iowa Press, 1993.
Pimentel, Alberto Figueiredo. *O aborto*. Rio de Janeiro: Livraria do Povo, 1893.
Pimentel, Alberto Figueiredo. *O aborto*. Rio de Janeiro: 7Letras, 2015.
Prendergast, Christopher. 'Negotiating World Literature', *New Left Review* 8 (2001): 100–21.
Prendergast, Christopher (ed.). *Debating World Literature*. London: Verso, 2004.
Reis, Maria Firmina dos. *Úrsula: romance original brasileiro*. São Luís: Tipografia do Progresso, 1859.
Reis, Maria Firmina dos. *Úrsula: romance original brasileiro*, edited by José Nascimento Morais Filho. Rio de Janeiro: Gráfica Olímpica; São Luís: Governo do Maranhão, 1975.
Schmidt, Rita Terezinha. 'Nineteenth-Century Brazilian Women Writers and Nation Building: Invisibilities, Affiliations, Resistances'. In *The Cambridge History of Latin American Women's Literature*, edited by Ileana Rodríguez and Mónica Szurmuk, 117–32. Cambridge: Cambridge University Press, 2016.
Schwarz, Roberto. 'The Importing of the Novel to Brazil and Its Contradictions in the Work of José de Alencar'. In *Misplaced Ideas. Essays on Brazilian Culture*, edited by John Gledson, 41–77. London: Verso, 1992.

Silva, Ana Cláudia Suriani da, and Márcia Abreu. *The Cultural Revolution of the Nineteenth Century. Theatre, the Book-Trade and Reading in the Transatlantic World*. London: I. B. Tauris, 2016.
Silva, Ana Cláudia Suriani da, and Sandra Guardini Vasconcelos (eds). *Books and Periodicals in Brazil 1768–1930*. London: Routledge, 2014.
Siskind, Mariano. *Cosmopolitan Desires: Global Modernity and World Literature in Latin America*. Evanston, IL: Northwestern University Press, 2014.
Sommer, Doris. *Foundational Fictions: The National Romances of Latin America*. Berkeley: University of California Press, 1991.
Taunay, Visconde Alfredo d'Escragnolle. *Inocência*. São Paulo: Martins Fontes, 2005.
Taunay,Visconde Alfredo d'Escragnolle. *Innocencia: A Story of the Prairie Regions of Brazil*, translated by James W. Wells. London: Chapman & Hall, 1889.
Teixeira e Sousa, Antônio Gonçalves. *A providência: recordação dos tempos coloniais*. Rio de Janeiro: Tipografia de M. Barreto, 1854.
Teixeira e Sousa, Antônio Gonçalves. *O filho do pescador*. São Paulo: Melhoramentos, 1977.
Treece, David, and Ray Keenoy (eds). *Babel Guide to the Fiction of Portugal, Brazil and Africa in English*. Oxford: Boulevard Books, 1995.
Treece, David, and Ray Keenoy (eds). *Babel Guide to Brazilian Fiction*. Oxford: Boulevard Books, 2001.
Trotsky, Leon. *History of the Russian Revolution*, Vol. 1, translated by Max Eastman. London: Sphere Books, 1967.
Warwick Research Collective. *Combined and Uneven Development: Towards a New Theory of World Literature*. Liverpool: Liverpool University Press, 2015.
Watt, Ian. *The Rise of the Novel: Studies in Defoe, Richardson and Fielding*. Berkeley: University of California Press, 1957.
Wellek, René. 'The Crisis of Comparative Literature'. In *Concepts of Criticism*, edited by Stephen Nichols, 282–95. New Haven, CT: Yale University Press, 1963.

1
Misterios del Plata: (Dis)Figuring History to Forge a Space for a Woman's Agency

Rita Terezinha Schmidt

> If the social contract, far from being that of equal men, is based on an essentially sacrificial relationship of separation and articulation of differences, which in this way produces communicable meaning, what is our place in this order of sacrifice and/or of language?
>
> (Kristeva 1981)

The novel *Misterios del Plata* [*Mysteries of the Plata*] by the Argentinian-born writer Juana Manso (Joana Paula Manso de Noronha, 1819–75) was first serialized in Rio de Janeiro from 4 January to 2 June 1852 in *O Jornal das Senhoras*. Although the title of the serial was Spanish, the work was published in Portuguese and contained a total of 26 instalments. The first Portuguese edition of the novel in book form was published in Brazil in 2014, with the subtitle 'Romance histórico contemporâneo' [Contemporary Historical Novel].[1] It is relevant to point out that Manso was the founder and director of *Jornal das Senhoras* during the years she lived in Rio de Janeiro, the city where her family lived in exile after having fled political persecution under the government of the dictator Juan Manuel de Rosas, who ruled Argentina from 1835 to 1852. A short time after her arrival in Rio, Manso married a Portuguese musician and left for the United States. She returned to Rio in 1848, when she became a Brazilian citizen. Her intent at the time was to enter medical school but, as she was turned down, probably for being a woman, she began working as a journalist. In 1853, she returned to Argentina, where she continued her work as a journalist, publishing essays in the newspaper *La Illustración*

Argentina. The following year, she founded her own periodical, *Album de Senõritas*, the first Argentinian journal in the nineteenth century dedicated to women's education. In that same year, Manso published *La familia del Comendador y otros textos* [*The Family of the Commander and Other Texts*], an abolitionist novel set in Rio de Janeiro. The novel was edited in book form in Argentina in 2006 and is part of the rare books collection of the National Library in Buenos Aires. In the late 1860s, the Argentinian president Domingo Sarmiento (1868–74) assigned Manso the position of director of the first mixed-gender public school in Argentina. Concerned about women's education and perhaps under Manso's influence, Sarmiento doubled the number of public schools in the country and founded around 100 public libraries. In Brazil today, *O Jornal das Senhoras* is considered a pioneer achievement in women's publishing.

Misterios del Plata had its first edition in Argentina in 1855 with the Americana Publishing House, Buenos Aires. It was also published in the Argentinian periodical *El Inválido Argentino* in 1867–8 under a different title, *Guerras civiles del Río de la Plata: una mujer heroica* [*Civil Wars in the River Plate: A Heroic Woman*]. Thirty years after Manso's death, in 1899, the second edition in book form bearing the original title was published in Buenos Aires by the Imprensa Los Mellizos. Comparing the original Brazilian serialized text kept in the archives of the Brazilian National Library with the 1899 Argentinian edition, Zahidé Muzart raises doubts in her introduction about the integrity of the text: she detected in the Argentinian version changes in structure and plot, and particularly concerning the role of the female protagonist. Along the same lines, Francine Masiello claims that the editor Ricardo Isidro López Muñiz, who organized the 1924 edition by Librería y Casa Editora de Jesús Menéndez in Buenos Aires, admitted having tampered with the manuscript, particularly the last chapters, and claimed that his changes had taken into account Manso's intention and style.[2] Masiello contends that Muñiz made the character named Adelaida (in the Brazilian edition her name is Antonia) a female warrior who enters into combat by acting as a double agent with the help of slaves, wet nurses and prison officials, and adds that 'the male editor's version of woman is interesting enough, not consonant with the pacifist course demonstrated in the earlier sections of Manso's novel'.[3] In her words, 'the editor confirms a common vision of women held by men in the nineteenth century, according to which women were seen as agents of deception, engendering transformations of nature and man'.[4] This case illustrates how writings by women in the past were often appropriated and modified by men of letters in positions of editorial authority.

The fact that the novel was published in two countries and that the author carried double citizenship fuelled some controversies among scholars about the status of the work vis-à-vis national literary systems. Luiza Lobo claims that, although the text in *O Jornal das Senhoras* was in Portuguese, it was probably a translation from Spanish and the novel deals with Argentinian history, something that would define it as part of the literary system of that country.[5] From the observations made by Zahidé Muzart about the 'civilizatory action'[6] carried out by Juana Manso while living in Brazil and about how her cultural influence extended over some Brazilian women writers at that time, it is possible to affirm her belonging to the tradition of women's writing in nineteenth-century Brazil. Manso also wrote another novel, *La familia del Comendador y outros textos*, which is set in Rio de Janeiro.[7]

Aside from these arguments, it is important to acknowledge that the 1852 original serialized text proves beyond doubt the status of the novel as a finished version. And it is precisely because of the last chapters that Manso's novel stands out as a pioneer text in terms of conceiving and portraying a woman's agency in public space. From this perspective, *Misterios del Plata* can be regarded as an example of how a nineteenth-century woman writer imprinted her own story into the collective history of nationhood and engaged in political debate on the project of nation-building by subverting the boundaries of female identity present in the normalized space of the masculine narrative order that traditionally underwrites the relation between nation and narration.

Borderline Territories: Fiction, History and Politics

The novel begins with a prologue in which Juana Manso presents a statement of purpose, with reference to the achievements of Walter Scott, considered the father of the modern historical novel, and to Eugène Sue's novel *Les mystères de Paris* [*The Mysteries of Paris*] published in serial form in the Parisian *Journal de Débats* between June 1842 and October 1843.[8] Acknowledging some debt to both writers, Manso claims that her intent is somewhat different, in a deliberate move to refuse subservience or resemblance to European models and to assert her independence. As she states: 'In this novel you will find what are still called very liberal ideas. … Unfortunately, I may never be servile, not in my opinions or in my writings. … I do not know how many formal defects there are in this novel; I have never paid attention to rules.'[9] The mysteries she intends to unravel emerge in a specific historical and geo-cultural space with a legacy of colonial rule, dictatorship and fratricidal wars. The prologue makes explicit the multi-layered aspects of her narrative project. Manso draws inspiration for the novel from her family's dramatic plight, that is, the family had to flee from Argentina and seek asylum in Brazil because of political persecution owing to the family's allegiance to the Unitarians' oppositional agenda to Rosas's regime. This explains why the locus of enunciation is not merely a formal stance of the narrative but the site where the writer projects and refracts herself as a narrator who organizes textual meanings that inscribe personal, social and historical elements in terms of what Julia Kristeva defines as 'ideologeme'.[10] According to Kristeva, the ideologeme is the centre of textual productivity and plays an intertextual function that discloses the dialogic nature of a literary work. On these terms, *Misterios del Plata* effects the presence of a historical and textual subjectivity overdetermined by a set of forces, of gender, class, nationality and political orientation, that shape the narrative through a series of discursive manoeuvres. Such moves are designed to engage the reader's civic feelings so as to enhance identifications that would grant validation to the novelist's intent: 'we write this novel in the agony of love for our homeland'.[11] Thus, the narrator's perception of the events during the bloodiest period of Juan Manuel de Rosas's regime, between 1838 and 1840, is not impartial. As a woman of a lettered class who opposed a government that turned constitutional access to power into a dictatorship, she conveys in the unfolding of the plot an obstinate belief in the right to occupy social and political positions which had been confiscated by state acts of violence. One may add that, according to the historian Jorge Myers, the social role of Latin American intellectuals during this period was to fight back against the loss of participation in political decisions and public life.[12] Myers affirms that the lettered class conceived itself as a privileged interlocutor facing the rise of new political powers and that in this condition it claimed not only to be the interpreter of the true essence of the society but also the right to participate in political decisions and public governance.

The novel's prologue presents a straightforward didactic and moralizing tone and, to a certain extent, a programmatic rationale, based on the foundation of Manso's narrative project, that is, to conceive a literary work that would denounce the downfall of her country, defined by the narrator as a 'gothic building', an image that encodes the irrationality and barbarism associated with Rosas's regime.[13] The compulsion to narrate a story that shows how government based on the principle of absolute power turns the body politic into a stage set for tragedy, a compulsion explicit in the prologue and the chapters that follow, leaves no doubt as to the author's affiliations with the liberal ideals of progress among the secular and urban class that emerged in the romantic period in Argentina as in other Latin American countries. Another feature of the prologue is the confluence of writer and narrator engendered by the assertion of national belonging and couched in the understanding that literature is a locus of identity formation deeply intertwined with the processes of nation-building. It is in this context that the narrator addresses the question of women's education, at a time when their role was confined to the domestic realm. Affirming that her account of heroic resistance proves the necessity of women's agency, Manso's narrator underscores her position as a discursive subject who positions herself as an agent of change, a position that accounts for the decisive role played out by this female character in the last chapters of the novel. Thus Manso's narrative project derives its strength from her belief in the role of literature in projecting a patriotic ethos associated with the idea of a social and political reconstruction of nationality fuelled by republican and democratic ideals. These ideals explain why she draws a fictional character based on the historical figure of Valentín Alsina (1802–69), a member of the Avelhaneda family and one of the most important politicians of the Unitary Party, who became a victim of persecution during Rosas's dictatorship. Alsina led the revolution of 1852 that overthrew Rosas from power and became governor of Buenos Aires in 1857.

The storyline of *Misterios del Plata* focuses on the events that followed the first capture and imprisonment of Dr Alsina and his wife Antonia and young son Rodolfo. An urban intellectual with a university degree, Alsina is a Unitarian leader who is condemned to death as an enemy of the country. To flee from Rosas's persecution, he and his family took refuge in Uruguay after he had received a death sentence in 1833. On his return to Argentina to settle down in Corrientes Province with his wife and son, he is betrayed by Oribe, the President of Uruguay, and captured in the Paraná River when his boat is heading to the Province. After a period in prison, Alsina manages to escape with the help of two men, a prison guard and an old friend, Simão. Antonia and their young son have been abandoned to their fate in the wilderness after they threw themselves into the river when trying to follow the boat in which Alsina was taken prisoner. However, two Italian sailors who have opposed Rosas's regime rescue both of them. Antonia then learns that Alsina has been taken to prison and is awaiting his execution in *Ponton*, a rotten boat sitting in Buenos Aires' dock. From this moment on, she schemes how to free her husband. With the help of old friends she manages to get him released. The family takes refuge in the Colony of Sacrament, where

Alsina continues to plan resistance against the central government. But he ends up being arrested once more and receives a death sentence. The prison guard and the friend who helped Alsina's first escape are two minor characters whose life stories converge with his family's history at a turning point in the narrative. Miguel is the prototype of the gaucho of the pampas turned into a soldier and for whom Rosas stands for humanity. Having exposed the hideout of the Alsina family, he undergoes a radical transformation after witnessing their sufferings and the injustice endured by one he considered to be the enemy of the nation, a savage Unitarian. Simão, meanwhile, is a disciplined and brave old soldier who in his youth consecrated his life to the cause of Argentinian independence, after 'the ideal of our great San Martin'.[14] For the naive Miguel, who entered the service without the least notion of Rosas's politics, Simão becomes a mentor as the keeper of the collective memory of a time of heroes whose names he honours, like Balcarce,[15] Belgrano, Olazabal, Rojas de Dias, Bessares and San Martin.

As narratives of nationhood, novels are hybrid texts, partly artistic–literary, partly historical–political, and *Misterios del Plata* fits this pattern. By performing a fictional transformation of a set of representations grounded in historical data, the novel is located in the field of forces of a double movement, of the politicization of the fictional and of the fictionalization of the political, producing an inter-discursive space in which the narrator is entangled in imaginary acts of memory and its processes of repetition, remembering, forgetting and reinvention. In this space, the narrator positions herself, defines her allegiances and appeals to identifications that will secure the conditions for a positive reception of her story. Thus the consciousness of moving in the field of a political discourse determines some of the narrator's strategies. One of these strategies is the use of self-reference by which the narrator seeks to enhance her authority on the subject matter and to emphasize the political voltage of the narrated events in order to gain the sympathy of the reader. Another strategy is the use of digressions, of philosophical evaluative nature, that illustrate the investment of the authorial voice in manoeuvres of persuasion. For example, there is a digression in the chapter entitled 'O Embaixador do rio Paraná' [The Ambassador of Paraná River] in which the narrator makes an analogy between the Argentinian Federation, the Holy Alliance and the Inquisition. The Holy Alliance was a coalition of monarchical European nations, first Russia, Austria and Prussia, joined later by the United Kingdom and France, that sought to control the spread of liberal ideas in the first half of the nineteenth century. Because of the fear of uprisings and revolutions on the part of people under the influence of the

Enlightenment, the governments of those nations formed a mutual aid bloc in order to uproot any attempt at rebellion. The narrator's definition of the Holy Alliance as a 'monster of a thousand faces' and the comparison with the 'Holy Cause of the Federation' highlight her position in relation to her country's history and reinforce moral judgement on Rosas's government as 'the cause' that came to 'destroy the young societies on the green margins of the River Plate'.[16]

Yet, there is more to be said about the narrator, who is torn between two distinctive poles, of reason, associated with the 'science of truth', and emotion, derived from the romantic ethos. On the one hand, she insists on the objectivity of her narration by referring to historical events; on the other, she acknowledges that the 'I' who narrates is driven by an unknown impulse, something within that she cannot explain: 'After all, I write because I have been carried away to this, I do not know how ... '[17] Thus the narrator's discourse embodies a subjective necessity that erases the postulate of truth that she advocates. In fact, there is a discursive instability in the oppositions embedded throughout the narrative – fiction/truth, reason/emotion, facts/invention – because, in the act of signification, the language is fraught with psychic content over which the narrator has no control. This means that the alignment of the narrator is both intellectual and affective, which accounts for the libidinal economy underlying the movement of the narrative: the desire for a reality beyond the limits set by historical contingency overrun by the pressing and inescapable necessity of narrating the nightmare of history.

To advance her project, Manso juxtaposes the trajectories of two families against the backdrop of the political dictatorship of Juan Manuel de Rosas in an attempt to probe into and explain the mystery of the 'Rosism' that divided Argentina in the nineteenth century, a mystery that, according to Cristina Iglesia, defies deciphering even today.[18] The divide between nation and home provides the dominant motif of the plot, in which two antagonistic national constituencies are figured in two male characters – the victim/hero (Dr Alsina) and the despot/ruler (Rosas). These characters foreground the correlation of forces between two distinct family scenarios: the private family in distress, outcast and homeless, threatened by extermination, and the public institutionalized family, cast as representative of the nation and a site for the exercise of absolute patriarchal power. The story of the private family folds back and forth against the backdrop of the official/state family; the private and the public spheres become at times intermingled, encouraging an allegorical reading of a double story, of family and nation. For the sake of making the historical context clear, it is necessary to add that during Rosas's regime there was an intense political struggle that divided Argentina: on one side were the Federalists, who counted on the support of the masses and stood for the hegemony of Buenos Aires and its control over the provinces; on the other, the Unitarians, members of an enlightened elite who held on to the liberal ideal of a civilized modern Argentina and regarded Rosas's politics as a setback for the country's development, a retreat into barbarism.[19] Given this context and the novel's historical subtext, some historical explanation is due. After independence in 1816, Argentina underwent a period of intestine struggle, mainly around the question of the status of the provinces, whose autonomy was being curbed by the rising power of Buenos Aires (central government). The provincial governments resented that centralism. The dispute among the provinces generated the conditions for the rising of Rosas, proclaimed head of state in 1828. He had the support of landowners and the urban masses, an illiterate and easily manipulated segment of the population, and ruled from 1835 to 1852. Under the dictatorship installed in the name of the Federation, Rosas suppressed the freedom of the press, dissolved Congress and forbade the free navigation of rivers such as the Paraná and the Uruguay. With the help of General Balcarce, Rosas also tried to subordinate the countries of Paraguay and Uruguay to the Argentinian Federation. Balcarce organized a secret society known as 'Mazorca', which had the goal of eliminating all those suspected of conspiring against the regime, producing a death toll of 22,000 victims in this period.

Misterios del Plata presents a pervasive haunted atmosphere in terms of sequence, character and actions, as well as descriptions of the natural landscape which overshadow scenes in which a realist mode of representation prevails. The first three chapters provide little clue to what the novel is all about, as the reader is plunged into descriptions and somewhat vague dialogues between Miguel, a simpleton soldier, and a judge about certain papers, in an atmosphere of unrest and secrecy. It is a picture of low life; the judge is represented as a ridiculous figure, described as 'a pack of flesh with no moral value'.[20] The initial scenes remind one of Sue's *Les mystères de Paris*, where from the start the narrator plunges the reader into the depths of Paris and the sinister low-life tavern on the Île de la Cité, where crime, prostitution and exploitation are rife. Upon the publication of the novel, Eugène Sue became a hero to the French working class and their political leaders and this may be one of the reasons why the novel is one of Manso's literary references in her prologue. Divided into two parts, the first with 15 chapters and the second with 13, the narrative develops unevenly; there are chapters with descriptions and dialogues that create suspense, delaying the unfolding of events, as well as chronological interruptions, movements forwards and backwards in time. The chapters differ in length and content in such a way that the reader may often find difficulty in connecting scenes with the storyline, particularly with the gallery of secondary characters who emerge at one point and then vanish from the story. There are chapters with only one or one-and-a-half pages, like Chapter 3 in Part 2, entitled 'O coronel Corbalán' [The Colonel Corbalán], Rosas's favourite officer, described as 'a desiccated living creature'.[21] Also in Part 2, in Chapter 9, 'O coronel Rojas' [The Colonel Rojas], the narrator presents detailed descriptions of the Colonel's role in the wars for independence as well as allusions to the mystery around his private life, there being doubts about whether his wife had been murdered or had committed suicide. The content of the chapter seems unrelated to the context of the story except for the fact that the Colonel plays a role in the outcome in a way that redeems somewhat the shadow hanging over his character.

In Part 1, two chapters stand out for their sombre poetical renderings of the natural landscape in tune with the atmosphere of doom that hangs over the members of Alsina's family. In Chapter 4, 'Os passageiros do barco *La Francesca di Rimini*' [The Passengers of the Boat *La Francesca di Rimini*], the narrator describes a family scene in which Alsina, Antonia and their son are on a boat that is peacefully gliding down the river. The detailed descriptions of nature charged with plastic expressivity as a backdrop for the love that unites the three human figures create a romantic tableau, idyllic scenery under a sky pure and serene until the sorrowful sound of a tropical bird named the *curucú* is heard. The narrator explains that this is a bird of bad omen according to the Guarani nation. Only later on, in Chapter 10, 'Lágrimas' [Tears], is it revealed that this boat ride ends with Alsina's first arrest. Another feature that adds to the sombre narrative mode are the recurring images of suffering and terrible deeds, a representation of life which strips bare the facade of social conventions to unveil conflicts that produce intense polarization. The majority of scenes are saturated with drama, incorporating standard features of romantic melodrama, such as the use of exaggerated rhetorical devices like hyperbole to convey images of lurid events, ominous threats and hostile landscape. An atmosphere of wrongdoing emerges out of the narrator's use of gothic tropes that produce effects both on the narrative structure and on the meaning of the narrated events: for example, deceit, secrecy, betrayal, torture, murder, vengeance, family doom, sadism, vandalism, debauchery and religious profanation.

The long account of the orgy of blood promoted by the Mazorca in Chapter 7 of Part 1 discloses the work of Rosas's secret society. The Mazorca was conceived to manipulate the mobs on the streets and incite them into acts of violence against Unitarian traitors. This group created the epithet repeated by political allies and by the chorus of the people on the streets: Rosas, the 'celebrated law-restorer'. Counter to that, the narrator compares Rosas's profile to Tiberius and Louis XVI, with eyes that bear the deadly attraction of the serpent. Since Rosas is being presented as a character in the novel, his private and public disposition is fully exposed. In the private sphere Rosas is shown to be a diabolical man who takes pleasure in watching the suffering of others, particularly in the grotesque and eschatological games he plays with his favourite fool. As a public figure he is depicted as a ruler with an iron will, indifferent to the fact that civilized conventions had been obliterated and the country had turned into a madhouse. There are references to the church tower of a convent in ruins, a convent that had been a symbol of colonial power in the past and became a fortress-prison under the regime of the despotic leader. The symbolic nature of this space is embedded in the historic analogy between the enslavement of Indians during the period of colonization by the missionaries, whose work sought to claim the Indians' body and soul in the name of God, and the dictatorial regime with its form of enslavement of the mind in the service of an idea of nationhood. In this analogy, the imagined nationhood is absent, an empty sign that fuels the insurgency of a desire for another time, another story.

The counterpoint to Rosas's demonization is the idealized representation of Alsina, a dignified man with a noble soul who looms larger than his party as an embodiment of the romantic aspiration of national brotherhood, inspired by the figure of José Martí, a hero for a time 'when wars were fought for a cause – the independence of America'[22] – and not for the service of men.[23] The narrator gives legitimacy to his dignified status by extolling his moral character, a reference that makes clear the narrator's political affiliations in relation to the oppositions engendered during the narrative, such as Unitarian versus Federalist, lettered versus ignorant, reason versus passion, civilization versus barbarism. These oppositions stand for two antagonistic political visions central to Manso's aesthetic–political project of textualizing history. From this point of view, the novel may be regarded as a symbolic act, a confrontation with the uncanny, the nation/home turned unfamiliar in a period of great social unrest, but also a form of structural repair to a personal and collective historical trauma that brought chaos to private and public life. In spite of the fact that the novel ultimately enacts an ethical opposition between forces defined as good and evil that derive from a melodramatic logic, the degree of sentiment involved in this is no mere emotional indulgence but a strategy that allows Manso to distance herself from self-centredness so as to emphasize the plight of the Alsina family and make the hero appealing to the reading public. In other words, Manso's discursive manoeuvres are designed to enhance identification with characters who are embodiments of virtue in distress.

Woman and Nation: Beyond Domestic Fiction

In nineteenth-century Latin American countries, the novel had a major impact in the constitution of the public sphere of social and political culture, for it was a genre that could satisfy the political and symbolic need to (re)tell identity stories that addressed the theme of nationality and, as such, it became an important channel for the constitution of national imaginaries.[24] It was a time when the transplantation of the ideals of European romanticism, embodied in notions such as unity, progress and nationhood, fed literary nationalism so that nationality became a narrative trope invested with the power to fulfil the historical need to establish a nexus of national belonging. Thus, closely allied to a nation-building project, the novel was regarded as the literary genre that could foster a system of cultural signification that would inspire a community of readers to imagine themselves as a network of people sharing a collective sense of belonging to a common place, time and language. In this capacity the novel became instrumental in fostering the political legitimacy of the new nation-states. As an affective mode of interpellation meant to engender subjects and subjectivities compatible with the logic of national belonging, the novel operated as a matrix enacting the pedagogical discourse of the many as one, giving the body politic a narrative of its 'imagined communities'.[25] Following along the lines of Benedict Anderson's work, Doris Sommer provides substantial insights into the development of the novel in Latin America, claiming that in canonical works of fiction the rhetorical solutions are the result of an analogy between erotic fulfilment and productive sexuality that engender allegories of the mutual dependence between family and state.[26] She makes a point, important to Manso's achievement, about the role of the novel in advancing the construction of nationhood as a distinctive form of male bonding, thus confirming Anderson's definition of nationhood as a 'deep, horizontal comradeship'.[27]

Contemporary discussions on the spaces of 'woman' and 'nation' have yielded insights into the boundaries of identity which the nation-state defined for women in the nineteenth century: they were definitely not invited to participate or even to imagine themselves as part of this horizontal brotherhood, except in their reproductive capacity. As Mary Louise Pratt remarks, 'women were literary subjects located at the border of nationalist ideologies, with one foot inside and another outside'.[28] With this statement Pratt reminds us that, though women were naturalized as the other of the nation, which explains why prevailing social conventions assigned female authorship a marginal status and writing was then regarded as an exclusively male affair, a generation of female writers did participate in the debates on nation-building. Deploying their own set of resources and concerns mediated by the particular circumstances of their lives, they appropriated the form of the novel to bring to light the conflictive identity claims of gender, race, class and nationality. Such a move is defined by Jean Franco as a paradigmatic moment in 'the struggle for interpretative power' at a time when existing conventions did not give credit to women who ventured into literary endeavours, least of all if they dealt with political issues.[29]

This power sustains Manso's project of nation/narration and secures its novelty. She not only engaged in the art of interpreting the dramatic circumstances and events of a divided nation; she also ventured into writing a historical novel at a time when novels by women usually fell into the category of domestic fiction, sometimes also referred to as 'sentimental fiction'. This was a type of popular novel that had a wide public of female readers because the plot usually centred on the plight of a young woman who learns to balance society's demands for self-denial with her own desire for autonomy. Marriage was the usual outcome and was not regarded as incompatible with the heroine's conviction of her self-worth, since her agency was so limited to the domestic sphere. Deviating from the trend of her time, Manso dared to address woman's agency not only by conceiving a self-conscious narrator identified with her gender but most of all by creating a female character who ends up performing a key role in a crucial moment in the plot and so brings about a decisive turn of events. With this move, Manso fashioned her intervention in the socio-semantic field of what were then defined as hegemonic narratives of masculine nationality. There is no doubt that the male character Alsina embodies the qualities of the hero who can fulfil the historical demands posed by the liberal project of nation-building, but the fact is that he plays an essentially passive role throughout the narrative. It is his wife Antonia who yields an image of empowerment as an active subject and who has the courage to venture into strange and sinister places to organize the plan to rescue her husband. She definitely plays a role beyond the confines of domestic life by taking on a patriotic mission that succeeds and that opens the possibility of a reversal of the nation's fate.

Her agency entails the process of restoration of a new social order, based on a right-acting government that could eventually guarantee democracy, freedom and dignity to its people.

The first description of Antonia appears in Part 1, Chapter 4:

> a beautiful woman ... of great intelligence in her mind and a heart of fire ... her education had been free from the mistakes and prejudices that disfigure and spoil the nature of the majority of women, so as a wife and mother she fulfilled these two noble missions with the intelligent response of someone who commands her actions by the force of duty and not by instinct, that sometimes confound ourselves.[30]

The references to the roles of mother and wife as well as to her fragility and delicate demeanour are compatible with the values of the patriarchal family at a time when women's social function was, as a rule, circumscribed by reproduction and domesticity. Her expression of love is defined in terms of duty, in conformity with the set of values attached to traditional female roles. However, it is worth observing that if, on the one hand, the oppositions between nature and culture and between private and public by which patriarchal ideology defines traditional gender roles remain the touchstone of female identity, on the other, they are worked out in the novel with a degree of subversion. Antonia's acts do not come into conflict with the liberal ideals of freedom, rationality and self-determination to which Manso explicitly subscribes. Denying the existence of the so-called 'female instinct', a notion that in the eighteenth and nineteenth centuries was assumed to be constitutive of female nature, Manso endows Antonia with the capacity to decide on two occasions to take action in order to fulfil her mission – to rescue her husband from prison and save him from a death sentence. Therefore, love, family and politics are deeply intertwined in the psychological structure of her character.

As a rule, in nationalist discourses, particularly those related to national formation, the family has played a central role in the construction of the nation's imaginary as a political self-determined entity, and maternity – reproductive and domesticated sexuality – has been regarded as a service to the nation. As Francine Masiello observes of both political parties during Rosas's regime, the Federalists and Unitarians, woman and the family became symbols associated with state power.[31] In the paternalist conception of the Federalists, women's activities were necessarily associated with functions of the state. Thus, female members of Rosas's family, such as his wife Encarnación, his sister Maria Josefa and her daughter Manuelita, took part in a web of espionage and information to help secure his power. For the Unitarians, women were the source of resistance, identified not with the forces of violence and male domination, but with the realm of feelings, of virtue and family ethics, strategic pillars of defiance against tyranny. Thus, maternity and the correlative functions in the private sphere acquired a new symbolic value in the struggle for power in Argentinian history. As Masiello states, 'if the masculine were identified with the dictator's reign, as a chartable, marked rhetoric and behavior located within the public sphere, the feminine was seen as strategically private, evasive and less formally determined'.[32] In relation to Antonia this definition is partially true. At a time when the national government responsible for collective well-being was associated with abusive power and the legitimacy of its authority has been put into question, domestic ideology and the stability of gender roles, particularly in the spaces of political dissent and resistance, were bound to change. Given the kind of femininity inscribed in the characterization of Antonia Alsina, her enshrinement as wife and mother in nurturing roles takes a twist to project on to the body politic the dynamic image of a self-determined, mindful and clever woman facing head-on a man's world.

Antonia's transformation begins in Part 1, in the note to Chapter 11 entitled 'O julgamento de um selvagem Unitário' [The Trial of a Savage Unitarian], when Alsina is taken prisoner for the first time and he and the family are kept at an abandoned monastery in a remote region along the Paraná River, where he undergoes interrogation and awaits his sentence. In the midst of her sorrow, Antonia has a sudden awakening, stops grieving and says to herself, 'to cry is not to love; to love is to save him from the horrors of being hanged under the orders of the tyrant or to die with him, because without him I cannot live'.[33] In a family scene of father, mother and son, described in detail, the atmosphere of pain and sadness does not give way to rhetorical sentimentalism; on the contrary, family love is fuelled by a psychic energy that spells out courage and serenity. In Chapter 13, 'Tentativa' [Attempt], which ends Part 1, Antonia finds a way to scheme an escape with the help of Simão and Miguel, a plan that includes her receiving and handling guns for self-defence, but the plan fails. Alsina is taken on a boat to Buenos Aires to be executed and Antonia throws herself with her son into the water after the boat, a suicidal gesture that seems incompatible with her previous depiction as a serene and rational woman, but is symptomatic of the extreme circumstances she and her son are experiencing. Rescued from drowning, she realizes that she must come to her senses to stand a chance of saving her husband.

Antonia's cold-blooded courage is emphasized by the narrator when she conceives a daring project to free Alsina, an almost infallible plan in her eyes. With the help of a sailor with whom she has not only shared her plans but also attended carefully to every detail to ensure its success, Antonia makes use of all her resources to achieve her goal. She uses dissimulation so as not to raise suspicion on the part of relatives and friends. She has secret meetings with men whom she has never met before, let alone had any familiarity with. She forges official papers and bribes a prison official. Last but not least, she disguises herself on two occasions. Once she dresses herself as a poor woman of the streets to access the harbour area in order to make contact with a sailor who will help her. Dressed as a man, she adopts the identity of an army captain, Manuel Torres, gains access to the prison of Ponton and finally manages to rescue Alsina.

The description of this groundbreaking episode of cross-dressing reveals Antonia's resolution as she moves surreptitiously to achieve her goal. The use of the present tense gives the scene a sense of urgency in tune with the suspense that attends the scene:

> Eight o'clock in the evening, the church bells ring. A man with a delicate figure, with short steps that he stretches as best he can, and enveloped in a military cap, moves to a neighbourhood far from the city to reach the riverbank – he is leading by the hand, underneath a coat, a boy who is nine or ten years old. The unknown man we're following crosses the street, turns his head to check whether he is being followed and, when he sees a crowd of men in a patrol, walks back and takes another street or goes into a house with its door open, walks along the corridor and avoids any encounter at all costs. After three-quarters of an hour of a fast walk, the man in the cap arrives at the corner of Sotoca. The store was full of sailors of all nations and had a red-light lamp hanging at the entrance where one could read in different languages 'Night Hostel'.[34]

When the boat reaches the prison of Ponton, bearing Antonia with a forged dispatch from the central government to free Alsina, she is examined in the lamplight by an official and the narrator describes her as follows: 'It was a young man with a delicate appearance, his face partly covered with a beard and a long black moustache; the brim of his military cap covered his forehead and eyes; his dress and badge were of a captain of hunters.'[35] Antonia's movement through public spaces at night transforms her into a political activist, a role that exceeds gender norms of behaviour and stands in opposition to the essentialist idea of woman which reduces her to the traditional domestic roles of wife and mother. Pretending to be a man in order to fulfil her mission, Antonia defies the patriarchal order with initiative, ingenuity, determination and bold courage, for she is intelligent enough to know that if she should fail she will bring doom upon herself and her son. It should be added that Antonia's acting in the name of a commitment to her marriage partner and the unconditional love they share is not couched in the rhetoric of devotional Catholicism that was strongly enforced in nineteenth-century Latin America. In fact, her actions constitute a sabotage of the religious imperative that enshrined marriage, childbearing and domesticity. *Misterios del Plata* postulates the idea that the dream of a democratic nation should be shared equally by both men and women and that a woman has the right to be a partner in making that dream come true, that is, her participation is not tangential but decisive to the achievement of what both desire.

Even if at times the narrator reproduces the discourse of the noble mission of maternity, Manso did not imprint into the consciousness of her character the idea that her intelligence should serve only the domestic sphere. With Antonia's proactivity in the resolution of the story, Manso conveys the message that a woman cannot be reduced to a mere adjunct role in history, whether in terms of her procreative powers, as a receptacle of prospective citizens, or as a repository of virtues to serve as a refuge to men after the hard battles for power are fought. By empowering Antonia, Manso inventively destabilized spaces and hierarchies ahead of her time, defied the idea that a woman participates in the horizontal brotherhood of nationhood only via her reproductive capacity and endowed her character with the status of heroine in the struggle against institutionalized despotic power. Furthermore, the character of Antonia perpetuates bravery as one of the ideals of literary feminism. As Ellen Moers points out, women novelists in the nineteenth century catered to

> the thrust toward physical heroics, toward risk-taking courage as a gauge of heroinism long after male writers had succumbed to the prevailing antiheroic, quiescent temper of the bourgeois century, and admitted, with whatever degree of regret or despair, that adventure was no longer a possibility of modern life.[36]

For Moers, this heroic impulse takes many forms, such as the intellectual and thoughtful female character, the passionate woman in love or the female traveller. What is key is that they all move, act, cope with vicissitudes, face adventures and survive risky situations.

As the founder of *O Jornal das Senhoras*, Manso was passionately engaged in addressing the condition of women in her time and place and was particularly concerned with women's education. In an essay,

'Emancipação moral da mulher' [The Moral Emancipation of Woman], published in her periodical on 11 January 1852, Manso contends that the very word 'woman' encodes, for society at large, the sum of human misery and that this is why the term incites contempt among men, except those few men of good faith.[37] Given that this was a dangerous obstacle to women's self-development, Manso warns, 'As long as man's education remains the same, without a reform, as long as he considers woman his property, we can accomplish nothing.'[38] In this essay, Manso manipulates discourse as a stylized weapon, making use of various rhetorical strategies, including humour and irony, in the form of questions and statements that turn the essay into a manifesto, of outrage but also of hope. Tackling the issue of women's situation in Brazil, she asks how a woman can have any influence on the family, on the nation, on the whole of humanity if her influence is reduced to her kitchen pans and her sewing machine. As a literary woman who had the opportunity to live in different places and cultural contexts, Manso had the means to compare the situation of Brazilian women with that of women in industrializing countries like France, England and the United States. In those places women, at least those who belonged to a certain class, not only had access to schooling but could also dedicate themselves to literature, to writing and publishing. On vigorously denouncing the condition of inferiority to which women had been relegated in Brazil, she emphasized to her readers the absolute need for women's access to education, which she regarded as the only weapon with which one could fight oppression and misery. On affirming her belief that woman was not inferior to man, she reiterated her commitment to fight for women's rights. It was a bold social and political stance for a woman in the nineteenth century to dare to question the cultural script that defined woman in terms of a natural procreative body propelled by instincts, a script composed of accumulated layers of history and knowledge in the Western world. Ultimately, her essay illuminates the problematic relationship of women with the modern nation-state and the defining lines of its construction of female subjectivity.

Manso's position as an essay writer is coherent with her fictional work in the sense that she acts as a performing subject in producing a political imaginary that signals to women the necessity of moving forward with acts of self-reinvention in order to claim their place as cultural, historical and political subjects in the socio-semantic and symbolic space of collective belonging. The potency of this imaginary lies in the fact that it engenders identifications and alliances that may lift the weight of prejudice and disclose what is sacrificial for women in the social contract so they can find the means and tools with which to act out their desire. Desire has been, for quite a time, the driving force of the feminist revolution. There can be little doubt that *Misterios del Plata* adds to the genealogy of women's writings as an example of the continuities and changes of the literary genre across geographical and temporal borders which highlight female agency, literary and fictional, in relation to dominant ideologies of nationhood that inform the canonical novels of the nineteenth century.

Notes

1. Zahidé Lupinacci Muzart organized the 2014 edition in Portuguese, which includes an introduction by Muzart, an afterword by Constância Lima Duarte, a chronology by Maria Julia de Giorgio and an explanation of the finalizing of the text with notes by Eliane Vasconcellos and Ivette Maria Savelli (Florianópolis: Editora Mulheres).
2. Masiello 1989.
3. Masiello 1989, 556.
4. Masiello 1989, 557.
5. Lobo 2009.
6. Muzart 2014, 34.
7. Manson 2006.
8. Sue 2015.
9. Manso 2014, 73. There is no translation of the novel into English. All quotes from the novel are my translations from this edition.
10. Kristeva 2005.
11. Manso 2014, 72.
12. Myers 1994.
13. Manso 2014, 73.
14. Manso 2014, 110.
15. The text raises doubt about the name Balcarce, since the narrator refers to the noble general who gathered those who were dissatisfied with the central government, which suggests that the name does not refer to the historical figure of the governor of Buenos Aires during Rosas's regime.
16. Manso 2014, 118–19.
17. Manso 2014, 73.
18. Iglesia 1998.
19. Halperin 2000.
20. Manso 2014, 81.
21. Manso 2014, 201.
22. Manso 2014, 170.
23. In *El espejo enterrado*, the historian Carlos Fuentes defines Rosas as the archetypical Hispano-American tyrant and argues that his ruling in the name of federalism reduced the idea of federation to a rhetorical figure. Fuentes 1992, 383–409.
24. Ricardo 1960.
25. Anderson 1983.
26. Sommer 1991.
27. Anderson 1983, 50.
28. Pratt 1993, 56.
29. Franco 1989, xi.
30. Manso 2014, 96.
31. Masiello 1989, 521–64.
32. Masiello 1989, 521.
33. Manso 2014, 159.
34. Manso 2014, 280–1.

35. Manso 2014, 284.
36. Moers 1985, 131.
37. This essay is included in 'Joana Paula Manso de Noronha' by Eliane Vasconcellos (1999). The quotes from this essay are my translations.
38. Manso 1999, 235.

Bibliography

Anderson, Benedict. *Imagined Communities: Reflections on the Origins and Spread of Nationalism*. London: Verso, 1983.

Franco, Jean. *Plotting Women: Gender and Representation in Mexico*. New York: Columbia University Press, 1989.

Fuentes, Carlos. *El espejo enterrado*. Buenos Aires: Aguilar, Altea, Taurus, 1992.

Halperin, T. D. *Historia de Argentina 3: De la revolución de la Independencia a la confederación rosista*. Buenos Aires: Prometeo Libros, 2000.

Iglesia, Cristina. *Letras y divisa: ensayos sobre literatura y rosismo*. Buenos Aires: EUDEBA, 1998.

Kristeva, Julia. 'Women's Time', translated by Alice Jardine and Harry Blake, *Signs* 1, no. 11 (1981): 13–35.

Kristeva, Julia. *Introducão à semanálise*, translated by Lúcia Helena França Ferraz. São Paulo: Perspectiva, 2005.

Lobo, Luiza. 'Juana Manso: uma exilada em três pátrias', *Gênero* 2 (2009): 47–74.

Manso, Juana. 'Emancipação moral da mulher.' In *Escritoras brasileiras do século XIX*, edited by Zahidé Muzart, 228–49. Florianópolis: Editora Mulheres; Santa Cruz do Sul: EDUNISC, 1999.

Manso, Juana. *La família del Comendador y otros textos*. Buenos Aires: Ediciones Colihue; Biblioteca Nacional de La Republica Argentina, Colleción Los Raros, n. 12, 2006.

Manso, Juana. *Misterios del Plata*. Ilha de Santa Catarina: Editora Mulheres, 2014.

Masiello, Francine. 'Between Civilization and Barbarism: Women, Family and Culture in Mid-Nineteenth Century Argentina.' In *Cutural and Historical Groundings for Hispanic and Luso-Brazilian Feminist Literary Criticism*, edited by Hernán Vidal, 517–64. Minneapolis: Institute for the Study of Ideologies, 1989.

Moers, Ellen. *Literary Women*. Oxford: Oxford University Press, 1985.

Muzart, Zahidé. 'Juana Manso, uma voz subversiva'. In *Misterios del Plata* by Juana Manso, 7–47. Ilha de Santa Catarina: Editora Mulheres, 2014.

Myers, Jorge. 'Literatura romantica y proyecto nacional, 1839–70'. In *América Latina: palavra, literatura e cultura*, edited by Ana Pizarro, Vol. 2, 221–50. Campinas: Editora UNICAMP, 1994.

Pratt, Mary Louise. 'Las mujeres y el imaginario nacional en el siglo XIX', *Revista de Crítica Literaria Latinoamericana* 38 (1993): 51–62.

Rojas, Ricardo. *Historia de la literatura argentina*, Vol. 2. Buenos Aires: Editorial Guillermo Kraft, 1960.

Sommer, Doris. *Foundational Fictions: The National Romances of Latin America*. Berkeley: University of California Press, 1991.

Sue, Eugène. *The Mysteries of Paris*, translated by Carolyn Bentenski and Jonathan Loesberg. New York: Penguin Books, 2015.

Vasconcellos, Eliane. 'Joana Paula Manso de Noronha'. In *Escritoras brasileiras do século XIX*, edited by Zahidé Muzart, 228–49. Florianópolis: Editora Mulheres; Santa Cruz do Sul: EDUNISC, 1999.

2
The Historical Significance of *Memórias de um sargento de milícias*

Edu Teruki Otsuka

Memórias de um sargento de milícias [*Memoirs of a Militia Sergeant*], the only novel of Manuel Antônio de Almeida, concerns the ways of life and the practical perspectives of the free poor people of Rio de Janeiro in the early nineteenth century; although restricted in social and geographical scope, it captures an essential aspect of class relations in the country as a whole. Comical in tone, unpretentious in its plotline and unconventional in its social ambience, *Memórias* is generally regarded as a work that diverges from the main trends of Brazilian fiction at the time. Although most novelists attempted to acclimatize the novel as a form in Brazil by writing sentimental stories with grandiloquent language, Almeida withdrew from prevailing romantic standards. By depicting the actions of people who were neither slaves nor owners, he succeeded in constructing a narrative framework that comprehends a decisive historical experience of nineteenth-century Brazilian society. Because of its distinctive features, as we shall see, Almeida's *Memórias* is an outstanding accomplishment in the early development of the Brazilian novel and is arguably one of the most penetrating works to appear before Machado de Assis's greater novels.

This chapter begins with a description of some general features of *Memórias de um sargento de milícias* and a brief overview of the main traditional readings of Almeida's work. Seen as a novel of manners or a picaresque novel, it has been praised because of its alleged accuracy in depicting popular customs in a lively, straightforward way. Thus, the initial critical responses to *Memórias* overemphasized its detachment from the prevailing romantic conventions of its time and, most importantly, gravitated around a loose sense of realism in their tentative critical assessments.

An innovative interpretation of *Memórias* was proposed in 1970 by critic Antonio Candido; his main argument is presented in the next section of this chapter. Candido contends against those traditional views on Almeida's novel and redefines the nature of its realism in order to characterize its literary and social relevance. According to him, *Memórias*'s narrative rhythm is established by a continuous oscillation of the main characters between order and disorder, which defines a structural feature corresponding to the fluctuation of the lower-class free population in nineteenth-century Brazilian society. In Candido's view, *Memórias*'s realism and literary effectiveness owe not so much to its accuracy in depicting detail as to its formalization of a general social dynamic.

Candido's analysis has provided the basis for an extensive discussion of both Almeida's novel and Brazilian society's particularities. In the following section, I discuss those connections further by examining a feature of *Memórias* that has been overlooked by previous readings: the profusion of dispute and acts of vengeance in virtually all the characters' relationships. Such widespread disposition to quarrel corresponds to the episodic narrative organization and is related to the organization of Brazilian society, marked by slaveholding, patron–client relationships and an extensive urge to affirm social superiority.

Finally, I focus on the role *Memórias* has played in the historical development of early Brazilian fiction. As the adjustment of the novel as a form to the specific social conditions of the country implied a disparity between the individualist and liberal values of the European plot, on the one hand, and the authority-based relations of Brazilian society, on the other, the first attempts to produce a national variety of the novel confronted problems that required a development of the literary material itself, so that its formal potentialities could come out. Almeida produced a particular formal solution to the maladjustment of European thematic and ideological conventions to local social relations by way of a comical rendering of the tension between modern norms and their 'colonial' infringement, thus grasping the specific historical experience of Brazilian society more effectively than other writers' attempts to juxtapose the European realistic plot and the local environment.

General Features

Memórias de um sargento de milícias first appeared anonymously in weekly chapters from June 1852 to July 1853, in *Correio Mercantil*, a Liberal newspaper in Rio de Janeiro, and was published in two volumes in

1854–5.[1] It begins by telling the fortunes and misfortunes of Leonardo Pataca, which gradually give way to the exploits of his son, a likeable rascal also named Leonardo, whose bustling life from birth to young adulthood is depicted in a series of loosely tied episodes. In his rambling route towards happiness, Leonardo is raised by his godfather the Barber, grows up as a scamp, falls in love a couple of times, gets in trouble repeatedly and is harassed by the Chief of Police, Major Vidigal, who eventually arrests Leonardo and turns him into a soldier; in the end, Leonardo is nominated a sergeant, marries his childhood sweetheart Luisinha and achieves social ascent.

As the novel follows the experiences of the main characters, it also describes human types and popular customs, sketching a picture of the social landscape of Rio de Janeiro 'in the time of the king',[2] that is, in the period when King João VI and the Portuguese court, fleeing from the Napoleonic army, settled in the colonial territory in Portuguese America (1808–21).[3] Being set in the past, *Memórias* has a semi-historical component, but most of the historical references as well as information about customs are counterbalanced by a fable-like treatment of events.

In fact, *Memórias* presents a combination of features that resemble traits of different types of writing, and so literary historians and critics have striven to categorize it according to available genre descriptions, and the effort to define its literary affiliations has given rise to stubborn controversy.

During Manuel Antônio de Almeida's lifetime, his novel did not arouse significant commentary from his fellow writers. Critical attention to it developed only after his death and especially from the late nineteenth century onwards.[4] Since then, it has been regarded as a novel of manners, since it presents social types and occupations, picturesque places, popular customs, religious festivities and other traditional cultural practices. Often praised because of its (alleged) accuracy in portraying popular manners in early nineteenth-century Rio de Janeiro, *Memórias* has also been considered a source of historical information, much like the books by foreign travellers who described places and customs in Brazil at the time.[5] Be that as it may, the (supposed) veracity of the register of customs has been taken as evidence of the novel's realism. Moreover, because it portrayed people of the lower middle class in demotic style, avoiding sentimental lavishness, excess of suffering and pompous language, Almeida's novel seemed to be disconnected from the main trends of romantic fiction. So much so that *Memórias* has been said to be a forerunner of the realistic or naturalistic novel.[6]

For sure, *Memórias* does to some extent provide a chronicle of customs, but, rather than a feature that deviates from romantic convention, or anticipates realism, the documentary vein can be considered something that Almeida's novel shares with romantic *costumbrismo*, a particular trend in the Spanish, Portuguese and Latin American literature of the period, which is characterized by a predilection for portraying scenes of local or regional customs and types.[7] *Memórias*'s connection with Brazilian romantic literature can be best grasped with reference to nationalism, for its description of local circumstances and details is part of a general tendency of the novel of the time to observe and depict multifarious aspects of the country as a whole, since literary nationalism was meant, above all, to write about local scenes and customs. As critic Antonio Candido has argued, the nineteenth-century Brazilian novel developed primarily as a literary device for investigating human and regional diversity and for disclosing unknown aspects of society, thus enhancing the country's knowledge of itself.[8]

Insofar as the novel's main character is a sort of cunning rogue and because of its episodic structure, *Memórias* has also been associated with the tradition of the Spanish picaresque novel of the *Siglo de Oro*.[9] In a loose sense, the picaresque genre comprises not only the earliest Spanish variety but also works such as Lesage's *Gil Blas* (1715), Defoe's *Moll Flanders* (1722) and Fernández de Lizardi's *El Periquillo Sarniento* (1816), to name just a few. These later 'picaresque' novels, however, employ only the external formal structure of the Spanish model, since the moral vision charged with disenchantment (*desengaño*) is replaced by a new system of values relating to the rising bourgeoisie.[10] To a certain extent, Almeida's *Memórias* may even be connected to this tradition, but, as far as historical transformations in social and ideological content can radically alter the meaning of the employment of a previous literary form, particular traits in it that deviate from the picaresque model may be more revealing than the similarities.

Narrative Rhythm and Brazilian Society

Antonio Candido's 'Dialética da Malandragem' [Dialectic of Malandroism][11] is admittedly the most important and influential modern interpretation of *Memórias*. Its point of departure is a discussion of *Memórias*'s literary affiliations, taking issue with both the critics who see Almeida's novel as picaresque and those who praise it for its documentary information.

Candido acknowledges that Almeida may have been acquainted with works that make use of the picaresque structure, but, proceeding to a comparison of *Memórias* with the picaresque genre, pointing out both affinities with and differences from it, he prefers to describe Leonardo not as a *pícaro* but as a *malandro*,[12] that is, a cunning rogue, 'coming from an almost folkloric tradition and corresponding ... to a certain comic and popular atmosphere of its time in Brazil'.[13] Rather than linking *Memórias* directly to a remote Spanish model, Candido investigates the particular elements that connect the novel to local cultural traditions. Firstly, he describes the *malandro* as a specimen of the mythical trickster, common to all folklores, including Brazilian popular stories (such as those about Pedro Malasartes). Secondly, Candido relates *Memórias* to local satirical writing in journalism, the emergence of caricature in Brazilian newspapers and the comic plays of Martins Pena.

Most decisively, Candido analyses the composition of *Memórias*, focusing on the system of relations in which Leonardo is involved in order to demonstrate how it is regulated by an internal rule of composition that articulates Almeida's novel to Brazilian society more effectively than does its descriptions of customs. Observing the social map of the fictional universe depicted in it, Candido describes the movement of the characters in the plot as a 'dialectic of order and disorder', that is to say, a permanent alternation between acceptance of established norms and transgression of those norms, between licit and illicit, between law and its infringement. This fluctuation can be grasped in the actions of Leonardo, who continuously shifts from one pole to the other; in the course of the story, he turns in succession from devilish child to dependant, from servant of the royal pantries to vagrant, from prisoner to soldier and from prankster to sergeant. This progression is not restricted to situations in which the main characters are involved, for most episodes in the novel, even those concerning secondary events, are ruled by this dynamic of order and disorder, which operates as an organizing principle of the novel's formal structure.

In a noteworthy passage of his essay, Candido analyses a scene near the end of the novel in which Major Vidigal, till then a central representative of order, is led to infringe the law himself, conceding a favour on behalf of Leonardo in exchange for personal satisfaction, as a result of an agreement with his former mistress. In the chapter 'Three Women on a Mission', Leonardo's godmother, Dona Maria (a wealthy matron) and Maria Regalada (Vidigal's former mistress) visit the Chief of Police in his house to plead for Leonardo's release from prison. Vidigal yields 'to the petition of an "easy" lady supported by a capitalist lady, in a smooth collusion of the two hemispheres [of order and disorder], on the initiative of a third lady, who circulates freely between the two'.[14] As Candido says, there is a particular feature in this scene that synthesizes, as a symbol, the combination of order and disorder and the final subversion of values:

> When the women arrive at his house ... the Major appears in a cotton print dressing gown and wooden clogs, in a slovenliness that contradicts the uprightness he has displayed throughout the narrative. Perplexed by the visit, dissolving in the smiles and chills of senile eroticism, he runs inside and returns arrayed in his uniform dress coat, properly buttoned up and shining in his gold braid, but with his everyday trousers and the same clogs pounding on the floor. And thus we have our severe dragon of order, the ethical conscience of the world, reduced to a lively image of the two hemispheres, because at that moment when he transgresses his own norms in the face of the seduction of his old and, perhaps, once again lover, he has really become the equal of any of the *malandros* he has persecuted.[15]

Candido also observes how Almeida's novel presents the characters' comings and goings between the social spheres of order and disorder in an open-minded fashion, without ascribing a positive or negative value to either order or disorder, and certainly not endorsing the conventional approval of established norms and admonition of transgressive practices. The narrative voice does repeatedly judge the characters' conduct, but the frame of evaluation is not stable, so that at times the narrator judges from the standpoint of the norm and at times from that of its infringement. By moving to and fro between the two poles, the narrator himself takes part in the general oscillation of the main characters. The result of this variation in the narrator's point of view is a 'moral neutrality',[16] or rather an incorporation of two diverging social viewpoints that cancel each other out.

Candido's main insight, however, pertains to the connection of this plot dynamic to Brazilian society. The characters' movement between order and disorder, he remarks, 'recalls the mode of formation of families, prestige, fortunes, and reputations in urban Brazil in the first half of the nineteenth century'.[17] Besides this general resemblance, Candido shows how the novel integrates, in its inner formal structure, a constitutive principle of society. *Memórias* is significant, he argues, not so much because of the documentary description or the exposition of customs, but because it is 'constructed according to the general rhythm of the society, seen through one of its sectors'. That is, the novel presents, at a deeper level, a hidden principle of composition that unifies the particular elements of the apparent level and also functions as a literary correlative of the social dynamic of Brazil at the time. It is the internal law of the plot, manifesting in the novel's narrative rhythm, that captures the rule of life crucial for the social reproduction of an entire class in a slave-owning society in which only a few free people worked, and the others lived in insecurity, gleaning the remnants of dependency relations, or surviving by contrivance or petty theft.[18]

Brazilian society at the time was composed of roughly three distinct social strata: at the top was a class of proprietors who could afford the goods of modern civilization as well as cultural novelties (an example in the novel is Dona Maria, the rich matron with whom Leonardo's family has connections); as an extension of this class, there was an institutional administration (embodied in the police system, of which Major Vidigal is the unequivocal representative). At the base was the multitude of slaves on whom the burden of manual work was imposed (this group is virtually absent from *Memórias*). Between these two classes – the essential ones from the point of view of economic organization – was an intermediary group of people who were neither proprietors nor slaves; this class comprised those who had a regular occupation (bailiff, barber) or worked as servants of the Royal House, and all those who lived in dubious conditions (like the necromancer, the Gypsies, swindlers, etc.). As the reader will readily find out, most of the characters in the novel belong to that intermediate, half-anomic social stratum. As a consequence of an economic organization based on slave labour, the situation of the poor free people was marked by particular problems, since they generally depended on the protection of the rich (even if they had regular jobs) or had to resort to unlawful activities for their livelihood.

In a newly independent country that was striving to build a modern nation, and thus imposed rigid control over any kind of misbehaviour or turmoil, but could not provide the material conditions for an entire class to live in accordance with the law, people could not do without order nor could they live in conformity to it. Refraining from the ideological desire for discipline and accepting the unruly exploits of the poor, *Memórias* expresses 'the vast general accommodation that dissolves the extremes, [and] confuses the meaning of law and order'. Because it mingles these disparate attitudes, Almeida's novel is, to quote Candido again, 'perhaps the only one in Brazilian literature of the nineteenth century that does not express the vision of the dominant class'.[19]

Quarrelsome Disposition

The society presented in *Memórias* is governed by relationships of favour and dependency;[20] as the narrator puts it, 'the use of influence, of connections among parents and godparents constituted a true mainspring within the entire working of society'.[21] Such relationships are decisive in the novel's denouement, in which, as already mentioned, the godmother, Dona Maria, and Maria Regalada make an arrangement with Major Vidigal so that Leonardo may be forgiven. As a consequence of this agreement, the Major not only releases Leonardo from prison and from the humiliating punishment of being whipped, but also promotes him to the position of sergeant (and finally manages his transfer to the militia so that Leonardo can marry Luisinha). This incident indicates the actual power relations that effectively interfere in the course of events and in the characters' fate.

A comparable instance of the significance of influence and connections occurs in an early episode, in which Leonardo Pataca is taken to the guardhouse after being caught in a necromancy ritual, and the godmother seeks help from a lieutenant colonel who, in turn, appeals to an influent nobleman who manages Pataca's release.[22] Most of the time, however, such power relations are only alluded to rather than developed in full narrative display. When the godmother finds a position for Leonardo in the royal pantries, the narrator suggests that she has attained it by means of unlawful patronage: 'How the *comadre* had been able to arrange such a thing for her godson is something that should be of little concern for us.'[23]

Even in the episode in which Leonardo becomes an *agregado*, that is, a dependant attached to the household of a family, the narrator comments on two general situations of the dependant in the family, but the specific problems relating to Leonardo and the matriarchs of Vidinha's household are only hinted at. At one point, Leonardo is arrested by Vidigal, and the matrons assume Leonardo must have hidden himself on purpose. Their indignation turns into 'intense hatred', insofar as they believe that such an attitude of Leonardo's would be a sign of his 'ingratitude ... toward those people who had so generously taken him in'.[24] Since the family have given shelter to Leonardo, the matrons expect him to be loyal and grateful to them, a reaction that implies that Leonardo's admission into the family entails the submission of the dependant to his protectors. However, as the plot unfolds, Leonardo becomes a soldier and the problems concerning the social and moral dilemmas of dependency break off without narrative development. Although favour and accommodation are prevailing relationships in the society depicted in

Memórias, most narrative scenes that actually show the characters' interrelations and actions are dominated by another kind of relationship, one characterized by a disposition to quarrel and revenge.[25]

Let us examine a sequence of events in the first part of the novel, in which a succession of revengeful actions occurs. Leonardo is raised by his godfather, the barber, who fancies a brilliant future for the child and yearns to see him eventually ordained as a priest. The godfather's babbling neighbour mocks him when she sees his unsuccessful attempts to teach Leonardo the Lord's Prayer. The godfather reacts, and an argument takes place, full of mutual insult and offence, until Leonardo appears and mimics the neighbour, avenging the godfather, who bursts into laughter.[26] Soon afterwards, Leonardo, now a sacristan, tricks the same neighbour in the church; she complains to the liturgy master, who gives the boy a hefty reprimand. In turn, Leonardo plans an act of vengeance against the liturgy master, making him almost miss his sermon; because he has arrived late, the liturgy master gets into a wrangle with the Italian Capuchin friar who has offered to improvise the sermon in his place, and dismisses Leonardo afterwards. As soon as the news reaches the neighbourhood, the annoying lady, avenged, nags Leonardo's godfather, and the altercation restarts all over again.[27]

Throughout the story, similar situations arise: Leonardo Pataca hires a ruffian, Chico Juca, to take revenge against the Gypsy girl; Leonardo's godmother defames José Manuel, who is contending with her godson for Luisinha's affection; Leonardo quarrels with the royal pantries' lackey and with Vidinha's cousins on account of a love dispute; Teotônio, a prankster, mockingly mimics Major Vidigal; etc. In all these episodes, the prevailing interpersonal relations are ruled by a peculiar disposition to quarrel, which ranges from mockery to physical assault. This propensity for quarrelling throughout the novel suggests that it is not merely an individual trait and is, rather, a socially determined behaviour. Thus, the majority of episodes, however diverse their apparent motifs, are similar in nature, for they are propelled by the quarrelsome disposition that establishes a pattern of successive revengeful actions in the dynamics of the plot and thereby defines a unifying structural principle of the novel.

The main conflict between Leonardo and Major Vidigal is itself tinged by revengeful feelings; the Chief of Police strives to arrest Leonardo not so much because of his commitment to maintaining order, but rather because of a personal dispute. When Leonardo gets a position in the royal pantries and seems to change his ways by living in conformity to the law, the Major thinks regretfully, 'I wonder if he is really changing … If he does change I lose my revenge.'[28]

Besides this conflict, which embodies the divergence between different social groups, most episodes in the novel concern rivalry and dispute involving characters who occupy near-equivalent social positions. In the context of a slave-owning society in which patron–client relationships prevail, the propensity to quarrel can be understood as a resource of the poor to imaginarily compensate for the subaltern position they are constrained to occupy. In *Memórias*, avenging oneself is not so much an action to get even as it is a way of demeaning others to affirm one's own supposed superiority. It is an imaginary compensation because the one who wins a dispute is momentarily raised to a position of fanciful pre-eminence which is not sustained by any real material basis. So much so that the one who is defeated will soon attempt to avenge himself and, if successful, will reverse the situation and affirm an imaginary superiority in turn.

Wealth and property are the material foundations of social power, sustaining the all-pervading web of favour and the social eminence of the owning class; but among the poor who are located in a roughly equivalent social rank, and especially when they are disconnected from the protection of actual sources of power, vengeance and rivalry are resources for obtaining a sense of social significance.

In *Memórias*, real power is exerted by Major Vidigal, the police authority and a surrogate of the proprietary class. His activity in the novel consists of patrolling the poor and punishing all irregular conduct, constraining them to live in conformity to a discipline they cannot adjust to in the conditions of the 'semi-colonial' country. Imbued with the prerogatives of his position, Vidigal acts as the 'absolute monarch' and 'supreme arbiter' of justice: 'he did as he chose, and no one called him to account'.[29]

This arbitrary will operates as a means to attest and reinforce the upper class's social superiority. Thus, Vidigal is never satisfied by merely arresting lawbreakers; he subjects them to humiliation, as in the scene in which the Major forces the participants in the necromancy ritual to continue dancing while the grenadiers ridicule them.[30] Moreover, Vidigal cannot bear in his vanity to be offended or demeaned in the eyes of others; that is what happens when Leonardo escapes detention: 'If Leonardo had not run away but had arranged his release some other way, Vidigal might even have become his friend in the end. But having been left in a bad light, the Major would now regard him as his inveterate enemy until he could get full revenge.'[31]

Likewise, the wealthy matron Dona Maria, who 'had a good heart, was generous, devout, a friend to the poor',[32] is prone to dispute as well; her mania for lawsuits is an expression of the way she takes care of those who disturb her exercising of her power. At one point, a story is heard in the town concerning a girl who had run off with a man when she was going to pray at the Stone Oratory, taking with her a 'goodly portion of gold pieces'.[33] The godmother makes a false accusation against José Manuel, suggesting he was the man with whom the girl had fled, and Dona Maria says, 'If I were a relative of the girl, I'd slap such a lawsuit on that monster as would teach him.'[34]

The profusion of quarrelsome and revengeful actions in *Memórias* suggests that characters of the lower social strata re-enact the belligerence and misconduct of the upper-class figures who have unlimited scope for arbitrary action, which is a sign of their social pre-eminence. The reproduction of the disposition to quarrel is, therefore, a result of the organization of society as a whole, in which rigid social hierarchy is continually reaffirmed. If the impulse for revenge is a psychological trait, it is also a socially mediated one and cannot be regarded solely as a problem of personal moral conduct.

This quarrelsome disposition can also be interpreted as a literary correlative of an actual tendency to conflict in mid-nineteenth-century Brazil, concerning the struggle for work in a society in which the free labour market was compromised by the predominance of slave labour. As historians have pointed out, master artisans preferred to train their slaves rather than free apprentices; by the same token, proprietors trained their slaves in skilled occupations, since this would increase the value of the slaves and of the wages they could earn as *negros de ganho* (blacks for hire). In these circumstances, since the early nineteenth century, poor whites had protested against the training of slaves as skilled craftsmen, which suggests that free whites could no longer compete with slaves to get work.[35] Moreover, at the time the novel was being written, there had been an expansion of social conflicts involving poor free whites, former slaves and *negros de ganho* who were fighting for work in the streets of Rio de Janeiro.[36] From this perspective, the self-generating movement of successive acts of vengeance in *Memórias* may also be related to a particular social dynamic of conflict among the poor, although the novel does not portray competition for work directly.[37]

Memórias de um sargento de milícias in the Development of the Early Brazilian Novel

Memórias played an essential role in the adaptation of the European novel to local conditions in Brazil. Because of the historical circumstances in which it appeared, however, Almeida's work could not solve all the literary problems posed by the social and cultural situation of his time, for the local tradition of the novel was not yet sufficiently developed for the literary material itself to be grasped in its full complexity.

In the formative period of Brazilian literature, as studied by Antonio Candido, local intellectuals were eager to participate in modern Western culture, leaving colonial seclusion behind, and at the same time were committed to building a national culture with an identity of its own. Thus, the development of cultural life in the country was and is guided by a perennial tension between universalism and localism.[38] The completion of the formative process implied the construction of a national literary system and the establishment of a local literary tradition, capable of self-reference, that is to say, capable of 'produc[ing] works of the first order, influenced by previous national examples, not by immediate foreign models'.[39] In the case of the novel, the establishment of a local tradition required a complete reworking of the materials writers had to deal with.

As the novel had become a prestigious cultural commodity and begun to be popularized in Brazil, some writers sought to bring about a national version of it, but the first attempts at creating works of prose fiction inspired by the European novel in Brazil were irreparably flawed.[40] Besides the obvious difficulties in mastering coherent plot development and accommodating literary language in the realm of daily prose, since the prevailing style was then deeply suffused by the dominance of poetry, there were particular problems concerning the way the novel as a form shaped empirical elements of social reality.

The basic difficulty for the adaptation of the European novel to local conditions was the fact that the social presuppositions of its form – relating to bourgeois ideology and resulting from the expansion of modern capitalism – did not exist, or were modified, in a slave-owning society ruled by patron–client relationships.[41] The main themes of the European novel of the time and the ideological coordinates that guided it did not find exact correspondence in nineteenth-century Brazilian society, since the reproduction of the 'semi-colonial' structure conditioned the accumulation of wealth and the cultural up-to-dateness of the upper class. Slaveholding, relationships of favour and peculiar forms of social interaction persisted, absorbing ideological and material demands from bourgeois civilization, which resulted in a complex historical experience. Relocated in this society, the novel would start to operate according to a different logic. Correspondingly, for the Brazilian novel to prosper a previous process of working out the literary material was necessary, adjusting it to this particular historical context.

The challenge of producing a local variety of the novel could not be solved by the mere juxtaposing of local setting and European plot, but to bring together those two conflicting elements was a crucial moment in the formation of the Brazilian novel, since the flaws so produced would disclose the real nature of the local social and literary materials.

After a number of lesser attempts at prose fiction by authors such as Pereira da Silva, Gonçalves de Magalhães, Joaquim Norberto and Teixeira e Sousa, who had written historical, sentimental and melodramatic stories,[42] Joaquim Manuel de Macedo had stabilized the novel as a form in Brazil. With the publication of *A moreninha* [*The Brunette*] (1844), he gave rise to a novel of manners which presented characters akin to the local bourgeoisie and contrived a diction and style adjusted to his social environment. Throughout his prolific career, Macedo generally repeated the formula of the sentimental plot. Although his novels were undeniably an improvement on previous efforts, his work was not without flaws. There remained a discrepancy between the portrayal of local characters and the employment of European romantic conventions. As Antonio Candido remarks, Macedo's work superimposes a romantic plot upon the depiction of socially plausible characters, resulting in an awkward combination; 'so much so that we wonder how it is possible for such ordinary people to get involved in the unforeseen happenings [Macedo] submits them to'.[43]

In the subsequent expansion of the urban novel, José de Alencar, following in Macedo's footsteps, developed the rearrangement of the European plot – now in a more realistic vein – in the local social setting. With greater analytical discernment and thematic sophistication, in novels such as *Senhora* (1875), Alencar left behind the provincial character of his predecessor's work, bringing the contemporary issues of money and individualism to the foreground. By doing so, however, he also deepened the incongruity between modern European themes and Brazilian social backwardness in the novel's composition. While the central conflict involving the main characters implies the coordinates of liberal–romantic values, the secondary characters are ruled by traditional patron–client relationships, producing a dissonance. The clash between the two incompatible elements, as Roberto Schwarz has shown,[44] resulted in a fractured or inconsistent form, suggesting that the formula of the European novel was not suited to depicting the logic of relationships in Brazil.

To be sure, the Brazilian novel could not do away with the discrepancy between European form and local social content, but it had to deal with it in such a way as to find a narrative structure capable of turning the incongruity itself into an element of the controlled logic of formal composition. For that to happen, however, it would be necessary for the literary raw material to be apprehended in its full complexity, understood not simply as supposedly pure local content, untouched by foreign elements, but rather as content that already contained the European form as an ineffective one. The Brazilian novel could only attain full realization when its literary material took in, 'at the level of content, the unsuitability of the European form'.[45]

In a different line of development, Almeida's *Memórias* belongs to a tradition of comic rendering of popular life. Almeida's main predecessor was Martins Pena, whose comic plays, such as *O juiz de paz na roça* [*The Justice of the Peace in the Countryside*] (1833) and *O inglês maquinista* [*The English Train Driver*] (1842), are similar in theme and diction to *Memórias*. Both Martins Pena and Almeida incorporate a popular social standpoint in their work and deal with modern bourgeois ideas and values with amusing nonchalance. Later, other comical novels, such as Macedo's *A luneta mágica* [*The Magic Eyeglass*] (1869) and Luís Guimarães Júnior's *A família Agulha* [*The Needle Family*] (1870), would come out, although with a somewhat different tone, closer to the local bourgeois viewpoint than to the popular one.

Almeida's main contribution to the development of the novel in Brazil is the creation of a narrative framework based on the actual social relations that prevailed locally; by doing so, he avoided the incongruency that the direct transposition of the European plot produced in other writers' works. Instead of clinging to the themes of the romantic or realistic novel, Almeida takes local relations as a point of departure and organizes the novel's plot in conformity to particular features of Brazilian society; thus, for instance, the motif of social ascent – a crucial one in the bourgeois realistic novel – acquires a different character in *Memórias*, since it functions according to the logic of relationships of favour.

The fact that the story of Leonardo is set in the past helps to render local social interaction and develop a narrative rhythm and structure suited to the depiction of traditional relationships. In *Memórias*, the narrator is located in mid-nineteenth-century Brazil and, as such, is partly imbued with modern values and a modern sense of morality. This viewpoint is embedded in some of the narrator's remarks but is absent from the characters' consciousness. Thus, for instance, when Leonardo becomes a dependant, a degrading condition from the point of view of the bourgeois idea of individual freedom and autonomy, the narrator remarks, 'Anyone older – or, to be precise, anyone with more sense and better rearing – would have been ashamed, and perhaps greatly so, at finding himself in Leonardo's position, but he did not give that a thought.'[46] Much of the novel's comical effect results from this tension between modern norm and 'colonial' infringement.

Nonetheless, the same features that enable *Memórias* to establish a narrative structure suited to depicting local social relations and avoiding formal incongruity also has a drawback, since they prevent the extensive incorporation of modern motifs and issues or the way they function in the local context. In *Memórias*, the achievement of a literary form adjusted to local particularities is obtained at the cost of cutting off the connection with the contemporary world.[47] Although the tension between modern moral sense and the arrangements of clientelism is embedded in the depiction of events, *Memórias* does not work out this tension thoroughly; it has not developed a literary form capable of dealing with contemporary issues and their displacement in Brazil.

Moreover, an effect of *Memórias*'s formal solution, according to Schwarz, is 'the suspension of determinate historical conflicts through a general expertise in the art of survival, which does not internalize these conflicts and has no knowledge of moral convictions or remorse'.[48] Although *Memórias* explores the movement and rhythm of a particular class, it also presents an attractive image of the country – based on conciliation and *malandragem* – in which historical conflicts are disguised.

The rhythm of continual reversibility between norm and its infringement, as well as the all-pervasive desire to affirm social distinction found in the disposition to quarrel, which Almeida transposes into the structure of *Memórias*, provided a crucial element of the literary materials Machado de Assis would later deal with in the composition of *Memórias póstumas de Brás Cubas* [*The Posthumous Memoirs of Brás Cubas*] (1880).[49] As Schwarz has shown, once adjusted to the social experience of the upper class, this rhythm 'is brought up to the Alencarian heights of a demanding, contemporary self-awareness'; conversely, the subjective aspirations of the individual self are adjusted to 'the lively merry-go-round, with no intention of reforming itself, that the literary tradition of a popular inspiration succeeded in inventing',[50] so that the combination of the backward system of relations and the modern normative demands results in reciprocal condemnation.

Thus, Manuel Antônio de Almeida's *Memórias de um sargento de milícias* marks an essential moment in the formation of Brazilian novel, since its comic deployment of particular patterns of social behaviour achieves a literary result that would be unattainable by means of the uncritical transposition of the prevailing models of romantic or realistic European plots. In exploring relationships of favour, disregard of bourgeois norms, and propensity to quarrel, *Memórias* has a consistent formal structure suited to capturing a significant component of the historical experience of nineteenth-century Brazilian society. As Candido suggests, Almeida presented a definite vision of Brazilian society with an acute sense of the potential and the limits of his art, and because of this he prefigured Machado de Assis's extraordinary literary self-consciousness.[51]

Notes

1. Manuel Antônio de Almeida (1831–61) was a 21-year-old student of medicine working on *Correio Mercantil* when he started writing *Memórias de um sargento de milícias*. It is generally accepted that some of the incidents of Almeida's novel were inspired by stories he heard from an older newpaper colleague, Antônio César Ramos, a retired sergeant who had worked under the real Major Vidigal.
2. Almeida 2000, 65; Almeida 1999, 7.
3. In 1808 João was still prince regent; he became King João VI in 1816, after the death of his mother, Queen Maria I.
4. The first substantial critical assessment of *Memórias* was by José Veríssimo (1894).
5. See, for instance, Pereira 1944, 54–5. Mário de Andrade stresses Almeida's skilfulness in representing folk culture and manners (Andrade 1974, 130–3). See also Galvão 1976.
6. Veríssimo, a critic who lived in the period of naturalism, suggests that *Memórias* was somehow a precursor of realism and naturalism (Veríssimo 1894, 117; Veríssimo 1963, 199); after him, a number of commentaries on the novel would reiterate his assertion.
7. See Merquior 1977, 71.
8. See Antonio Candido 1993b, Vol. 2, 97–105.
9. Andrade has claimed that *Memoirs* is not a precursor of realism, but rather belongs to a tradition of works that emerge on the margins of the dominant trends of their time, such as the Spanish picaresque novel (Andrade 1974, 136–8). Various critics have since explored the affinity between *Memórias* and the picaresque novel. See, for instance, Montello 1955; González 1994.
10. See Carpeaux, Vol. 2, 682–91. See also Prado 2003.
11. Antonio Candido 1993a; Antonio Candido 1995, 79–103. For a thorough commentary on Antonio Candido's essay, see Schwarz 1987.
12. In common usage, *malandro* refers to a Brazilian social type, a rogue or a scamp who usually does not work and lives on the margins of legality, employing astute means to survive.
13. Antonio Candido 1993a, 25; Antonio Candido 1995, 83 (translation slightly modified).
14. Antonio Candido 1993a, 43; Antonio Candido 1995, 94.
15. Antonio Candido 1993a, 43–4; Antonio Candido 1995, 94 (translation slightly modified).
16. Antonio Candido 1993a, 52; Antonio Candido 1995, 101.
17. Antonio Candido 1993a, 52; Antonio Candido 1995, 101.
18. See Antonio Candido 1993a, 45; Antonio Candido 1995, 95.
19. Antonio Candido 1993a, 51; Antonio Candido 1995, 99–100.
20. On the centrality of favour or patron–client relationships in nineteenth-century Brazil, see Schwarz 1977; Schwarz 1992.
21. Almeida 2000, 319; Almeida 1999, 158.
22. Almeida 2000, 112–13, 121–3; Almeida 1999, 33, 40–1.
23. Almeida 2000, 282; Almeida 1999, 134.
24. Almeida 2000, 295; Almeida 1999, 142.
25. See Otsuka 2016, 61–95; Otsuka 2007; Otsuka 2008.
26. Almeida 2000, 125–9; Almeida 1999, 42–5.
27. Almeida 2000, 131–47; Almeida 1999, 50–5.
28. Almeida 2000, 282; Almeida 1999, 134.
29. Almeida 2000, 91; Almeida 1999, 22–3.
30. Almeida 2000, 93–5; Almeida 1999, 24.
31. Almeida 2000, 276; Almeida 1999, 130 (translation slightly modified).

32. Almeida 2000, 166; Almeida 1999, 64.
33. Almeida 2000, 210; Almeida 1999, 92.
34. Almeida 2000, 214; Almeida 1999, 94.
35. See Karasch 2001, 276; Karasch 1987, 199–200. See also Algranti 1988, 91.
36. See Alencastro 1988, 50.
37. For a full account of this connection, see Otsuka 2016, 61–95.
38. See Antonio Candido 1993b; Antonio Candido 1980. See also Schwarz 2012, 36–40.
39. Antonio Candido 1987, 153; Antonio Candido 1995, 131.
40. See Antonio Candido 1993b, 106–20.
41. The main sources for this section on the development of the Brazilian novel are Roberto Schwarz's 'A importação do romance e suas contradições em Alencar' (Schwartz 1977, 29–60), translated as 'The Importing of the Novel and Its Contradictions in Alencar's Novel' Schwartz (1992, 41–77), and *Um mestre na periferia do capitalismo* (1990, 207–27), translated as *A Master on the Periphery of Capitalism* (2001, 149–64).
42. For a description of the early Brazilian fiction, see Daniel (2006, 127–36).
43. Antonio Candido 1993b, 124.
44. Schwarz 1977, 48–51; Schwartz 1992, 64–8.
45. Schwarz 1977, 51; Schwartz 1992, 68. See also Schwarz 2012, 33–53.
46. Almeida 2000, 244; Almeida 1999, 112.
47. In this aspect, the limitation of Almeida's formal solution resembles that of Machado de Assis's first novels, although for quite different reasons. See Schwarz 1977, 65; Schwarz 1990, 219; Schwarz 2001, 158.
48. Schwarz 1987, 133; Schwarz 2012, 15. See also Schwarz's 'Outra Capitu' (Schwarz 1997, 133–4), translated as 'Another Capitu? Helena Morley's Diary' (Schwarz 2012, 181).
49. Assis 1988; Assis 1998.
50. Schwarz 1990, 224; Schwarz 2001, 161–2.
51. See Antonio Candido 1993b, 199.

Bibliography

Alencastro, Luiz Felipe de. 'Proletários e escravos: imigrantes portugueses e cativos africanos no Rio de Janeiro, 1850–1872', *Novos estudos CEBRAP* 21 (1988): 20–56.

Algranti, Leila Mezan. *O feitor ausente: estudo sobre a escravidão urbana no Rio de Janeiro*. Petrópolis, RJ: Vozes, 1988.

Almeida, Manuel Antônio. *Memoirs of a Militia Sergeant*, translated by Ronald W. Sousa. New York: Oxford University Press, 1999.

Almeida, Manuel Antônio. *Memórias de um sargento de milícias*, edited by Mamede Mustafa Jarouche. Cotia, SP: Ateliê Editorial, 2000.

Andrade, Mário de. 'Memórias de um sargento de milícias'. In *Aspectos da literatura brasileira*, 5th edn, 125–39. São Paulo: Martins, 1974.

Antonio Candido. 'Literatura e cultura de 1900 a 1945'. In *Literatura e sociedade: estudos de teoria e história literária*, 6th edn, 109–38. São Paulo: Companhia Editora Nacional, 1980.

Antonio Candido. 'Literatura e subdesenvolvimento'. In *A educação pela noite e outros ensaios*, 140–62. São Paulo: Ática, 1987.

Antonio Candido. 'Dialética da malandragem'. In *O discurso e a cidade*, 19–54. São Paulo: Duas Cidades, 1993a.

Antonio Candido. *Formação da literatura brasileira: momentos decisivos*, 7th edn. Belo Horizonte: Itatiaia, 1993b.

Antonio Candido. *On Literature and Society*, translated by Howard S. Becker. Princeton, NJ: Princeton University Press, 1995.

Assis, Machado de. *Memórias póstumas de Brás Cubas*. Rio de Janeiro: Garnier, 1988.

Assis, Machado de. *The Posthumous Memoirs of Brás Cubas*, translated by Gregory Rabassa. New York: Oxford University Press, 1998.

Carpeaux, Otto Maria. *História da literatura ocidental*, 3rd edn. Brasília: Edições do Senado Federal, 2008.

Daniel, Mary L. 'Brazilian Fiction from 1800 to 1855'. In *The Cambridge History of Latin American Literature*, Vol. 3, edited by Roberto González Echevarría and Enrique Pupo-Walker, 127–36. Cambridge: Cambridge University Press, 2006.

Galvão, Walnice Nogueira. 'No tempo do rei'. In *Saco de gatos*, 27–33. São Paulo: Duas Cidades/SCCT-SP, 1976.

González, Mario M. 'Nos primórdios da neopicaresca: *Memórias de um sargento de milícias*'. In *A saga do anti-herói: estudo sobre o romance picaresco espanhol e algumas de suas correspondências na literatura brasileira*, 278–96. São Paulo: Nova Alexandria, 1994.

Karasch, Mary C. *Slave Life in Rio de Janeiro, 1808–1850*. Princeton, NJ: Princeton University Press, 1987.

Karasch, Mary C. *A vida dos escravos no Rio de Janeiro (1808–1850)*, translated by Pedro Maia Soares. São Paulo: Companhia das Letras, 2001.

Merquior, José Guilherme. *De Anchieta a Euclides: breve história da literatura brasileira*. Rio de Janeiro: José Olympio, 1977.

Montello, Josué. 'Um precursor: Manuel Antônio de Almeida'. In *A literatura no Brasil*, edited by Afrânio Coutinho, Vol. 2, 37–45. Rio de Janeiro: Sul Americana, 1955.

Otsuka, Edu Teruki. 'Espírito rixoso: para uma reinterpretação das *Memórias de um sargento de milícias*', *Revista do Instituto de Estudos Brasileiros* 44 (February 2007): 105–24.

Otsuka, Edu Teruki. 'Rixas no tempo do rei', *Revista USP* 79 (September–November 2008): 132–41.

Otsuka, Edu Teruki. *Era no tempo do rei: atualidade das Memórias de um sargento de milícias*. Cotia, SP: Ateliê Editorial, 2016.

Pereira, Astrojildo. 'Romancistas da cidade: Manuel Antônio, Macedo e Lima Barreto'. In *Interpretações*, 48–113. Rio de Janeiro: Casa do Estudante do Brasil, 1944.

Prado, Raquel de Almeida. *A jornada e a clausura: figuras do indivíduo no romance filosófico*. Cotia, SP: Ateliê Editorial, 2003.

Schwarz, Roberto. *Ao vencedor as batatas: forma literária e processo social nos inícios do romance brasileiro*. São Paulo: Duas Cidades, 1977.

Schwarz, Roberto. *Que horas são?* São Paulo: Companhia das Letras, 1987.

Schwarz, Roberto. *Um mestre na periferia do capitalismo: Machado de Assis*. São Paulo: Duas Cidades, 1990.

Schwarz, Roberto. *Misplaced Ideas: Essays on Brazilian Culture*, edited by John Gledson. London: Verso, 1992.

Schwarz, Roberto. *Duas meninas*. São Paulo: Companhia das Letras, 1997.

Schwarz, Roberto. *A Master on the Periphery of Capitalism: Machado de Assis*, translated by John Gledson. Durham, NC: Duke University Press, 2001.

Schwarz, Roberto. *Two Girls and Other Essays*, edited by Francis Mulhern. London: Verso, 2012.

Veríssimo, José. 'Um velho romance brasileiro'. In *Estudos brasileiros: segunda série (1889–1893)*, 107–24. Rio de Janeiro: Laemmert, 1894.

Veríssimo, José. *História da literatura brasileira: de Bento Teixeira (1601) a Machado de Assis (1908)*, 4th edn. Brasília: UnB, 1963.

3

A providência, recordação dos tempos coloniais and the Novel in Brazil

Marcus Vinicius Nogueira Soares

The novel *A providência, recordação dos tempos coloniais* [*The Providence, Remembrances of Colonial Times*], by Antônio Gonçalves Teixeira e Sousa, was first published in the Carioca[1] newspaper *Correio Mercantil, e instrutivo, político, universal* between 26 January and 17 June 1854. It was the sixth and last novel by the author, whose first was *O filho do pescador* [*The Son of the Fisherman*], published in 1843. In the newspaper, the text appeared in the feuilleton section, usually on the first page, although it was occasionally found on the second. It was divided into five volumes and 61 chapters, including the prologue and conclusion.

The novel came out as a book in the same year, in five volumes printed by Tipografia de M. Barreto, with the same number and order of chapters as in the newspaper. One could say that *A providência* is the most ambitious novel by Teixeira e Sousa, not only because of its length but also because of its structure, which includes various subgenres of the novel (historical, gothic, didactic, adventure, etc.) and also other literary and non-literary genres, such as the sermon, the essay and the melodrama. It thus constitutes a kind of compendium of Western literature from the seventeenth century onwards. This chapter will explore the presence of the historical novel – especially the Luso-Brazilian reception of the Scottian model – and the sermon in the construction of possible meanings for *A providência*.

The Historical Novel

Although the novel's title immediately refers the reader to a religious discourse, a fitting starting point for this chapter is provided by the subtitle,

'Remembrances of Colonial Times', since it indicates a possible classification of Teixeira e Sousa's narrative as a historical novel. The assumption is that the subtitle is a paratextual resource that circumscribes what will be read within a genre, which, in turn, guides the reading. To assess the debate around this type of novel in the Brazilian mid nineteenth century, two articles by the Fluminense[2] historian and novelist João Manuel Pereira da Silva (1817–98), both published in *Jornal dos Debates, políticos e literários*, deserve attention.

In 'Revista Dramática' ['Theatre Review'], published on 8 July 1837, Pereira da Silva comments on the staging of a French version of Gaetano Donizetti's opera *Lucia di Lammermoor* (1835), based on Walter Scott's *The Bride of Lammermoor* (1819), and stresses the importance of the Scottish writer as the creator of 'a new literary genre', which he named 'historical novels'.[3] He praises Scott's ability to promote Scotland as a great European nation by presenting to the world 'its glorious bards, its interesting chronicles, its picturesque legends, the originality of its clans and its customs different from those of other peoples in Europe'.[4]

In 'Os romances modernos e sua influência' ['Modern Novels and Their Influence'], published on 23 September 1837, Pereira da Silva approaches Scott's work once more. He starts by showing the importance of the novel in the cultural origins of peoples: 'Through novels, almost all literatures start; peoples' infancy is always rocked in the cradle of fiction and in games of imagination.'[5] After briefly presenting the development of the genre from the ancient Hebrews to the late eighteenth century, the author points out a rupture in the nineteenth century, reaffirming his view of Scott's decisive contribution: 'The man who entirely changed the shape of the novel and gave it some historical spirit, some form of the philosophical ideal of Beauty, that man was Walter Scott.'[6] He then evaluates the legacy of the Scottish novelist in different cultural milieux, from Alessandro Manzoni's Italy to Victor Hugo's France and James Fenimore Cooper's United States.

Before the end of the article, Pereira da Silva highlights another subgenre, not a historical one, that expresses the 'praise of intimate feeling'[7] and finds in Johann Wolfgang von Goethe its creator and in Friedrich von Schiller, Bernardin de Saint-Pierre and François-René de Chateaubriand its main players. Pereira da Silva's treatment of the genre issue, the privileges he attributes to the novel, and specifically to the historical novel, may have been associated with the need for a properly national literature as was sought by the literati in the first half of the nineteenth century. After all, if literature starts with the novel, Brazilian literature had not yet started – a situation that would change when Pereira da Silva himself published, from 1839 on, various fictional historical narratives in the royal court's periodicals.

Sixteen years later, something similar would be articulated in the Brazilian press. In the introduction to his novel *Calabar: história brasileira do século XVII* [*Calabar: Seventeenth-Century Brazilian History*], part of which was published by *Correio Mercantil* in 1853 and the whole of which was published by the same paper and in book form a year later, Portuguese writer José da Silva Mendes Leal Júnior (1820–86), takes upon himself the task suggested by Jean-Ferdinand Denis 30 years earlier: the writer wishing to create a Brazilian literature should look to the national historical tradition for raw material.[8] Says the author of *Calabar*,

> The very rich elements of Brazilian history, disseminated and scattered, need collecting and coordinating by competent hands, a robust mind, and a systematic and philosophic spirit. It is a beautiful enterprise, which will certainly tempt someone with a strong will and a conscientious knowledge. Brazil will also have its Alexandre Herculano, as France had its A. Thierry.[9]

This is not, though, a denial that a national literature is underway. Leal Júnior does cite Gonçalves Dias's poetry, although he considers it almost an exception among 'babbling creations'[10] that only mirror European works. Actually, 'Brazil does not have yet, to the author's knowledge, a national novel.'[11] And it does not have it because the country is still in a phase between 'youth' and 'virility' in its trajectory as a nation.

Correlating, thus, literary genres and the different phases in the development of a national literature, Leal Júnior points out that 'lyric is the first literary manifestation'[12] of a people, a natural and inherent expression of the soul. Following the metaphor of the physiological development of a national body, he goes on to associate legends and fairy tales with infancy, 'chants of war and love'[13] with youth and, finally, 'the austere and grand epopee, the vast and wise poem that inherits the gifts from the past and prepares the seeds of the future'[14] with the period of manhood.

If the accomplishment of this process depends on profound historiographical endeavour, it must not be limited to the collector's or the archaeologist's work, or that of the professionals of universities and monasteries, since their erudite publications would be almost incomprehensible and unenjoyable for a larger public. Hence the importance of the novel as a mediating form: 'All know today that the novel is not history but an incentive to it, or a way to understand it, not in its chronology but in its thought and spirit, as an attraction that favours perception.'[15] As Leal Júnior sums up, if 'meridional America has its Washington … it still lacks its Cooper'.[16] Like Pereira da Silva, Leal Júnior devised a platform for the historical novel based on the work of this genre's Scottish creator: 'a modern critic says, "Scotland owes more to Walter Scott than to all of its chroniclers"'.[17]

Thus, *Calabar* would be the Portuguese contribution to the formation or, more exactly, the consolidation of Brazilian literature. From the huge collection of historical events available to writers, Leal Júnior selected the well-known episode of treason by the *mameluco*[18] Domingos Fernandes Calabar during the Dutch occupation of Pernambuco. The novel covers the period between 1630, when the occupation started, and 1635, when Calabar was captured and executed by the Luso-Brazilian resistance. It is interesting to note that, in spite of the title, the narrative comes from another historical character, João Fernandes Vieira, who, in the novel, ends up in a love triangle with Calabar and Maria Cesar, the daughter of the aristocrat Francisco Berenguer de Andrade – personalities included in the historiography of Pernambuco.

The novel is riddled with meticulously described battles and grand heroic gestures, all in gorgeous natural landscapes, where native peoples and the Catholic Church are in evidence, the former participating directly in combat and the latter represented by the Society of Jesus through Friar Manuel de Moraes (who, incidentally, is the protagonist of a novel by Pereira da Silva published in 1866). In spite of the differences – after all, the Fluminense author was concerned with properly starting a national literature and not just producing a single novel – both Pereira da Silva and Mendes Leal Júnior understood Walter Scott's importance within universal parameters. They did so not only in terms of the breadth of his influence, reaching beyond European borders, but also in relation to the consolidation of a literary structure that would work in various cultural environments, providing a model available to any writer interested in rebuilding the past through the history of the nationality one intends to constitute.

In that sense, Georg Lukács suggests a particular reading of Walter Scott's novel that could be applied to *Calabar*. According to Lukács, Scott includes in his narratives the 'great crises of [the] historical life'[19] of a people, within which heroes of the middle ground move between opposing parties, bringing to light not only the elements of a general conflict, but also what remains afterwards: everyday life as 'an important foundation for the continuity of cultural development'.[20] In his novel, Leal Júnior chooses the crisis precipitated by the Dutch invasion of Pernambuco as the moment when consciousness of a new nationality germinated from the alliance between the Portuguese and the native Brazilians to expel the aggressor.

In contrast to Scott, in Leal Júnior such consciousness does not depend on the participation of the lower strata of society.

When it was published by the *Correio Mercantil*, the first chapter of *A providência* was expected to be a sequel to *Calabar*, interrupted six months before. A brief note followed the presentation of the new novel on 26 January 1854: 'Once Mr. Teixeira e Sousa's novel is published, we hope to continue and conclude the publication of Mr. Mendes Leal's *Calabar*.'[21] Ten years later, when *Calabar* was finally published in its entirety as a book, the editors would write about the importance of history in establishing a Brazilian nationality: 'The Dutch war, the struggle of a handful of undisciplined warriors, almost helpless against powerful Holland, an unremitting fight of patriotism against foreign domination, is an example that must be remembered today.'[22] Moreover, their note also points out the specific contribution of Leal Júnior as well as the effects of the mediating role of a historical novel as indicated by the Portuguese writer:

> However, if such facts already arouse enthusiasm in their silent simplicity, what effect will they have when recounted by Mr. Mendes Leal's fecund ingenuity, rich imagination, with all the galas of poetry, a trained pen, in style as in all the beauties of our language?[23]

The immediate reception of *A providência* was much more consistent with an archaeological matrix than with a properly historical one. In the introduction to the novel in the *Correio Mercantil* of 26 January 1854, the author, supposedly quoting a respectable opinion, writes that the merit of Teixeira e Sousa's work rests on his 'engendering it in a way that conveys many of our customs, uses, and habits from colonial times, thus granting the author the designation of archaeologist of our old traditions and still deeply missed uses'.[24]

A similar evaluation would appear the following year, in the review 'Reparos sobre um romance' [Notes on a Novel], published in *O Guanabara, revista mensal, artística e literária*. There the critic highlights 'three things in the novel: the fidelity to the uses of the time when the story unfolds, the convenience of its characters, and the local colour always lively, always brilliant'.[25] Finally, Teixeira e Sousa himself shows an interest in archaeology. Just after describing 'the meadows, woods, hills, and valleys of Campos-Novos',[26] the Cabo Frio region where the plot develops, he writes, 'The archaeologist, looking at the society of a century ago, hidden deep in that dust, finds himself between his contemporary society and the past one, two worlds almost opposed through their differences!'[27]

Considering the critical appreciation of both novels over the span of a decade, one may perceive a distinction between the historical and the archaeological within the Scottian pattern. The former entails a greater commitment of the novelist to historiography, thus to engaging with previously established narratives legitimated by a field of knowledge deemed able to describe the history of the country. Hence the need to include events that are historically recognized and amid which the novel's plot unfolds with the effective and direct participation of historical characters, as protagonists or otherwise, as is the case in *Calabar*. As in Scott's work, the historical crisis described in Leal Júnior's narrative aims to evoke historical consciousness of a nationality.

From an archaeological perspective, though, historical elements compose a large frame in which the plot develops. The recording of past habits and customs prevails, presenting the formative process of a people's cultural tradition. However, *A providência* does not, as Scott's novels do, treat crises as themes, nor does it develop their importance for the above-mentioned historical consciousness. Notwithstanding that the story takes place in the first half of the eighteenth century and in Brazil, the plot is not based on any historical fact nor are there historical characters; instead there are merely allusions to historical situations in which fictional characters were present, none of which alters the story.

In the chapters where Felipe, father of the young Narcisa, talks to his two guests, Pedro and Justino, he recalls his origins in Lisbon and tells the saga of his arrival in Brazil. To do so, he goes back to the stories of the explorer Fernão Mendes Pinto and the Portuguese presence in the Far East during the sixteenth century in order to highlight the importance of Macao, where his grandfather arrived in 1646 and became a rich trader. When his father and grandfather died, Felipe travelled to Macao to take over the business; he stayed there for five years before finally deciding to go back to Portugal. A heavy storm wrecked his ship and he was rescued by a Spanish vessel, but he entertained the idea of suicide, having lost his entire fortune. As if that were not enough, the vessel was taken by the Moors and all aboard became prisoners until they were rescued by a Portuguese ship.

Once free, Felipe arrived in Rio de Janeiro in 1707. After a few questions about the narrative he has just heard, Pedro asks Felipe if he has experienced any interesting episode in Brazil. He answers, 'Oh! Such long stories! I witnessed our shame, or rather the affront to us by the celebrated Duguay-Trouin, and the infamous and cowardly behaviour of Francisco de Morais. Don't you know the details of that story?'[28] Although Pedro does not know the episode, the report is postponed: 'I'll tell you on another occasion.'[29] In fact, the story of the successful French invasion of Rio de Janeiro in 1711, headed by the French pirate René Duguay-Trouin and causing the flight of Francisco de Castro Morais, governor of the captaincy, will be told not by Felipe but by Maria, his former lover, whom he believed to have been killed in Macao.

More than 40 years after the incidents in Asia, Maria shows up at the wedding party of Batista and Narcisa, one of the central female characters. She is disguised as an old wanderer who calls himself Providence and reveals to the guests the true story of Felipe, whose real name is Afonso Aranda. The circumstances of the French invasion, briefly presented by her, become just a scenario to reiterate the insidious character of Aranda: 'And what was Afonso Aranda doing through that night of ruin, disgrace, and desperation? He was stealing from his master, who had already done him much good and who had a blind and limitless trust in him.'[30]

Outside the dominant model of the historical novel adopted by nineteenth-century writers, as in Mendes Leal Júnior's *Calabar* or indeed in other novels by Teixeira e Sousa, such as *Gonzaga ou a conjuração de Tiradentes* [*Gonzaga or the Conspiracy of Tiradentes*], published in 1848, the author does not take as 'scenario for his work a fact already established in history'.[31] In that sense, Teixeira e Sousa has built a more properly 'archaeological novel', to adopt the term used by his contemporary critics.

In his examination of the novels of the author from Cabo Frio, Antonio Candido recognizes in the subtitle – 'Remembrances of Colonial Times', also employed in another book of the author's, the 1846 *As fatalidades de dois jovens* [*The Fatalities of Two Youngsters*] – a more adequate expression of the 'quasi-historical' character of *A providência*.[32] It is worth noting that the archaeological qualifier does not exclude the historical dimension, since it corresponds to a historically oriented type of fiction with the fundamental trait of redeeming cultural manifestations of the past in specific regions or even nationally, although without attempting to insert into the narrative any events from national historiography, whereby memorable personages would act as characters in the novel's plot.

In spite of references to various places in the world, from Lisbon to Santa Catarina and Macao, the narrative of *A providência* basically unfolds between two locations: the city of Rio de Janeiro and the surroundings of Cabo Frio, the author's hometown. The narrator presents the habits and social mores that would be distinctive of the inhabitants of those two locations. In the prologue, a young man goes to the Beco do

Cotovelo, in Rio, where Maria Rita lives, in order to escort her to another residence, in the Rua dos Ferradores, where her services are urgently expected:

> Mrs. Maria Rita took an old *lemiste*[33] skirt, tightened her faded *cabuya*[34] doublet and wrapped her shoulders in a *droguete*[35] cloak; thus dressed, she took a branch of rue from a big, dirty cup on top of an old table and, once out, got on the sedan chair, voluptuously sprawling in it with the air of a great Chinese lady in a superb palanquin.[36]

As soon as the retinue comprising Maria Rita, two slaves and the young man departs, the narrator intervenes: 'Although the narrator has not previously reported that a big fat cross was painted on the door of her house, the reader will perhaps have understood that Mrs. Maria Rita was a midwife.'[37]

What follows is a roster of city streets that the group perambulates to reach its destination. The triviality of the scene is marked by the narrator's interest in presenting old practices in Rio de Janeiro, here associated with a professional activity. The goal is reached by a series of cultural signs, such as the clothing and the cross painted on the door or the branch of rue, to which a magical protective power was attributed. At the time, midwives would use the plant as a talisman for newborns, as seen in another novel of archaeological vocation, *Memórias de um sargento de milícias* [*Memoirs of a Militia Sergeant*], set in the early nineteenth century. Published in the same *Correio Mercantil* in 1852–3 and in book form in 1854 and 1855, the novel by Manuel Antônio de Almeida describes how Leonardo's godmother, who had brought him into the world, uses rue at the end of the christening ceremony: 'The party did not end until late; the godmother was the last one to leave, bestowing a blessing upon her godson and placing on his bellyband a sprig of rue.'[38]

Still referring to eighteenth-century Rio de Janeiro, the narrator of *A providência* also considers 'half a dozen bad habits, so harmful, so vulgar, and so stupid, if you will excuse the language, that they were worth elimination, even at the cost of tiny sacrifices if necessary'.[39] In a situation involving a duel between Geraldo de Pina and Arcanjo for the hand of Rosa Branca, daughter of João Batista, one of the contenders is supposedly late and the narrator ponders the need to change the bad cultural habit of tardiness. According to him, the bad habit of leaving people waiting is not restricted to Rio de Janeiro, but can be found in 'all of our provinces'.[40] Almost the whole chapter, 'To Wait! ... To Wait! ... Oh What a Torment!', deals with examples of everyday situations that highlight this bad behaviour, both archaeologically and anthropologically, involving all social types, from bricklayers to doctors and public employees.

As for the northern region of the province, it is worth highlighting the Passos procession, a religious ceremony, occurring on the second Friday of Lent in the village of São Pedro, founded by Mem de Sá in 1630 with the help of native tribes. The narrator also refers to the renown of the Lord of the Passos d'Aldeia as a worker of miracles, which would explain, according to him, the presence of thousands of people at the ceremony, from a variety of social groups and status and coming by land or sea from distant locations.

Among this multitude, the native peoples stand out with their brief presentation of cultural objects and Tupi idioms to designate native trees, all of which serves the narrator's aim of preserving the region's memory, since 'very little is left from the race that owned this beautiful land':[41] 'Native families on foot, women loaded with children and baskets containing their provisions, men ahead, taking only a formidable *mangual*,[42] as they called it, made of *tinguaciba, gurumarim, ipê do campo, camará*, or *imbuia*.'[43] A little later, Teixeira e Sousa describes the procession from the moment it leaves the church to the closing sermon, through various aspects of the ritual mixed with dialogues among its participants, especially that in which the faithful attempt different comic interpretations of the acronym SPQR[44] stamped on the banner. It is one of the few moments in the novel in which a satirical tone is evident.

Mystery Story

All the considerations presented thus far have been drawn from the subtitle 'Remembrances of Colonial Times'. However, the semantic field such considerations establish, involving history and more specifically archaeology – in the sense employed by the author's contemporary critics – does not seem to be sufficient to cover the meaning of *A providência*. There is another narrative layer that may be inferred from the title: the mysterious shape of the novel and its possible correspondence with religious and also historical discourses.

Let us start with a summary of the plot. Although the narrator warns that he does not want to 'openly designate'[45] the main action and the story's hero, owing to the importance attributed to various characters, it would not be inappropriate to identify a certain leadership in the figure of Father Chagas, not only because of his providential interventions throughout the narrative, which grant him some degree of heroism, but also because of the key position he occupies in the genealogical tree of many characters, along with João Batista.

Father Chagas was born in Lisbon to a noble family. In 1683, aged 22, he decides to try his luck as a trader in his uncle's shop in Rio de Janeiro, along with his childhood friend, the Marrano Renato, who was called Ismael when he was still a Muslim. This friend becomes involved in a love affair and soon becomes the father of a boy also called Renato. Soon afterwards he is accused of theft and imprisoned. Chagas takes care of the boy when the father escapes and disappears. Around the same time, Chagas meets Rosa, falls in love and, within 13 months, marries her. As this marriage to a poor commoner was without his father's consent, Chagas returns to Portugal to seek paternal forgiveness, while, in his absence, Rosa dies giving birth to the twins Rosa and Branca. The daughters are left with their uncle and aunt, and Chagas enters a Jesuit seminary. As soon as he is ordained, he leaves with a mission for the Brazilian backlands to catechize the native peoples.

In 1698, he goes to India, and on his journey back he meets his old friend Renato, who has reconverted to Islam and now works as an enslaver of Christians. Back in Rio de Janeiro in 1713, he finds his daughter Branca pregnant with the child of a now dead suitor. The child is born in the same year and named Benedito. To fulfil a promise, the Jesuit priest travels to holy places in Europe and the Middle East. In Nazareth, he meets Renato once again, now an ordained Franciscan friar, who weeps for 'the errors of the impostor from Mecca'.[46] Father Chagas returns to Rio de Janeiro in 1716. In 1724, Benedito is sent to Europe to study and, soon after, João Batista marries Branca. Their daughter is named Rosa Branca.

The summary above reveals very intricate aspects of the plot, especially regarding family relations. But the plot is much more complicated than this. João Batista raped Branca before the wedding. When they meet again, though, neither of them remembers the other. Moreover, the episode occurs right after another ill-fated love affair: Batista loves the young Alexandrina, who was promised by her father to another man, Graciano. Graciano knows his wife does not love him, for he knows of the passion between the old lovers, which explains why he keeps humiliating his rival. In revenge, when Graciano's travels take him away from Rio de Janeiro, Batista and Alexandrina meet in secret and conceive a child, Vicente, who is born as soon as the betrayed husband returns to the city. A month later, without any explanation, Alexandrina dies.

As soon as he is informed of the death of his beloved, Batista leaves town, fearing Graciano will make an attempt against his life. Hidden on the Island of Governador, he drinks and goes hunting with friends and saves a young woman, Branca, from a wild dog. He ends up raping her, as Batista himself describes:

> The woman comes to me, says Batista; I send the dog away and throw myself to her, uttering brutal niceties … Terrified, she backs off, repels me, and tries to escape … I lock one of her arms and woo her; she resists, pushes me, tries to yell; in vain, as I cover her mouth … and, after a brief struggle, almost unconscious, she was mine.[47]

In other words, Benedito is actually the son of João Batista and not of the suitor who died before he could marry Branca. There is more: Arcanjo is also a son of Batista, since he is a twin of Benedito, and both are brothers of Rosa Branca. The separation of the newborns occurred right after the delivery, Arcanjo being born six hours after Benedito. He is sent to the family of the Moor Renato, specifically to Renato's son, also a Renato, and his wife, who assisted Branca during her labour. This fact, known not by Batista or Father Chagas, but only by the couple and the midwife, comes to light at the end of the novel, when Renato delivers to the priest a revealing letter written by Branca.

The first troubling obstacle resulting from the genealogy of *A providência* is incest. The illegitimacy of the relationships produces many bastard children, dangerously close in daily life, an underground network that is woven on the border of crime. As soon as Benedito comes back from Europe, Rosa Branca falls in love with him. Arcanjo was also interested in marrying the same young woman, hence the failed duel with another suitor, Geraldo de Pina, Chagas's nephew, who, after all the revelations, ends up marrying the girl. Illegitimacy also pervades the novel in a dynastic sense, related to the maintenance or rupture of lineages that have been fully established. When Geraldo, a descendant of a noble Portuguese family, proposes to Rosa Branca, João Batista's response indicates that social inequality may be linked not necessarily to class differences, but to lineage:

> My family is more obscure than you think! My father did not know his parents and, what's more, he was not born a legitimate son! Maybe my daughter is of the impure race of a bastard generation; maybe she comes from a black-skinned African grandmother or from a dark-skinned Tamoio or Tupi:[48] aren't these black-skinned people reduced to slavery for that sole motive?[49]

Later in the narrative, the problem resurfaces with Benedito. Father Chagas, in collusion with Rosa and Batista, starts to meddle in the relationship between the newly arrived young man and Rosa Branca in order to prevent their contact exceeding mere friendship. Feigning ignorance, the narrator wonders about such intervention: 'But why and what for? The girl who could be the wife of Arcanjo or Geraldo de Pina could not marry Benedito?!'[50] His speculation falls into the mystery of ascendancy: 'Illegitimacy was then a shame, or a reproach that led children to expiate the parents' weaknesses.'[51]

What follows is a philosophical consideration of how ancient societies dealt with kinship regulations, through control mechanisms targeting human reproductive instincts, based on the legal punishment of deviation: the legitimacy of the union and the descendants' rights to inheritance were not recognized. On one hand, the narrator considers valid and fair 'the severity of ancient society towards bastard children'.[52] On the other hand, he points out a limit to such severity, since illegitimacy might well be pondered within a Christian sphere:

> But the ideas presented above are appropriate to aristocrats or to people very severe about the purity of their births, and not to a minister of God, who professes humility, and must not only close his eyes to the weaknesses of his neighbour, but also forgive them.[53]

Let us remember that Chagas, of noble descent, also deviated from his family's order, but redeemed himself by becoming a priest and committing to missionary tasks. As a 'minister of God', he acts as one capable of forgiveness and of inspiring forgiveness in others.

The second obstacle pertains to treason. The villain of the novel – the character Graciano – is established on this basis. After murdering his wife, Graciano proceeds to create a web of vengeance. Incidentally, the prologue is precisely about Graciano's return to Rio de Janeiro around the time of Vicente's birth – the scene previously mentioned with the midwife Maria Rita – and Alexandrina's death. However, nothing is revealed about the identity of the son or the circumstances of her death:

> A month after Graciano's return, Death added one more name to her large and terrible book. Alexandrina, in her blossoming years, in the adorable freshness of all her charms, mourned by her husband, almost suddenly fell from being into nothing.[54]

The enigma of the prologue does not find a solution in the subsequent chapters. The narrative skips 28 years and goes from Rio de Janeiro to Cabo Frio, presenting new characters who apparently have nothing to do with those summarily presented in the prologue.

Such dislocation puts on the stage the pretty and ambitious Narcisa and her parents, Felipe and Maria. Justino and Pedro, two outsiders welcomed by the generous family after a storm, are introduced as well. The year is 1738, the starting point of the story that now unfolds. The reader is immediately informed that the names of the newly arrived are not Justino and Pedro. But the narrator deliberately omits their real names:

> The two strangers whom the reader saw arriving at the house described in the previous chapter were not both Portuguese, as the older one said. He was, but the younger one was not. Also, the name of the older one was not Justino, nor was the younger named Pedro: but as they wish to be called thus, let us obey their will, knowing them by the names they themselves chose, until their true names can appear before us.[55]

In the same chapter, when reporting how and when the two characters met in Santa Catarina, the narrator again denies having any information, now concerning Pedro's family and a godfather who lives in Rio de Janeiro and is responsible for sending him to Coimbra. The journey occurs under the tutelage of Justino, who guides Pedro through the most vicious and dissolute situations, in a sort of upside-down coming-of-age story.[56] After years in Europe, both return to Santa Catarina. The young man's father is dead and his mother is dying. She requires the presence of her son and a priest in order to confess, but Justino intervenes in order to prevent any contact between Pedro and his mother, and guides the priest at the time of the confession, fearing the possible revelation of an important secret. The priest asks, 'But what secret is that?'[57] The answer is whispered: 'Justino leaned over the priest, and, in fear that even the auras would listen, deposited his secret in that old ear.'[58]

Although adhering to the facts, the narrator filters out his omniscience in favour of allowing the scene to be mysterious. Thus, the auras and the readers are momentarily ignorant of the secret. However, if information is needed in order to deliver an effect, the narrator promptly provides it. In the episode of the duel between Geraldo de Pina and Arcanjo, the failure of the clash owes to the intervention of a hooded man who attacks Arcanjo before the duel. The mysterious man is hurt, but manages to flee and finds shelter at a farmhouse on Santa Luzia beach, where he is welcomed by the foreman. Father Chagas is called to provide confession for the dying man, who tells the tale of a travelling salesman who would have interfered in the duel. The following day, when the Jesuit goes back to the farmhouse to check on the patient's health, he is informed that the man has died. In spite of the foreman's poor explanation, the priest believes the story. But the narrator intervenes:

> It will be good for the reader to know it was a scandalous lie. The supposed patient dictated it to the foreman, who, thanks to some silver coins and a few threats in case he did not do a good job, played the role perfectly well.[59]

In spite of hiding the identity of the injured man, who is in fact Justino, the narrator informs the reader that he is still alive. This piece of information is indispensable not only for the progression of the plot, but also to demonstrate the narrator's capacity for machination and interference in the causal logic of events.

Such narrative strategies characterize most of Teixeira e Sousa's novel: the evidence presented in the plot is in fact the narrator's prerogative, not the narrated facts. Instead of clues being made available within the narrative, pertaining to the world the narrative refers to, as usually happens in such narratives of detection as contemporary detective stories and novels, in *A providência* the clues depend on an interventionist narrator.[60] Thus, the narrator's omniscience is manifest or hidden, depending on the mysterious effect he intends to have on the reader. Such an effect can occur in two ways: explicitly omitting or revealing a piece of information, as seen in the previous examples; or surreptitiously pointing out inconsistencies, drawing the reader's attention to connections that will be revealed only later. In this case, the narrator does not omit information, but neither does he clearly provide it. Examples of the first of these narrative strategies have already been given; in the following, attention is given to the second narrative strategy of alluding to inconsistencies or possible connections.

In one of his visits to Rosa Branca's home, Geraldo is confronted with a scene in which the narrator signals a connection between the characters that would ordinarily sound merely speculative, but this is not unreasonable within the plot: 'From the dining room, Mr. de Pina saw Rosa Branca gently strolling beside Arcanjo, and with such familiarity that one could say they were brother and sister!'[61] Or when the narrator refers to Rosa as 'a serious matron, maybe the head of the family',[62] a position she does not in fact occupy, as the reader will find out later.

Both alternatives are typical of the hide-and-seek game that constitutes *A providência*. After all, not all underground threads duly woven could surface from the start in a novel that intends to be mysterious. The main thread, as the reader realizes when they have finished the book, relates to Justino and Pedro, whose real names are, respectively, Graciano and Vicente. The latter will only become aware of his origin at the end of the narrative. Justino's efforts to keep the secret not only from the reader, but also from Pedro, are understandable: to get close to him, to become his tutor, to educate him in the vices and pleasures of a dissolute life, and then lead him to Cabo Frio, where his father, João Batista, lives – all of it constitutes a plan for vengeance, a web woven by an agent who denies providence not only because of his atheism, but also because he believes himself able to intervene in the order of events.

With the exception of the intrigues in the past of some characters (already mentioned above), almost all the conflicts and misunderstandings in the novel result from Justino's treacherous albeit concealed intervention. The villain acts, but not in the open. He needs to be inserted into the daily life of the people he plans to hurt without letting his true face be recognized. Hence the mask, the equivocal character of his personality, the duplicity of the name, and the intelligence needed to manipulate people based on knowledge of their psychology and their relationships. Omniscience, omnipresence and persuasion are his weapons, all attributes that give him a demonic nature. On the verge of convincing himself of the need to murder João Batista, Pedro desperately asks himself, 'Justino ... man or devil!!!'[63] A little while later he concludes, 'Oh! What a horrible idea! Devil. ... devil!'[64]

Christian Preaching

It seems appropriate to associate the mysterious form of *A providência* with a series of subgenres of the novel that appeared from the eighteenth century onwards, in particular the gothic novel. As Daniel Serravalle de Sá states, this novelistic mode consists of 'an essentially hybrid manifestation, a link between romance and novel, in which prevails an atmosphere of mystery, affliction and terror'.[65] Such an atmosphere certainly pervades Teixeira e Sousa's narrative, fed as it is by natural phenomena such as torrential storms and devastating gales, shipwrecks, eerie landscapes and ghostly apparitions, with and without natural explanations. All these components serve the impression of terror that is peculiar to the gothic mode: 'Indeed, great is the terror of this stormy night.'[66] No less convincing is the presence of the French melodrama, a theatrical genre full of 'gusty episodes and complicated machinations',[67] not to mention the hyperbolic gestures of characters in *A providência*, as when Pedro is dying and asks for his father's forgiveness: 'Batista fell on his knees by this bed of pain and remorse, his hands raised to the skies, and cried: "My God, forgive him as I do!"'[68]

Here it is worth giving some attention to the mystery suggested in the novel's title, which, as mentioned above, is connected to Catholic religious discourse: in Teixeira e Sousa, providence corresponds to 'dispositions through which God leads His creation'[69] towards a future perfection. God created the world but transcends it, although sustaining his presence in his creation. In spite of his omnipresence, God cannot be completely seen; his signs on the earthly plane are not easily recognizable. In *A providência*, gothic and melodramatic effects may sometimes inspire terror but actually construct a mystery akin to the providential presence of the divine, which brings the novel closer to another genre: the sermon. This definition of providence may be associated with the rhetorical position of mystery in the Baroque period, in particular in Padre Antônio Vieira's sermons, as noted by the critic Alcir Pécora:

> To an author such as Vieira, it seems appropriate to state that God provides the world with sensitive signs of His presence precisely to keep human desire, within the limits of its own weakness, as a legitimate search for His Being. Mystery works as a beacon to mark occasions for free will and signals the direction of the divine will.[70]

It is worth recalling that the sermon is not an activity intended to be merely reflexive or contemplative. Associated with a 'militant Church'[71] engaged in the Counter-Reformation, and linked to Jesuit precepts, it also presupposes a 'sacramental, ceremonial, and public practice'[72] in order to attain salvation. It is a circumscribed practice, one that requires some competency, whereas the law is better endorsed by the presentation of specific events: 'The reality of cases embodies the law more precisely than its generic or aprioristic formulation.'[73]

All chapters of *A providência* are introduced by epigraphs, as in two other novels by its author: *O filho do pescador* (1843) and *As fatalidades de dois jovens* (1846). This format brings the 1854 novel closer to the sermon model. In the nineteenth century, most authors used epigraphs cited from various sources, articulated alongside the content of the book, chapter or poem. In sermons, the matrix is almost all biblical. Teixeira e Sousa chooses his own dictums. The epigraph of the prologue provides an example:

> Do not despise facts, small though they may seem in their origin; because some events, which may appear meaningless, start growing so much that they become extraordinary, like the waves of a river that increase as they distance themselves from the source, rolling bigger and seething with foam.[74]

This chapter narrates the birth of Vicente, the return of Graciano to Rio de Janeiro and the death of Alexandrina. Apparently isolated in the narrative, it is actually the origin of the character of Justino, who will become the main axis of the conflicts that structure the whole story. If such an origin is not immediately perceptible, as a result of its apparent irrelevance, the reader must pay attention to the fact that events are not self-contained, with no impact beyond their immediate occurrence: the real meanings of things in the world transcends immediate experience, since they are situated on a divine plane that must be continually unveiled on the earthly plane, even if partially, as vestiges. For both planes have distinct and thus irreducible natures – the finite substance of earthly things does not include the infinitude of what is divine. From that perspective, the nexus between epigraph and chapter happens between, respectively, a principle of universal value, thus from the order of the law, and a particular case that materializes it into action: 'The testimonial of the Scripture is unanimous: the divine providence's solicitude is *concrete* and *direct*, takes care of everything, from minimal things to the great events of the world and history.'[75]

Once the connection between epigraph and text is established, the latter requires an interpretation that goes beyond the banality of everyday scenes. After Arcanjo learns from Renato that he is Chagas's grandson, the young man immediately asks whether it is possible that he is a cousin of Rosa Branca. The reverend answers, 'Rosa Branca is your sister.'[76] Arcanjo's reaction is one of total despair. In the chapter that follows, the narrator tries to anticipate the reader's possible reaction to the unlikelihood of Arcanjo's behaviour – presumably he should be happy about his kinship with Chagas instead of lamenting this fraternal link to Rosa Branca. Says the narrator,

> A reader tends exclusively towards these trivial scenes of humanity, which happen almost every day or all days; he is less wont to deepen the human heart in the mysteries of its pleasures and pains; he might express some disapproval, which will appear fair at first, but will cease to be so following slight reflection.[77]

What follows is a reflection on the 'enlightened', 'respectful' and 'pure' love[78] that must be devoted to one woman and that resembles the divine in its 'graces' and 'mysteries'.[79] Thus, from the minutiae of everyday life to obviously grandiose or sublime manifestations, the world is a field of ordeals the human being crosses while seeking to decipher the divine design. However, the 'occasions for free will' that properly correspond to human action may lead, without suitable guidance, to deviations, the worst of which is atheism.

Besides the villain Justino, two other characters advocate disbelief in divine providence: Pedro and Felipe. The former, as seen, was instructed by Justino's thirst for revenge, while Felipe not only inherited the criminal nature of his family, but also suffered numerous misfortunes before arriving in Brazil. When narrating his adventures, Felipe always ends by 'cursing or denying the Divinity, or its Providence'.[80] When he tells such adventures at Batista and Narcisa's wedding party, Father Chagas and Maria, the latter disguised as a mysterious old man, are listening. At the end, Chagas intervenes:

> Felipe … Felipe, allow me to call you thus, because of my age and because of my being a priest! If the story of your ancestors, your age, and your disgraces have made you prudent and reasonable … woe to your soul! Felipe, why do you blaspheme against Divinity or deny its Providence? Our disgraces are not the same, my son, since mine, I believe, are incomparably larger than yours; and the more they thundered over my head, the more I saw in them the hand of God! Stop, inconsiderate and unjust elder, stop denying Divinity and blaspheming against its Providence! … Stop, and in your misfortunes seek whether there is some justice from the omnipotent hand that regulates the worlds, rather than an injustice from Providence, which is always just in its design![81]

The priest's diction is that of a preacher and is legitimated by an acceptance of the occult meaning of a superior order that 'regulates the worlds' towards just perfection, especially in moments of great ordeal. Therefore, the mystery of Teixeira e Sousa's novel is expressed rationally, since providence consists in the possibility of attributing to earthly things the cause that finds its reason for being in God. As it is an ongoing task of hermeneutics, the narrative resembles the archaeological posture in which writing is based on events of the past as vestiges that must be unveiled but do not necessarily depend on historiography.

In Teixeira e Sousa's *A providência*, mystery is not just a means to inspire angst and fear in the characters and in the reader, although such sentiments contribute to the perception of the existence of supersensitive phenomena. It is mainly a means for historical interpretation and preaching, with the goal of materializing the cultural past and constantly affirming Christian morality.

Notes

1. 'Carioca' is the demonym for those native to the city of Rio de Janeiro.
2. 'Fluminense' is the demonym for those native to the province (now state) of Rio de Janeiro.
3. Silva 1837, 74. Unless otherwise indicated, all the translations are mine.
4. Silva 1837, 74.
5. Silva 2003, 43.
6. Silva 2003, 45.
7. Silva 2003, 46.
8. Denis 1826.
9. Leal Júnior 1863, 4. Book edition cited. With the exception of some differences in the order of paragraphs, it reproduces the 1853 edition in *Correio Mercantil*.
10. Leal Júnior 1863, 9.
11. Leal Júnior 1863, 9.
12. Leal Júnior 1863, 9.
13. Leal Júnior 1863, 9.
14. Leal Júnior 1863, 9.
15. Leal Júnior 1863, 15.
16. Leal Júnior 1863, 18.
17. Leal Júnior 1863, 6.
18. A *mameluco* is a man of mixed (white and indigenous) race.
19. Lukács 1983, 36.
20. Lukács 1983, 37.
21. *Correio Mercantil, e instrutivo, político, universal*, 26 January 1854, 1.
22. Leal Júnior 1863, 62.
23. Leal Júnior 1863, 62.
24. *Correio Mercantil*, 26 January 1854, 1.
25. 'Reparos sobre um romance' 1855, 153.
26. Sousa 1854, Vol. 3, 49.
27. Sousa 1854, Vol. 3, 50.
28. Sousa 1854, Vol. 1, 47.
29. Sousa 1854, Vol. 1, 47.
30. Sousa 1854, Vol. 3, 45.
31. Sousa 1848, 2.
32. Antonio Candido 1981, Vol. 2, 133.
33. *Lemiste* is a thin black fabric made of wool.
34. *Cabuya* is a natural fibre from the leaves of the fique plant (*Furcraea andina*), native to the Andean regions of Colombia, Ecuador and Peru. Its range extended to Venezuela and the Brazilian coast.
35. *Droguete* is a cheap, low-quality fabric of wool, cotton or silk.
36. Sousa 1854, Vol. 1, 5.
37. Sousa 1854, Vol. 1, 5.
38. Almeida 1978, 8; Almeida 1999, 11.
39. Sousa 1854, Vol. 2, 35.
40. Sousa 1854, Vol. 2, 35.
41. Sousa 1854, Vol. 2, 15.

42. A *mangual* is a kind of flail attached to a large stick.
43. Sousa 1854, Vol. 2, 6. *Tinguaciba*, *gurumarim*, *ipê do campo*, *camará* and *imbuia* are kinds of wood from native trees.
44. The acronym comes from the Latin phrase *Senatus populusque romanus*, which translates as 'Roman Senate and People' (Faria 1982, 499). The phrase was the official name of the Roman Empire and appeared on the banners of Roman legions, as well as on the banner of the procession of Our Lord of Passos described by Teixeira e Sousa.
45. Sousa 1854, Vol. 1, 8.
46. Sousa 1854, Vol. 4, 36.
47. Sousa 1854, Vol. 5, 45.
48. Tamoio and Tupi are Brazilian indigenous nations.
49. Sousa 1854, Vol. 2, 26.
50. Sousa 1854, Vol. 3, 17.
51. Sousa 1854, Vol. 3, 17.
52. Sousa 1854, Vol. 3, 18.
53. Sousa 1854, Vol. 3, 18.
54. Sousa 1854, Vol. 1, 8.
55. Sousa 1854, Vol. 1, 17.
56. The reference here is to the *Bildungsroman*, a type of novel pioneered by Johann Wolfgang von Goethe with the publication of *Wilhelm Meister's Apprenticeship* in 1795–6 (Goethe 1995). Goethe's work describes the protagonist's transformation resulting from adversities he faces in his trajectory through the world, which constitutes him, objectively and subjectively, as a socially configured individual.
57. Sousa 1854, Vol. 1, 22.
58. Sousa 1854, Vol. 1, 22.
59. Sousa 1854, Vol. 2, 63–4.
60. Although Norman Friedman's well-known concept of 'editorial omniscience' could be employed to deal with this aspect of the narrator of *A providência*, I prefer to adopt the idea of intervention, since my focus is on the control of omniscience by the narrator in order to produce enigmas.
61. Sousa 1854, Vol. 2, 27.
62. Sousa 1854, Vol. 2, 16.
63. Sousa 1854, Vol. 4, 60.
64. Sousa 1854, Vol. 4, 60.
65. Sá 2006, 21.
66. Sousa 1854, Vol. 1, 13.
67. Thomasseau 2012, 21.
68. Sousa 1854, Vol. 5, 32.
69. *Catecismo da Igreja Católica* 2000, 90.
70. Pécora 2001, 14.
71. Pécora 2001, 12.
72. Pécora 2001, 12.
73. Pécora 2001, 15.
74. Sousa 1854, Vol. 1, 5.
75. *Catecismo da Igreja Católica* 2000, 91.
76. Sousa 1854, Vol. 4, 63.
77. Sousa 1854, Vol. 5, 5.
78. Sousa 1854, Vol. 5, 5.
79. Sousa 1854, Vol. 5, 6.
80. Sousa 1854, Vol. 3, 38.
81. Sousa 1854, Vol. 3, 41.

Bibliography

Almeida, Manuel Antônio de. *Memórias de um sargento de milícias*. Rio de Janeiro: LTC, 1978.

Almeida, Manuel Antônio de. *Memoirs of a Militia Sargeant*, translated by Ronald W. Sousa. New York: Oxford University Press, 1999.

Antonio Candido. *A formação da literatura brasileira: momentos decisivos*. Belo Horizonte: Itatiaia, 1981.
Catecismo da Igreja Católica. São Paulo: Loyola, 2000.
Denis, Jean-Ferdinand. *Résumé de l'histoire littéraire du Portugal, suivi du Résumé de l'histoire littéraire du Brésil*. Paris: Lecointe et Durey, Libraires, 1826.
Faria, Ernesto. *Dicionário escolar latino-português*. Rio de Janeiro: Fename, 1982.
Goethe, Johann Wolfgang von. *Wilhelm Meister's Apprenticeship*, translated by Eric A. Blackall with Victor Lange. Princeton, NJ: Princeton University Press, 1995.
Leal Júnior, José da Silva Mendes. *Calabar: história brasileira do século XVII*. Rio de Janeiro: Tipografia do Correio Mercantil, 1863.
Lukács, Georg. *The Historical Novel*, translated by Hannah and Stanley Mitchell. Lincoln: University Nebraska Press, 1983.
Pécora, Alcir. 'Sermões: a pragmática do mistério'. In *Sermões 2*, edited by Alcir Pécora, 11–27. São Paulo: Hedra, 2001.
'Reparos sobre um romance', *O Guanabara, revista mensal, artística e literária*, August 1855, 152–66.
Sá, Daniel Serravalle. 'O gótico tropical: o sublime e o demoníaco em O guarani'. MA dissertation, Universidade de São Paulo, 2006.
Scott, Walter. *The Bride of Lammermoor*. Edinburgh: Archibald Constable, 1819.
Silva, João Manuel Pereira da. 'Revista dramática', *Jornal dos debates, políticos e literários*, 8 July 1837, 2–3.
Silva, João Manuel Pereira da. 'Os romances modernos e sua influência', *Matraga* 15 (2003): 43–6.
Sousa, Antônio Gonçalves Teixeira e. *Gonzaga ou a conjuração do Tiradentes*. Rio de Janeiro: Tipografia de Teixeira, 1848.
Sousa, Antônio Gonçalves Teixeira e. *A providência: recordação dos tempos coloniais*. Rio de Janeiro: Tipografia de M. Barreto, 1854.
Sousa, Antônio Gonçalves Teixeira e. *O filho do pescador*. São Paulo: Melhoramentos, 1977.
Thomasseau, Jean-Marie. *O melodrama*, translated by Cláudia Braga and Jacqueline Penjon. São Paulo: Perspectiva, 2012.

4
Maria Firmina dos Reis and the First Afro-Brazilian Novel[1]

Eduardo de Assis Duarte

> What must be demanded of the writer above all is a certain intimate feeling that makes him a man of his time and his country, even when dealing with themes remote in time and space.
>
> (Machado de Assis 1873)

Introduction: Maria Firmina dos Reis's Historical Context

The nineteenth-century canon of novelists constructed by Brazilian literary history has always featured names like José de Alencar and Machado de Assis. Both authors appear as major stars in a context in which Joaquim Manoel de Macedo, Bernardo Guimarães, Aluísio Azevedo and Raul Pompeia are also remembered, among others regarded as minor. Women's writing – including that of Maria Firmina dos Reis – traversed the nineteenth and twentieth centuries practically forgotten both by the textbooks of literary history and by criticism in general. It has taken a lot of effort, mainly over the last few decades, to recover texts by female authors and make them available to readers and thereby to challenge the predominant masculinity of the Brazilian literary canon.

Maria Firmina dos Reis is a case in point. An Afro-descendant born in 1822 in the remote province of Maranhão, this author did not have access to regular school education, nor did she attend university. A poor and orphaned woman, she lived most of her 95 years in the countryside, finding in reading the bridge to connect to the problems and predicaments of her time, among them slavery. Self-taught and a voracious reader of everything that came within her reach as a primary school teacher, Maria Firmina dos Reis published *Úrsula* [*Ursula*] in 1859, a moment in which the Brazilian novel was taking its first steps. This feat makes her not only the author of the first abolitionist novel of Brazilian literature, but also, if I'm not mistaken, the first woman to publish an abolitionist novel in Portuguese and the first Afro-descendant woman to publish a novel throughout the whole of Latin America. Perhaps owing to the forcefulness of certain passages, *Úrsula* was not reissued in the nineteenth century and had to wait no less than 116 years for a second edition to be released in 1975.[2]

Before Maria Firmina dos Reis, other Brazilians, such as Nísia Floresta, spoke against slavery through poems, *crônicas* and other writings, but without risking writing novels. Nineteenth-century Latin American female authors such as the Cuban-Spanish Gertrudis Gómez de Avellaneda, the Argentines Juana Paulo Manso de Noronha and Juana M. Gorriti, the Peruvian Mercedes C. Carbonera and Clorinda Matto de Turner and the Bolivians Lindaura Anzoátegui, Adélia Zamudio and Maria Josefa Mujía wrote and published novels, but they were white women who belonged to the economic and social elites of their respective countries.

Maria Firmina dos Reis innovated not only in highlighting the inhumanity of a system that transformed men and women into commodities, but also in assuming the perspective of the enslaved and thus evading the stereotypes deriving from the slaveholding mindset that reduced Africans and their descendants to inferior beings in all senses. In doing so, she came much closer to the writings of black female authors published in England and the United States than to those of her white counterparts in Latin America.

The nineteenth century witnessed the publication of dozens of 'slave narratives' – mostly autobiographical accounts, printed on both sides of the North Atlantic to fuel the ongoing abolitionist campaign in the United States. Dramas experienced by Olaudah Equiano (in the eighteenth century), Frederick Douglass, Mahommah Gardo Baquaqua and Solomon Northup, among others, add to the accounts of Harriet E. Wilson, Kate Drumgoold, Harriet A. Jacobs and Frances Ellen Watkins Harper in denouncing the cruelty of slavery from the perspective of its victims. In these writings, autobiographical testimony generally prevails, and does to the end of the nineteenth century, as a way of recording a past that everyone wants to see superseded but which leaves its consequences in the form of racism and social inequality.

If men's slave narratives favoured the form of autobiography, among women's writing fiction took a prominent place. Knowing the appeal of the romantic novel, authors such as Maria Firmina dos Reis and Harriet Wilson questioned slavery through strategies similar to those used in the *roman-feuilleton* – a genre widely accepted among the readership of their time.

The subject of the enslaved black person had been present in Western women's writing since Aphra Behn published *Oroonoko, or the Royal Slave: a True History* in 1688. Behn is considered to be the first woman in England to make a profession of literature. The plot of this novel of hers is situated in the Caribbean and revolves around Oroonoko – an African who becomes the object of white curiosity owing to his 'primitive' knowledge in dealing with nature. But this happens only up to the moment when he rebels against his condition and is then arrested and tortured to death in a public square.

Another nineteenth-century novel that deals with the issue of the enslaved black is *Sab*, written by the Cuban-Spanish Gertrudis Gómez de Avellaneda. Published in 1841, *Sab* tells the story of the impossible love between an enslaved young man and a master's daughter. Even though it does not criticize the regime of slavery, the book was banned from circulating in Cuba, a Spanish colony at the time. This was because the ideas it conveyed opposed the hegemonic European doxa that depicted black people as subhuman beings dominated by instincts and devoid of reason and feelings.

However, none of these publications had the same repercussion as Harriet Beecher Stowe's *Uncle Tom's Cabin; or, Life among the Lowly*, published in 1851 and translated into Portuguese two years later, obtaining great circulation in Brazil. A white and Christian author, Stowe saw her text win the crowds and turn into a great manifesto against slavery. President Abraham Lincoln even asserted that Stowe's narrative 'provoked the civil war' that divided the country and led to the abolition of slavery. But *Uncle Tom's Cabin* has a benevolent and idealized tone when it comes to slavery, a tone marked by the image of the good lord and the slave reconciled to the destiny that God gave him. This led some critics to regard the black women's writing published after *Uncle Tom's Cabin* as a response to the romanticized slavery constructed by Stowe's narrative.

A classic example is Harriet E. Wilson's *Our Nig: Sketches from the Life of a Free Black* (1859), considered the first novel by a black female author, not only in the United States but in any English-speaking country.[3] Like *Úrsula*, *Our Nig* was relegated to oblivion for more than a century, being reissued only 124 years later, thanks to Henry Louis Gates, Jr, who signed the introduction of the new edition along with R. J. Ellis. This historical erasure constitutes the first point of contact between the texts of Wilson and Reis.

Colonial Black Reason

In his essential study of the history of the meanings of the word 'black', the Cameroonian philosopher Achille Mbembe[4] maps and questions what he calls 'black reason': a set of mythical, philosophical and even 'scientific' narratives that aim to build a knowledge that establishes a 'paradigm of subjection'. Since its beginning, at the dawn of the era of European navigation and discovery, the goal of this metanarrative was always to confine black people in a permanent 'attribute of inferiority', intended to transform them into subhuman beings, that is, 'differentiated' by being devoid of reason and dominated by instinct.

Once naturalized and internalized, this attribute works by forging what Mbembe calls a 'psycho-oneiric complex', which in many cases is assimilated by the victims themselves. Such a set of beliefs, 'a kind of giant cage', links the noun 'black' to an intricate and perverse network of qualifiers that have in the idea of 'race' one of their main foundations. As a 'form of primal representation', the idea of race establishes what the philosopher calls a 'perverse complex' that affects both Europeans and Africans. Its consequence is the generation not only of a 'colonial system of exploitation and depredation', but also of 'fears and torments ... especially of infinite sufferings and, ultimately, catastrophe'.[5]

One of these catastrophes is 'altruicide', that is, the 'constitution of the Other not as similar to oneself but as a menacing object'[6] – therefore as someone that, even when exploited as submissive workforce, must be repudiated, watched and if necessary incarcerated and eliminated. In this context, the myth of racial superiority that came from Europe marked indelibly the age of discovery and the expansion of mercantile capitalism. It served thereby the Western Hemisphere's strategies of power, since it produced in the enslavement of Africans and their descendants, and in the narratives that supported slavery, what Mbembe describes as the 'baptismal fonts of modernity'.[7]

To do so, from the mid fifteenth century onwards it was necessary to 'produce Blackness'[8] and, consequently, 'produce race' as a result of what Mbembe calls 'fantasizing' – and we need to stress that the word 'race' at that time served to designate only non-European human groups. In parallel, it was also necessary to produce a locus – a space and an origin – in which this Other could be located. This locus came to be Africa, although it has always been known that not every black is African and not every African is black. It was necessary, still, to produce a discursive system that could make of these people a group marked by a 'social link of subjection' and a '*body of extraction*',[9] both male and female.

Thus, as 'a system of narratives and discourses of academic pretensions', European black reason also designates a cluster of practices that involved the 'daily work' of constructing an image – and a meaning – of savagery, of 'moral disqualification and practical instrumentalization', that is, a 'reservoir that provided the justifications for the arithmetic of racial domination'.[10] As one can see, for centuries have been reproduced statements, comments and myths that, however disparate they may be, end up confining the black person within a frame of permanent subhumanity. Achille Mbembe's book only maps and ratifies something previously known. From a historical point of view, it is established that, just as the East has always been a Western construction – to engage with the ideas of Edward Said (1978) – the black person, as depicted in Europe, has always been a construction of white people interested in exploiting them. In that regard, statements of Hegel in *The Phenomenology of Spirit* (1807) may be recalled, as well as ones in his *Lectures on the Philosophy of History* two decades later.[11] The *Lectures* simply exclude Africa from the 'universal spirit', that is, from the civilized world, owing to the supposed inability of its inhabitants to attain the 'Idea of Reason'. Ethnocentrically viewed by Hegel as a 'childish world, wrapped in the blackness of the night', Africa was plunged into ignorance and cannibalism, uncultured and without religion, submerged in a 'sensual arbitrariness' that approximates humans to animals. Thus, as a 'species' that 'hesitates' between these two forms of life – human and animal – the black person constructed by the Hegelian narrative appears to be a 'statue without language' and without 'self-consciousness', therefore 'devoid of universality'. For Mbembe, this whole discourse is nothing more than the result of an 'imaginary relationship' with Africa, sustained by a 'fictional economy'.[12]

It is evident that such manipulation, historically interpreted as true, concealed behind it political and economic interests linked to the establishment, especially in the Americas, where colonization was based on forced labour, whether of the native peoples or trafficked Africans. In *The Phenomenology of Spirit*, Hegel idealizes the enslaved as those who hand over their freedom in order not to lose their life, thus granting to the enslaved free will over their own actions and future, as if this option really existed for the millions of Africans deported to the Americas. In another book, *The Philosophy of Right* (1821), the philosopher remarks,

> Yet if a man is a slave, his own will is responsible for his slavery, just as it is its will which is responsible if a people is subjugated. Hence the wrong of slavery lies at the door not simply of enslavers or conquerors, but of the slaves and the conquered themselves.[13]

Widely known, these excerpts speak for themselves. Let us leave the discussion there, as far as Eurocentric discourse is concerned. In opposition to this white dimension of black reason there is that written by the blacks themselves, as a result of the 'Black conscience of Blackness',[14] within which black people strive to rescue, activate and revitalize their traditions and their memory, in order to finally rediscover the 'truth of the self no longer outside of the self but standing on its own ground'.[15] This new current was strengthened in nineteenth-century abolitionism, and later in anarchism, Marxism and other anti-capitalist movements. The twentieth century witnessed the slow and progressive blossoming of the vast worldwide network that has formulated the modern black imaginary.

At the Beginnings of a New Black Reason

From the beginning of *Úrsula*, Maria Firmina dos Reis uses Christian axiology to stigmatize the slave regime and its methods. The narrator's voice and that of almost all the characters are pervaded by belief in Catholicism and its values. The text thereby appeals to the convictions of its readership at the same time that it indirectly targets the hypocrisy of the Church that gave moral support to slavery: 'Lord God! When will Thou enclose in men's breast Thy sublime maxim – love thy neighbour as thyself – and cease to oppress with so reprehensible injustice Thy fellow! … that who was also free in his country … that who is Thy sibling?!'[16]

The narrator's outlook is made clear in the first pages of the book, where is staged the meeting of a slave with an elite young man lost on a deserted road. By depicting whites and blacks as 'brothers', the novel turns Christian discourse against its alleged adherents inhabiting the colonial slave master's house.

The particular treatment Maria Firmina dos Reis gives to the racial relationship between blacks and whites pervades the novel from beginning to end. In the first chapter, the young Túlio, in whose veins runs 'African blood',[17] sees a man lying unconscious on the road, the victim of an accident in which he has ended up under the carcass of a horse. The man's name is Tancredo and he and Úrsula will later form the romantic pair who star in the narrative. Under the scorching tropical sun, Túlio feels pity 'before the painful scene that was being offered to him', since 'slavery had not brutalized his soul'.[18] It should be emphasized at the outset that the author does not condemn slavery solely because a specific slave has a noble character, as one can read in abolitionist narratives of the time, both Brazilian and foreign. It is a question of condemning slavery as a system that defies religion and morality, which the author does by resorting to the the very kind of speech deriving from white hegemony.

The composition of the character indicates the perspective that guides the representation of the coexistence of masters and captives in this novel. Slavery is 'hateful', but it does not harden the young black man's sensibility. This is the key to understanding the authorial strategy of combating the regime without overly attacking the convictions of white readers. Túlio is victim, not tormentor. His revolt is experienced in silence, for he has no means to confront the power of the masters.

The first chapter aims to present the two male characters who will embody the moral centre of the text: one white, one black. Thus they make their appearance on the scene: first Tancredo; then Túlio. By using the artifice of the accident, the author makes the latter take the place of the former to stand out as a character. From the beginning, the reader comes to know Túlio for his virtues, while the other is known only for the mental shock that caused his fall. So the black man tries in every way to revive the horseman. He succeeds in his efforts and successfully transports the wounded young man to the farm's main building. When Tancredo awakes from his faint, he finds the black man in front of him. In spite of the daze that begins to dim his senses again, Tancredo sees in the slave the good man who saved him. It is worth mentioning the first words exchanged between these two characters:

> – Who are you? – asked the young man to the slave as soon as he had come out of his lethargy – Why do you show such interest in me?
>
> – Sir! – stammered the black man – Your state… I – he continued with shame, generated by slavery – I suppose I can render you no service, yet I wish I could be useful to you. Forgive me!
>
> – I? – said the gentleman with great gratitude – I, forgive you! *May all hearts resemble yours.*[19]

Thus, already in the opening scene, the text reveals the foundations of the worldview that sustains it. Faced with Tancredo's question, the slave hesitates, because he knows he is before a representative of a high social rank. Yet Tancredo is grateful to the one who has saved him; later on the reader will find out that Tancredo was betrayed by his own father, who has abused his trust and filial love. In the face of this, Tancredo's voice carries a very special meaning: it is the young and sensitive white man – the ideal of a new man, for a new society – who finds in the unknown black man nothing less than a *model of virtue*:

> Despite the rising fever, the gentleman began to coordinate his ideas, and the slave's statements, and the services that he had rendered him, touched his heart. *The fact is that feelings as noble and generous as those that animated the young black man's soul burned in his heart*: so, in a moment of intimate and generous gratitude, the young man, pulling off his glove, extended his right hand to the man who had saved him.[20]

The scene is unique in Brazilian literature of the period. At the height of the slavery regime in Brazil, the unusual gesture of this white man – to greet the slave as an equal – has a paradigmatic meaning in the face of the reduction of black people to the inferior attributes identified by Mbembe. The outstretched hand of the white man crowns the elevation of the black man as the moral reference of the narrative. Charles Martin, analysing the scene, aptly points out that the author makes the slave the 'basis of comparison for the young white hero'.[21] The humane gesture seems natural before the noble morality of Túlio, who thanks God for having arrived at the scene of the accident at that moment. From then on, the novel demonstrates the strong empathy that binds the black man to the white man depressed by the patriarchal order. It suits, moreover, the title of the chapter: 'Two Generous Souls'.

The narrative then highlights the embarrassment experienced by Túlio before the gesture of the injured man. Owing to his enslaved condition and the 'distance that separates them', he wants to kiss the white hand stretched out in front of him. Tancredo responds, 'Were you not, by chance, my saviour?' and then shakes the slave's 'coarse hand', in which he 'discovered with satisfaction, loyalty and purity'.[22] Tancredo adds, 'Túlio, my friend, I evaluate the uncured pain you carry in your soul, I understand your bitterness, and I curse in your name the first man who enslaved his neighbour.'[23] Surprised by the gesture, the black man cannot conceal his happiness. The narrative voice concludes, 'He was the first white man who had said such sweet words to him.'[24]

According to the omniscient narrator, the black man is, therefore, a parameter of moral elevation. Such a posture reverses the values of the slave society and argues against the 'scientific' theories about the 'natural inferiority' of Africans. The discourse of the novel shows, from the beginning, commitment to the dignifying of black people's character, while at the same time expressing the cultural and axiological territory that it claims: that of Afro-descendants' commitment to opposing the hegemonic black reason of the author's time. This perspective can be seen in the sympathy the text gives to Túlio and the other characters submitted to captivity. Thus, the discourse of Maria Firmina dos Reis stands at the antipode of the Eurocentric doxa and against the altruicide mapped by Achille Mbembe, which carries within it the whole historical charge of ethnocide and also of epistemicide.

By harbouring the wounded horseman at his mistress's house, Túlio enables their meeting and also the beginning of the passion that leads them to a brief happiness. Once again, the zeal and the dignity of the young black man stand out. He ends up gaining manumission as a sign of gratitude from the white man. A strong bond of friendship comes to unite them. From then on the black man becomes an inseparable companion to the young white one. And Túlio plays the role of the good young lad, who respects the lady for not having mistreated him, while he feels indebted to the one who freed him. However, his new condition is questioned by Mother Susana when she ironizes the 'freedom' of the freed – which will eventually lead him to his death – comparing it with the life she used to live in Africa:

> You! You free? Oh, do not deceive me! – exclaimed the old African woman, opening her eyes wide … Freedom? I enjoyed it in my youth! – Susana went on bitterly. Túlio, my son, no one has enjoyed it more broadly than I, there was no woman more blessed than I.[25]

In addition to reinforcing the Afro-Brazilian identity of the text itself, the introduction of the old African woman increases the density of political layering. The territory of origin is mentioned bluntly, contrary to what is seen in other writings of the nineteenth century, including those signed by Afro-descendants. What emerges is the diasporic condition experienced by characters who got torn from their lands and families to live in exile the imprisonment represented by forced labour. According to Zahidé Muzart, 'it is Mother Susana who will explain to Túlio, freed by the gentleman, the meaning of true freedom, which would never be that of a man freed in a racist country'.[26] Of the tension that defines the central conflict of the novel, Cristina Pinto-Bailey remarks,

> In *Úrsula*, the only concrete solution to redress the injustice of slavery is the manumission of a particular slave, Túlio, by the white hero. … This could be seen as one of the flaws of the novel, for it does not offer any structural solution to the question of slavery. It can be argued, however, that the main social function of a literary work is not to solve problems, but simply to denounce them and expose them, which Maria Firmina does very well and with great appeal to the readership.[27]

Literature by itself could not interfere in the structure of the slavery regime that had dominated the country since colonial times, in order, like a magic trick, to alter reality. The author's narrative acts on another front by exposing by confrontation the ethnic tensions then in force and by denouncing – using white and Christian morality – all the unjust brutality of that mode of labour exploitation. This becomes explicit when the narrative makes space for the story of the African Susana, which occupies the whole of Chapter 9:

> Harvest time had come, and corn and yam and peanut were abundant in our fields. It was one of those days when nature seemed to indulge in gentle pleasure; it was a smiling and beautiful morning, like the face of an infant, though I had a heavy weight in my heart. …
>
> I had not yet overcome two hundred metres of road when a whistle, reverberating through the woods, informed me of the impending danger that lay before me. Immediately two men appeared, and tied me with ropes. I was a prisoner – I was a slave! It was in vain that I begged them in the name of my daughter to restore my freedom: the barbarians laughed at my tears, and looked at me without compassion. I thought I would go crazy, I thought I would die, but I could not … fortune lay still a lot of fighting in store for me. …
>
> They put me and three hundred companions of misfortune and captivity in the narrow and infected basement of a ship. Thirty days of cruel torments, and absolute lack of all that is necessary to life we spent in this grave until we approached the Brazilian shores.[28]

Among the scenes in which blacks are depicted in nineteenth-century Brazilian literature, especially women, this one is undoubtedly the most shocking. The imprisonment and the kidnapping of Susana have, in my view, the same importance and the same symbolism as the scene in *Memórias póstumas de Brás Cubas* [*The Posthumous Memoirs of Brás*

Cubas], written 31 years later. There, Machado de Assis has his protagonist, still a child, ride on the back of the boy Prudêncio as if on horseback, a perfect allegory of the situation of the black in the slave-based regime: poor little Prudêncio is made to get down on all fours and serve as a mount for the heir of the master's house, who assaults him and also calls him 'beast'.

On the other hand, Firmina adopts a different, straightforward tone, without the ironic subtleties of Machado de Assis's discourse when he relates Brás's 'joke'. In *Úrsula*, the person who speaks in the first person is an adult African, born free, married, the mother of a family, an inhabitant of a structured community; in short, a human being who knows her duties in coexistence with her equals. She does not hesitate to call her captors 'barbarians' when she loses her 'homeland, husband, mother and daughter'.[29] In so doing she not only assumes the indignation of the unjustly imprisoned human being but also reverses the attribute of inferiority inherent to the doxa present in European black reason: barbaric is the one who kidnaps ... barbaric is the one who enslaves.

The tone of confrontation against hegemonic thought could not be more explicit. Let us remember that this is the first time that the capture and enslavement of Africans are depicted in Brazilian literature. *Úrsula* is the inaugural gesture of an entire abolitionist lineage in Brazilian letters. Published more than a century and a half ago, but not recorded by the manuals of literary historiography, the novel stands out by the forcefulness with which it exposes the methods of those who transform human beings into merchandise and submissive labour force. The diegesis, tone and even the choice of vocabulary make explicit the authorial perspective, identified with the sufferings of the victims.

The agents of this 'nefarious trade' at the service of European mercantile and colonial interests are readily classified as inhumane, unmasking the civilized image flaunted by the settlers in the narratives that had circulated since the age of discovery. The woman transformed into an object has her humanity highlighted, like the social relationships she is forced to abandon: 'homeland, husband, mother and daughter'.[30] The novel thus establishes itself as a phenomenon previously unheard of in Brazilian literature. For the first time, Africa is thematized and emerges as a *space of civilization* in which the individual and the community are harmonized, in which one plants and harvests, marries and bears children, in which there are values and feelings of family and homeland. This space is suddenly invaded by traffickers at the service of the most nefarious aspect of European expansion, albeit a practice that had been usual since the beginning of the discoveries of new lands.

Besides Africa – and, above all, the aggression suffered by its inhabitants – another space also appears for the first time in Brazilian literature: the slave ship's hold. Described in detail, this place immersed in pain is the stage on which are exposed the methods adopted to address the complaints of the chained – hungry and thirsty women and men:

> They gave us filthy, rotten water, given with pettiness; the food was bad and even dirtier: we saw many companions die beside us for want of air, food and water. It is horrible to remember that human creatures treat their fellow men like this and that their conscience does not hurt for taking them to their grave asphyxiated and hungry.[31]

The impetus to denounce is evident both in the crudeness of the description and in the ethical appeal. In both, an unprecedented first-person narrative voice expresses the drama of the victims in order to accuse and judge their abductors. This subjugated black *self* soon transmutes into an *us* in order to amplify the historical anchoring of the plot. Both the commitment to inform through the means of the novel and the effort to narrate from *inside the problem* are made explicit, in order to configure another interpretation and another meaning of the regime that was the central foundation of the mode of production adopted by colonial expansionism in the Americas. In accordance with this purpose, the tone of the narrative approaches orality. In spite of its grammatical correctness – a requirement of the literary norm of the time – it resorts to noun and verb repetitions, among other devices, to strengthen verisimilitude. This strategy is successful and marks in vivid colours both the voice of the character – which attains the status of a testimony – and the narrated facts:

> In the last two days there was no more food. The people suffering most began to scream. Good God! From the hatch they threw upon us boiling water and pitch, which scorched us and came to kill the leaders of the riot.
>
> The pain of losing homeland, loved ones and freedom was smothered on this journey by the constant horror of such atrocities.
>
> I still do not know how I resisted – God wanted to spare me to prove the patience of His servant with new torments that awaited me here.[32]

Mother Susana's narrative mixes the account of imprisonment and resistance with the adjudicative power of Reis's anti-slavery discourse.

The text reiterates the accusation that blames the colonizer not only for the abduction of human beings, treated by their captors as 'ferocious animals of our forests that are used by the potentates of Europe as recreation',[33] but also for the atrocities committed during the voyage. Barbarism is met with resistance, which attests to the humanity of the prisoners, aware of the risk and the high price they will pay for their protest. It should be noted that the ship and its hold are configured as *places of memory*, as Pierre Nora teaches us. For him, the main reason for the place of memory to exist is 'to stop time, to block the work of oblivion, to fix a state of affairs, to immortalize death, to materialize the immaterial – gold is the only memory of money –, capturing maximum sense in a minimum of signs'.[34]

By naming the hold as 'grave', Reis's text echoes the designation of 'tomb ship' (in other words, slave ship) for the vessel used to carry 'human commodity'. According to Nei Lopes, this designation ('tomb ship') 'alludes to the conditions in which enslaved Africans were transported to the Americas'. It also refers to the procedure of taking the dead to their grave.[35] The term, therefore, suggests the constitution of a semantic field marked by the signs of agony and death. In such a way the text brings to the Portuguese language the voice – and the perspective – of the Africans through attentive listening to what they have lost: civilization, freedom, homeland, family and, for many, their own lives. And it does so without losing sight of the perspective of those who survived to tell the story.

The position of *subject of remembrance* immediately emerges, in which the personal joins the collective. It is the voice of the Other making the voice of the enslaved heard. The novel advances with realistic description outweighing fiction. Thus, while the text achieves historical and human density, it loses something in terms of psychological depth and the development of the plot, which is interrupted to provide the perspective of the victims. The narrative of Mother Susana's life in Africa and her imprisonment takes up the whole of Chapter 9 and is inserted precisely at the moment when the liberation of a young captive is depicted, putting Túlio's manumission into perspective as the victory of freedom.

This reading is corroborated when compared with, among others, the memories of Mahommah Gardo Baquaqua – called José da Costa in Brazil – a slave who arrived in the Brazilian northeast in 1845 and two years later travelled to the United States, where he succeeded in escaping from his master and gaining freedom. Literate in English, Baquaqua wrote an autobiography, becoming one of the first Africans to publish his memoirs. Considered a precious document, his text precedes by five years the novel of Maria Firmina dos Reis and often confirms the tone and various details of the hell narrated by the Brazilian novelist. Describing the crossing of the ocean, he says,

> The only food we had during the voyage was corn soaked and boiled. I cannot tell how long we were thus confined, but it seemed a very long while. We suffered very much for want of water, but were denied all we needed. A pint a day was all that was allowed, and no more; and a great many slaves died upon the passage. … When any one of us became refractory, his flesh was cut with a knife, and pepper or vinegar was rubbed in to make him peaceable (!) I suffered, and so did the rest of us, very much from sea sickness at first, but that did not cause our brutal owners any trouble. Our sufferings were our own, we had no one to share our troubles, none to care for us, or even to speak a word of comfort to us. Some were thrown overboard before breath was out of their bodies; when it was thought any would not live, they were got rid of in that way.[36]

Thus, fiction and autobiography are illuminated and converge in both the description of the trafficking and the condemnation of its inhumanity. The similarity of the two texts, distant from each other linguistically and geographically, is astonishing: it can be seen in the indignant tone transposed into a discursiveness that appeals to God as a greater emblem of justice, in the denunciation of murder as a form of coercion and in the horrific details of the 'grave' and the 'tomb ship'. Reis and Baquaqua emphasize the brutishness of the traffickers in the sadistic and prolonged torture as well as in the burning of corpses. The distinction of the biographical narrative from the fictional one dissolves in the holds where the memory of pain dwells. The distance that separates Detroit – the place of publication of Baquaqua's writings – from São Luís do Maranhão disappears in the shared histories of the Black Atlantic to inaugurate a transnational perspective in which fiction and testimony come together to build another vision of the history of the African diaspora in the Americas.

Seemingly isolated voices, Reis and Mahommah Baquaqua are united by the hand that seeks a political gesture in writing, and in the construction of a diasporic identity that refers back to Africa and repudiates enslavement. Both texts cause the reader to ask questions about barbarism and about who is truly civilized. It is noteworthy that the account of experience, which in Baquaqua's case is true to his memories and central to his narrative, is also present in *Úrsula* as a documentary source of a fiction committed to critiquing the mode of production still in force at that time in many parts of the Americas.

Inscribed in the fiction as a testimony, the voice of Susana contests Western black reason and demystifies it. It starts from the point of view of those who have lost their freedom in order to detail the cruellest moments of that process and question the logic that reduces the humanity of Africans so as to justify their imprisonment and commercialization. Upon arriving in the world in which she will now live, the newly enslaved woman 'freezes with horror' and pities her siblings, the victims of a vicious master and his instruments of torture and the prisons where he 'buried them alive', 'chained in iron'.[37] The semantic field of death is thus amplified. It extends now to a whole life of submission and annulment of the self – the new destiny of those who have just arrived. Charles Martin remarks,

> Maria Firmina dos Reis evidently makes a definitive contribution to abolitionist literature: it represents a standpoint of opposition to the general tendency, providing the Negro with their own mental pattern in the context of the New World. This means a revolution in the depiction of the other and in the depiction of authority. Not only does the other come to have a self, but they also come to express themselves. When Mother Susana and Antero remember, they are at the same time self-representing. In other words, they not only show themselves, but are also shown.[38]

On the other hand, Reis's voice is skilful in avoiding the Manichaeism so common to the feuilleton. The narrated conflicts are not subject to generalization that puts all virtue on one side and all villainy on the other. This makes it possible for Mother Susana to recognize that there is goodness and compassion among the oppressors, which mitigates but does not extinguish her suffering. The slave devotes to the young Úrsula a motherly love which only heightens her humanity. Nevertheless, she does not forget her losses: 'The pain that I have in my heart only death can erase! – my husband, my daughter, my land … my freedom.'[39]

In addition to the painful memories of the old woman and the Christian frame that presides over the existence of Túlio, *Úrsula* also addresses another type of slave: one who loses his self-esteem and indulges in addiction. Here emerges the decrepit figure of Father Antero, a good-hearted man, but dominated by alcoholism. Missing the customs of his land and the 'palm wine' that is drunk in the African ritual of weekly rest – which Reis names 'fetish feast' – Antero functions as the dramatic counterpoint to Túlio's noble morality. By highlighting this character's addiction, the text seeks to avoid an excessive idealization – of either black or white people – which had become a rather common feature of Brazilian romantic fiction.

With Antero, the structure led by Mother Susana is closed, and the black triad gradually mobilizes the attention of the reader and supersedes in importance the predictable love triangle of the white characters. On the other hand, the reference to palm wine and the African festival reinforces a textual link with traditions erased by colonization and absent from the hegemonic discourse. Once again, the fictional text acts as a place of memory by referring to practices left behind during the process of enslavement. Of the representation of slaves in the novel, Juliano Carrupt do Nascimento remarks,

> Túlio, Preta Susana and Antero add moral characterizations that distinguish them from the stereotypes articulated by the cultural and literary processes of the nineteenth century. Their roles as characters force upon the narrative events that would not be possible if they were constructed differently. … Their voices appear in dissonance with the traditional historical and literary discourses, because they characterize themselves as African and persuasive, and do not appear only as voices of slaves who accept subordination to the patriarchal and slaveholding power.[40]

The incidents the black people are involved in are part of a novelistic structure based on embedded narratives in which characters narrate their life stories. They almost always experience extreme situations, marked by chance and abrupt changes of fate. The plot is linear and the characters lack great psychological complexity. By setting *Úrsula* in the context of the feuilleton narrative, one can assess to what extent the writer appropriates the techniques of the popular novel for the purposes of her project of dignifying the oppressed – and not only the enslaved.

Intersectionality and the Critique of Patriarchal Reason

The love triangle formed by Úrsula, Tancredo and the Commander (the uncle who appears as the incarnation of all evil on earth) occupies centre stage. Besides murdering her father and abandoning the protagonist's mother who had been confined to bed for years, the Commander cuts the sadistic figure of the cruel master who exploits his captive workforce to the limits of their strength.

This old and immoderate uncle embodies the incestuous passion typical of what Northrop Frye[41] calls 'romance'. Other traits of this genre are still dear to the general public: multiplicity of time, space and actions; Manichaeism in the construction of protagonists and villain; exaggerated feelings; remorse and madness as punishment; the myth of love at first sight (love can both harm and heal); overabundance of feelings in scenes characteristic of romanticism (sadness kills, unpleasant surprises lead to fainting); all of which is crowned by a narrative strategy marked by flash-forwards and forebodings of all kinds to capture the reader's attention.

At the end, maddened with jealousy, the Commander kills Tancredo on the very night of his wedding to Úrsula, which causes the heroine's madness and death and the inconsolable remorse that also leads her uncle to his death, but not before he releases his captives and is confined in a convent. Discarding a happy ending, the text opts for the schemes enshrined in the gothic novel, to which may be added a path full of obstacles to be overcome.

The novel situates slavery in a context of the supremacy of the master's will as absolute power. In this context a female character is also seen as a nullified individual and as submissive, in short, a person shaped for obedience, in an unprecedented intersection between gender and ethnicity. Úrsula is the typical white woman attached to land ownership and her orphan status. Something similar is true of her mother, whose being in the world is aggravated by illness. By sheltering Tancredo and foreseeing the possibility of love that will bind him to her daughter, she thanks God for the arrival of a potential bridegroom, the only possibility of altering her destiny and that of the heroine. On the other hand, through the voice of the young man, the author points out the 'tyranny' of marriage according to the patterns established by the slave-owning patriarchy of those times as incapable of producing love. Thereby the novel denounces the social triangle at whose apex is placed the will of the master as untouchable, oppressing those under his tutelage: the *woman* and the *enslaved*.

It is, therefore, as a woman and an Afro-Brazilian that the author narrates the drama of young Úrsula and her unfortunate mother. To that are added the misfortunes of Tancredo and the tragedy of Túlio, Susana and Antero, whose narrative treatment is marked by an *internal point of view* based on a faithful rendering of the unofficial history of the African diaspora in Brazil.

Thus, between the positivity and naive goodness of the young Afro-Brazilian, the negativity represented by the decadence of the elderly African and the permanent harassment by patriarchal power against a defenceless woman, Reis makes room for the voice of Mother Susana, a living connection to ancestral memory and to the consciousness subalternized by the regime. A sort of alter ego of the novelist, Susana configures that feminine voice which is the bearer of historical truth. She also intersperses the action with moralizing comments and interventions, sometimes as an oracle weaving the past, present and future through foreshadowing that, on one hand, prepares the reader and accelerates the progress of the narrative and, on the other, encourages reflection and criticism. Susana's voice, thus, arises from the margins of the story's action and gives it density, just as *Úrsula*'s author arises from the margins of Brazilian literature to add to it an instigating supplement of meaning: Afro-Brazilianness. By establishing a discursive difference from the hegemonic abolitionism in the Brazilian literature of her time, the author of *Úrsula* seeks to establish the place of an Afro-Brazilian literature of female authorship.

The discourse of emancipation runs through almost all Reis's work. Her short story 'A escrava' ['The Slave Woman'] published in *Revista Maranhense* in 1887, at the height of the campaign for abolition, also contains the testimony of an aged captive, the character Mãe Joana. This African voice brings to Brazilian literature the supplementary meaning configured by an ancestral trace coming from another continent and another civilization, apparently left behind, and perhaps for this very reason repressed by the hegemonic discourse.

Both characters – Mãe Susana and Mãe Joana – refuse the role of objects ready to satisfy the sexual appetite of the master and his equals. Thus they disrupt roles imposed by customary practices implanted since colonization, among which was to serve as an *enjoyable body*, as is evident in the etymology of the term *mucama* – which comes from the Kimbundu language [*mukama*] and can be translated as 'concubine',[42] a 'slave mistress of her master'.[43]

Brazilian literature has always foregrounded the figure of the sexy Afro-descendant woman who is always available to the white man. Moreover, Brazilian literature has distinctively constructed the image of the black woman with all the trimmings of pleasure without consequence or commitment. This was done in a subtly disguised way because, especially for 'mulatto women', sex never leads to procreation. However, the opposite happens with the characters of Maria Firmina dos Reis. Besides lacking the charm of the 'sensual mulatto women', both Susana and Joana figure as procreators and zealous mothers. Susana mourns until the end the absence of her daughter who was left behind in Africa; Joana witnesses the growth of her children, suffers at the treatment they receive from the overseer and goes mad when she sees her children sold and sent to an unknown place.

The image of a zealous and caring mother is also portrayed in Harriet E. Wilson's *Our Nig: Sketches from the Life of a Free Black*.[44] That, like *Úrsula*, *Our Nig* was forgotten for more than a century is a first point of connection between these texts. Wilson's novel also engages with the reality of racial relations in her time. The book has been described as a mixture of novel and 'third-person autobiography'.[45] The similarities with *Úrsula* emerge even in the words that precede the beginning of the narrative. Wilson shows humility in her foreword and appeals to the reader's complacency:

> In offering to the public the following pages, the writer confesses her inability to minister to the refined and cultivated, the pleasure supplied by abler pens. It is not for such these crude narrations appear. … My humble position and frank confession of errors will, I hope, shield me from severe criticism. Indeed, defects are so apparent it requires no skillful hand to expose them.[46]

Maria Firmina dos Reis adopts a very similar stance to Harriet E. Wilson's. This modest tone was very common among female writers of the nineteenth century. In her foreword, Reis describes *Úrsula* as a 'petty and humble book' written by a 'woman, a Brazilian woman, of poor education and without the manners and conversation of enlightened men'. She also conceals her authorship, signing only as 'Uma Maranhense'.[47]

Our Nig features a child as its main character, Frado. She is abandoned by her mother in a white family's home – the Bellmonts'. Although there is no formal slavery in the Bellmonts' home and her lady is an alleged Bible scholar, catechist and teacher of religion, Frado experiences the presence of the 'shadows' of the old regime. Each in its own way, both novels are centred in the condition of woman – poor or enslaved. In *Úrsula*, Susana is imprisoned and loses her children and family. In *Our Nig*, Mag is forced to abandon her daughter because of the destitution that has haunted her since she was a child. Herself abandoned in the past, Mag will repeat the same behaviour, leaving her daughter behind to the care of others. Thus, the conditions of class, gender and ethnicity are articulated to provide both plots with a historical and social foundation. The superficial construction of the characters is very evident – a popular trait in nineteenth-century novels.

Harriet Wilson's narrative focuses on the trajectory of Frado, a child who is adopted but exploited, having to do demanding jobs incompatible with her age. In the narrative, slavery exists not in the cruelty of the slave trade, but indirectly, in the 'shadows' it casts on the white family's behaviour and in the rough treatment meted out to the girl. This is something Frado endures from the age of six till she is 18 years old. Thus she experiences 12 years of a kind of slavery, that of the 'dependant' – a subaltern human being who, though not formally enslaved, lives in a condition of dependency in a patriarchal household. The 'dependant' was a very well-known figure in the context of nineteenth-century patriarchy, in both Brazil and the United States. Túlio in *Úrsula* is an example of a 'dependant' who, though free, dies attempting to save the white man who released him from slavery.

In *Our Nig*, the shadows of the ideology of slavery are present in the smallest details and draw a frame in which the characters' behaviour is ruled by the most harmful consequence of this ideology: racism – a mindset and posture that have survived the end of the slavery regime, the American Civil War and all the movements of ethnic affirmation in the United States throughout the twentieth century. In the novel, Mrs Bellmont does not allow Frado to attend religious services, even though she is a teacher of religion and should, theoretically, be intent on expanding her 'flock'. In the absence of her husband and children, the villain has no difficulty in expressing how much she discriminates against black people: 'Religion was not meant for niggers.'[48]

In Chapter 4, there is a climax of physical aggression in the scene in which Frado brings pieces of firewood to the fireplace, but never the small pieces required by Mrs Bellmont. The girl cries quietly, already knowing what awaits her, since there is no more firewood of the required size:

> As she expected, Mrs. Bellmont, enraged, approached her, and kicked her so forcibly as to throw her upon the floor. Before she could rise, another foiled the attempt, and then followed kick after kick in quick succession and power, till she reached the door. Mr. Bellmont and Aunt Abby, hearing the noise, rushed in, just in time to see the last of the performance. Nig jumped up, and rushed from the house, out of sight.[49]

The scene shocks the reader for its cruelty and makes *Our Nig* similar to *Úrsula* and also to autobiographical accounts, such as Solomon Northup's *Twelve Years a Slave* (1853), that are equally marked by the absurd punishments imposed on the enslaved.

The boundaries between autobiography and fiction are tenuous when it comes to narratives of black and female authorship, especially those produced in the nineteenth century. In *Our Nig* and *Úrsula* the historical foundations upon which the plots are built are clearly evident. Wilson and Reis anchored these texts in memory that is individual but also collective; a memory that exists in the orality of Afro-Brazilian *causos* and American tales – oral narratives transmitted through generations of people of African descent.

Thus, the Afro-Brazilian and African-American narratives are very similar in the means of resistance they both mediate. They are also close to each other in opposing the submission that marks the depiction of Afro-descendants imprisoned by servility. Each in her own way, the authors are women of 'their time and country' (as Machado de Assis says) in search of a perspective other than that of the oppressor, to slowly create the 'Black conscience of Blackness'[50] that would flourish in the twentieth century. They do so by resorting to memory, both individual and collective, and by appropriating a European invention – the melodramatic *roman-feuilleton* – a genre that provoked so much shedding of tears, until people awoke from the centuries-old nightmare through which the New World was built.

Notes

1. This chapter reproduces previous writings, especially the afterword to the seventh edition of *Úrsula* (Reis 2018). Translation by Harion Custódio.
2. Morais Filho 1975.
3. Gates 1983, xiii.
4. Mbembe 2017.
5. Mbembe 2017, 10.
6. Mbembe 2017, 10.
7. Mbembe 2017, 13.
8. Mbembe 2017, 18.
9. Mbembe 2017, 18.
10. Mbembe 2017, 27.
11. Hegel 2002; Hegel 1989.
12. Mbembe 2017, 12.
13. Hegel 1955, paragraph 57, 122.
14. Mbembe 2017, 30.
15. Mbembe 2017, 29.
16. Reis 2018, 32.
17. Reis 2018, 32.
18. Reis 2018, 32.
19. Reis 2018, 33, emphasis added.
20. Reis 2018, 34, emphasis added.
21. Martin 1988, 11.
22. Reis 2018, 34.
23. Reis 2018, 35.
24. Reis 2018, 36.
25. Reis 2018, 101–2.
26. Muzart 2000, 266.

27. Pinto-Bailey 2017.
28. Reis 2018, 103–4.
29. Reis 2018, 103.
30. Reis 2018, 103.
31. Reis 2018, 103.
32. Reis 2018, 103–4.
33. Reis 2018, 103.
34. Nora 1993, 22.
35. Lopes 2004, 659.
36. Baquaqua 2001, 43–4.
37. Reis 2018, 104.
38. Martin 1988, 13.
39. Reis 2018, 104.
40. Nascimento 2009, 101.
41. Frye 1957.
42. Lopes 2004, 456.
43. This role is remembered, even with some nostalgia, by Gilberto Freyre in *Casa-grande e senzala* [*The Masters and the Slaves*] when he emphasizes the role of the 'mulatto woman who initiated us in physical love and transmitted to us, on the creaking of the bed, the first utter sensation of being a man' (Freyre 1984, 283).
44. Gates 1983, xiii.
45. Gates 1983, xiii.
46. Wilson 2005, 5.
47. Reis 2018, 23.
48. Wilson 2005, 38.
49. Wilson 2005, 25.
50. Mbembe 2017, 30.

Bibliography

Baquaqua, Mahomah Gardo. *Biography of Mahommah G. Baquaqua, a Native of Zoogoo, in the Interior of Africa*. Text transcribed by Apex Data Services, Inc. Text encoded by Apex Data Services, Inc., Elizabeth S. Wright and Natalia Smith. Chapel Hill: University of North Carolina at Chapel Hill, Academic Affairs Library, 2001.

Freyre, Gilberto. *Casa-grande & senzala*. Rio de Janeiro: José Olympio, 1984.

Frye, Northrop. *Anatomia da crítica*, translated by Péricles Eugênio da Silva Ramos. São Paulo: Cultrix, 1957.

Gates, Jr, Henry Louis. 'Introduction'. In *Our Nig, or Sketches from the Life of a Free Black*, edited by Henry Louis Gates, Jr and R. J. Ellis. New York: Vintage Books, 1983.

Hegel, G. W. F. *The Philosophy of Right*, translated by T. M. Knox. Chicago: Encyclopædia Britannica, 1955.

Hegel, G. W. F. *Lecciones sobre la Filosofia de la História Universal (1837)*, translated by José Gaos. Madrid: Alianza, 1989.

Hegel, G. W. F. *Fenomenologia do espírito*, translated by Paulo Menezes with Karl-Heinz Efken and José Nogueira Machado. Petrópolis: Vozes, 2002.

Lopes, Nei. *Enciclopédia brasileira da diáspora africana*. São Paulo: Selo Negro, 2004.

Martin, Charles. 'Uma rara visão de liberdade'. In Maria Firmina dos Reis, *Úrsula*, edited by Luiza Lobo. Rio de Janeiro: Presença; Brasília: INL, 1988.

Mbembe, Achille. *Critique of Black Reason*, translated by Laurent Dubois. Durham, NC: Duke University Press, 2017.

Morais Filho, José Nascimento. *Maria Firmina, fragmentos de uma vida*. São Luiz: COCSN, 1975.

Muzart, Zahidé Lupinacci. 'Maria Firmina dos Reis'. In *Escritoras brasileiras do século XIX*, edited by Zahidé Lupinacci Muzart. Florianópolis: Editora Mulheres, 2000.

Nascimento, Juliano Carrupt do. *O negro e a mulher em* Úrsula, *de Maria Firmina dos Reis*. Rio de Janeiro: Caetés, 2009.

Nora, Pierre. 'Entre memória e história: a problemática dos lugares', translated by Iara Aum Khoury. *Projeto História* 10 (December 1993): 7–28.

Pinto-Bailey, Cristina Ferreira. 'Na contramão: a narrativa abolicionista de Maria Firmina dos Reis', 2017. http://www.letras.ufmg.br/literafro/29-critica-de-autores-feminios/316-na-contramao-a-2017

Reis, Maria Firmina dos. *Úrsula*, edited by Eduardo de Assis Duarte. Belo Horizonte: Editora PUC Minas, 2018.

Said, Edward. *Orientalism*. New York: Pantheon Books, 1978.

Wilson, Harriet E. *Our Nig, or Sketches from the Life of a Free Black*, edited by Gabrielle Foreman and Reginald H. Pitts. London: Penguin Books, 2005.

5
'A suspicious sound interrupted the gentle harmony': *Iracema* by José de Alencar[1]

Thiago Rhys Bezerra Cass

Incongruities

Gerald Martin once remarked that, although all societies emerge from waves of miscegenation, 'only Latin Americans have been so deeply and inescapably aware of this'.[2] He should have added that such awareness is often marred by ambivalence.[3] *Iracema* (1865), by José Martiniano de Alencar (1829–77), fictionally instantiates the hesitancy and tentativeness that tend to permeate the assessment of miscegenation in Brazil, since this still widely read novel simultaneously posits and mitigates the violence pervading the country's history of racial and cultural intermixing. In little more than 200 pages, printed in crown octavo (190 × 125 mm),[4] *Iracema* refigures the colonial encounter with a marriage plot that harkens back to the formula codified in British and Irish unionist novels, such as those by Susan Ferrier. In a story of star-crossed lovers, a Tabajara priestess and a Portuguese conquistador satisfy their reciprocated sexual desire and end up producing a biracial son, a type who had not been imagined in paradigmatic novels set in the Americas which circulated in nineteenth-century Brazil. The drive to connubial union of the protagonists of *Iracema* renders narratable the process of conquest and displacement of indigenous populations.[5] As any meagre paraphrase will show, interracial coupling in *Iracema* imposes unequal obligations to Amerindians, something that had not (quite) taken place in Alencar's earlier so-called Indigenist novel, *O guarani* [*The Guarany*] (1857). Compensatively or not, *Iracema* departs from Alencar's former strategy of inscribing in linguistic terms racial and cultural tensions, a strategy long associated with Walter Scott's historical novels. Rather, *Iracema* is famously, or notoriously, overridden by a heightened poetical language, reminiscent of *Ossian*, that makes narrator and characters speak, if not in unison, at least with indistinguishable voices. This ostensible monologism seems to interfere, the reception of the text indicates, with readers' capacity to apprehend *Iracema*'s unpleasant core.

One of the recurrent pitfalls of comparison, Juliet Hooker has recently argued, is that 'it assumes, or constructs, an illusion of coherence and distinctness of the units being compared'.[6] To unpack thus *Iracema*'s interplay of form, style, politics and readerly response, Alencar's novel had to be interrogated by means of multiple texts from divergent national backgrounds and generic affiliations. This sequential juxtaposition of apparently unrelated materials not only demonstrates the radicalism of Alencar's literary experiment; first and foremost, it disentangles incongruities and unleashes dissonances that otherwise would have been eclipsed.[7]

Archery

Iracema is a misleadingly straightforward novel.[8] Fewer than five pages into the 1865 edition are necessary to bring the couple together. 'Iracema, the maiden with lips of honey, whose hair was darker than the *graúna*'s [rice grackle] wings and longer than her torso', is resting in a forest clearing after bathing in a river.[9] 'The pearly drops of water still bedewed' Iracema's body when 'a suspicious sound interrupted the gentle harmony' of her prelapsarian existence. Iracema lifts her eyes and sees 'a strange warrior' with cheeks as white as 'the sands that border the sea' and eyes as blue as the waters of the deep. It is Martim. Scared by his odd-looking appearance, Iracema aims her bow at him and injures his face. Instead of attacking back, he smiles at her. To his 'mother's religion', the narrator tells us, women are symbols of 'tenderness and love'.[10] The arrow metaphorically marks their bonding and, in a less obvious way, a withdrawal from the initial mythical register. Before the fatal shot, Iracema was roaming in the woods in the historical present. This timeless world is brought abruptly to an end by the introduction of the past tense when 'the arrow set in the bow flew'.[11]

Iracema repents the assault and brings Martim to her father's hut in order to tend him. There, as a sign of peace, she breaks 'the murderous arrow', handing 'the shaft to the stranger, keeping the barbed point'.[12] Unsurprisingly, Martim's presence is resented by the Tabajaras.

Notwithstanding the hospitality granted by *pajé* [shaman] Araquém, who happens to be Iracema's father, Martim is threatened by the champion of the Tabajaras, Irapuã. An irascible and vengeful warrior, Irapuã has long courted Iracema and is only refrained from killing Martim by her intervention. On the eve of Martim's departure, the white and the native consummate their erotic yearnings for each other.[13] With the help of Poti, a Pitiguara whom Martim calls brother, the couple flee the heights of the Tabajaras and head to the shores, a territory under Pitiguara control. Irapuã and his followers chase the lovers, but are repelled by Poti's men. Iracema takes part in the fight and kills many of her tribespeople. The arrow, formerly a symbol of bonding, now stands for betrayal: 'the Christian only defended himself, but the arrow ready in his wife's bow protected the warrior's life against the enemy's thrusts'.[14] To protect Martim, she will unhesitatingly shed the blood of her brother, Caubi.[15] Iracema's break with her Tabajara past soon finds an asymmetrical equivalent in Martim's ritualistic metamorphosis, through which he goes native by painting his body and taking a Tupi name: Coatiabo, the creature who has painted itself.[16]

> The foreigner, having adopted the homeland of his wife and his friend, must pass through that ceremony in order to become a red warrior, son of Tupã …
>
> Martim opened his arms and his lips to receive the body and the soul of his wife.
>
> 'My brother is a great warrior of the Pitiguara nation: he needs a name in the language of his nation.'
>
> 'Your brother's name is on his body, where your hand placed it.'
>
> 'Coatiabo!' exclaimed Iracema.
>
> 'You have spoken it: I am the painted warrior, the warrior of his wife and of his friend.'[17]

Having both renounced their erstwhile identities, Martim and Iracema beget a son, who is neither Amerindian nor European, but Brazilian. More specifically, Cearense: 'the first child born in [the province of] Ceará'.[18] Iracema names him 'Moacir, the child born of my suffering'.[19]

Alencar had a record of tinkering with allegorical narratives of interracial love. His first literary splash, *O guarani* (1857),[20] brings together the generous but slightly spoiled Cecilia de Mariz, the daughter of a Portuguese knight who has taken refuge in the hilly outskirts of Rio de Janeiro, and the unflinchingly heroic Pery, a Goytacaz who has given up his chiefdom in order to serve Cecilia. Their story concludes with biblical overtones. Only Cecilia and Pery survive an attack of hostile Aymorés to the forest abode of the Mariz family. She asks him to procure cotton and furs. She intends to dress like a native and live with Pery in the bush: 'Pery cannot live with his sister in the city of the white men; his sister will remain with him in the wilderness amid the forests.'[21] Freed from the constraints of her family's prejudice, Cecilia realizes what the reader has known all along: that she is desperately in love with Pery. They kiss under torrential rain, escaping a flood in a hastily made canoe that is compared by the narrator to Noah's Ark.[22]

With such upbeat dénouement, *O guarani* rehearses, even if not smoothly, the unionist plots that had saturated Irish and British fiction in the early decades of the nineteenth century.[23] Examples abound. In an aptly titled novel by Susan Ferrier, *Marriage* (1818), the matrimony of Mary Douglas and Colonel Lennox optimistically puts an end to intergenerational misunderstandings between Scottish and English characters. Their union is forcibly presented as an instrument for social regeneration: 'And the poor, the sick, and the desolate, united in blessing what heaven had already blessed—this happy Marriage.'[24] *Iracema* purveys a much more nuanced version of this conciliatory structure. The protagonists' sexual drive is potent enough to overcome the themes of interdiction and sterility that had beset narratives of interracial love set in the New World, such as René de Chateaubriand's *Atala* (1801)[25] and James Fenimore Cooper's *The Last of the Mohicans* (1826).[26] In the latter, the mere suggestion of an afterlife marriage between Cora, the mulatto daughter of a colonel of the British Army, and Uncas, the last 'pure-blood' Mohican, is condescendingly rejected as the error of a 'simple creed'.[27] In *Atala*, the eponymous character, a mixed-race Christian girl, craves sexual intimacy with Chactas, a Natchez who has hitherto rejected overtures to embrace Christianity:

> Sometimes, as I fixed my eyes upon you, my desires would go to the wildest and most forbidden extremes. I wanted to be the only living creature on earth with you; or else, feeling some divinity restraining me in my dreadful ecstasies, I longed for the annihilation of the divinity, if only, clasped in your arms, I could plunge through endless depths along with the ruins of God and the universe![28]

She is, however, admonished by a priest, Aubry, who considers 'these intense emotions … unworthy of your innocence'.[29] Distraught, and shackled to an oath that has consecrated her virginity, Atala commits suicide lest she gives in to her desire. In contrast, Iracema's characterization does not rest upon martyred maidenhood. Despite having sworn celibacy like Atala, she quite willingly forfeits her vows. Martim asks Iracema to drink from a ceremonial hallucinatory liquor, *jurema*, so that he can be, in his dreams, 'with Iracema and gather from her lips the kisses that luxuriated there among smiles, like fruit in the flower's corolla'.[30] Martim thus possesses 'the image of the maiden' and, in his reverie, 'gently' intones Iracema's name. This will make her cast her lot irrevocably with Martim:

> The *juriti* [field dove], wandering through the forest, hears the tender cooing of its mate; it beats its wings and flies to find shelter in its warm nest. So did the maiden of the interior nestle in the warrior's arms.
>
> When morning came, it still found Iracema enfolded there, like a butterfly that has slept in the bosom of a shapely cactus.[31]

Franklin Távora, an acerbic detractor of Alencar's oeuvre, describes this scene as an act of 'villainy', scoffing at the idea of drinking an elixir 'in order to use without *abuse*'.[32] Relishing in his infamous tongue-in-cheek sanctimony, he compares Iracema to a dove and Martim to a kite, flesh-eating even when 'asleep and inert'.[33] Blinded by his notions of decorum, Távora cannot come to terms with Iracema's active sexuality. And yet such sexuality is far from being narratively sanctioned. The trajectory of Cecilia and Pery is not to be replayed. Eventually, Iracema will face the same tragic ending assigned to dark-skinned heroines such as Atala and Cora.[34]

The optimism of the 1850s, which had informed so much of the regenerative utopianism of *O guarani*, was long gone. The Conservatives, together with their rallying cries for stability and political pacification, were ousted from power in 1863.[35] Cabinets quickly succeeded one another in an atmosphere marked by factionalism and an impending sense of crisis, a situation to which the War of the Triple Alliance (1864–70) greatly contributed. A conservative by temperament and party affiliation, Alencar portrayed the current state of affairs as a 'very painful predicament' in a series of open – albeit anonymous – letters to the Emperor, *Cartas de Erasmo* (1865).[36] To Alencar, a once 'vigorous Empire' no longer strode along the 'path towards progress'.[37] Contradictions that could be miraculously washed away in the days of *O guarani*, by dint of a providential flood, now resurface with full force in *Iracema*.[38]

After the triumph of the Pitiguaras over Irapuã and the Tabajaras, Poti guides Iracema and Martim to his ancestral lands. But Iracema does not want to stay as an exiled outcast in the village of her people's hereditary enemies, and asks Martim to leave. Poti follows them in a journey 'without destination', with no planned movements along the domains of the Pitiguaras.[39] As they march towards the Maranguab range, they arrive at a hut near the Pirapora stream. It has a sole tenant: Batuireté, Poti's grandfather. Though Martim had fondly anticipated palavering with Batuireté as an opportunity for praising his valiant grandson, the meeting is totally anticlimactic. Batuireté breathes his last when he contemplates his multiracial visitors:

> The old man half opened his heavy eyelids and ran his lusterless gaze from his grandson to the foreigner. Then his chest heaved and his lips whispered: 'Tupã has willed that before losing their sight these eyes should see the white hawk beside the *narceja* [snipe].'
>
> The wise old man's head dropped to his chest, and he spoke nor moved no more.[40]

An authorial note explains Batuireté's metaphoric last words as a prophecy of 'the destruction of his race by the white race'.[41] From this juncture onwards, the hitherto unhampered conjugal plot begins to undermine itself. Martim, Poti and Iracema settle near a sandhill by the estuary of a river. Immediately afterwards, Iracema realizes, to her desperation, that her husband's passion towards her is rapidly weakening. His heterosexual bond with Iracema is overshadowed by his homosocial partnership with Poti as they enlist together in the wars against Dutch settlers.[42] Lest he should be softened by his wife's sorrow, Martim joins the military expedition without bidding her farewell. Significantly, the archery motif is once more mobilized, now to convey forsakenness and dereliction. Before setting off, Poti chooses one of the arrows Iracema brought with colourful feathers to her husband and leaves it as a sign to Iracema not to follow Martim's trail. The arrow is then adorned with 'a twig of the passion-flower, the flower of remembrance'.[43]

Iracema endures 'many days of longing and abandonment' before Martim's return.[44] Feeling forsaken, she descends into depression, which is not relieved even by her pregnancy or by Martim's revived love, inspired by his imminent fatherhood. By the time of the birth of Moacir, the so-called child of her suffering, Iracema is too debilitated to lactate. When she is at last able to feed her son, after offering her breasts to be suckled by tayra pups, her milk is tinged with blood. She agonizes alone, since Martim is far away fighting the Dutch. Only reluctantly he decides to quit the field and go back to his wife. He arrives too late, to see only the final moments of Iracema's withering demise. She places the child in his father's arms and asks him to have her body buried beneath his favourite coconut tree: 'When the wind from the sea blows among its leaves, Iracema will think it is your voice rustling through her hair.'[45]

Poem

To our latter-day sensibilities, trained in Marxist, cultural and post-structuralist criticism, *Iracema*'s brutal subtext is indisputable.[46] The erotic coming together of Martim and Iracema, producing a mixed-race offspring, may represent an allegory of miscegenation. But such allegory cannot obfuscate the fact that the encounter of Europeans and indigenous populations almost invariably resulted in disproportionate destruction of native lives, such as those of Iracema and the Tabajaras. And yet, rather predictably, many of Alencar's contemporaries failed to acknowledge the latent violence of the text. In fact, *Iracema* was almost immediately deemed to be a celebratory work.[47] One example will suffice. In the fourth year (1868) of the War of the Triple Alliance, a series of articles on the experience of the southern front found their way on to the pages of the daily paper *Correio Paulistano*. The author, a medical volunteer named Joaquim de Paula Souza, is not usually included in Brazil's long and unillustrious lineage of openly racist intellectuals. With his unsympathetic account of a 'strange land' peopled by 'Indians from the Chaco', however, he penned a very eloquent document of mid-nineteenth-century prejudice against South American indigenous peoples.[48] It is difficult to discuss it without causing offence. Professedly scandalized over the modes and mores of the inhabitants of Corrientes, Paula Souza falls short of depriving them of their humanity. Men are dismissed as simply 'ugly', whereas women, probably because of their perceived nakedness, are depicted as 'horrendous, ignoble, disgusting, with their loose hair covering their backs, swinishly; torn loincloths, showing their dirty legs, uncovered bosom'.[49] He notices how swiftly Brazilian 'gold and civilization' are changing the landscape, but bemoans that this new influx of progress and enlightenment hasn't had the strength to drive away 'these Indians of the Guaycuru race … so ugly, stupid and ignoble'.[50] He can't understand why these 'hordes' have been admitted into town. Overwhelmed and carried away by his intolerance, Paula Souza finds fault not merely with the local authorities for allowing such trespass against his racist sense of propriety. He berates 'the poets' who 'have dared to paint' Indians beautifully and heroically. To Paula Souza, these poets, by not characterizing Indians as 'ugly and bestial', are like proverbial swindlers selling a pup. 'To me, they may even paint [Indians] with heavenly hues, that it won't dispel the disfavour that has stayed with me, after seeing them in the backlands of São Paulo, Chaco, and Paraguay.'[51] Among these supposedly insincere poets, Paula Souza lists Alencar:

> Imperceptibly, they [the indigenous populations] brought back to my mind that beautiful poem by Mr Alencar – Iracema – in which he makes the Indian so beautiful, intelligent and poetical, when we always see them so ugly, stupid and swinish. I lamented that such a towering intelligence had offered itself such an object, and I wish I could have extracted him from it, at least for a while. I confess that I found myself inveighing against Iracema the Indian – What have you done, Iracema?
>
> You have distracted the strength of a superior white warrior, and turned him into a painted Indian! The one who aspires to great deeds … is bound to you, and settles in the backlands, Iracema! Iracema, sometimes I wish you had died and spared the vigour of the warrior, spared him of toiling, which I find useless, among stupid Indians, when our fathers are so great and so beautiful. Sometimes, as I contemplate such beautiful work, Iracema, in a trance I forgive you as I admire it! What a delicate needlework in its smallest details! Such pretty embroideries and arabesques! Everything it says is engraved with a chisel![52]

In a few repetitive lines, this nauseating piece of unbridled bigotry foregrounds – probably unbeknownst to its author – *Iracema*'s aestheticized language, which, to many of Alencar's contemporaries, diluted the contradictions that ultimately unravel the novel's conciliatory structure. Such modulations, as Paula Souza indicates, frequently transfigure the narrative into 'a beautiful poem', whereby even the text's sacrificial closure may be discarded as irrelevant or non-existent.

Voice

Throughout his literary career, Alencar regarded the novel as 'a poem of real life',[53] consistently labelling the genre as 'congenial' to an 'adolescent' country such as post-independence Brazil, with its 'indecisive, vague, and multiple physiognomy'.[54] In one of his earliest critical-cum-theoretical pronouncements, his merciless debunking of Domingos José Gonçalves de Magalhães's neoclassical epic about the 1556 Tamoyo revolt against

Portuguese settlers,[55] we can find Alencar already 'persuaded' that a novel à la Walter Scott, if it tackled similar materials and themes, would be much more engrossing than Magalhães's state-sponsored epic:

> I am strongly persuaded that, if Walter Scott translated these Portuguese [Magalhães's] verses in his correct and elegant style, if he turned this poem into a novel, he would have given it a charm and appeal that would compel the reader who skimmed through the first pages of the book to read it with interest and pleasure.[56]

To a large extent, Alencar's first fictional incursion into Brazil's indigenous past, *O guarani*, programmatically fulfils such conviction.[57] Drawing from chronicles and characters of colonial times, *O guarani* presents itself as a historical novel, edited and forwarded by a somewhat watered-down version of Jedediah Cleishbotham, professing to have uncovered a manuscript eaten up by termites.[58] More importantly, *O guarani* re-enacts Scott's strategy of using linguistic stratification, or heteroglossia, to inscribe social, cultural and intranational disputes galvanized by a pre-modernity that refuses to be superseded.[59] In *Waverley; or Tis Sixty Years Since* (1814),[60] for example, the vernacular inflections in Evan's invective against the members of an Edinburgh court who rejected his offer to face the gallows in lieu of Fergus Mac-Ivor, translate in linguistic terms the centuries-old cleavage between Highlanders and Lowlanders:

> 'If the Saxon gentlemen are laughing,' he said, 'because a poor man, such as me, thinks my life, or the life of six of my degree, is worth of Vich Ian Vohr, it's like enough they may be very right; but if they laugh because they think I would not keep my word, and come back to redeem him, I can tell them they ken neither the heart of a Hielandman, nor the honour of a gentleman.'[61]

Like *Waverley*, *O guarani* invites the reader to approach 'the text as linguistic as well as a cultural amalgam'.[62] But instead of incorporating vernacular forms by recording multiple demotic variations of what was perceived as the same language, Alencar worked, throughout *O guarani*, within long-established notions about the peculiarities of 'primitive' expression. These notions permeated his rendition of indigenous voices. In the Americas, ideas such as Hugh Blair's, whose *Lectures on Rhetoric and Belles-Lettres* (1783) were carefully read by Alencar, had enormous resonance.[63] In his early writings, in which he analysed the poems attributed to Ossian, Blair maintained that 'those times which we call barbarous are favorable to the poetical spirit. That state, in which human nature shoots wild and free, though unfit for other improvements, certainly encourages the high exertions of fancy and passion.'[64] By the time Blair published his *Lectures*, he substantially expanded the argument in a discussion on the origins of languages. Here, concepts such as 'savage' become patently racialized:

> [A]ll Languages are most figurative in their early state … Language is then most barren; the stock of proper names, which have been invented for things, is small; and, at the same time, imagination exerts great influence over the conceptions of men, and their method of uttering them; so that, both from necessity and from choice, their Speech will, at that period, abound in Tropes. For the savage tribes of men are always much given to wonder and astonishment. Every new object surprises, terrifies, and makes a strong impression on their mind; they are governed by imagination and passion, more than by reason; and, of course, their speech must be deeply tinctured by their genius. In fact, we find, that this is the character of the American and Indian Languages; bold, picturesque, and metaphorical; full of strong allusions to sensible qualities, and to such objects as struck them most in their wild and solitary life. An Indian chief makes a harangue to his tribe, in a style full of stronger metaphors than a European would use in an epic poem.[65]

Thus, in *O guarani*, the figurative rendering of Pery's voice sets him apart from the prosaism of the 'band of adventurers' who, 'united together by ambition for wealth', served Dom Antônio de Mariz, Cecilia's father, in his 'explorations and expeditions into the interior'.[66] These adventurers speak, in their lower echelons, the bald idiom of colonialism, recurrently evoking money, commerce, silver mines and the necessity of mounting lines of defence against uncooperative natives, disparagingly referred to as 'savages', 'barbarians' and *Bugres*. Demanding from the adventurers a 'duty of passive obedience'[67] and a lion's share of their profits (50 per cent), Dom Antônio, obsequiously emulated by Dom Diogo and Álvaro de Sá, couches the parlance of his subordinates in a paternalistic terminology of chivalry, loyalty, discipline and devotion to the House of Braganza.[68] Conversely, the ventriloquism of the Goytacaz voice is premised on disfluency in these mundane affairs. More precisely, Pery's dialogues and interventions are entangled in the luxuriant rainforest that surrounds him. His speeches are engendered by environmental metaphors and similes, conjuring up images of streams, flowers and palm trees. He tells Álvaro that he loves the young man because he makes Cecilia smile. 'The reed, when it is by the water side, is green and merry ... You are the river.'[69] And, of course, Cecilia is supposed to be the reed. According to the narrator, Pery is a 'primitive poet' who sings 'nature in the very language of nature'.

> His word is the one God has written with the letters that form the book of creation; it is the flower, the sky, the light, the color, the air, the sun; sublime objects which nature created smiling. His style flows like the meandering brook, or leaps like the river dashing down the cascade; at times it rises to the summit of the mountains, at others it descends and creeps like the pretty, diminutive insect.[70]

In his rancorous literary testament, 'Como e porque sou romancista' ['How and Why I Am a Novelist'] (1873), Alencar argued that, 'in *O guarani*, the lyricism of a young imagination overflows, having the fault of exuberance as its first foliage; everywhere, the lymph, wanting in sap, produces flowers or leaves'.[71] He repudiated the perennially repeated insinuation that he had modelled his first Indigenist novel on *The Last of the Mohicans*. 'In *O guarani*, the savage is an ideal, whom the writer intends to poetize, undressing him from the vile crust with which chroniclers had wrapped him, and tearing him from the ridicule that the remnants of an almost extinct race project upon him.'[72] To Alencar, 'the eminent American novelist' did not indulge in these flights of poetization. 'Cooper considers the Indian from a social point of view, and he was a *realist* in the description of their customs.'[73] His works, Alencar claimed, had 'the simplicity and the parsimony of the prose writer, who does not allow himself to enraptured by fantasy; quite the contrary, he castigates it.'[74] Scholars have intensely debated the accuracy of these retrospective assessments.[75] It is clear that Alencar downplays his own constructive device of framing the so-called 'poetry' of his Amerindians with an ostensibly realist prose. This discursive duality was also present in *The Last of the Mohicans*. The 'bloody and inhumane' narrative of the 'pages of colonial history' is contrasted to the beauty of Mohican voices:

> It is impossible to describe the music of their language, while thus engaged in laughter and endearments, in such a way as to render it intelligible to those whose ears have never listened to its melody. The compass of their voices, particularly that of the youth, was wonderful; extending from the deepest bass, to tones that were even feminine in softness. The eyes of the father followed the plastic and ingenious movements of the son with open delight, and he never failed to smile

> in reply to the other's contagious but low laughter. While under the influence of these gentle and natural feelings, no trace of ferocity was to be seen in the softened features of the Sagamore.[76]

Those voices, however, are marked for annihilation, being engulfed in the long run by 'sounds of hostility'.[77] In *O guarani*, quite remarkably, heteroglossia does not stand in the way of the narrative's mythical closure. Rather, realist conventions authenticate and legitimize Pery's emergence as 'the king of the wilderness, the lord of the forest'. Speaking a 'poetic language', he finally wins Cecilia's hand by promising her that she will never be alone. Even if he goes on an errand, he will leave his soul behind, in a flower, to watch over her.[78] Eight years later, when this sort of unproblematic resolution seemed no longer tenable, Alencar definitively abandoned his technique of inscribing colonial tensions in linguistic discontinuities.

At first glance, *Iracema* is distinctly monologic.[79] In spite of being written in Portuguese, and unmistakably addressed to a Portuguese-speaking readership, the text is advertised by an authorial persona, in a postscript titled 'Letter to Dr. Jaguaribe',[80] as a 'translat[ion] into his language' of indigenous images, thoughts, terms and phrases. As much as Blair had correlated poetic endowments with a restrictive lexicon, since it induced 'primitive' poets to make use of metaphorical circumlocution, the 'Letter to Dr. Jaguaribe' claims that Alencar was able to infuse the Portuguese language with the beauty of 'savage' expressions by simply providing literal translations to the Tupi vocabulary he had mined in etymological dictionaries. *Piguara*, it is argued, could have been unceremoniously translated as 'guide'. Nevertheless, 'master of the pathway' is preferred, thereby turning Brazilian Portuguese into an Adamic or motivated language.[81] In other words, *Iracema* is 'an experiment in prose', whereby 'the civilized language' is professedly moulded, as much as possible, 'to the primitive simplicity of the barbaric tongue'.[82] To attain such 'simplicity', European and Amerindian voices, whose limits were so strenuously demarcated in *O guarani*, collapse into one in *Iracema*. Martim arrives at the tribe of the Tabajaras already fluent in Tupi:

> The warrior spoke …
>
> 'Who has taught you, white warrior, my brothers' tongue? From where have come to these woods, which have never seen another warrior like you?'
>
> 'I come from far away, daughter of the forests. I come from the lands that your brothers once possessed and which my own now have.'[83]

As a result, rhetorical devices that once pertained exclusively to indigenous characters now impregnate the dialogues ascribed to a European. Iracema, as one might expect, retains Pery's penchant for piling up figures of speech. But she also develops a propensity for repeating them with minimal variations, re-signifying them or suggesting unanticipated connotations.[84] Hence Iracema, whose name, an authorial note explains, combines the etyma of honey and lips, tells Martim after the battle against Irapuã and the Tabajaras that she 'bears all for her warrior and master. The sugar apple is sweet and tasty, but when it is bruised it sours. Your wife wants her love to fill your heart with the sweetness of honey.'[85] Pages later, when she notices her husband pulling apart from her, she summons the same saccharine images, but now to express sourness:

> Your lips have become barren to your wife; so does the sugarcane, when the long sunny days blaze, lose its honey, and its withered leaves no longer sing the passing breeze. Now you speak only to the wind of the shore, so that it may carry your voice to the hut of your fathers.[86]

Martim, symptomatically, partakes of the same images. Initially, he wants 'to sip, like the hummingbird, the honey' of Iracema's lips, but as he later becomes indifferent towards his wife he reproaches her for letting sadness embitter her once honeyed lips.[87] Martim's very introduction to Araquém, Iracema's father, displays the white warrior's full immersion in Amerindian discursive practices. He makes reference to the Latin etymology of his name, explaining that 'Martim' 'in your language means son of a warrior'. He alludes to the 'tree of friendship' that he planted with Poti, brother of Jacaúna. He uses a synecdoche when he recounts how 'three suns ago' he and Poti 'left for the hunt' and he, wandering alone, got lost and ended up in 'the land of the Tabajaras'. Above all, he uses a periphrasis to ascertain his origins, declaring that he is a man in whose veins flows the 'blood ... of the great people who first saw the lands of your country'.[88]

This vocal uniformity is supported and reinforced by a narrator constructed in accordance with Alencar's (and Blair's) preconceptions about indigenous utterance. From *Iracema*'s very outset, one notices a rhetorical and prosodic apparatus generally associated with poetry. Chapter 1 opens with an apostrophe to the 'Green, tempestuous seas of my native land'.[89] The mere personification of an environmental element would certainly be enough to sever *Iracema* from realist protocols. But in Portuguese these lines are also rhythmically and aurally layered and can be almost entirely scanned as rendondillas suffused with alliteration and assonance:

> Verdes **ma**res bra**vios**/ de **mi**nha **te**rra na**tal**,/ onde **ca**nta a jan**daia**/ nas **fron**des **da** carna**ú**ba;
> Verdes **ma**res, que bri**lhais**/ como **lí**qui**da** **es**mer**al**da/ aos **raios** do **sol** nas**ce**nte,/ perlon**gan**do as **al**vas **praias**/ ensom**bra**das de co**quei**ros;[90]
>
> [Green, tempestuous seas of my native land, where the *jandaia* sings amid the carnauba fronds:
> Green seas, that gleam with liquid emerald in the rays of the rising sun, skirting alabaster beaches shaded by coconut trees:][91]

Such hypertrophied poetical dialect is sustained throughout *Iracema*. In Chateaubriand's *Atala*, events unfold through Chactas's conventionally figurative pre-modern voice. But this voice is assessed through filters within filters: 'Chactas, son of Outalissi the Natchez, told this story to René the European. Fathers have repeated it to their children, and I, a traveller in far-distant lands, have faithfully set down what I received from the Indians.'[92] In *Iracema*, prosaism is completely displaced into paratexts: prefaces, postscripts and annotations. All in a verbose authorial register, these paratexts provide etymological, geographical, historical and ethnographical information while decoding symbols, metaphors, similes and prophecies. More relevantly, they provide an apology for Alencar's literary experiment.[93] In some measure, this strategy of encompassing a poetically charged, or 'primitive', composition with bulky paratextual paraphernalia can be found in James Macpherson's *Ossian* (1760–73),[94] with which Blair's name was closely associated.[95] Macpherson, whom Alencar praises in his early writings as a model for singing the traditions of the fatherland,[96] tames the text's heterodox diction, imagery and syntax, all purportedly drawn from Gaelic sources, with extensive data about the language, culture, history and customs of the ancient Celts.[97] To illustrate: in *Fingal*, the first Ossianic epic, the adumbration of 'four stones' that 'rise on the grave of Catbath' is complemented by a sprawling note stating that

> This passage alludes to the manner of burial among the ancient Scots. They opened a grave six or eight feet deep: the bottom was lined with fine clay; and on this they laid the body of the deceased, and, if a warrior, his sword, and the heads of twelve arrows by his side. Above they lay another stratum of clay, in which they placed the horn of a deer, symbol of hunting. The whole was covered with a fine mold, and four stones placed on end to mark the extent of the grave. These are the four stones alluded to here.[98]

And as much as is the case with *Ossian*, *Iracema* pushes mediation to the margins of the text and frees the narrator's 'primitivism', or indigeneity, to present itself as unconditioned and uncontained. Narration, thus, is constituted in a voice indistinguishable from Iracema's or Martim's. When Martim's love wanes, overwrought honeyed metaphors and similes reappear, as when the conquistador is compared to a satiated hummingbird:

> The hummingbird drinks its fill of nectar and perfume, then sleeps in its white nest of down until the season of flowers returns the next year. Like the hummingbird, so too does the soul of the warrior saturate itself with happiness and have need of sleep and repose.[99]

Unsurprisingly, scholars have debated whether *Iracema* is a novel or a prose poem. Antonio Candido's ingenious presentation of *Iracema*, as a 'lyrical narrative of the amours between a Portuguese man and an Indian woman, written as a prose poem', is indicative of the text's competing generic tendencies.[100] Alencar himself was reticent on the labelling of his most ambitious, and most acclaimed, work of fiction. It is subtitled as a legend – a legend from Ceará, collected from forlorn 'ditties of the fatherland' and 'traditions that lulled the infancy of the people'.[101] In the 'Letter to Dr. Jaguaribe', the authorial persona deliberately eschews tight typologies, calling the 'book' an 'exhibit' of Alencar's 'ideas about Brazilian literature', brimming with 'poetry entirely Brazilian, absorbed from the language of the savages'.[102] Later in life, Alencar acrimoniously complained that *Iracema* was his only novel (his only work 'within this genre') to be honoured by the periodical press.[103] Novel or not, *Iracema* does engender a novelistic plot of intercultural love, such as emerged in Britain in the early decades of the nineteenth century and started gaining traction in the Americas in the 1820s with Cooper's *The Last of the Mohicans*.[104] Alencar himself had picked up this genre with *O guarani*. With the prestidigitation of such a plot, *Iracema* addresses and (unsuccessfully) struggles to fictionally dispel racial antinomies legated by colonialism.[105] And yet, one may argue that this novelistic articulation of conflict often goes unnoticed by *Iracema*'s readers. The text's aestheticizing homogeneity ultimately muffles the voice of the invader and colonizer, a member of 'the great people who first saw the lands of your country'. Furthermore, by blurring the sonic limits between narrator and characters, Alencar deflates the agency of the latter, as if inserting their trajectories in a higher, transcendental order. Overarching cadences and tropes both exculpate Martim and naturalize Iracema's death. Or, to slightly misquote Paula Souza, this homogeneity renders the novel's unequivocal violence 'so beautiful, intelligent and poetical'.

Notes

1. This research was generously funded by a Coordenação de Aperfeiçoamento de Pessoal de Nível Superior (CAPES) Postdoctoral Fellowship awarded by the Department of Literary Theory and Comparative Literature at the University of São Paulo (grant number 607.722).
2. Martin 2006, Vol. 1, 638.
3. For an empirical and statistical account of miscegenation and, more specifically, interracial marriages in Brazil, see Telles (2004, 173–93).
4. See Alencar 1865. All other references to *Iracema*, unless indicated, are to Clifford E. Landers' translation (Alencar 2000).
5. Sommer 1991, 5–6.
6. Hooker 2017, 19.
7. On textual juxtaposition as a productive critical method, see Hooker (2017, 19–25).
8. 'The plot is deceptively simple' (Treece 2000, 194).
9. All translations in this essay are mine, except for those of *Iracema*, *O guarani* and *Atala*.
10. Alencar 2000, 3–4.
11. Alencar 2000, 5. Although extremely competent, Clifford E. Landers' translation of *Iracema* does not do justice to Alencar's subtle temporal shifts. In a 'Translator's Note', Landers states that 'the author's use of the historical present, which occurs frequently but not consistently throughout the text, has been translated uniformly into the past tense' (Alencar 2000, xxvi). See Cass 2013, 225.
12. Alencar 2000, 5.
13. Even after intercourse, the narrator still deems Iracema to be both virginal and chaste, as in 'The waters of the river bathed the chaste body of the new [wife]' (Alencar 2000, 51). Such designations are dropped only when she turns her back to the Tabajaras (Franchetti 2006, 29). Curiously, in the passage just cited, Landers translates *esposa* [wife] as 'bride'.
14. Alencar 2000, 61.
15. Alencar 2000, 61.
16. On the asymmetrical sacrifices of Martim and Iracema, see Wasserman (1994, 211).
17. Alencar 2000, 81–2.
18. Alencar 2000, 111.
19. Alencar 2000, 101. On the offspring of Iracema and Martim, see Anderson (1998).
20. References to *The Guarany* are from James W. Hawes's translation (Alencar 1893).
21. Alencar 1893 [22, no. 131], 544.
22. Marco 1993, 73–91.
23. Donovan 2010, 22–96; Connolly 2015, 216–33.
24. Ferrier 1997, 468.
25. Chateaubriand 2007. All other references to *Atala* are from Irving Punter's translation (Chateaubriand 1952).
26. Wasserman 1994, 194; Cooper 2009.
27. Cooper 2009, 391.
28. Chateaubriand 1952, 61.
29. Chateaubriand 1952, 61.
30. Alencar 2000, 50.
31. Alencar 2000, 50.
32. Távora 2009, 222.
33. Távora 2009, 222.
34. Wasserman 1994, 209.
35. Neddell 2006, 214ff.
36. Alencar 2009.
37. Alencar 2009, 10, 16. On the chronology of Alencar's output, see Lima (2010).
38. Treece 2000, 193.
39. Alencar 2000, 71.
40. Alencar 2000, 75.
41. Alencar 2000, 127, n. 8.
42. See Pitt 2006, 137; Lemaire 1989, 64.
43. Alencar 2000, 89.
44. Alencar 2000, 93.

45. Alencar 2000, 109.
46. Arguably, the most resonant instances of this sort of symptomatic reading of *Iracema* are Santiago (1982, 104) and Bosi (1993, 189ff).
47. To Tracy Devine Guzmán, *Iracema* has become a model for uncritical renderings and theorizations of miscegenation (Guzmán 2013, 131–9).
48. Later in the year, Paula Souza's articles were collected in book format and published by Typographia Imparcial (Souza 1868b).
49. Souza 1868a, 2.
50. Souza 1868a, 3.
51. Souza 1868a, 3.
52. Souza 1868a, 3.
53. Alencar 1958b, 139.
54. Alencar 1958a, 698.
55. Magalhães 2007.
56. Moreira and Bueno 2007, xlii.
57. On the relationship between Scott and Alencar, see Vasconcelos (2008; 2016, 212).
58. For instance, Antônio de Mariz, one of the actual founders of Rio de Janeiro, is rendered as Cecilia's indulgent but overly protective father.
59. See Duncan 2015, 315–22.
60. Scott 2010.
61. Scott 2010, 428.
62. Crawford 2000, 129.
63. On Blair and Alencar, see Martins (2005, 1–25, 117–59). On Blair and Cooper, see Rivett (2017, 262–70).
64. Blair 1996, 345.
65. Blair 2005, 150.
66. Alencar 1893 [21, no. 121], 544.
67. Alencar 1958c, 38. There is no equivalent to this passage in James W. Hawes's translation of *The Guarany*. In Chapter 2 of Part 1, at least two paragraphs were excised from the 1857 text.
68. Marco 1993, 53–7; Bosi 1993, 241–2.
69. Alencar 1893 [21, no. 125], 531.
70. Alencar 1893 [21, no. 125], 532. Hawes translates 'poeta primitivo' as 'a born poet.'
71. Alencar 1958b, 149. Some time ago, scholars would have unhesitatingly approached a passage like this as an eloquent manifestation of Alencar's penchant for 'glorifying' Brazil's Amerindian populations, overlooking the inherent Eurocentrism of any formulation that essentializes, even if by ascribing extraordinary qualities, a 'primitive' Other (see Stafford 1996, 81).
72. Alencar 1958b, 149.
73. Alencar 1958b, 149.
74. Alencar 1958b, 149.
75. See, among others, Bellei 1991, 105; Bastos 2014, 104–8.
76. Cooper 2009, 225–46.
77. Cooper 2009, 375.
78. Alencar 1893 [22, no. 131], 539–40.
79. Incidentally, this is also true of Alencar's last novel with indigenous themes and characters, *Ubirajara* (1874).
80. It has been annexed to every reprint of *Iracema* since 1870 (Martins 2010, 248).
81. Alencar 2000, 135. See Campos 2004, 161.
82. Alencar 2000, 133–6.
83. Alencar 2000, 5.
84. Franchetti 2006, 67ff. I have taken my cue from Franchetti's analysis of the modulations of the images of honey throughout *Iracema*.
85. Alencar 2000, 67.
86. Alencar 2000, 96.
87. Alencar 2000, 23, 97.
88. Alencar 2000, 8.
89. Alencar 2000, 1.
90. Alencar 1979, 11.
91. Alencar 2000, 1.
92. Chateubriand 1952, 76. See Franchetti 2006, 60.

93. On Alencar's paratexts, see Abreu (2011).
94. Macpherson 1996.
95. Rizza 1991.
96. Moreira and Bueno 2007, cxxi.
97. For a thorough account of *Ossian*'s paratexts, see Moore (2016).
98. Macpherson 1996, 57, 421–2, n. 42.
99. Alencar 2000, 84.
100. Antonio Candido 2004, 59.
101. Alencar 1958a, 697.
102. Alencar 2000, 137.
103. Alencar 1958b, 153.
104. Donovan 2010, 1–21. According to Doris Sommer, 'Latin Americans rewrote Cooper's books in so many *ways*' (1991, 55).
105. On novels providing fictional solutions to antinomies posed by actuality, see Jameson (1981, 83).

Bibliography

Abreu, Mihriane Mendes de. *Ao pé da página: a dupla narrativa em José de Alencar*. Campinas: Mercado de Letras, 2011.

Alencar, José de. *Iracema: lenda do Ceará*. Rio de Janeiro: Typographia de Vianna & Filhos, 1865.

Alencar, José de. 'The Guarany. From the Portuguese of Jose Martiniano de Alencar' translated by James W. Hawes, *Overland Monthly and Out West Magazine* 21, no. 121 to 22, no. 131 (1893).

Alencar, José de. *O Guarany: romance brasileiro*. Rio de Janeiro: Empreza Nacional do Diario, 1857.

Alencar, José de. 'Bênção paterna'. In *Obra completa*, Vol. 1, 691–702. Rio de Janeiro: José Aguilar, 1958a.

Alencar, José de. 'Como e porque sou romancista'. In *Obra completa*, Vol. 1, 125–55. Rio de Janeiro: José Aguilar, 1958b.

Alencar, José de. 'O guarani'. In *Obra completa*, Vol. 2, 27–399. Rio de Janeiro: José Aguilar, 1958c.

Alencar, José de. *Iracema*, edited by M. Cavalcanti Proença, 2nd edn. São Paulo: Edusp, 1979.

Alencar, José de. *Iracema*, translated by Clifford E. Landers. Oxford: Oxford University Press, 2000.

Alencar, José de. *Cartas de Erasmo*, edited by José Murilo de Carvalho. Rio de Janeiro: Academia Brasileira de Letras, 2009.

Anderson, Cathleen E. 'Moacir: The Forgotten Son in José de Alencar's *Iracema*', *Romance Notes* 38, no. 2 (1998): 139–47.

Antonio Candido. *O romantismo no Brasil*. São Paulo: Humanitas, 2004.

Bastos, Alcmeno. *Alencar, o combatente das letras*. Rio de Janeiro: Faperj – 7 Letras, 2014.

Bellei, Sérgio. 'A fundação racial da nacionalidade em Cooper e Alencar', *Fragmentos* 19, no. 1 (1991): 100–32.

Blair, Hugh. 'A Critical Dissertation on the Poems of Ossian'. In *The Poems of Ossian and Related Works*, edited by Howard Gaskill, 345–99. Edinburgh: Edinburgh University Press, 1996.

Blair, Hugh. *Lectures on Rhetoric and Belles Lettres*, edited by Linda Ferreira-Buckley and S. Michael Halloran. Carbondale: Southern Illinois University Press, 2005.

Bosi, Alfredo. *Dialética da colonização*. São Paulo: Companhia das Letras, 1993.

Campos, Haroldo de. *Malandragem & outras metas*. São Paulo: Perspectiva, 2004.

Cass, Thiago Rhys Bezerra. *Sombras no paraíso: dos poemas de Ossian à prosa indianista de José de Alencar*. São Paulo: Nankin, 2013.

Chateaubriand, René de. *Atala*. In *Atala/René*, translated by Irving Punter. Berkeley: University of California Press, 1952.

Chateaubriand, René de. *Atala*. In *Atala – René*, edited by Jean Claude Berchet. Paris: Librarie General Française, 2007.

Connolly, Claire. 'The National Tale'. In *English and British Fiction 1750–1820*, edited by Peter Garside and Karen O'Brien, 216–34. Oxford: Oxford University Press, 2015.

Cooper, James Fenimore. *The Last of the Mohicans*, edited by Paul C. Gutjahr. Peterborough, ON: Broadview, 2009.

Crawford, Robert. *Devolving English Literature*, 2nd edn. Edinburgh: Edinburgh University Press, 2000.

Donovan, Josephine. *European Local-Color Literature: National Tales, Dorfgeschichten, Romans Champetres*. New York: Continuum, 2010.
Duncan, Ian. 'Walter Scott and the Historical Novel'. In *English and British Fiction 1750–1820*, edited by Peter Garside and Karen O'Brien, 312–331. Oxford: Oxford University Press, 2015.
Ferrier, Susan. *Marriage*, edited by Herbert Foltinek. Oxford: Oxford University Press, 1997.
Franchetti, Paulo. 'Apresentação'. In José de Alencar, *Iracema*, edited by Leila Guenther, 9–83. Cotia: Ateliê, 2006.
Guzmán, Tracy Devine. *Native and National in Brazil: Indigeneity after Independence*. Chapel Hill: University of North Carolina Press, 2013.
Hooker, Juliet. *Theorizing Race in the Americas: Douglass, Sarmiento, Du Bois, and Vasconcelos*. New York: Oxford University Press, 2017.
Jameson, Fredric. *The Political Unconscious: Narrative as a Socially Symbolic Act*. Ithaca, NY: Cornell University Press, 1981.
Lemaire, Ria. 'Re-reading *Iracema*: The Problem of the Representation of Women in the Construction of a National Brazilian Identity', *Luso-Brazilian Review* 26, no. 2, (1989): 59–73.
Lima, Israel Souza. *José de Alencar*. Rio de Janeiro: Academia Brasileira de Letras, 2010.
Macpherson, James. *The Poems of Ossian and Related Works*, edited by Howard Gaskill. Edinburgh: Edinburgh University Press, 1996.
Magalhães, Domingos José Gonçalves de. *A confederação dos tamoios: edição fac-similar seguida da polêmica sobre o poema*, edited by Maria Eunice Moreira and Luís Bueno. Curitiba: Editora UFPR, 2007.
Marco, Valeria De. *A perda das ilusões: o romance histórico de José de Alencar*. Campinas: Editora da Unicamp, 1993.
Martin, Gerald. 'The Novel of a Continent: Latin America'. In *The Novel*, edited by Franco Moretti, Vol. 1, 632–76. Princeton, NJ: Princeton University Press, 2006.
Martins, Eduardo Vieira. *A fonte subterrânea: José de Alencar e a retórica oitocentista*. Londrina: Eduel; São Paulo: Edusp, 2005.
Martins, Wilson. *História da inteligência brasileira*, Vol 3. Ponta Grossa: UEPG, 2010.
Moore, Dafydd, '"A Comparison Similar to This": Ossian and the Forms of Antiquity', *Journal for Eighteenth-Century Studies* 39, no. 2 (2016): 171–82.
Moreira, Maria Eunice, and Luís Bueno. 'Polêmica sobre *A confederação dos tamoios*'. In Domingos José Gonçalves de Magalhães, *A confederação dos tamoios: edição fac-similar seguida da polêmica sobre o poema*, edited by Maria Eunice Moreira and Luís Bueno, i–ccx. Curitiba: Editora UFPR, 2007.
Neddell, Jeffrey D. *The Party of Order: The Conservatives, the State, and Slavery in the Brazilian Monarchy, 1831–1871*. Stanford, CA: Stanford University Press, 2006.
Pitt, Kristin. 'Disappearing Bodies: The Nation and the Individual in José De Alencar's *Iracema*', *Latin American Literary Review* 34, no. 67 (2006): 128–47.
Rivett, Sarah. *Unscripted America: Indigenous Languages and the Origins of a Literary Nation*. Oxford: Oxford University Press, 2017.
Rizza, Steve. 'A Bulky and Foolish Treatise? Hugh Blair's *Critical Dissertation* Reconsidered'. In *Ossian Revisited*, edited by Howard Gaskill, 129–46. Edinburgh: Edinburgh University Press, 1991.
Santiago, Silviano. *Vale Quanto Pesa*. Rio de Janeiro: Paz e Terra, 1982.
Scott, Walter. *Waverley*, edited by Susan Kubica Howard. Peterborough, ON: Broadview, 2010.
Sommer, Doris. *Foundational Fictions: The National Romances of Latin America*. Berkeley: University of California Press, 1991.
Souza, Joaquim de Paula. 'Itinerario de S. Paulo ao Paraguay', *Correio Paulistano*, 18 July 1868a, 2–3.
Souza, Joaquim de Paula. *Itinerario de S. Paulo ao Paraguay*. São Paulo: Typographia Imperial, 1868b.
Stafford, Fiona. 'Primitivism and the "Primitive" Poet: A Cultural Context for Macpherson's Ossian'. In *Celticism*, edited by Terence Brown. Amsterdam: Rodopi, 1996.
Távora, Franklin. *Cartas a Cincinato*, edited by Eduardo Vieira Martins. Campinas: Editora Unicamp, 2009.
Telles, Edward E. *Race in Another America: The Significance of Skin Color in Brazil*. Princeton, NJ: Princeton University Press, 2004.
Treece, David. *Exiles, Allies, Rebels: Brazil's Indianist Movement, Indigenist Politics, and the Imperial Nation-State*. Westport, CT: Greenwood Press, 2000.

Vasconcelos, Sandra Guardini Teixeira. 'Figurações do Passado: o Romance Histórico em Walter Scott e José de Alencar', *Terceira Margem* 18 (2008): 5–37.
Vasconcelos, Sandra Guardini Teixeira. 'Tropical Gothic: José de Alencar and the Foundation of the Brazilian Novel'. In *Tropical Gothic in Literature and Culture: The Americas*, edited by Justin D. Edwards and Sandra Guardini Vasconcelos, 198–217. New York: Routledge, 2016.
Wasserman, Renata R. Mautner. *Exotic Nations: Literature and Cultural Identity in the United States and Brazil, 1830–1930*. Ithaca, NY: Cornell University Press, 1994.

6

Displaced Experience and Magic Compromise

Jorge de Almeida

> The formal realism of the novel allows a more immediate imitation of individual experience set in its temporal and spatial environment than do other literary forms.
>
> (Ian Watt 1957, 35–6)

As in other peripheral national literatures in the eighteenth and nineteenth centuries, Brazilian writers and literary critics from the start faced the problem of how to interpret the value and originality of literary works that had foreign (mainly French and English) novels as implicit or explicit models. 'To study Brazilian literature always entails doing comparative literature,' argued the great Brazilian critic Antonio Candido.[1] Literary historians in Brazil have to deal with the specific contradictions of Brazilian authors, who in the past simultaneously tried to follow European models and strived to create a genuine Brazilian literary experience. This problem began with the exotic Brazilian pastorals and epics of the neoclassical eighteenth century, pervaded Brazil's peculiar 'realist' romanticism and shaped its contradictory nationalistic–cosmopolitan modernism, culminating in the anthropophagic movement of Oswald de Andrade in the 1920s, which advocated the ritual cannibalization of foreign literary forms and cultures.

With regard to the novel, a genre that has been international by nature since its beginnings, there are two important topics concerning its subgenres and displacement throughout the world: (a) how the genre arose in different countries and (b) how its forms acclimatized in historical conditions other than those of modern Europe.

To understand the rise of the Brazilian novel, and the contradictory works it produced, Ian Watt's book *The Rise of the Novel* is of fundamental interest. The book is now part of the basic bibliography in many literature courses and has had several editions since its first translation into Portuguese in 1990. What interests the Brazilian critics is the way the specific relation between form and social process in Watt goes beyond the analysis of influences. Retrieving the dialectic aesthetics of Hegel and Georg Lukács, Watt argues that, to understand the rise of the novel as a new genre, we must understand how new historical situations demand new forms of literary representation.

Watt's theses on the rise of the novel have recently become very controversial. They are frequently attacked by the French, for having reduced the importance of the revolutionary *roman philosophique*; by the Spanish, for having overlooked Miguel de Cervantes as the real founder of the novel; by Asian critics, for foregrounding a Eurocentric vision of the development of the genre; by medievalists, for not acknowledging the continuity between romance and novel; by classicists, for forgetting that the novel began with the Greeks.[2]

Ian Watt's main argument, consolidated from a historical perspective in the second chapter of his book, is condensed, in the first chapter, into the concept of 'formal realism', which encompasses several features: the rise of the individual, related to the rise of an urban middle class; the spread of secularism; the philosophy of the Enlightenment; and the rise of capitalist social and economic relations. This individual – the novelty of the novel – struggles for autonomy, acting in an enlightened way (in the sense of a free, conscious and precise articulation of means to obtain certain ends) in a world whose traditional norms and behaviours are being challenged by the 'novelties' of the market, modern science, new labour relations and the rise of what came to be called the 'public sphere'.

Formal realism is configured as a set of literary procedures that aim to represent this new individual 'experience'. This involves new conceptions of characterization, new models of plot, new depictions of time and space and a new prosaic style. Watt stresses that the novel incorporates and gives new meaning and form to previous literary and non-literary genres (such as journalism, travel writing, correspondence, legal narratives, memoirs and so on). Following his analysis of early English novels, we can see that Watt is much less dogmatic and much more dialectical than many of his critics suggest.

Watt's book sheds particular light on the rise of the Brazilian novel, not because it explains it, but because it shows the impossibility of understanding it according to the criteria Watt adopted to interpret early

European novels. The historical situation in nineteenth-century Brazil was obviously very different from that of eighteenth-century England, but we should not forget that the early Brazilian writers mainly used foreign novels, written and developed on the basis of the 'formal realism' described by Watt, as models for their writing. In this sense, the way Watt is read in Brazil and the way that part of the Brazilian critical tradition mindful of the dialectic between literary form and social process engages with his work can also facilitate the correct evaluation of his importance. In his comprehensive examination of the many works devoted to the topic, Nicholas Seager comes to the conclusion that 'in the course of my reading for this study I have found a considerable extent of misprision and, what is worse, misrepresentation of *The Rise of the Novel*. It has unfortunately become a book more often caricatured than consulted.'[3]

Members of an educated elite, Brazilian novelists were committed to providing the new nation with a national literature, that is, to write, in Brazil, in a literary genre that, to quote Watt, 'allows a more immediate imitation of individual experience set in its temporal and spatial environment'.[4] The attempt to do so in a completely different social context, on the periphery of capitalism, gave rise to new problems, some of them of great literary interest. As Roberto Schwarz has argued: 'Because we do not have our own tradition, we imitate, but as we do not know how to imitate well, something else results, an involuntary difference which is itself creative, innovative in its own way.'[5]

Macedo's Works and Contradictions

To understand the scope of these contradictions, we will examine one specific case in the rise of the novel in Brazil, focusing on an author who is considered the real first Brazilian novelist, Joaquim Manuel de Macedo (1820–82).

It is important to bear in mind some aspects of Brazil's complex history to grasp the context in which Macedo evolved as an intellectual and wrote his many novels and plays. Brazil achieved its independence from Portugal in 1822, when the son of the Portuguese king Dom João VI, allying with local elites, became the first Brazilian emperor. A decade of regional insurrections demanded a great effort to maintain the political unity of Brazil's immense territory. Owing to a serious political crisis in Portugal, Dom Pedro I of Brazil had to return to Europe in 1823, becoming Dom Pedro IV of Portugal, and left as heir to the crown his five-year-old son, Dom Pedro II, who would be the emperor of Brazil from 1831 to 1889.

During the long reign of Dom Pedro II, the court of Rio de Janeiro flourished, sheltering a core of artists and intellectuals (national and foreign) engaged (the term is very relevant in Brazilian literary criticism) in providing the 'young' country with everything a nation needed to create its own identity in the romantic nineteenth century.

We know how much romanticism is linked to this consolidation of the idea of nation. In the periphery, in Brazil specifically, this process was much more intense, since the romantic ideal, as opposed to the universality of neoclassical aesthetics, devoted greater attention to the particular, to history recreated as heroic fact. Antonio Candido has noted that

> Brazilian Romanticism was initially and above all nationalism (and to a certain extent remained so to the end). And before anything else nationalism meant writing about local topics. Hence the importance of fictional narrative in prose, the most accessible and current way of presenting reality, offering the reader a greater amount of verisimilitude and thereby bringing the text closer to their personal experience.[6]

One of these romantic intellectuals in service of the new nation was Joaquim Manuel de Macedo.[7] Graduating in medicine, with a thesis on the history and effects of melancholy, he never practised, and ended up joining the intellectual group of the Instituto Histórico e Geográfico Brasileiro (IHGB) [Brazilian Historical and Geographical Institute], with the mission, encouraged by the Emperor, to provide the country with everything necessary for its consolidation as a nation: a national history, a national geography, a national music and also a national literature.

Macedo was the author of the first successful Brazilian novel of manners. Published in 1844, *A moreninha* [*The Brunette*] tells a love story in which a cunning young brunette, in contrast to the current European literary pattern of blonde female beauty, manages to win the heart of and finally marry a young medical student, accustomed to love conquests, whom she has known since their childhood. There is nothing original about the plot, but one of the reasons for the interest and success of the book (in its time and in posterity) was its attentive description of Brazilian landscape and customs. As Antonio Candido points out: 'Brazilians seemed to enjoy the descriptions of places, customs, and the kind of people whose reality they could appraise and gave them the encouraging feeling that their country could be promoted to the compelling domain of literary art.'[8]

Macedo continued his career by writing several novels of manners and comedies for the theatre, portraying the incipient middle class who lived around the court in Rio. Like many other contemporary intellectuals, he participated intensely in the political life of the Empire, even becoming a member of parliament for the Conservative Party. Enjoying the favour of the Emperor, he was appointed as professor of Brazilian history in the prestigious Colégio D. Pedro II, the school that formed the young elite the new nation needed. In 1860, he published his *Lições de história do Brasil* [*Lessons of Brazil's History*], updated in successive editions, a book that would become the basic history textbook in Brazilian schools for generations, up to the first decades of the Republic. In the 1850s, the public of Rio de Janeiro, enthused about the novelties coming from Europe, began to consume more elaborate literature, moving away from the simple sentimentality of *A moreninha*. At that same time, disillusioned with the course that national politics was taking, Macedo tried his hand at a first comic novel, *A carteira de meu tio* [*My Uncle's Wallet*] (1855), criticizing the vices of a young man who, sponsored by his rich uncle, is sent to study in Europe, like so many of his generation. When he returns, arrogant and Europeanized, he is intent on following a political career, not exactly to help the country, as his uncle would wish, but simply to have a good job in which he would not have to work. The uncle cuts off his allowance and forces him on a journey through the hinterland of Brazil so that he can get a closer look at the ills of this backward country run by inept politicians.

The same character is taken up again in *Memórias do sobrinho de meu tio* [*Memoirs of My Uncle's Nephew*] (1868). He is now older and has finally inherited his uncle's fortune. This sequel of the previous novel, written with even more mordant irony, denounces the corruption of Brazilian politics, marked by constant selfishness and little attention to the problems of the country. The main character confesses to following the ideology of the cynical 'School of the I', in which one learns to lie and dissimulate in order to achieve the tranquillity of a wealthy marriage and a public job. The narrator comments, 'Do not think that this philosophy is mine alone: no! It belongs to a very noble philosophical school: the head of the school is the government of Brazil.'[9]

The Ironic Eyeglass

In 1869, Macedo published *A luneta mágica* [*The Magic Eyeglass*]. In this novel, as in many others during the complex 'rise of the novel' in Brazil, the country's social tensions come into view as formal tensions in an effort to represent characters who have not yet been completely formed through individual 'experience'. Since the eighteenth century, this kind of experience had been taken for granted in European novels, which shaped characters who were distanced from literary types and beginning to be represented as rational individuals in newly developed literary forms. In Macedo's novel, however, magic is the means to realistically configure the contradictions of the small and fragile Brazilian urban middle class, deprived of autonomous individuals in the European sense. The problem is posed in the first paragraph:

> They call me Simplício [Simpleton] and my natural condition is sadder than my name. I was born under the sway of an evil star, I was born with the sign of misfortune. I'm short-sighted. Worse than that: [I'm] doubly short-sighted, morally and physically. Physical short-sightedness: I can't distinguish a sunflower from a violet at the distance of two inches. That's why I walk through the town and don't see the buildings. Moral short-sightedness: I am always enthralled by someone else's ideas. Because I could never coordinate two ideas of mine. That's why when I go to the parliament and the senate, I consecutively and decidedly agree with all the orators who speak in favour and against the topic under scrutiny. If only I weren't conscious of my moral short-sightedness ... But a deep conviction of such a misfortune is the light that shines cloudlessly within my spirit.[10]

Here, we can already trace many of the European models, such as Voltaire's *Candide* and the ironic French *roman philosophique*, that would portray a naive character as counterpoint to society in order to reveal the lack of sense and the moral faults of the world. Far away from Europe and from the philosophical debates of the eighteenth-century European Enlightenment, in the Brazilian novel this kind of naive character acquires new and interesting features, with political, literary and historical significance.

Irony is crucial here, and relates to the gap between the narrator's remarks and the world perceived by the readers. However, in the Brazilian novel such ironic mediation operates via the development of the first-person perspective of the protagonist. The consequences are compelling, as we can read in the following extract, in which Simplício comments on the advice he receives from his brother. Instead of a contraposition between the common-sense view and the Leibnizian perspective of a foolish sage like Pangloss – who argues (even under the worst circumstances) that we are all living in the best of all possible worlds – the main character in Macedo's novel is a rich myopic man surrounded by a world in which everyone seems to follow the 'dynamics of economic individualism' studied by Watt as a principal driver of the genre:

> My brother Americo has been a perennial well of consolation. Nevertheless, I am haunted by the unhappiness of not being able to appreciate the wisdom that comes from his lips. I've already told you how he used to comfort me from my physical short-sightedness. But his kindness went beyond: when he listened to my complaints about my moral short-sightedness, he would hold my hand and talk to me thus: 'Thank God for this misfortune. You're free from countless sorrows, endless responsibilities, and unrelenting torments. You can't think. But I think for you and me. You could barely take care of your affairs. But I take care of both yours and mine. You suffer less than I suffer. Because I suffer for you and me.' What a saintly soul my brother has![11]

The first turning point occurs when Simplício buys a magic eyeglass, in a kind of Faustian episode, a gothic scene that displays the usual romantic pact with the devil, and receives this piece of advice from an Armenian wizard who has just arrived in Rio de Janeiro: 'I give you a magic eyeglass. You'll see through it as much as it pleases you. You may see a lot. You may see too much.'[12]

The first part of the book shows the magically 'enlightened' Simplício seeing the world as it supposedly really is. Looking through his magic eyeglass, Simplício abandons his naivety and finally acquires some knowledge of the society in which he lives. Through the 'experience' provided by magic, he becomes wise, in this particular sense:

> The knowledge of evil has operated on me a striking change of ideas and sentiments. I know now it is necessary to pretend: I know it. … I shall therefore lie and dissimulate. That's the first lesson of the science of evil that I have received, the first step on to the tortuous path towards demoralization. But that's inevitable, because it is necessary to lie and dissimulate in order to defend myself from unloving and perfidious relatives and, cautious and safe, carry out projects that, over the past few minutes, have been burning within my spirit exalted by resentment. In the wars of this world I shall fight with the appropriate weapons: lies against lies, dissimulation against dissimulation.[13]

The world reveals itself through magic as a place in which all the other characters strive for power, money and fortune, following literally Adam

Smith's liberal conception of individuals living in a modern market-oriented capitalist society – the exact historical situation that shaped the origins of the novel as described by Ian Watt. But in a country in which economic and social relations were so permeated by slavery, the possibility of representing society as a group of individuals who act rationally and pragmatically will be considered, in the novel, too scary and almost impossible to deal with.

We are not in England, and therefore the novel needs, from a Brazilian elite writer's point of view, the magical 'correction' of a second part. After Simplício breaks his evil eyeglass in despair, he remembers the advice of the Armenian wizard: 'You will be convinced that it is better to be blind than see too much.'[14] In this second part, he goes back to the wizard and receives from him a second eyeglass, which shows only the good intentions and compassion of all of his relatives and countrymen.

The eyeglass works really well at the beginning, but, like the first one, it also has terrible consequences, because honesty and goodwill are not 'realistic' enough to enable the protagonist to act reasonably in the world. Giving his money to everyone who asks him, seeing genuine love in cunning prostitutes, unable to distinguish evil in those who take advantage of him, Simplício puts his inherited fortune in danger. Just as he had been hated before for using the first eyeglass, now he is taken by public opinion to be ridiculous:

> Ridicule! ... Ridicule is a fall into a quagmire; it is disgrace without compassion; it is the pillory a thousand times worse than the scaffold; it is the scourge more cruel than the guillotine; it is death by contempt ... I'd rather be persecuted by hate than be accompanied by ridicule.[15]

This second bout of despair sends Simplício to the heights of Corcovado Mountain (where today Christ the Redeemer blesses the city of Rio de Janeiro), where he finally understands the consequences of his actions:

> Through the vision of evil or through the vision of good, through hate or through the love of humanity; through the bad judgement of all or through the good judgement of all, the two magic eyeglasses have led me to the same danger, to the same end, to the same calamity.[16]

Simplício is about to commit suicide when the Armenian wizard wisely intervenes, arguing that there is neither absolute evil nor absolute good, for humanity is essentially imperfect. And he gives Simplício a third eyeglass, that of common sense. The lesson is taught, the example is given and the novel ends with a call for reason: 'Society must accept each man with his qualities and faults, exploring both of them to its profit.'[17]

Comparative Ironies

'Its profit' ... This very liberal statement was of course misplaced – and politically and ideologically violent – in a slaveholding society like Brazil. There was little room there for the growth of a modern middle class whose members could be 'accepted' and represented as 'individuals'. The Brazilian intelligentsia, who in other works were trying to write foundational novels, could never be entirely critical and were always (and have been even in recent times) committed to participating in necessary 'modernization' processes. The final moral message of a constricted Moll Flanders, the revealing irony of any love relationships in a Jane Austen novel, the philosophical garden cultivated by Voltaire's Candide, and the sociological urban explorations of Balzac's characters are very far from the perspectives historically imposed on the writers who sought to establish the novel in Brazil. In the particular case of this novel of Macedo's, it is as if only through magic could this contradictory reality be shown and literarily grasped by a novel.

We can analyse the specific differences by taking as examples two French works that were very successful in Brazil at the time and were cited in a newspaper article written by the famous Brazilian novelist José de Alencar:[18] *Le lorgnon* (1832) by Madame Émile de Girardin[19] and *Les mémoires du diable* by Fréderic Soulié (two volumes, 1836–8).[20] In this *crônica*, Alencar's narrator mentions a visit to a new optical shop in Rio where, among a number of items, he discovers an antique eyeglass which on examination he finds to be magical. He buys it for a bargain and on reflecting about his purchase he wonders how that magic glass, lost in antiquity and then found by Soulié in *Les mémoires du diable*, could now be in his pocket; he conjectures what misfortune had brought Delfina Gay's *lorgnon* as far as Rio, to end up in that shop, 'unknown, ignored by all'.[21] A flurry of ideas takes hold of him; fantastic visions suddenly come to him. After lunch, he remembers he is a writer and assesses the enormous reach that magic glass could have for him: 'Three or four *coups de lorgnon* would suffice to write a review that before would rob me of hours of rest and tranquillity.'[22] While Alencar's reference to both works testifies to their circulation in the imperial capital at the time, it is not implausible to think that Macedo may also have been familiar with them, since they both use as literary trigger a magic eyeglass or monocle, capable of revealing what is kept concealed in society and in the world.

In the novels of Girardin and Soulié, the tone of social critique does not tend towards moralizing compromise. Magic as a literary device for realist representation ends up as a critique of modern urban society in Europe. That is why, after a great deal of confusion and sharp moral observation of the hypocrisy of Parisian society, Girardin's tale closes with the following piece of advice:

> M. et madame de Lorville sont encore possesseurs de ce lorgnon; ils le cachent avec soin aux méchants et aux ambitieux; prudence inutile, ce talisman serait sans puissance entre leurs mains; car il faut avoir l'esprit libre et le cœur pur pour juger le monde tel qu'il est; il faut n'avoir rien à désirer pour regarder sans illusion, rien à cacher pour observer sans malveillance.[23]

In Soulié's novel, which was hugely successful in Brazil, Baron François-Armand de Luizzi, a kind of Faustian character, sells his soul to the devil to obtain the satisfaction of all his desires. He will escape damnation only if he can prove that he has known true happiness. Borrowing the devil's magic eyeglass and using other magical devilish devices, Baron Luizzi experiences a series of picaresque adventures that reveal every hidden corner of the depraved French society, exposing scenes of kidnapping, rape, murder and adultery. The ironic and cynical devil comments coldly on all the episodes, demonstrating that hell is not far from our world.

In both cases, we have characters living, through a magic device, genuine 'experiences' of the world, framed by the 'formal realism' described by Watt. The characters are fully formed modern individuals, who rationally seek their goals in the world, a world that reveals itself 'as it really is', by means of magic.

This could not happen in Brazil, especially in the hands of the *bom moço* [nice fellow] Macedo, a conservative teacher and official of the Empire, who could never shock his readers as his European models might have done. To discover Paris to be a debauched society was very appealing for Brazilian readers who would not feel the same if similar revelations occurred in provincial Rio de Janeiro. Therefore, the critics stressed that in his novels Macedo never deepens the psychological analysis of his characters. The narrator always predominates over the characters, mere types and moral exempla, and their actions are displayed through 'summary judgment and no nuance', as Candido notes.[24]

In his late novels, Macedo tries to get closer to realism, like so many of his generation, but yet remains strongly marked by romantic traits. The Brazilian public, accustomed to reading his works as those of a candid romantic author, do not welcome the novelty of his ironic novels, despite their moralistic and compromised endings. Tania Serra, author of the most important monograph on Macedo's works, remarks, 'By proposing a philosophy of "good sense", in place of the ideology of evasion, Macedo, strictly speaking, is beginning to tread the path of public decline. It is the beginning of the end.'[25]

The shift from romanticism to realism is indeed tricky in imperial Brazil, because it cannot really combine the tradition of the novel of manners with an effective critique of society. In the same year that Macedo published *A lanterna mágica*, affected by debts that led him to despair, he published another novel, based on the hereditary deterministic theories in vogue in France. Trying to catch up with the latest literary trends, and surrounded by the abolitionist wave spreading all over the country, Macedo addressed the subject of slavery in the novel *As vítimas–algozes. Quadros da escravidão* [*The Victims–Executioners. Pictures of Slavery*] (1869). He writes in the preface,

> Following two opposite paths, one arrives at the spot we have been aiming, at the profound condemnation that slavery must inspire.
>
> One of these paths extends amidst extremely severe wretchedness, and the slave's incalculable sufferings, amidst this life of endless woe, of barren desert without an oasis, of everlasting hell in the black world of slavery. It is the picture of the harm the master does the slave, even if unintentionally.
>
> The other shows to its sides the ignoble vices, the perversion, the hate, the ferocious instincts of the slave, the natural and spiteful enemy of his master, the miasmas, let us say so, the moral syphilis of slavery infecting the house, the farm, the masters' families, and his concentrated anger, but always in latent conspiracy striking against the fortune, the life and the honour of his unaware oppressors.[26]

The difficult balance that marks his other works is also present here. He admits that slavery does harm to the slave, but his main purpose in the novel is to show how it corrupts the local elite, depicted by Macedo as the actual victims while the slaves are depicted as the perverse tormentors of their owners. Macedo stresses the inherent violence of the situation, but resorts again to a moral tale. His peculiar views on the realist school that arrived in Brazil in the 1860s are voiced by a character from *Nina*, his 1869 novel:

> In literature, Firmiano, the realist school teaches that the novelist must be the faithful copyist of life in society, of feelings, of passions and of customs; consequently, the scrupulous and subtle scrutinizer of the hearts, the informer of the tendencies and character of the times, in one word, the moral daguerreotype of the society and of the family.[27]

If the novel as a realist genre has always tried to show what is behind the façade, in Macedo's novels this intent is accompanied by a moralistic feeling, appropriate to the 'Fluminense' (small and provincial) scale of the Brazilian middle class in Rio de Janeiro. Antonio Candido again:

> Instead of analyses, [Macedo] passes summary and unnuanced judgements, [and is] ready to abruptly change them when circumstances demand, and even when they do not, giving evidence of a good nature that migrates from life to literature. ... His novel is situated, therefore, in the intersection of the two tendencies – one tributary of petty realism, the other, of implausible idealization.[28]

Unlike other Brazilian novelists of the time, who were successful in exploring the exotic characteristics of the immense country, revealing its types and landscapes, Macedo insisted on writing about the incipient urban middle class of Rio de Janeiro, sandwiched between the great landowners, who held the real political and financial power, and the slaves, who were worked to exhaustion. How to think of a middle class in a society where the idea of work was despised by the social order? By remaining faithful to the subgenre of the sentimental urban novel, yet unable to develop more realistic approaches, Macedo would never be able to portray his characters as individuals capable of real 'experiences' in the sense that Watt considers fundamental to the rise of the novel. The situation of realism in Brazil was very different from that in modern European countries, as summarized by Antonio Candido:

> Balzac, for example, could without leaving Paris cover an extensive range of long-matured groups, professions, strata, whose interaction came to enrich, on the level of behaviour, those options and alternatives ... which constitute the very flesh of high standard

fiction. In Brazil, richness and variety were sought out through the displacement of the imagination in space, searching for a kind of exoticism that stimulates the writer's observation and the reader's curiosity.[29]

Resuming our argument, we can see how Ian Watt's ideas – by emphasizing the relationship between the rise of the novel and the socio-historical conditions – function as a 'negative' parameter for the analysis of the rise of the novel in nineteenth-century Brazil. Displacement, here, is dialectically perceived not as lack or deficiency, but as tension between the historical and ideological assumptions consolidated in the form of the novel and the way the Brazilian elite availed themselves of the genre to try to 'realistically represent' the society in which they lived.

In this sense, Brazilian criticism (especially Antonio Candido's historical systematic approach and Roberto Schwarz's dialectical studies of the ironic realism of Machado de Assis[30]) has stressed the disparity between the realistic expectations of the novel (brilliantly analysed by Ian Watt) and the specific Brazilian social context, which could only plausibly configure literary representations of displaced individual experiences. Such a difficulty is at the core of the rise of the novel in many (peripheral) literatures and needs to be continually perceived by critical readers.

Notes

1. Antonio Candido 1993, 211. Unless otherwise indicated, all translations from Portuguese are my own.
2. Cf. Moretti 2001–3 (the five volumes of this work are abridged in two volumes in the English edition (*The Novel*. Princeton, NJ: Princeton University Press, 2006); Seager 2012.
3. Seager 2012, 189.
4. Watt 1957, 32.
5. Schwarz 2018, 74.
6. Antonio Candido 2002, 39–40.
7. From here on 'Macedo', as he is known in Brazil.
8. Antonio Candido 2002, 44.
9. Macedo 2011, viii.
10. Macedo 1987, 7.
11. Macedo 1987, 11.
12. Macedo 1987, 34.
13. Macedo 1987, 51.
14. Macedo 1987, 26.
15. Macedo 1987, 205.
16. Macedo 1987, 204.
17. Macedo 1987, 231.
18. Alencar 1960.
19. Girardin 1832, Vol. 2, 249–50.

20. Soulié 1876.
21. Alencar 1960, 773.
22. Alencar 1960, 773–4.
23. Girardin 1832, Vol. 2, 126.
24. Antonio Candido 2017, 457.
25. Serra 2004, 149.
26. Macedo 1991, 4–5.
27. Macedo 1871, Vol. 1, 23.
28. Antonio Candido 2017, 457.
29. Antonio Candido 2017, 434.
30. Schwarz 2001.

Bibliography

Alencar, José de. 'Ao correr da pena'. In *Obra completa*, Vol. 4, 771–7. Rio de Janeiro: Editora José Aguilar, 1960.

Antonio Candido. 'Literatura comparada'. In *Recortes*, 211–15. São Paulo: Companhia das Letras, 1993.

Antonio Candido. *O Romantismo no Brasil*. São Paulo: Humanitas FFLCH/USP, 2002.

Antonio Candido. *Formação da literatura brasileira: momentos decisivos 1750–1880*. São Paulo: FAPESP; Rio de Janeiro: Ouro sobre Azul, 2017.

Girardin, Delphine Gay de [Madame Émile de Girardin]. *Le lorgnon*. Paris: Gosselin, 1832.

Macedo, Joaquim Manuel de. *Nina*. Rio de Janeiro: B. L. Garnier, 1871.

Macedo, Joaquim Manuel de. *A luneta mágica*. São Paulo: Círculo do Livro, 1987.

Macedo, Joaquim Manuel de. *As vítimas-algozes*. Rio de Janeiro: Fundação Casa de Rui Barbosa; São Paulo: Scipione, 1991.

Macedo, Joaquim Manuel de. *Memórias do sobrinho de meu tio*. São Paulo: Penguin/Companhia das Letras, 2011.

Moretti, Franco (ed.). *Il Romanzo*. Turin: Einaudi, 2001–3.

Schwarz, Roberto. *A Master on the Periphery of Capitalism*, translated by John Gledson. Durham, NC: Duke University Press, 2001.

Schwarz, Roberto. 'Antonio Candido'. In *Antonio Candido 100 anos*, edited by Maria Augusta Fonseca and Roberto Schwarz, 72–7. São Paulo: Editora 34, 2018.

Seager, Nicholas. *The Rise of the Novel: A Reader's Guide to Essential Criticism*. London: Palgrave Macmillan, 2012.

Serra, Tania. *Joaquim Manuel de Macedo. Os dois Macedos: a luneta mágica do II Reinado*. Brasília: UNB, 2004.

Soulié, Frédéric. *Les mémoires du diable*. Paris: J. Le Clerc, 1876.

Watt, Ian. *The Rise of the Novel: Studies in Defoe, Richardson and Fielding*. Berkeley: University of California Press, 1957.

7
Brazilian Landscape: A Study of *Inocência*[1]

Eduardo Vieira Martins

Space: Landscape and the Backlands

The novel *Inocência* [*Innocencia*][2] (1872), by Alfredo d'Escragnolle Taunay (1843–99), opens with a chapter entitled 'The Sertão and the Sertanejo' in which the narrator portrays himself as a learned traveller who, from a panoramic perspective, depicts the extensive natural scenery that advances westwards from the meeting point of the provinces of São Paulo, Minas Gerais, Goiás and Mato Grosso: 'The road from the town of Sant'Anna do Paranaíba to the abandoned pass of Camapuan crosses a little-known and thinly-inhabited zone of the south-east part of the vast province of Mato Grosso.'[3]

The use of the word *sertão* to designate this specific region is not typical of current usage but relates to the meaning the term had in the nineteenth century. It was used in reference to sparsely populated areas of the countryside. According to Antonio de Morais Silva, the most prestigious Brazilian lexicographer of the period, *sertão* meant 'inland, the heart of the land', 'the woods far away from the shore'.[4] In a more elaborate way, the French botanist Auguste de Saint-Hilaire, for whom Taunay had great admiration, explained that 'the noun *sertão* or "desert" does not designate any political division of land; it only indicates a somewhat vague and conventional area determined by the particular nature of the region, mainly by the scarcity of its population'.[5] For this reason, he goes on to say, 'the various provinces, perhaps all of them have their *sertão*, which are their most deserted areas'.[6] In his *History of Brazil*, published between 1810 and 1819, referring to *Sertoens*, Robert Southey remarked, 'The word requires explanation. *Sertam*, or *Certam* (as it is sometimes spelt), in the plural *Sertoens*, means the interior of the country. An inhabitant of the interior is called *Sertanejo*. I do not know the origin of the word.'[7] In the same vein, James W. Wells, author of the nineteenth-century translation of *Inocência*,[8] chose to keep the word in Portuguese rather than use the terms 'backlands' or 'highlands', as *sertão* was usually translated: 'The term Sertão (pronounced Sair-toung)', he explains in a footnote, 'expresses any very thinly-peopled prairie region in the distant interior of Brazil, and the inhabitants, *Sertanejos* (pronounced Sair-tahn-ái-jous), invariably follow the occupation of cattle breeding.'[9]

In line with the understanding of *sertão* as uninhabited desert, regardless of its specific geographical features, such as climate, vegetation or precipitation patterns, the charting of this space is characterized in the opening of *Inocência* as a dive into the void. In his wanderings along the thoroughfare from 'the town of Sant'Anna do Paranahyba to the abandoned pass of Camapuan', the imaginary traveller who trails through that inhospitable region sees houses and villages that become gradually more spaced out from each another. Subsequently he passes by the 'ranch of João Pereira' to enter, finally, the 'Sertão Bruto', a term that, according to the note appended by the translator, signifies 'The Wild Sertão or Wilderness'.[10] Many years after the publication of *Inocência*, in a passage of Taunay's memoirs in which he recounts his journey from Mato Grosso to Rio de Janeiro, bringing news of the military expedition sent to liberate the distant province from Paraguayan invaders,[11] the author once again indicates that the retreat and the village are the limits of the deep *sertão*: 'On 30 June [1867] we were in the large ranch of Mr. José Pereira ... the first resident we met at the exit of the *harsh sertão* of Camapuã and at the entrance of Sant'Ana do Paranahyba, a place slightly more inhabited.'[12] Elsewhere in the narrative, Taunay notes that the village is situated 'at the entrance of the more effectively inhabited region, once the *vast interposed solitudes* are traversed',[13] an image that aptly encapsulates the meaning assigned to the region in the nineteenth century: one that is understood as a kind of border to civilization. Indeed, the *sertão* was perceived as a space in constant motion, which, like the Far West in the United States, was encroached upon by the rare regions that were more densely populated and were advancing step by step with the gradual conquest of the territory.[14]

In *Inocência*, despite the narrator's efforts to delineate the *sertão* with precision, the region's elusive character persists because its contours depend exclusively on the way in which the territory was occupied by the colonizer. It is worth noting that João Pereira's retreat is a landmark not because there is any remarkable geographical change in its immediate surroundings, or because it signals entry into a specific kind of land, but simply because beyond this area habitation becomes even more sparse. For this reason, which in a way betrays the narrator's determination to establish clear points of reference, it seems that the *sertão* slips inevitably through his hands to the extent that, when referring to the 'predominating element of the soil' – sand – he ends up using another phrase that accurately captures the essence of the territory's overriding image: 'In some places it is so soft and loose that the hoofs of animals of travelling troops sink in it to their fetlocks, and many a horse or mule falls exhausted with the fatigue of a journey in such terrible *heavy ground.*'[15] In fact, *sertão* can be described as a shifting and 'uncertain terrain', one that resists any clear definition. This is so particularly because as soon as some consistent line is chosen to establish its boundaries, it is as if they dissolve in the air and the object one sought to apprehend disappears before one's eyes.

In *O Brasil não é longe daqui* [*Brazil Is Not Distant from Here*], Flora Süssekind argues that the narrator of the nineteenth-century Brazilian novel was shaped through direct conversation with the genre of travel narratives, being always ready to interrupt the account and indulge in lengthy descriptions of nature, thus adopting a naturalist's gaze. Through this lens an inventory of plant and animal species is produced in a mapping and cataloguing exercise characteristic of the romantic project, whose attention was focused on constructing the nation's image.[16] At the opening of *Inocência*, in line with Süssekind's perspective, the narrator constructs a broad panorama of the region, allowing the reader to contemplate the diversity of landscapes (forests, fields, woods and heaths) and then portraying the rare inhabitants of this immense space. Traditionally, the critics associate Taunay's descriptive method with his experience as a traveller, which enabled him to walk through that particular landscape at length. Although the setting constructed in the novel owes much to observations made by the author in his peregrinations through the interior of the country, the role of the literary conventions that permeate such descriptions becomes evident in the way the narrative conceptualizes the objective and subjective elements of the 'landscape'. As Alain Roger puts it, a landscape is never located solely *in situ*, but always and necessarily *in visu*. In other words, it does not rest solely on the objective data of the region, but depends on the perspective of the person contemplating and conceptualizing it.[17] Defined as an 'extension of the territory that the gaze is able to reach in a glance',[18] the landscape is constituted by the 'gaze' of the observer and determined not only by their viewpoint, but mainly through the cultural prism that, so to speak, refracts the elements gathered by the senses. According to Michel Collot,

> the landscape is not the territory, but a certain way of seeing it or painting it in a 'glance' perceptually and/or aesthetically organized ... Therefore, in order to understand or evaluate an artistic or literary 'landscape' it becomes less important to compare it to its eventual referent ... than to consider the way by which it is 'attained' and expressed.[19]

Taunay, who was born and educated in a family of painters,[20] observes with pride that he was the only member of the military expedition to Mato Grosso who had enough sensibility to admire the magnificent paintings that nature uncovered to him during his trip.[21] At the request of his father, he tried his hand at exercises in landscape painting along the route – pieces later collected in an album exhibited in Rio de Janeiro.[22] In *Inocência*, the epigraphs of the first chapter, taken from Goethe and Rousseau, point out to the reader the erudite perspective from which the narrator contemplates nature. Nature is conceived as a space of recollection and solitude and described by means of a set of commonplaces that refer to the concepts of the picturesque and the sublime. In addition, it brings out the hidden aspects of the scenery and the superhuman grandeur of its elements. In the long description of the setting two important literary tropes can be identified: firstly, the idea that fields consumed by fire become magically reborn with the first rainfall, and, secondly, the analogous theme of the *sertão* as having two faces – one melancholic with 'grim perspectives' (during the dry season), and the other similar to an enchanted garden (in the rainy season). Similar tropes can be found in texts as diverse as *O sertanejo* (1875), a novel by José de Alencar, who helped decisively to build up the idealized image of the wilderness, and *Os sertões* (1902) [*Rebellion in the Backlands*], in which, to denounce the crimes committed by the army during the destruction of the village of Canudos, Euclides da Cunha constructs an impressive interpretative essay on Brazil, encompassing its physical and human formation and its history.[23]

Conversely, the fact that the narrator of *Inocência* describes the scene in the opening of the novel before the action begins brings him closer to the canon of the nineteenth-century novel, in which the setting is traditionally constructed to accurately reflect the events about to take place and is often a moral index of the characters who inhabit it. As Maria Lydia Maretti observes, the first chapter of the novel works as a musical overture, adopting a perspective that progresses from the general to the particular. According to Maretti, it moves 'from the *sertanista* as a regional type to the singular novelistic characters that will represent the *sertanista* in the narrative'.[24] From this perspective, the twofold nature of the *sertão*, alternatingly the harsh and the paradisiac, can be read as an index of Pereira's voluble character. In the course of the narrative, Pereira, the father of Inocência, assumes two contradictory faces: from the likeable figure of the talkative citizen of Minas Gerais, frank and hospitable, emerges the brutal father who has his daughter's lover killed in order to wash with blood the family's stained honour. Given the relationship between the description of the scenery and the construction of the characters, the narrator refers to Inocência's love as 'the new sentiment, which, really unknown to her, was as suddenly born in her breast as the flowers of the campos burst into bloom after the rain'.[25]

The image of the *sertão* and the *sertanejo* outlined by the narrator in the first chapter of *Inocência* is clearly positive. Throughout the novel, this image is nuanced by the different kinds of gaze the characters cast upon the space. In this context, Pereira, a man of the *sertão*, despite his complaints about the lack of people with whom he can talk, is perfectly capable of appreciating the value of local customs, especially when contrasted with those of the city. At the beginning of the action, the reader is informed that it was in the 'fever-stricken and decadent town of Sant'Anna do Paranahyba' that Inocência contracted malaria. For Pereira the insalubrity of the air corresponds to the immorality of the urban customs: 'Why, they say now, that up in the cities—Uumph! Detestable!—there is no girl, no matter how poor she is, who does not know how to read and scratch a pen on paper ... That is altogether too much.'[26]

All the same, this picturesque *sertão*, adventurous and forthright, safeguarded by physical distance from the influence of urban modernization, is ingrained with a dangerous trap that has its roots in ancient customs: violence. In the first encounter with Cyrino, anticipating the end of the novel, Pereira warns,

> beware of these people of the Sertão, not exactly of those who live in decent homes, you know, but rather of casual strangers, muleteers, carriers, and such like, for they are more often than not only gangs of gamblers, armed with marked cards and all kinds of shuffling tricks, and for a mere straw they will stick a knife into the stomach of a Christian, or let fly the contents of a pistol at the head of a companion as if it were a rotten melon.[27]

From Pereira's perspective, danger is found not among the region's inhabitants who live orderly lives, but in those who are constantly on the move, like 'casual strangers, muleteers, carriers'. In *Inocência*, violence arises not out the plot of cheating 'gamblers', but from the conflict between the code of honour of the *sertanejos* and urban customs. When Meyer, the naturalist-traveller who travels through the region cataloguing the flora and fauna, asks Pereira if Inocência will get married, an annoyed Pereira replies in the affirmative, but to 'a man of the Sertão, one who would grind his knife into the bowels of whoever would interfere with his wife'.[28] Cyrino tries to convince Pereira to consult Inocência before she is handed over to Manecão Doca, to whom her hand is promised in marriage. However, to the father's astonishment, the hopeless 'doctor' quickly corrects himself: '"Ha! Ha!" said he with a simulated smile. "It is true. I was quite thinking of the customs of the city. Here in the Sertão you Sertanejos have very different ideas."'[29]

As in many nineteenth-century Brazilian novels, the action of *Inocência* starts with a journey. At the beginning of the second chapter, on 15 July 1860, a 'day clear, serene, and fresh',[30] Pereira and Cyrino meet by chance on a road and Pereira takes the young 'doctor' to his home, where that same night the German Meyer will arrive. The journey not only features in the opening, but plays a prominent role in the plot and the thematics of *Inocência*. Conversely, the novel's dramatic action is structured upon a moment of stasis: during their journey, Cyrino, Pereira and Meyer meet at Pereira's house, where they remain for more than a month. It is there that they establish relationships and perform actions that will determine their respective destinies. In his scientific excursions in the fields, Meyer (suspected by Pereira of attempting to seduce his daughter) drags the father with him and opens the way for the meeting of Cyrino and Inocência. In this sense, the very country roads that bring the characters together also take away Manecão Doca, whom the girl was supposed to marry, thus delaying Manecão's arrival and allowing the love affair between the protagonists to emerge. Finally, it is on a road that Cyrino is murdered by Manecão, while awaiting Antonio Cesario, Inocência's godfather, who was supposed to meet him if he agreed to intercede for the couple.

In this crisscross of roads and paths, of itinerant doctors and muleteers, 'life is but a journey', as the simple Manecão Doca philosophizes.[31] But though all the characters may agree on the idea that 'life is but a journey', the journey acquires different senses in each of their lives. Described as a strong and fearless man, 'the type of a captain of muleteers',[32] Manecão appears only in the final chapters of the novel, but from the beginning his shadow looms always over the lovers as a threat. His journeys, however, keep Manecão away, allowing the meetings between Cyrino and Inocência and consequently the birth of their love. According to Pereira, Manecão 'is accustomed to go [sic] with the droves of cattle to S. Paulo'; 'he rides throughout all these *Sertões* and drives such herds of cattle as would astonish you'.[33] In this sense, Manecão becomes one of the possible updates of the generic type described in the first chapter, being a countryman who cuts through inland roads completely oblivious of the natural beauty around him, oriented exclusively towards the demands of his journey, which is his daily bread and butter.

Despite not being originally from those parts, Cyrino is a man used to trailing through the wilderness. He plays a central role not only as protagonist of the love story but also as a mediator between Pereira and Meyer, the foreigner who is unaware of the *sertanejo*'s code of conduct, which he repeatedly infringes. Born in the countryside of São Paulo, which at the time was a vast *sertão*, Cyrino was educated at the College of Caraça, an important religious educational institution in Minas Gerais which remained open until the twentieth century. Expelled from college by the priests, who had not received the inheritance they hoped for from the boy's godfather, Cyrino started working in a pharmacy in Ouro Preto, the capital of the province of Minas Gerais. Subsequently, 'with some medicines in his trunk, he one day set out on a voyage of discovery in the neighbouring districts in search for patients requiring his services'.[34] Immediately after leaving the 'drug store', Cyrino joined the School of Pharmacy of Ouro Preto, but even before he had been awarded a 'diploma of chemist and druggist' 'he proceeded to travel through the inhabited regions of the Sertão, to cure, bleed, cut, and slash, uniting to a limited knowledge of some value such ideas as his experience indicated or that popular opinion or superstition called for'.[35] In his first meeting with Pereira, Cyrino says that he has 'no certain destination'. In the face of the mistrust that this statement produces, he explains, 'I am travelling about these distant regions curing agues and severe fevers.'[36] Furthermore, when no more patients are left to be treated in Pereira's house, he must depart again. As with Manecão, the journey is part of Cyrino's work and a source of financial resources, besides making it possible to live freely. Nonetheless, like Meyer, the pharmacist also sees the journey as an opportunity to enhance his knowledge of 'indigenous medicinal herbs'.[37] When he travels to the house of Inocência's godfather in search of an ally to help him win the young woman's hand, Cyrino justifies his sudden departure by explaining that he needs to collect more remedies and see new patients.

As he is a good romantic traveller, Cyrino's state of mind emulates all aspects of the landscapes he traverses: when the road is 'shady and pleasant' he is confident about the possibility of succeeding in his undertaking and his love life; whereas when he is crossing 'sandy plains, weltering in the scorching heat of the sun', he becomes discouraged and despondent.[38] To be sure, the moment he leaves the village of Sant'Anna do Paranahyba in the direction of Antonio Cesario's house, after his encounter with Manecão Doca, 'the route was transformed into a path of torments through which he craved to fly with furious velocity, yet slowly, withal, seemed to him to pass the varied landmarks of his journey'.[39] Similarly, the time he spends in Pereira's house and his experience of first love completely transform him; consequently, the afflicted young man who departs from the village of Sant'Anna in Chapter 25, 'The Journey', is no longer the same man who travelled light-heartedly along sandy roads in Chapter 2, 'The Traveller'.

Wilhelm Tembel Meyer, the 'doctor in philosophy of the University of Leipizig'[40] who came to Brazil on a mission to search for and catalogue plants, insects and animals, is undoubtedly the great traveller figure portrayed by Taunay in *Inocência* and one of the greatest strengths of the novel. In the words of Cyrino, he is a 'travelling zoologist' or, as he calls himself, a 'travelling naturalist'.[41] When Meyer arrives at Pereira's house, he has already been travelling for 23 months. The letter of recommendation that he carries, coincidentally signed by Pereira's brother, presents him as 'a Senhor of great learning, and who goes to the wild Sertão travelling and studying the countries'.[42] When asked by the incredulous Pereira if it is 'actually true that the Senhor is wandering all over these Sertões just to stick "innesects" [sic]', Meyer explains, 'in my country they are very valuable for purposes of science, and for placing in museums and collections. I am travelling by order of my government, and already I have forwarded many cases all full. They are very precious indeed.'[43]

Meyer plays important roles in the plot. In the gallery of characters, the zoologist and his servant Juca are, along with the narrator, the only characters completely foreign to the region. Despite his scientific knowledge, the naturalist-scholar is completely unaware of the customs of the *sertanejos* and continuously disregards the local rules of conviviality. By openly praising Inocência's natural and unassuming beauty, he raises Pereira's suspicions and vigilance. While worriedly watching him, Pereira leaves the path open for Cyrino and his charming patient to become more intimate. Meyer also illustrates the comic aspects of *Inocência*: his caricatural type, his indiscreet frankness and the humiliations to which he is submitted when attempting to capture his insects must certainly have entertained the first readers of the novel, and even today these aspects retain their freshness. Finally, but equally important, through the lens of Meyer the narrator makes clear the dialogical relationship the novel establishes with travel narrative.

The Novel's Plot and Characters

The plot of *Inocência* is simple and progresses in a straightforward manner, without too many parallel episodes which could interrupt the main action, and without major advances or flashbacks in time, with the exception of Chapter 3, 'The Doctor', in which a flashback tells us about the protagonist's background. At the beginning of the narrative, Cyrino, a practising apothecary (in fact, a 'healer, simply a healer') who is journeying through the *sertão* with his medicines treating patients, comes across Pereira, a small farmer who takes Cyrino to his home so that he can treat his daughter, Inocência, who has contracted malaria. When Cyrino meets the 'gentle patient'[44] he falls in love with her. Thus he betrays Pereira's trust, since he has already been warned to look upon Inocência only as a patient, not as young woman, she being pledged to marry Manecão Doca, the herdsman whose main activity is to trail through the *sertões* driving cattle to São Paulo. The passion between the doctor and the patient sets up a love triangle that will lead inexorably to a tragic end. This sentimental plot is permeated by the adventures of Meyer, who stays in Pereira's house in order to carry out his research into the local fauna and flora, and who through his incautious praise of the beauty of Inocência ends up drawing upon himself the suspicion of the wary Pereira. This situation clears the path for the romance between the apothecary and his patient. The gallery of principal characters is completed by Tico, a mute dwarf who watches over Inocência as a loyal guardian and eventually reveals the true identity of the young woman's lover, playing a major role in the resolution of the plot, and Antonio Cesario, Inocência's godfather, who represents the only hope the couple has of discouraging Pereira from giving his daughter's hand in marriage to Manecão Doca. There are also a few minor characters, including Maria Conga (Pereira's slave), Juca (Meyer's servant), Cyrino's two patients (Coelho and Garcia) and Major Melo Taques, a historical character who was an acquaintance of Taunay's in real life and to whom he refers in his *Memórias* [*Memoirs*].[45]

From a structural viewpoint, the narrative can be divided into three parts. The first introduces the characters and outlines the initial situation of stability. It covers Chapters 2 to 12, where, through a series of casual encounters, Cyrino and Meyer meet in Pereira's house and get to know Inocência. The second part comprises Chapters 13 to 23 and recounts the events involving these characters during their stay at Pereira's house. This section centres on the romance between Cyrino and Inocência and breaks the stability of the first part. In parallel, it also records from a comic perspective the adventures of Meyer as he conducts his research.

The third part comprises Chapters 24 to 30 and the epilogue and is significantly smaller than the previous two parts. This is the only section that does not feature Pereira's farm as the setting, recording instead the consequences of the tensions that developed on the farm: on the one hand, the efforts of Cyrino and Inocência to work around the crisis triggered by their love, which eventually leads to their death; on the other, the consecration of Meyer in Germany, where he triumphantly displays the wonderful butterfly discovered in the *sertão* of Brazil, which he has named *Papilio innocentia*.

At the centre of *Inocência*'s plot is the drama of the lovers who are prevented from being together, a topos that is familiar to nineteenth-century romanticism but has its roots in a rich European literary tradition, as some of the chapters' epigraphs indicate. These are taken from the tragedy *Romeo and Juliet*, by William Shakespeare, and *Paul et Virginie* [*Paul and Virginia*], a short novel by Bernardin de Saint-Pierre, which has captured the imagination of generations of readers since its publication in 1788.[46] The relationship of the so-called *sertaneja* narrative to Saint-Pierre's famous novel did not go unnoticed among the nineteenth-century public. In the preface that James W. Wells wrote for his English translation he quotes the opinion of a friend, H. W. Bates, who observes, 'The plot is very simple, but not simpler than that of the famous *Paul et Virginie*, and there is great pathos in the story – not artificially worked up, but coming out quite naturally.'[47] Taunay himself, expressing the hope that his book will reach the readers of the future, aligns his work to Saint-Pierre's classic novel: 'My ambition for *Inocência* is the fate of *Paul et Virginie*! This is my posthumous aspiration.'[48]

In *Inocência*, contrary to what happens in the literary models provided by Shakespeare and Saint-Pierre, the impediment to the couple's union is not the hatred between families or the social and spatial distance that separates them, but the prejudices of the *sertanejos*, who consider woman to be an inferior being, one who is placed in a submissive position in the patriarchal family and is subordinated first to the father and then to the husband. From this perspective, *Inocência* is a drama generated by the clash between the culture of the *sertanejo*, patriarchal and intransigent, in which a word once given cannot be broken, and an urban culture that presses for a more liberating space for women in the family and in social relationships. In the fabric of the plot, the traditional world of the countryside, whose seclusion is symbolized by the architecture of Pereira's house, is shaken by the urban civilization that sees women from a new perspective, treating them in a way that is significantly different from unrestrained repression. The arrival of the foreign characters challenges the *sertanejo* code of conduct and causes the crisis that culminates in a bloody outcome. This confrontation between two spheres, the *sertanejo* and the urban, is explicit in the dialogues of Cyrino and Pereira about women's education and the father's obligation to find, as quickly as possible, a suitable match for his daughter. According to Pereira, 'with petticoat people you never can rely on anything'.[49] It is in this context that the novel's urban narrator, assuming the position of interpreter of *sertanejo* customs, comments,

> This injurious sentiment with regard to women is common throughout the Sertão, and brings for immediate and practical consequences the rigorous seclusion in which they are maintained, the pre-arranged marriage of children by relatives, and, above all, the numerous crimes committed. Yet, withal, seldom is suspected the possibility of an intrigue between members of a family and a stranger.[50]

For Pereira, since Inocência was promised to Manecão, she already belonged to him as his wife. In essence, this is very clear in the conversation the father has with the young apothecary before Inocência is introduced to him: 'when I saw the girl assume the proportions of a woman, I at once set about getting her married'.[51] When Cyrino asks if she 'is married', the zealous father clarifies, 'She is, and yet she is not. The thing has been talked about.'[52] From the *sertanejo*'s perspective there is no difference between a 'thing that has been talked about' and an accomplished fact. According to this parameter, Inocência and Cyrino are instantly guilty of adultery and as such they must be punished. Crucially, the duty of avenging the affront and washing the family honour with blood belongs to the herdsman: 'this is a business that belongs to me', says Manecão; 'the Senhor is the father, it is true, but I am the bridegroom'.[53] After Tico reveals that it was not Meyer but Cyrino who seduced Inocência, Pereira despairs and begs Manecão, 'show that you are now the owner of this house and do what you please. I deliver myself to you bound hand and foot. Everything here belongs to you. While the honour of a Mineiro is not redeemed I will not raise my head. Meu Deus! meu Deus! What a disgrace!'[54]

If, on the one hand, the tragic romance between the protagonists allows the insertion of the plot in the literary tradition that combines love and death, a theme dear to the romantics, on the other hand, it clears the way for the incorporation of local colour into the story, starting with the representation of women in the society of the *sertão*. Despite the relatively restricted role that Inocência plays in the action, it is upon her the actions of all the characters and the interest of the reader converge, which is one reason why the novel has her name, not that of Cyrino, who is at the centre of the events. Through Inocência's story the narrator is able to reflect on the way that women were tyrannized by father or husband, systematically locked in their own homes without access to formal education, prevented even from acquiring literacy and without a voice to determine their personal destiny. In the novel, the condition of women is articulated with the question of honour, an ethical principle that transcends the internal organization of the patriarchal family. Honour also has repercussions in the social circle, manifesting both in the rationale of the given word that cannot be taken back ('Mecê knows not what means the word of a Mineiro,' says Inocência to Cyrino; 'iron breaks, but that never')[55] and in the notion of hospitality, a sacred duty that ties the hands of Pereira and prevents him from expelling Meyer from his house. Meyer carried a letter of recommendation signed by Pereira's elder brother, to whom Pereira owed almost filial respect and obedience.

In enabling the description of local customs, these themes provide an element of the picturesque, which certainly helped to awaken interest among the national and international nineteenth-century public, as we can see from the words of James W. Wells in the preface to his translation:

> I found my attention attracted, not only by the interest of the story, but also by the life-like picture it conveyed to me of the characters of the people and the scenery of the backwoods of Brazil. Here, thought I, in the compass of this short narrative, any reader can obtain a better idea of the rural life and scenery of inland Brazil than he could gain by studying the whole library full of books of travels in that country.[56]

Arguing in the same vein, H. W. Bates stresses in a short comment about his friend's translation that he appreciates the 'novelty and charm in the scenes and characters of *Innocencia*' and adds, 'The groundwork of the tale is its graphic picture of scenery, life, and character in rural Brazil, and the characters are drawn with wonderful truth and simple force.'[57]

It is only in the sixth chapter, after the reader has been introduced to the scene of action and to two of its main characters, Cyrino and Pereira, that Inocência enters the stage, an appearance meticulously prepared by the various speeches of her father describing her to the young apothecary. Pereira's house, where most of the episodes take place, is conceived as a labyrinth or, better, a cloister that protects and hides his daughter.

The account of the route the characters take to reach Inocência's bedroom enables the evocation of such a cloister, one that is physically separated from the room designated to receive and accommodate guests who do not belong to the family circle. The latter is the room where Cyrino is already installed and that shortly after will accommodate the German naturalist: 'leaving the room [Cyrino] accompanied Pereira, who proceeded by a roundabout way towards the back door of the house, and in order to do so he had to pass through two fences that shut off the rear portion of the premises from the front. Facing the back of the house an orchard of magnificent orange-trees.'[58] Later, when an analogy is established between Inocência and the butterfly discovered by Meyer, the architecture of the house connotes a cocoon, a perfect allegory of the state of isolation in which the young woman has been kept, severely aloof from any contact with strangers.

After crossing the areas designated for visitors, Cyrino, led by Pereira, penetrates the intimate, secluded space where the young patient rests. When the first encounter between the protagonists takes place, it is night ['it was so dark'[59]], a time romantically enchanted in which things cannot be seen with clarity and the eyes of reason, always limited and imperfect, must withdraw and give way to deeper and truer insights, more pertinent to the heart and to feelings. The description is constructed like a framed picture, as made explicit by James W. Wells, who in his translation changed the passage considerably by inserting a direct comparison with painting: 'Her [Inocência's] face was Madonna-like in its form and sweet expression – such an [sic] one as the old masters loved to depict for their saints and Virgin Maries.'[60] In addition to the comparison with the Virgin Mary's face, the pictorial description is reinforced in the English edition by the inclusion of a picture, with the caption 'The doctor contemplated his patient', that portrays the scene of the first encounter between Cyrino and Inocência, observed by Tico, who is sitting at the foot of the bed.

In the original version of the novel, Inocência is glimpsed in her bed amid a play of light and shadows which reinforces her paleness and beauty: 'Despite the pallor of illness and the dim, flickering light of the candle, now placed on a bracket against the wall above her, it was easily seen that Inocência was really dazzlingly, bewilderingly beautiful.'[61]

In the room, barely lit by the candle, the heroine's face emerges from the shadows and casts a glow that fascinates the young doctor, who is overwhelmed by her 'dazzling' beauty and by the expression that 'radiated' from her face,[62] two terms that connote brightness. Inocência's portrait is painted from the perspective of Cyrino, whose 'dazzled' eyes seek to apprehend the image by means of a movement between the whole and the parts that make it up. Initially, the narrator depicts Cyrino's patient by concentrating on the shadows that envelop her – her face, brow and head – recording, simultaneously, the impression she makes: 'Inocência was bewilderingly beautiful.'[63] Subsequently, in close-up he describes the details of the picture: first the 'face' (a part of the whole), in which he distinguishes the 'sweet expression', the 'long lashes', the 'delicate nose', the 'little mouth', the 'graceful contour of her cheeks'; secondly the 'neck of alabaster whiteness' (another part of the whole).[64] Owing to the linear nature of verbal language, which must submit to the succession of time what is simultaneously perceived in space and represented in a painting, Inocência's face is depicted from top to bottom, from the eyes down to her chin. In the paragraph that follows this portrayal, the narrator emphasizes the effect the image has on Cyrino: as he is stunned by the beauty radiating like a strong light from the young woman, 'Abundant reason therefore had Cyrino to suddenly feel his hand become cold and somewhat tremulous as he endeavoured to examine the pulse of so gentle a patient.'[65]

The three epigraphs that open Chapter 6, 'Inocência', which narrates Cyrino and Inocência's first encounter, are very revealing. The first, from Moysés Sefardy's *Da amizade ou Livro de Henoch* [*Of Friendship, or The Book of Henoch*], is a commentary on the meaning Inocência will have for Cyrino, anticipating the tragic end of their love: 'It is in this maiden that my life and my death come together.'[66] The two other epigraphs, taken respectively from George Sand and Walter Scott, allude to essential elements of the composition of the heroine's portrait: in the quote from the Scottish novelist, the idea of a woman as similar to a 'miniature';[67] in the French writer's epigraph, disease: 'Never had I seen something so perfect as her pale face, her eyes garnished with thick silky lashes, her mien sweet and sickly.'[68] As George Sand appears to imply, it is the disease that lends beauty to Inocência and makes her irresistible in Cyrino's eyes. When the narrator starts to draw her portrait, he observes that her paleness and thinness do not detract from her stunning beauty. Later, the narrator will note again that Inocência appears to the apothecary like a 'fever-stricken maiden, yet so beautiful even with the pallor of illness'.[69] Thus, it is possible to suggest that it is not 'in spite' of the illness but because of it that the patient fascinates the young doctor. This suggestion gives the novel a touch of morbidity which is in perfect harmony with the conception of love as an illness that takes lovers by storm and drags them to death, an 'abyss sown with torments'.[70] Overcome by this feeling, and despite his attempts not to, Cyrino allows his symptoms to emerge: restless and unable to eat or sleep, he ends up exchanging the day for the night. When Inocência mentions that she is cured, he instantly answers, 'Ill am I now. It is I who am now about to die, for you have bewitched me, and no remedy can I find for my sickness.'[71]

Closely associated with the soil and painted with the colours of Brazilian nature, Inocência is romantically invested with pleasant qualities. In Taunay's novel, the integration of the heroine with the natural environment, besides being suggested by the character's physical description and marked by comparisons to birds and plants, is also allegorized by the splendid butterfly discovered by Meyer and christened with her name:

> Without contestation, it was a most beautiful specimen, a wonderful caprice of the splendid nature of those regions. In the very exuberance of his contentment, Meyer could not keep quiet a moment.
>
> 'This butterfly,' said he, as if his listeners were two professors of the science, 'belongs to the family of Papilionidae, or swallow-tails, and I at once denominated it Papilio Innocentia, in honour of the daughter of Senhor Pereira, who has treated me so well.'[72]

Inocência, whose name is descriptive of her character, is also 'a wonderful caprice of the splendid nature of those regions', and just like the butterfly discovered by the naturalist she is 'a new species—a new one, a new one!'[73] Spotted in their habitat and admired in all their brilliance and beauty, both Inocências die – the butterfly pierced by the pin of the naturalist, and the girl by the feeling that tears her apart and makes her break the social and cultural conventions she has been subjected to. This outcome functions as an allegory of beauty and purity destroyed by the hands of the stranger who intrudes into such a peculiar world whose preservation depends on its very insulation. As Süssekind explains, 'the friendly figure of Meyer, the German naturalist who systematically hunts, classifies, and collects butterflies … is a kind of comic double of the travelling narrator, who caricatures him in *Inocência*, and in this case, there is no margin for hesitation: naming and killing represent to him inseparable actions'.[74]

Romantic Topoi

Reading *Inocência*, one cannot ignore Taunay's use of romantic clichés to weave the novel's plot and construct his characters: the heroine is kept in a kind of cloister and guarded by some kind of monstrous being (Tico the dwarf, compared by Pereira to a 'little devil' or 'a sort of little dog for 'Nocencia');[75] the inexperienced young lady awakened by love; the couple prevented from coming together by obstacles external and superior to their strength; the love triangle; and the relationship between beauty, illness, love and death. The novel's great appeal partially owes to the skill with which Taunay took advantage of these topoi, adapting them to his goals by telling a love story that is entirely conventional but renewed by the setting and by the characters which he collected from the deep *sertão*. The construction of the novel is based on a meticulously elaborate technique that articulates the plot with epigraphs opening each chapter and the use of footnotes containing comments and additional information about the text.

This paratextual material provides clues to the worldview that presided in Taunay's work and comprises fragments that, as in a mosaic, recreate the cultural context of the time. In his analysis of the novel, José Maurício Gomes de Almeida remarks that the epigraphs not only function as an indirect commentary on the narrative and a guide to show how it should be received, but also aim to situate the local plot in the European literary tradition. The *sertanejo* matter was thus to be raised to a noble status. This strategy of establishing a paratextual counterpoint to the main body of the work became 'one of the outstanding features of its originality in the context of the Brazilian novel of the time, as well as of the interest that the modern reader can still find in it today'.[76]

The procedure of textual annotation, a frequent feature of the period, also helps us to uncover the principles that governed Taunay's literary endeavour. In *Inocência*, to the extent that the narrative incorporates local colour through language register and the description of places, people and customs, the footnotes explain and reinforce the meanings of these elements. Most of the novel's 123 footnotes contain comments and explanations about language, as in the chapter 'The Dyspeptic Patient', where the meaning of 'inziminar' is explained as a 'local corruption of "examinar", to examine'.[77]

Characteristically, through this kind of procedure, Taunay's travelling experience enables him to compose a small but authoritative and credible glossary intended to clarify and comment on regional words and expressions virtually unknown to the urban reader. While the epigraphs are similar to the key signature on a musical score, the discourse of the footnotes can be compared to the voice of a translator, converting as they do the unknown elements of the universe of the *sertanejo* into the language of the urban audience. Besides their specific explanatory function, the footnotes arguably also establish the character of the author-narrator (two categories that were not clearly distinguished at the time) as an experienced traveller, one who is familiar with the universe he portrays. In this way, the footnotes function as a kind of authentication that the author is telling the truth. Similarly, as important as the information conveyed in the footnotes is the effect produced by the whole set of them. Among other things, they help to construct the image of the narrator as a perceptive and judicious man, one who selectively observed and collected the elements that underpin his account. In a similar manner to naturalist-travellers like Meyer, such well-versed travellers systematically collected material on their journeys that could reconstitute the strange and fascinating new world they encountered to the learned European.

In essence, emphasizing Taunay's direct knowledge of the *sertão* and the *sertanejo*, twentieth-century literary criticism and history have consistently considered *Inocência* to be a novel highly representative of the aesthetic changes that were at work in the 1870s. In this period the overtly imaginative elements of romanticism were problematized by the new principles of observation and fidelity professed by young writers emerging on the literary scene. Taunay himself drew attention to the distance separating him from some of his predecessors, like José de Alencar, whom he respected but believed to be lacking in knowledge of 'Brazilian nature'.[78] In his view, such a fault had been corrected by *Inocência*, considered by the author to be 'the basis of true "Brazilian Literature"' because of its careful style and truthful descriptions 'in which I attempted to accurately reproduce impressions gathered in the heart of the Sertão'.[79]

In conclusion, if the assessment of *Inocência* as a novel inspired by direct knowledge of the *sertão* and the *sertanejo* explains part of its success, we should not forget that its documentary content is counterbalanced by Taunay's craft of literary composition, which adapts the information gathered from observation to the internal requirements of the narrative. Thus, even though he was in tune with the literary trends of his generation, which prioritized observation over imagination, Taunay was not affected by the trend towards documentary depiction. Instead, he engaged all his narratorial skills to shape this small book, which, despite its appearance of simplicity, he considered to be one of his major works.

Notes

1. Translated by Elton Uliana (University College London).
2. Taunay 1889, 1. In his *Memórias*, Taunay comments on this translation, 'The engineer James Wells ... transposed that novel of mine into English, or produced an adaptation that really pleased the London public; so it has been said in magazines and newspaper articles.' Taunay

n.d., 161. In his translation, Wells omitted all the epigraphs. All quotations from the book are from Well's translation.

3. Taunay 1889, 1–2.
4. Silva 1813.
5. Saint-Hilaire 1975, 307. When not otherwise specified, translations from the Portuguese are Elton Uliana's.
6. Saint-Hilaire 1975, 307.
7. Southey 1810–19, Vol. 2, 565, n. 8.
8. 'Innocencia; is also the name of the protagonist in Wells's translation.
9. Taunay 1889, 1.
10. Taunay 1889, 2. At the end of the narrative, when Cyrino is travelling towards the house of Innocencia's godfather, the village of Sant'Anna is described as situated 'on the edge of the wild moorlands of the Sertão of Mato Grosso' (Taunay 1889, 244).
11. At the end of 1864, the Paraguayan army invaded a region that today belongs to the state of Mato Grosso do Sul, starting a long and deadly war that lasted until 1870. In January 1865, Taunay departed from Rio de Janeiro as a member of the commission of Brazilian army engineers sent to liberate the province, initiating in this way a long journey that only ended two-and-a-half years later.
12. Taunay n.d., 270.
13. Taunay n.d., 258, my emphasis.
14. The idea of the *sertão* as a frontier that came after the advance of colonization and its comparison to the American West appear, among other examples, in *Explorations of the Highlands of Brazil* (1869), by Richard Francis Burton, the legendary military and English explorer who lived in Brazil in the 1860s. In the account of his journey along the São Francisco River, when referring to the town of Curvelo, in the countryside of the province of Minas Gerais, the explorer observes, 'built upon the *Campo*, and being the last town in this region, it is supposed to demarcate the *Sertão*, or Far West' (Burton 1969, Vol. 2, 156–7).
15. Taunay 1889, 3. In Portuguese, the phrase is *terreno incerto* [uncertain, unfamiliar, unreliable, insecure terrain]. My emphasis.
16. Süssekind 1990, 60.
17. Roger 1997, 16ff.
18. Houaiss 2001.
19. Collot 2005, 12.
20. The author was the grandson of Nicolas Antoine Taunay, a French painter who emigrated to Brazil with his family in 1816, after the fall of Napoleon Bonaparte. The children of Nicolas Antoine were also painters, among them Félix Émile Taunay, father of the novelist, who became close to the emperor Dom Pedro II and held the position of director of the Academy of Fine Arts.
21. 'With the artistic education I had received from my father … I was the only one among my companions … who was looking at the charms of the great natural paintings and showing them proper appreciation.' Taunay n.d., 131.
22. Entitled *Viagem pitoresca a Mato Grosso* [*Picturesque Journey to Mato Grosso*], this album of paintings is available on the website of the Institute Hercule Florence: http://www.ihf19.org.br. Mentioning his 'talents as innocent landscape artist', Taunay comments, 'I have reproduced with considerable success and fidelity a number of curious perspectives that are worthy of attention.' Taunay n.d., 155.
23. See Chapter 10 of the first part of *O sertanejo* (Alencar 1977b) and Chapter 4 of 'A terra' [The Land] in *Os sertões* (Cunha 1985).
24. Maretti 2006, 236.
25. Taunay 1889, 147.
26. Taunay 1889, 58.
27. Taunay 1889, 32.
28. Taunay 1889, 210.
29. Taunay 1889, 214.
30. Taunay 1889, 23.
31. Taunay 1889, 251.
32. Taunay 1889, 250.
33. Taunay 1889, 56.

34. Taunay 1889, 40.
35. Taunay 1889, 41.
36. Taunay 1889, 27.
37. Taunay 1889, 42.
38. Taunay 1889, 242–3.
39. Taunay 1889, 258.
40. Taunay 1889, 104. 'University of Iena' in the original.
41. Taunay 1889, 85. In the translation, Meyer simply repeats, 'Travelling zoologist!'.
42. Taunay 1889, 108.
43. Taunay 1889, 103.
44. Taunay 1889, 65.
45. Taunay n.d., 276.
46. Fragments of *Romeo and Juliet* are taken as epigraphs to Chapters 18 and 23, symbolically entitled 'Idyll' and 'The Last Interview'. Chapter 18 contains an epigraph from *Paul et Virginie*. Chapter 21, 'Papilio Innocentia', also include in its opening a fragment from Bernadin de Saint-Pierre, this time taken from *Harmonies of Nature*.
47. Wells 1889, vii. Brito Broca considers that 'there was an obsession among the writers of the new continent … to make a *Paul et Virginia* of America', an idea that would have guided Taunay in the writing of *Inocência*, which had the theme of 'the supremacy of rural life over the artifices of civilization'. Broca 1991, 206.
48. Taunay n.d., 161.
49. Taunay 1889, 58.
50. Taunay 1889, 58.
51. Taunay 1889, 56.
52. Taunay 1889, 56.
53. Taunay 1889, 293–4.
54. Taunay 1889, 297–8. [My God! my God!].
55. Taunay 1889, 234. [Mecê = you].
56. Wells 1889, v–vi.
57. Wells 1889, vii.
58. Taunay 1889, 62.
59. Taunay 1889, 64.
60. Taunay 1889, 65.
61. Taunay 1889, 64–5.
62. Taunay 1889, 65, my emphasis.
63. Taunay 1889, 63.
64. Taunay 1889, 65.
65. Taunay 1889, 65.
66. Sefardy 1928.
67. 'Her countenance resembled a most beautiful miniature; and there was a quickness, decision, and fire, in Fenella's look, and especially in her eyes.' Scott 1823.
68. 'Je n'avais jamais rien vu de si bien achevé que son visage pâle, ses yeux … bordés de soies très épaisses, son air doux et fatigué.' Sand 1853.
69. Taunay 1889, 117.
70. Taunay 1889, 96.
71. Taunay 1889, 190–1.
72. Taunay 1889, 217–18.
73. Taunay 1889, 218.
74. Süssekind 1990, 220.
75. Taunay 1889, 67–8. Wilson Martins draws attention to 'the sudden popularity of the monsters' at the beginning of the 1870s, a fashion suggested by the model of Victor Hugo and exemplified by Brás, the character in José de Alencar's *Til* (1872), and by Tico, the dwarf of *Inocência*. See Martins 1976. On the theme of the damsel in distress, see Praz 1996, 102ff.
76. Almeida 1999, 106.
77. Taunay 1889, 163.
78. Taunay n.d., 166.
79. Taunay n.d., 168–9.

Bibliography

Alencar, José de. *O gaúcho. O tronco do ipê*. Rio de Janeiro: José Olympio, 1977a.

Alencar, José de. *Til. O sertanejo*. Rio de Janeiro: José Olympio, 1977b.

Almeida, José Maurício Gomes de. *A tradição regionalista no romance brasileiro*. Rio de Janeiro: Topbooks, 1999.

Antonio Candido. 'A sensibilidade e o bom senso do Visconde de Taunay'. In *Formação da literatura brasileira*. Belo Horizonte: Itatiaia; São Paulo: Edusp, 1981.

Broca, Brito. 'Inocência'. In *Papéis de Alceste*. Campinas: Ed. UNICAMP, 1991.

Burton, Richard Francis. *Explorations of the Highlands of the Brazil*. New York: Greenwood Press, 1969.

Collot, Michel. *Paysage et poesie du Romantisme à nos jours*. Paris: José Corti, 2005.

Cunha, Euclides. *Os sertões*, edited by Walnice Nogueira Galvão. São Paulo: Brasiliense, 1985.

Houaiss, Antônio. *Dicionário Houaiss da língua portuguesa*. Rio de Janeiro: Objetiva, 2001.

Maretti, Maria Lídia L. *O Visconde de Taunay e os fios da memória*. São Paulo: Unesp, 2006.

Martins, Wilson. *História de inteligência brasileira, Vol. 3 (1855–1877)*. São Paulo: Editora Cultrix, 1976.

Praz, Mario. *A carne, a morte e o diabo na literatura romântica*. Campinas: Ed. UNICAMP, 1996.

Roger, Alain. *Court traité du paysage*. Paris: Gallimard, 1997.

Saint-Hilaire, Auguste de. *Viagem pelas províncias de Rio de Janeiro e Minas Gerais*. Belo Horizonte: Itatiaia, São Paulo: EdUSP, 1975.

Saint-Pierre, Bernardin. *Paulo e Virgínia*, translated by Rosa Boaventura. São Paulo: Ícone, 1986.

Sand, George. *Les maîtres sonneurs*. Paris: A. Cadot, 1853. https://beq.ebooksgratuits.com/vents/Sand-sonneurs.pdf

Sefardy, Moysés. *Da amizade; ou, Livro de Henoch*, translated by Moses Bensabat Amzalak. Lisbon: n.p., 1928.

Scott, Sir Walter. *Peveril of the Peak*. Edinburgh: Archibald Constable, 1823.

Silva, Antonio de Moraes. *Dicionário da língua portuguesa*. Lisbon: Tipografia Lacerdina, 1813.

Southey, Robert. *History of Brazil*. London: Longman, Hurst, Rees & Orme, 1810–1819.

Süssekind, Flora. *O Brasil não é longe daqui*. São Paulo: Companhia das Letras, 1990.

Taunay, Alfredo d'Escragnolle. *Innocencia*, translated by James W. Wells. London: Chapman & Hall, 1889.

Taunay, A. E. *Inocência*. São Paulo: Martins Fontes, 2005.

Taunay, A. E. *Memórias*. São Paulo: Melhoramentos, n.d.

Taunay, A. E. *Viagem pitoresca a Mato Grosso*. http://www.ihf19.org.br

Wells, James W. 'The Translator's Preface'. In A. E. Taunay, *Innocencia*. London: Chapman & Hall, 1889.

8

Silences and Voices of Slavery: *A escrava Isaura* and *Incidents in the Life of a Slave Girl*

Heloisa Toller Gomes

Introduction: The Abolitionist Literature, Hybrid Forms

> Reader, if you do not disdain
> Coming down to the slave quarters,
> Exchanging cushions and salons
> For a heinous whorehouse,
> Come with me, but ... beware ...
> That your embroidered dress
> Is not stained by the floor
> The floor of the filthy brothel.
>
> (Castro Alves, 'Tragedy in the Home')[1]

We will discuss in this chapter two texts that present literary perceptions of slavery in Brazil and in the United States. They are the novel *A escrava Isaura* [*Isaura the Slave Girl*] by Bernardo Guimarães (1875), a success of Brazilian romantic literature, and the slave narrative *Incidents in the Life of a Slave Girl* by Linda Brent (1861).[2] Bernardo Guimarães (1825–84), novelist, poet, dramatist and journalist, led a bohemian life in his youth and was well known in Brazilian literary circles in his lifetime, being a member of the white elites during the monarchical years; 'Linda Brent' is the pen name of Harriet Jacobs (1818–96), who, using pseudonyms to protect the characters in the book, chronicled her early life as a slave and the ordeals of her concealment and escape from slavery to the free states of the North of the United States.

Important points in common unite *Incidents in the Life of a Slave Girl* and *A escrava Isaura* and invite a comparative approach. One of them is that slavery was a living institution in the two countries where the respective authors were born and lived. Another is that both works belong to the sphere of abolitionist literature, a branch of the thesis genre. *Isaura* is explicitly a thesis novel. *Incidents*, on the other hand, is a slave narrative and autobiography. As such, it shows similarities and differences with respect to the standard thesis literature.

According to Susan Suleiman, in *Le roman à these: ou l'autorité fictive*, thesis literature demands a complicity of ideas uniting author, text and reader, since the assumptions orienting the text precede the text and go beyond it. The thesis text must refer to the world of experiences of the reader, who will ideally apply, in real life, the lessons learned or confirmed in the reading of the work. Descending from the parable, the *récit exemplaire* and the philosophical or political allegory, and akin to the discourse of modern publicity, the thesis genre is a didactic, doctrinarian literature that follows an aesthetic of verisimilitude – the reader must accept the textual action as a representation of reality.[3] The function and truth of thesis literature and of its sub-genres, or branches, are to reveal a motivation exterior to the work: the idea that created and structured the dramatization of facts. In *A escrava Isaura* and *Incidents in the Life of a Slave Girl*, the idea that orients the flux of the narrative is that slavery is abominable.

This does not mean that the thesis genre has always been at the service of good causes: in the South of the United States, for example, in the years before the Civil War (1861–5), an abundant pro-slavery literature was written and published by influential Southern poets and novelists as part and parcel of the defensive ideology of slavery as a 'positive good'. Examples include poems by William Grayson ('The Hireling and the Slave') and novels by William Gilmore Simms (*Woodcraft: or, Hawks about the Dovecote*) and J. W. Page (*Uncle Robin in His Cabin in Virginia and Tom without One in Boston*). In the twentieth century, in the same line, Thomas Dixon was famous for his fictional trilogy, *The Leopard's Spots, The Clansman, The Traitor* (1902–7).[4]

In this chapter's endeavour, we stand on the blurred frontiers between fiction and non-fiction. As we bring together a fictional work (*Isaura*) and a self-identified non-fictional work (*Incidents*), the first words of Linda Brent's 'Preface' sound like a warning: 'Reader, be assured this narrative is no fiction.'[5] Nevertheless, I am well aware that works of fiction frequently contain autobiographical elements and 'several well-known novels adopt the form of the autobiography in that their fictitious protagonists give first-person accounts of their life stories'.[6] It is worth noticing the wide interest increasingly shown in the interchangeability of fictional and documentary techniques, of fiction and non-fiction, in literary, cultural and social studies in recent decades.

The slave narrative and the autobiography are genres that merge together. *Incidents* belongs to both categories, having the specific characteristics of autobiography and of slave narrative.[7] *Isaura*, in turn, is a novel elaborated according to the romantic canons then prevailing in Brazil and, as a thesis novel, incorporates factual elements in its fictional nature.

To help us in relation to these points, I refer to the concept of 'hybrid forms' developed by Luiz Costa Lima. According to the Brazilian critic, 'the heterogeneity of literature allows it to encompass works that initially had another destination'.[8] Costa Lima defines as 'hybrid' those literary forms that possess a 'double inscription', as he puts it. Having a former, distinct inscription recognized, 'they admit a literary inscription for their specific treatment of language'. To perceive this, it is necessary to recognize 'the permanence of the efficacy of the marks of the first [inscription], together with the supplementary presence of the second'.[9] The comprehensive denomination of literature encompasses works that, having lost their original destination, change their function.[10] An ample capacity of imaginary re-creation confers upon these works, even if they be primarily non-fictional, a literary quality.

Thus, *Incidents in the Life of a Slave Girl*, with a clear, deliberate political purpose, may also be seen as a fictional work (manifest in the changes of names, locations and other novelistic details), and it shares common ground with *Isaura* – which too is bound to a specific historical context and may be considered in the tradition of the *roman-feuilleton*, or, beyond that, as a courageous pamphlet throwing into relief intolerable situations in the social universe of slavery.[11]

After the separate discussions of *Isaura* and *Incidents* that follow we will bring the two texts together in a comparative commentary in relation to the *play of differences* they express, drawing for theoretical support upon the thought of Jacques Derrida.

A escrava Isaura

> a woman created of by and for darkness
>
> (William Faulkner 1972)

> They are so naked, you imagine
> them closed in the stuff of tears.
>
> (Cecília Meireles 1972)

In Bernardo Guimarães's novel, a lot of space is given to the evils of slavery but, paradoxically, very little place given to the black person. Much of its interest derives from the fact that *A escrava Isaura* is one of the few abolitionist works of fiction in Brazilian literature. Owing to its fame and success, some called it 'the Brazilian *Uncle Tom's Cabin*'.[12] The undeniable popularity it still enjoys today comes from the agility with which the author manipulates situations and from a certain easy charm in the construction of environments and melodramatic conflicts. The fiction of Bernardo Guimarães, according to Antonio Candido (referring to that author's novels in general), 'expresses an essentially romantic psychological conception reducible to few situations and fundamental types, schematically represented according to current representations of hero, heroine, father and villain'.[13]

There is another way to explain the immediate success of the work: Bernardo Guimarães was very careful when describing the horrors of slavery impacting on Isaura, a slave exceptional in all respects. Thus, he did not offend the sensibility of the reading public he had in mind – a public more able to feel pity when witnessing the oppression of an apparently white slave rather than an ordinary one.

It is true that Isaura has African blood, but nothing in her appearance reveals it. She looks like 'an Andalusian from Cadiz', or a 'Neapolitan girl',[14] as the bewitched villain Leôncio suggests. Besides her fine features, Isaura has a 'noble figure radiating beauty and angelic serenity'.[15] Her late mistress took a personal interest in educating her. So, after learning 'to read and to write, to sew and to pray', Isaura had masters 'of music, of dance, of Italian, of French, of drawing'.[16] Isaura accumulates so many perfections that the result is not very convincing.

Of course, in romantic literature women tend to be idealized, but Isaura has to be doubly idealized – as the heroine of the novel and as compensation for her mixed blood. She has to be idealized in order to correspond to the ideal heroine; she has to look white so that readers can identify with the pure love of Álvaro, who wishes to marry her. As the text makes it clear that there is African blood in Isaura's veins, it is necessary to compensate for this 'deficiency' by means of idealization. Álvaro, Isaura's lover, is described as 'one of these privileged beings upon whom nature and fortune seem to have wished to pour all their treasures'.[17] He is, thus, the equivalent to Isaura, who, in his own fervent words, 'is not a woman; she is a fairy, an angel, a goddess!'[18]

In truth, racial prejudice is present in the narrative voice and in the characters – including Isaura herself. As she weeps about her sad destiny, she laments, 'it would be better for me to have been born brutal and ungainly, as the lowest of the negresses'.[19] Her friendly mistress Malvina, while ignoring the sexual advances of her husband, Leôncio, towards Isaura, tries to comfort her with these words: 'You are lovely and have such a beautiful color, that no one would say there is a single drop of African blood in your veins.'[20] In the text, virtue and beauty are intimately associated with whiteness. No wonder, then, that the idea of Isaura having sexual intercourse with a black man constitutes the worst of all threats: 'I will make you the wife of the vilest, most hideous of my Negroes,' vituperates her master Leôncio when she refuses his advances.[21]

Isaura differs from the other slave women in every respect. Her 'stamp of superiority' alienates her from the women with whom she shares the misfortunes of slavery. She is a royal bird among vulgar fowls, says the narrator. The opposite pole of Isaura is Rosa, an 'envious, malevolent' mulatto girl, 'malicious and revengeful'.[22] Rosa is unscrupulous and promiscuous and for a long time was Leôncio's mistress – 'an easy conquest for him'.[23]

The novel considers different types of women and, in doing so, provides us with grounds for examining how nineteenth-century fiction expressed the sexual attitude of white men towards white and coloured women. Malvina embodies the virtuous wife, the ideal 'marriageable' woman. Her husband, however, looks for sexual satisfaction with the mulatto women in the story, Rosa and Isaura. The former is readily available; the latter is as unattainable as a star. But Leôncio lusts for Isaura, as he lusted for Rosa before. Both women are seen as prey, meant for his pleasure. In Leôncio's eyes, Rosa and Isaura belong to an essentially different species from that of his wife: they are sexual objects.

Rosa has two characteristics entirely absent in Isaura: sensuality and features revealing her African descent. The description of Rosa is one of the high points in the novel, when she transmits the vivacity lacking in the pale Isaura, whose face is 'calm and smooth like polished marble'.[24] Rosa is presented as follows:

> Svelte and flexible of body, she had a gracious face, lips somehow thick but well shaped, voluptuous, wet and red like chrysanthemums just blossomed in the April morning. … If it were not for the little golden ear-rings trembling in her small and well-framed ears, and the turgid, panting bosom which, like two mischievous little kids, jumped from below the transparent shirt, one would take her for a tricky, petulant lad.[25]

In describing Rosa, the author indulges freely in his erotic fantasies. The narrator treats her with a crudeness absent in descriptions of Malvina or Isaura. The direct motivation is Rosa's 'depravity': she is devoid of modesty and loyalty. But there are social and cultural motivations deriving from traditional patriarchal Western male (and female, for that matter) racial views. All the repressed sexuality in the text is concentrated on Rosa, the prototype of the perfidious sensual mulatto woman. In all cases, the text blocks the development of its female characters and, as commonly happens with clichés and stereotypes, the written product expresses the author's fantasies rather than a consistent sense of characterization.

The other black characters lack any individuality and endorse a plain sense of inferiority before the ruling class. Thus, André, the page, is sorry for Isaura, 'a girl so nice and gracious', being treated as one of the 'kitchen negresses'.[26] The slave quarters replicate the ideology of the salons. The slaves do not see themselves as a community and readily accept the spaces reserved for them. Only Isaura complains of her private fate – her 'sad destiny'. She has not a word to say about the fate of the other captives.

In quick brushstrokes, several aspects of slave society in Brazil are portrayed. It is here that the textual scene is amplified, leaving Leôncio and Malvina's farm in Campos, in the province of Rio de Janeiro, for the aristocratic salons of Recife. This allows the entrance of Álvaro, the romantic hero and mouthpiece of the abolitionist authorial discourse.

There are several references to the artificiality of life in metropolitan centres: Recife, for example, where the salons were 'temples of pleasure, of laughter and frivolity'.[27] Leôncio appears, at the beginning of the novel, to have just come from Europe 'with an empty mind … a corrupted soul and the heart damaged by habits of depravity'. Paris is mentioned as that 'vast pandemonium of luxury and pleasure';[28] there, Leôncio, a famed 'lion of the boulevards', seldom paid attention to the 'eloquent lectures of the great masters of the time and was never seen in museums, institutes of learning and libraries'.[29] While the text emphasizes Parisian licentiousness, in nostalgic opposition to the alleged purity of the Brazilian countryside, it also bows to European culture – including the scientific fashions of the time. So, the narrator gives credit to racist notions here embodied by Kaspar Lavater and his ideas, and insists on the 'correctness and nobility of Isaura's features' that correspond to Caucasian traits.[30] The denunciation of slavery is allied to the ethnocentric vision of society peculiar to the Europeanized Americas of those days, the actual life of the enslaved black community in the slave quarters being utterly ignored. It is as if slavery were basically the result of inhuman legislation operating in a vacuum and cruel enough to strike even an 'angel fallen from God's hand upon this earth', like Isaura.

However, in a moment of surprising lucidity, Bernardo Guimarães's novel insinuates that the preoccupation with praising the protagonist is to the detriment of reason – as we may see in this passage about Isaura: '[Her facial features] are so pure and delicate that they fascinate the eye, dazzle the mind and paralyse all analysis.'[31] On the level of plot, here, the narrative voice is describing the heroine; at another level, however, the text may be speaking of its own limitations, admitting that a spell of fascination is interposed between subject matter and analytical capacity.

Incidents in the Life of a Slave Girl

> All this, and much more, I thought of, as I sat at my loop-hole, waiting for the family to return from the grave; sometimes weeping, sometimes falling asleep, dreaming strange dreams of the dead and the living.
>
> (Linda Brent 1973)

The slave narrative which flourished in the United States mainly during the abolitionist campaign had as its primary goal to obtain the sympathy of the white readers. Thus, slave writers were encouraged by their sponsors to adopt conventional literary values, techniques and language, so much so that the authenticity of their production was often called into doubt. Contemporary re-evaluations of the slave narratives, however, have increasingly affirmed their importance as historical records and rich sources of learning.

Long recognized as a distinctive literary genre worthy of scholarly investigation, the slave narrative was influential in the work of African-American authors born in the twentieth century, including Langston Hughes, Richard Wright, James Baldwin, Alice Walker and Gayl Jones.[32] They appropriated and subverted the imposed literary forms through ironic humour and diverse linguistic devices, among them the creative transposition of the oral traditions coming from African cultures and often passed by word of mouth in customs and ceremonies. James Weldon Johnson, who was also the editor of pioneering anthologies of black American poetry and spirituals, emphasized the 'fusion of Negro idioms with Bible English' as he poetically transcribed the eloquence of old-time black preachers in his masterpiece, *God's Trombones* (1927).[33]

One of the last and the few slave narratives written by a woman, *Incidents in the Life of a Slave Girl* starts its story when the protagonist is very young ('I was born a slave' are the first words of Chapter 1, 'Childhood')[34] and ends with her as the mother of two children. She tells how she was able to save her life and her children when slavery was still a reality in half of the United States; in between, she narrates (always in the first person, as 'Linda') her previous life as a slave in South Carolina, the circumstances of her concealment, and her escape to the North. *Incidents* is a woman's book in which the theme of slavery revolves around a woman slave, her family ties and the dramatic links with the family who owned them. 'My mother's mistress was the granddaughter of my grandmother's mistress,' she explains in the initial chapter. Always the text emphasizes the role played by women, white and coloured: 'She was the foster sister of my mother; they were both nourished at my grandmother's breast. In fact, my mother had been weaned at three months old, that the babe of the mistress might obtain sufficient food. They played together as children.'[35]

The publication of *Incidents* was made possible by the help of another woman, Lydia Maria Child – a white Northern abolitionist who faithfully 'revised her manuscript', as she stated in her 'Introduction' to the book. Child explains her reasons for helping: 'I do this for the sake of my sisters in bondage, who are suffering wrongs so foul, that our ears are too delicate to listen to them'; she thus appeals to the 'reflecting women at the North [and] to a sense of their duty in the exertion of moral influence on the question of Slavery, on all possible occasions'.[36] So, in its genesis and fulfilment, one woman renders the narrative to another who will then expand the reading circle to encompass Northern women readers. The author, in turn, explains in the 'Preface' that she did not only want to tell the story of her own trials and tribulations. Her aim was to enlarge the scope of the narrative to illustrate the horrors of slavery as experienced by 'two millions of women' still enslaved in the South at that time, and 'to arouse the women of the North'.[37]

First and foremost in that 'pit of abominations'[38] that was slavery stood the fear and the reality of sexual abuse. The narrator/protagonist in *Incidents* establishes a sharp contrast between the perennial uncertainties and misery of black women's lives and those of 'happy women whose purity ha[d] been sheltered from childhood', as she pictures the life of white women.[39]

She was not wrong. In *Casa-grande e senzala* [*The Masters and the Slaves*] (1933), sociologist Gilberto Freyre confirmed, 'It was their bodies [slave women's] – at times, tiny ten-year-old bodies – that, in the moral architecture of Brazilian patriarchalism, constituted a formidable block of defense against bold attacks by Don Juans on the virtue of white ladies'.[40]

Freyre was referring specifically to slave society in Brazil, but his comment is pertinent wherever slavery existed. In the South of the United States, Linda Brent knew quite well what she was talking about when she wrote horrifying lines about the slave woman's life: 'She will become prematurely knowing in evil things. Soon she will learn to tremble when she hears her master's footfall. She will be compelled to realize that she is no longer a child.'[41]

More recently, Trudier Harris discussed the historical role played by power and family life in the United States, remarking that '[t]he white male's function, ostensibly, was to protect his home and especially the white woman who was the center of it'.[42] But even if 'the white man's craving for power' was stronger than his efforts to prevent 'mongrelization', as the author argues – and all this went on long after slavery was over– the constant fear of sexual exploitation and rape among black women was an everyday reality, described in history and in literature, fiction and non-fiction alike. William Faulkner was well aware of this when he wrote, in *Absalom, Absalom!*, of the 'baronial splendor' of Thomas Sutpen – and of the implications of such power for women, black or white, slave or free.[43]

In *Incidents*, even though female solidarity in suffering is a strong point to stress, Brent also took pains to depict other kinds of women, distant from her own plight. Cruelty was not a privilege of the masters only. Her Southern mistress, for instance, is described as follows:

> Mrs. Flint, like many southern women, was totally deficient in energy. She had not strength to superintend her household affairs; but her nerves were so strong, that she could sit in her easy chair and see a woman whipped, till the blood trickled from every stroke of the lash.[44]

Minute details are added to the picture:

> If dinner was not served at the exact time on that particular Sunday, she would station herself in the kitchen, and wait till it was dished, and then spit in all the kettles and pans that had been used for cooking. She did this to prevent the cook and her children from eking out their meagre fare with the remains of the gravy and other scrapings.[45]

Religious hypocrisy is part and parcel of that female cruelty: '[Mrs. Flint] was a member of the church; but partaking of the Lord's supper did not seem to put her in a Christian frame of mind.'[46] The issue of religiosity is strong in *Incidents*, and Christian teachings are shown as strategically enforced in the slaves' lives, in a sort of instruction that took two main things for granted: the assumed 'depravity of the slaves' hearts' and the hope of potential salvation from 'serving [their] masters faithfully'.[47] The chapter 'The Church and Slavery' starts crudely in these terms: 'After the alarm caused by Nat Turner's insurrection had subsided, the slaveholders came to the conclusion that it would be well to give the slaves enough of religious instruction to keep them from murdering their masters.'[48]

The awareness of the role played by religious education shows the intellectual independence of *Incidents* – remarkable, considering the circumstances and the time in which the book was published. The narrator/protagonist comments on the sermons and attitudes of Episcopal, Baptist and Methodist clergymen with a great deal of irony – observing, for instance, that the Episcopal preacher was 'kind enough' to offer a separate service on Sundays for the slaves' benefit.[49] A clear evaluation of the attempts to inculcate fear and subjection on the slaves pervades the text, and irony amounts to sarcasm in the reference to the 'touching proof of the attachment between slaveholders and their servants' shown by Mrs Flint, once present at a slave's funeral: 'and tender-hearted Mrs. Flint would have confirmed this impression, with handkerchief at her eyes'.[50] Simultaneously, the narrative voice denounces the ever-present prejudice about African spirituality, always associated with 'the practice of conjuring, or hoodooing, African magic' – a subject often present in sermons with the recurrent warning, 'Although your masters may not find you out, God sees you; and he will punish you.'[51]

The strong relationship of the slave community with death and religion – often through music – would later be appropriated in African-American fiction and poetry, as stated above. In *Go Tell It on the Mountain* (1952), James Baldwin wrote about modern church life in Harlem, New York, and the impact of religious practices on the black congregation:

> On Sunday mornings the women all seemed patient, all the men seemed mighty. ... then the tambourines began again, and the voices rose again, and the music swept on again, like fire, or flood, or judgment. Then the church seemed to swell with the Power it held, and, like a planet rocking in space, the temple rocked with the Power of God.[52]

At the dawn of the twentieth century, W. E. B. Du Bois had also acknowledged 'the deep religious feeling of the real Negro heart' in the ambiguous freedom of a second-class citizenship. Du Bois praised the force of the black music coming from the slave past: 'In these songs', he wrote in *The Souls of Black Folk*, 'the slave spoke to the world'.[53] In fact, he was anticipated by Linda Brent, who, in *Incidents*, ended musically the chapter 'The Church and Slavery':

> No wonder the slaves sing, –
> Ole Satan's church is here below;
> Up to God's free church I hope to go.[54]

Critical/Theoretical Issues: Jacques Derrida's *Supplement*

> Thus it is always possible for a text to become new, since the blanks open up its structure to an indefinitely disseminated transformation. The whiteness of the virgin paper, the blankness of the transparent column, reveals more than the neutrality of some medium; it uncovers the space of play or the play of space in which transformations are set off and sequences strung out.
>
> (Jacques Derrida 1982)

Voices of slaves were rarely taken into consideration in the hegemonic political emancipation campaigns and the corresponding literary production. Such voices were ignored, misused, or neutralized as replications of the whites' discourse.

Abolitionist leaders considered the perspectives of the black community to be unnecessary for the exposition of anti-slavery ideas and militant abolitionism. Illustrative of this are statements from the great Brazilian abolitionist Joaquim Nabuco in his *O abolicionismo* (1883). 'The abolitionist campaign, in fact, is not addressed to the slaves,' he wrote. 'It is not to the slaves that we speak, it is to the free.'[55]

The black abolitionist poet, lawyer and orator from Bahia, Luiz Gama (1830–82), wrote in one of his satirical poems,

> Sciences and letters
> Are not for thee,
> Darkies from the Coast
> Are not people here.
> ...
> I am sorry, my dear friend,

> I can give you nothing;
> In this land where the whites command,
> They deprive us even of thinking![56]

In the United States, black journalists like John Russwurm and Samuel Cornish, editors of the first black newspaper (*Freedom's Journal*, established in 1827 to promote abolitionism), were also extremely sensitive about this interdiction, and theirs was a voice of intellectual rebellion: 'Too long have others spoken for us. Too long has the publick been deceived by misrepresentations.'[57]

The eloquent silence of slaves and of the black community in general is manifest in mainstream abolitionist literature in the Americas – in the United States, for instance, in the poetry of Henry Wadsworth Longfellow ('The Witnesses') and of John Greenleaf Whittier ('The Panorama' and 'The Slave-Ships').[58]

In the course of the nineteenth century, the progress of black journalism, as well as the publication of slave narratives and autobiographies in the United States – many of them instantly valued by readers, active abolitionists or not, in the free states – helped to draw critical attention to the scarcity of black voices in the cultural and political milieu; and to highlight inherent tensions, inevitably exposed and denounced by the ever more abundant writings of black male and female authors in different American countries.[59]

These days, we investigate such rigid separations and limitations – the result of intricate games of knowledge and power in colonial and postcolonial societies – as we approach past cultural materials with new interpretative tools. In doing so, we discover that the seeming obstacle of textual gaps and empty spaces may be converted into an analytical tool, since the textual blanks – actually part and parcel of any discursive structure – open the text up to indefinitely disseminated transformation, as Jacques Derrida explains in *Dissemination*.[60] According to Silviano Santiago, '[a] text always gives itself in a scene of representation and, thus … what is manifest is always a *dissimulation*, masking the original sense of the text, which never offers itself whole and present'.[61]

Both *A escrava Isaura* and *Incidents in the Life of a Slave Girl* condemn the social world in which slavery reigned supreme. They belong to distinct literary forms and were written by authors with different genders, nationalities, racial origins and social backgrounds. In interpretation, however, one must be careful when faced by disparate discursive perspectives not to attempt to achieve some sense of completion and thus fall into the 'metaphysical trap' well described by Jacques Derrida.

According to Derrida, since Plato, Western philosophical thought has been characterized by the desire for an ultimate principle of truth or reason and the concomitant idea of a centre – an origin, a truth, an ideal form, a fixed point, a 'transcendental signified' – as a guarantee of all meanings.[62] This thinking constitutes, in Derrida's terms, a logocentric *logic of the complement* that attempts to repress difference (and *différance*) in favour of identity and presence; and it endorses classic dichotomies or mutually exclusive dualities like within/without, good/evil, true/false, essence/appearance, central/marginal, abolitionism/slavery.[63] In literature, this dichotomy is found, par excellence, in the thesis genre by way of the eternal opposition it establishes between right and wrong.

Decentred thought, as proposed by Derrida and supported by much postmodern, postcolonial criticism, argues that binary oppositions, with their inherent hierarchies and sense of exclusion, repress the limitless instability of language. What a deconstructive reading envisages, instead, is the endless proliferation of different interpretations in a 'multiplicity of possibilities' among the uncertainties of signification.[64]

We will not attempt here any sort of 'conclusive' reading of the two texts under consideration – for the simple reason that definitive readings do not exist. *Isaura* and *Incidents* do not 'complement' one another, since neither text is intended to 'complete' the other, or our comprehension of the other or, in this case, of slavery in its 'totality', since each text acts upon differences. What is really of interest is the *play of textuality* discussed specifically by Derrida in his concept of the '*supplement*', and the great value of this concept in and for comparative endeavours such as this chapter's.

The *supplement* is an addition, a disposable signifying that is added to replace and suppress a lack on the side of the signified, and to provide a necessary excess. The *logic of the supplement* can only be contemplated in decentred thought. The absence of a centre (or 'transcendental signified': the fixed origin, the point of presence, as stated above) makes the game of replacements possible in the field of language. In fact, the text corresponds to a game of absence and presence, since there is always the possibility to relocate an occasional 'centre', or position of reference. So, each act of interpretation opens up to others, and so on, infinitely. In this way, there is an endless supplemental movement in the *play of textuality,* which always has a plurality of different meanings: the text is nothing but a *play of differences;* and 'difference is therefore no longer a matter merely of distinctions; as an empty space it operates both as a divider and as a stimulus for the linking of what has been divided'.[65]

Final Remarks: *Isaura*, *Incidents*

> Leôncio had blown his brains out with a pistol shot.
>
> (Bernardo Guimarães 1998)

The considerations above lead us to characterize the textual attitudes towards slavery and the respective writing strategies not as complementary – as a hurried reading might suppose – but rather as supplementary. Our joint approach to *Isaura* and *Incidents* will therefore privilege not the evident textual oppositions (black female author versus white male author) but, rather, the *play of differences* that the respective textualities display and a comparative reading enhances. Some textual aspects will, thereby, be emphasized, as they stand out in their similarities and differences. They are: religiosity; family and communal life; motherhood; the literary treatment of slavery. The notion of the authorial *speaking position* is fundamental at this point, as we shall see in what follows.

In Djamila Ribeiro's words, the notion of a speaking position or, in more specifically critical terms, the standpoint theory was initially developed by the black feminist movement as a refutation of traditional historiography and knowledge as resulting from social hierarchy. Ribeiro draws attention to the production of historically marginalized groups, especially in structures of oppression such as slavery and colonialism; groups that now speak as political subjects.[66] In the same vein, Patricia Collins has suggested that the place of marginality traditionally occupied by black women in society demands creativity in the development of theories and thought reflecting these women's viewpoints and perspectives – i.e., their standpoint.[67] We may now go back to our two texts and see how their respective speaking positions interfere in the textual dynamics when we consider the topics listed above.

In *Isaura*, spirituality is practically non-existent – except at the moment when Isaura prays to the 'Virgin of Mercy, Holy Mother of God', begging to be delivered from her torturer.[68] Isaura's prayer is the only reference to spirituality in the whole novel. The conjunction of religious faith and familial love provides, here, a brief touch of warmth in the gloomy sequence of events. It is when the heroine is praying that her father, the Portuguese labourer Miguel, reappears on the scene and tells his daughter of his plan for their escape. Miguel is all the family that Isaura has on this earth; his paternal presence remains strong throughout the rest of the narrative. He is also her only friend: Isaura is virtually isolated, since the divide between her and the slave community is enormous, if not absolute. The narrative voice is entirely oblivious of the slave quarters and their inhabitants, as we have seen, and a heavy silence prevails as regards the slaves' personal and communal lives.

Incidents, on the other hand, incorporates in its discursive texture the strength coming from the religious practices of the enslaved community. We have already seen the boldness with which the narrative criticizes the strategic imposition of Christianity on slaves and the emphasis on black religion, black attitudes in relation to Christianity and particular forms of expression in dealing with this life and the hereafter. Moreover, a sense of sturdy dignity permeates the dialogues between the protagonist and her peers – family and friends, literate or illiterate. All this gives the slave community the comfort and solidarity of a cohesive group, since their troubles are shared by all.

These striking differences between the two works have to do with the speaking position that each author and the corresponding narrative perspective occupy – *Isaura* being the work of an erudite writer who taught philosophy and foreign languages in different schools in Minas Gerais; *Incidents* a text written by a slave woman, whose critique of slavery was rooted in female experience not as a solitary individual but rather 'from within an intricate network of family relations'.[69] In Linda Brent's text, the authoress/narrator/protagonist assumes the risk 'of the speaking act with all its implications' – to paraphrase the lucid words of Lélia Gonzalez.[70] On the other hand, women are virtually silent in *Isaura*, as we have seen. They do not have a voice of their own, and suffer the infantilism of having others speak for them.[71]

Another aspect that deserves comparative attention is motherhood – an issue about which there is also a deafening silence in *Isaura*. The protagonist and the enslaved women Isaura is supposed to represent are not pictured as mothers and there is no textual indication that Isaura will ever be one, in spite of her eventually happy love affair with Álvaro. *Isaura* is a novel without children. This is not just an authorial option in the construction of the plot. Rather, we can observe that nineteenth-century Brazilian literature (as well as American literatures in general) found it extremely difficult to deal with the theme of mixed-race progeny. Inter-racial motherhood was, for centuries, a complicated issue, especially in relation to characters of African descent; the treatment given to Indians, in Brazilian literature, was quite different.[72] Until relatively late into the twentieth century, the hegemonic, canonical literature involving African-Brazilian characters tended to be childless.[73] In the nineteenth century, the plot never went beyond the prospective wedding day of the hero and heroine (the case for *Isaura*); or it offered, instead, a disastrous outcome, as in the abolitionist play *Mãe* [*Mother*] (1860) by José de Alencar and the naturalist novel *O mulato* [*The Mulatto*] (1881) by Aluísio Azevedo. In Azevedo's novel, the white Ana Rosa suffers a bloody miscarriage when she sees the dead body of her mulatto lover. In *Mãe*, the slave protagonist – the mother in the title – dies so that the wedding of her son to a white woman may happen without her troublesome presence.[74]

In *Incidents* – as an African-American writing – this theme is treated very differently. Linda, the protagonist, is the proud mother of two children by a white man (about whose character and behaviour there are rather ambiguous allusions). On the other hand, the slave families and their homes and ambiance are represented, as well as children of different racial and social groups. The narrative in *Isaura* never crosses the threshold of the slave quarters, and concentrates its descriptions and action in the rooms of the big house inhabited by Leôncio and Malvina, the salons in Recife, and the dungeon where Isaura is imprisoned and chained to the wall.

Discussion of slavery itself is limited in *Isaura*. There is only one debate about the slave system, which occurs in the conversation between Álvaro and the experienced lawyer Dr Geraldo (Chapter 15). They discuss the judicial aspects of slavery and Geraldo tries to persuade Álvaro that, according to current Brazilian legislation, there are no legal means by which his friend may set Isaura free from her legitimate owner – about which the lawyer is absolutely right.

My comparative reading will, at this point, go beyond abolitionist feelings and moral or legal allegations about slavery – present in both texts – in order to examine how the *play of textuality* functions differently in the two works in relation to the respective outcomes. There is a happy ending in *Incidents*, directly addressed to the reader: 'Reader, my story ends with freedom; not in the usual way, with marriage. I and my children are now free!'[75] *Isaura* ends with Leôncio's suicide and, in so doing, provides us with a richly symbolic outcome. The novel transcends the limitations that circumscribe its social, political achievement, offering as compensation the sudden, unexpected annihilation of the villain – to the astonishment of characters and readers alike.

Bernardo Guimarães's fictional work does not anticipate the end of the slave regime. It does not indulge, either, in final sentimental scenes and words of love between the heroine and her saviour. It presents, instead, the self-inflicted death of an unrepentant slave master – which sounds like the outcome of a feuilleton rather than of a romantic, abolitionist thesis novel. The last sentence in the text (reproduced in the epigraph of this section) means death and destruction – and the story does not finish 'in the usual way with marriage', we might add, in Linda Brent's words.

With Leôncio's suicide, the narrative justifies its trajectory, the blank spaces of silence confirm their efficacy as interpretative instruments and *A escrava Isaura* redeems itself.

Notes

1. Alves 1953, 457. In this chapter, all translations into English are my own, unless otherwise specified.
2. Guimarães 1998; Brent 1973. The texts under analysis will be referred to as *Isaura* and *Incidents*, respectively.
3. Suleiman 1983, 153–4.
4. Gomes 2009, 153–8.
5. Brent 1973, xiii.
6. Vallade 1996, 9.
7. Carson 1992, 228.
8. Costa Lima 2006, 350.
9. Costa Lima 2006, 352.
10. Costa Lima 2006, 348.
11. Baldick 1996, 83; Antonio Candido 1975, Vol. 2, 243.
12. Bosi 1974, 159.
13. Antonio Candido 1975, 238.
14. Guimarães 1998, 24.
15. Guimarães 1998, 26
16. Guimarães 1998, 19–20.
17. Guimarães 1998, 81.
18. Guimarães 1998, 74.
19. Guimarães 1998, 55.
20. Guimarães 1998, 13–14.
21. Guimarães 1998, 69.
22. Guimarães 1998, 52.
23. Guimarães 1998, 50, 52.
24. Guimarães 1998,12.
25. Guimarães 1998, 48.
26. Guimarães 1998, 147.
27. Guimarães 1998, 68.
28. Guimarães 1998, 16–17.
29. Guimarães 1998, 16.
30. Guimarães 1998, 102.
31. Guimarães 1998, 12
32. Vallade 1996, 336.
33. Johnson 1955, 9.
34. Brent 1973, 3.
35. Brent 1973, 5.
36. Child 1973, xii.
37. Brent 1973, xiv.
38. Brent 1973, xiv.
39. Brent 1973, 54.
40. Freyre 1986, 455.
41. Brent 1973, 27.
42. Harris 1998, 299–300.

43. Faulkner 1972, 39.
44. Brent 1973, 10.
45. Brent 1973, 12.
46. Brent 1973, 10.
47. Brent 1973, 70.
48. Brent 1973, 69.
49. Brent 1973, 69.
50. Brent 1973, 150.
51. Brent 1973, 150.
52. Baldwin 1953, 15.
53. Du Bois 1982, 270.
54. Brent 1973, 77.
55. Nabuco 1977, 71.
56. Gama 1974, 41–2.
57. Litwack 1968, 207.
58. Gomes 2009, 170. I consider the poetry of Castro Alves to be a remarkable exception to that prevailing nineteenth-century tendency. See Gomes 1988, 67–77.
59. In Brazil, Maria Firmina dos Reis, Luiz Gama, José do Patrocínio and the symbolist poet Cruz e Sousa were some of the pioneers in the configuration of the Afro-Brazilian literary canon in the nineteenth century – together with the great novelist Machado de Assis. See Duarte 2011.
60. Derrida 1982, 345.
61. Santiago 1976, 93.
62. Santiago 1976, 14, 71, 84; Baldick 1996, 125.
63. The concepts of logocentrism and *différance* will not be discussed here, although their importance in Derrida's thought must always be acknowledged.
64. Iser 1993, 74.
65. Iser 1993, 229.
66. Ribeiro 2017, 30, 49, 64.
67. Collins 2000, 45.
68. Guimarães 1998, 71.
69. Carson 1992, 228.
70. Gonzalez 1984, 225.
71. Ribeiro 2017, 13.
72. Gomes 1988, 25–31.
73. Queiroz Junior 1982, 122.
74. Gomes 2009, 164–5.
75. Brent 1973, 207.

Bibliography

Alves, Antonio Castro. *Poesias completas*. São Paulo: Edição Saraiva, 1953.

Antonio Candido. *Formação da literatura brasileira (momentos decisivos)*. Belo Horizonte: Itatiaia, 1975.

Baldick, Chris. *The Concise Oxford Dictionary of Literary Terms*. Oxford: Oxford University Press, 1996.

Baldwin, James. *Go Tell It on the Mountain*. New York: Dell, 1953.

Bosi, Alfredo. *História concisa da literatura brasileira*. São Paulo: Cultrix, 1974.

Brent, Linda. *Incidents in the Life of a Slave Girl*. New York: Harcourt Brace, 1973.

Carson, Sharon. 'Incidents in the Life of a Slave Girl'. In *Masterpieces of African-American Literature*, edited by Frank N. Magill, 226–9. New York: Salem Press, 1992.

Child, L. Maria. 'Introduction'. In Linda Brent, *Incidents in the Life of a Slave Girl*. New York: Harcourt Brace, 1973.

Collins, Patricia Hill. *Black Feminist Thought: Knowledge, Consciousness and the Politics of Empowerment*. New York: Routledge, 2000.

Costa Lima, Luiz. *História. Ficção. Literatura*. São Paulo: Companhia das Letras, 2006.

Derrida, Jacques. *Dissemination*, translated by Barbara Johnson. Chicago: University of Chicago Press, 1982.
Duarte, Eduardo de Assis. *Literatura e afrodescendência no Brasil – antologia crítica*. Belo Horizonte: Editora UFMG, 2011.
Du Bois, W. E. B. *The Souls of Black Folk*. New York: NAL Penguin, 1982.
Faulkner, William. *Absalom, Absalom!* New York: Vintage Books, 1972.
Freyre, Gilberto. *The Masters and the Slaves: A Study in the Development of Brazilian Civilization*, translated by Samuel Putnam. Berkeley: University of California Press, 1986.
Gama, Luís. 'No álbum do meu amigo J. A. da Silva Sobral'. In *Trovas burlescas*, 39–42. São Paulo: Editora Três, 1974.
Gomes, Heloisa Toller. *O negro e o romantismo brasileiro*. São Paulo: Atual Editora, 1988.
Gomes, Heloisa Toller. *As marcas da escravidão: o negro e o discurso oitocentista no Brasil e nos Estados Unidos*. Rio de Janeiro: EdUERJ, 2009.
Gonzalez, Lélia. 'Racismo e sexismo na cultura brasileira'. *Revista Ciências Sociais Hoje* ANPOCS (1984): 223–44. https://www.academia.edu/27681600/Racismo_e_Sexismo_na_Cultura_Brasileira_-_L%C3%A9lia_Gonzales.pdf
Guimarães, Bernardo. *A escrava Isaura*. Porto Alegre: L&PM Editores, 1998.
Harris, Trudier. 'White Men as Performers in the Lynching Ritual'. In *Black on White: Black Writers on What It Means to Be White*, edited by David R. Roediger, 299–304. New York: Schocken Books, 1998.
Iser, Wolfgang. *The Fictive and the Imaginary: Charting Literary Anthropology*. Baltimore, MD: Johns Hopkins University Press, 1993.
Johnson, James Weldon. *God's Trombones: Seven Negro Sermons in Verse*. New York: Penguin Books, 1955.
Litwack, Leon. 'The Black Abolitionists'. In *Black History: A Reappraisal*, edited by Melvin Drimmer, 206–20. New York: Doubleday, 1968.
Meireles, Cecília. 'Ballad of the Ten Casino Dancers', translated by James Merrill. In *An Anthology of Twentieth-Century Brazilian Poetry*, edited by Elizabeth Bishop and Emanuel Brasil, 39–41. Middletown, CT: Wesleyan University Press, 1972.
Nabuco, Joaquim. *O abolicionismo*. Petrópolis: Vozes, 1977.
Queiroz Junior, Teófilo de. *Preconceito de cor e a mulata na literatura brasileira*. São Paulo: Ática, 1982.
Ribeiro, Djamila. *O que é lugar de fala?* Belo Horizonte: Letramento, 2017.
Santiago, Silviano (ed.). *Glossário de Derrida*. Rio de Janeiro: Francisco Alves, 1976.
Suleiman, Susan. *Le roman à these: ou l'autorité fictive*. Paris: Presses Universitaires de France, 1983.
Vallade III, Roger M. *The Essential Black Literature Guide*. Detroit, MI: Visible Ink Press, 1996.
Whittier, John Greenleaf. 'The Slave-Ships'. In *Complete Works of Whittier*, 265–7. Boston, MA: Houghton Mifflin, 1984.

9
The Construction of Pseudo-Modern Individuals in *Senhora* by José de Alencar

Maria Eulália Ramicelli

José de Alencar's Views on Writing Novels in Brazil

In 1872 in Rio de Janeiro the famous writer-journalist-politician José de Alencar launched his latest novel, *Sonhos d'ouro* [*Golden Dreams*].[1] The narrative is preceded by a text entitled 'Bênção paterna' [Paternal Blessing], dating from 23 July 1872, in which Alencar presents his ideas about writing novels in Brazil.

The central point of 'Bênção paterna' is the claim that Brazilians have the right to have their own literature, written in the Brazilian form of the Portuguese language and shaped by the particular socio-cultural circumstances that underpin the formation of the Brazilian nation. Upon this premise, Alencar systematizes his own fiction by grouping his novels according to broad geo-historical themes that comprise formative past and present aspects of Brazilian people and culture. Besides considering specific aspects of the Brazilian context, Alencar makes several remarks about the novel, which he believes to be the literary genre most suited to the contemporary moment, given its lighter content and unobtrusive form.

Alencar's arguments can be better understood if considered against the broad context of literary production in Brazil. It was not until the late 1830s that Brazilian fiction (initially in short form) began to be produced systematically. At the time, the country was going through a turbulent phase in consolidating its political independence after Portugal had attempted to recolonize Brazil and provincial revolts against the central government in Rio de Janeiro had threatened the country's territorial unity. The serious threat of disintegration was particularly felt by politicians and writers based in Rio de Janeiro. In this context of strong political and economic instability, nationalism (a key idea of European romanticism) was an important ideological principle to Brazilian writers, who worked intensively to cultivate a national sensibility. Brazilian writers from Rio de Janeiro used fiction to make the different Brazilian regions and their inhabitants known to readers (however few in number they were). Furthermore, writing fiction entailed the praise of certain historical events and persons (considered heroic for their unifying purposes and principles) and of the beauty of the unique Brazilian natural landscape (regarded as the hallmark of the new country). In short, producing fiction, especially novels, was central to the Brazil's nationalist literary programme in the nineteenth century.

José de Alencar played an interesting and complex role in this political–literary context. Although his fiction certainly contributed to the consolidation of Brazilian literature (notably the Brazilian novel) in line with the romantic nationalist trend, he nevertheless also opened the way for a critical perspective on the strong national bias of Brazilian literary critics and writers who insisted that local colour was an indispensable element in Brazilian literature. In 'Bênção paterna' the author asserts that Brazilian novels do not need to have 'that piquant flavour of the land'.[2] He goes on to argue that what Brazilians call 'national literature' is the result of the inevitable and continuous importation of foreign ideas and cultural forms. It is worth remarking that José de Alencar first considered the question of the 'imitation of models' in Brazil in a letter to Machado de Assis (dated February 1868) in which he introduced Castro Alves, then a promising young poet just arrived from Bahia. In this text, Alencar affirmed that Castro Alves was a disciple of Victor Hugo but that his poetry already expressed the 'feeling of nationality'.[3] In March 1873, Machado de Assis published an essay in which he used a slightly different term – 'national instinct' – to develop the discussion about the creation of a national sensibility in literature.[4] Machado's essay has been more frequently cited by scholars than Alencar's letter. In this regard, I would like to highlight the work of the Brazilian literary critic Valéria De Marco, who selected this letter and other important texts of José de Alencar in order to analyse his trajectory as a critic.[5]

The importance of 'Bênção paterna' resides in the fact that it presents Alencar's more detailed discussion of the matter and his understanding of the implications and difficulties of producing literature in Brazil. Alencar maintains that Brazilian literature, just like Brazilian society, is the positive result of the continuous importation of foreign material which then mingles with the 'American sap'. This process was started by the Portuguese colonists and became more intense with increased 'contact with other peoples and [the] influx of civilization'. As Alencar remarks, the new Brazilian society and its sense of nationality were being formed through the mixing of 'traces of other nationalities – the English, the Italian, the Spanish, the American, but most notably the Portuguese and the French'.[6] Consequently,

> The struggle between local spirit and foreign invasion is reflected in *Lucíola* [*Lucíola*], *Diva* [*Diva*], *A Pata da Gazela* [*The Foot of the Gazelle*], and in you, little book, which is going to travel the world under the title of *Sonhos D'Ouro*.
>
> To accuse these books of being of foreign confection is, begging critics' pardon, to reveal a profound ignorance of carioca society, which is, right here, showing off its Parisian bows and frills, and speaking the universal tongue, the language of progress, a jargon littered with French, English, Italian and now German terms. How can we hope to photograph this society without copying down its features?[7]

Alencar's statement about the amalgamation of foreign and local elements in the making of Brazilian literature matters because the nature and the degree of this process have been a contentious issue in discussions of the formation of Brazilian literature and culture. When we turn to Alencar's output as a novelist, this issue becomes even more interesting and significant because his novels articulate, with a higher level of accomplishment, the trial-and-error process of combining imported and local content. In other words, Alencar's novels pose the problem of the direct use of successful European formulations of the novel to represent the Brazilian context in a more productive way.

The modern novel has a complex and multifaceted history in Europe. Central to the large variety of themes, narrative forms and techniques that constitute this history – in and across the different European contexts – is the representation of the *individual*. In his indispensable work about the beginnings of the modern novel in England, Ian Watt emphasizes the growing interest in and the centrality of the individual in the modern period.[8] Watt also outlines the historical and philosophical conditions that led up to this socio-cultural–economic–political scenario. It is no coincidence that Watt stresses these issues in the opening section of his chapter on *Robinson Crusoe*, whose protagonist is a powerfully resourceful individual. When presenting the socio-cultural grounds for the emphasis on the individual, Watt states that this condition can only exist in a society characterized by 'individualism':

> [The concept of individualism] posits a whole society mainly governed by the idea of every individual's intrinsic independence both from other individuals and from the multifarious allegiance to past modes of thought and action denoted by the word 'tradition' – a force that is always social, not individual. The existence of such a society, in turn, obviously depends on a special type of economic and political organization and on an appropriate ideology; more specifically, on an economic and political organization which allows its members a very wide range of choices in their actions, and on an ideology primarily based … on the autonomy of the individual, irrespective of his particular social status or personal capacity. It is generally agreed that modern society is uniquely individualist in these respects, and that of the many historical causes for its emergence two are of supreme importance – the rise of modern industrial capitalism and the spread of Protestantism, especially in its Calvinist or Puritan forms.[9]

England was the first country to create the basic conditions for the emergence of an individualist society in the terms presented by Watt. At different paces and with particular features, other countries in Europe and elsewhere underwent this highly influential historical process. In this context, literature – mainly the novel – successfully contributed to the construction of the figure of the autonomous individual. The realist tradition in literature has been very important to the construction of the most enduring values that have shaped the modern individual and their mode of life. Those values became central to bourgeois society. As Franco Moretti explains: 'In the course of the nineteenth century, once the stigma against "new wealth" had been overcome, a few recurrent traits clustered around this figure [the bourgeois]: energy, first of all; self-restraint; intellectual clarity; commercial honesty; a strong sense of goals.'[10]

In broad terms, this is the foreign (i.e., European) socio-cultural–economic–political process formalized by the novel, which reached Brazil as a sign of modernity and civilization. As Alencar himself affirms in his preface to *Sonhos d'ouro*, by reading (or listening to someone reading) and by writing novels in Brazil, one was in tune with the prevailing system of ideas and cultural forms in the Western world. However, cultural and literary forms cannot simply be reproduced in different contexts as if they were abstractions of their own context of production. In this regard, *Senhora: perfil de mulher* [*Senhora: Profile of a Woman*] (Alencar's urban novel after *Sonhos d'ouro*) provides rich material with which to reflect on important implications of writing novels in Brazil in the nineteenth century.[11] On the basis of an analysis of internal focalization and the protagonists, I will discuss the problematic representation of the modern individual in *Senhora* and argue that the friction between foreign and local elements is at the centre of this narrative.

Senhora: The Complex Adjustment of European Models of the Novel to the Brazilian Context

Senhora is one of the most important nineteenth-century Brazilian novels. Considered by Brazilian literary critic Roberto Schwarz to be 'one of Alencar's most carefully constructed books',[12] *Senhora* is the main subject of his in-depth discussion of the challenges experienced by the first Brazilian writers who tried to write *Brazilian* novels. José de Alencar is confirmed as a pivotal figure because the shortcomings of his fiction express nodal conflict points of the Brazilian milieu after independence.

First published in 1875, *Senhora* is divided into four parts with titles that characterize the story of Aurélia Camargo and Fernando Seixas's marriage as one of commercial transaction: 'The Price', 'Redress', 'Possession', 'Ransom'. The narrative is thus shown to be about the determining power of money in people's lives, a common theme in European novels because of its centrality in modern societies.

From the beginning, the protagonists' romantic relationship is marked by their different attitudes towards money and feeling. Seixas is a civil servant and a newspaper contributor with economic and political ambitions, who lives as a man about town but without the means to afford his costly lifestyle. The narrator affirms that Seixas is driven by gallantry and that he has 'aristocratic instincts and the panicky terror of toil and mediocrity'.[13] These personal traits explain why the 'indolent' Seixas[14] leaves poor Aurélia with an eye to a lucrative marriage with Adelaide Amaral. In turn, Aurélia has a strong aversion to the mercantilization of people. For instance, when still an impoverished young lady, she accedes to her sick mother's entreaties that she stand by the window in order to attract the attention of some eligible young man, but Aurélia feels uncomfortable in this situation:

> This public display of her beauty, with an eye to marriage, was a cruel torture for the girl. She overcame the repulsion at such a display of wares and endured the humiliation for love of the woman to whom she owed her being and whose only thought was for her happiness.[15]

Even after inheriting a fortune from her paternal grandfather (Lourenço Camargo), Aurélia considers money degrading because it corrupts the human soul: 'she considered the gold a vile metal that debased men; and in her heart, she felt deeply humiliated thinking that to all these people who surrounded her, she, herself, merited none of the flattery that they dedicated to each of her thousands in capital'.[16] As a result, Aurélia despises and publicly humiliates most of her suitors. More importantly, she uses her money and pulls strings in the marriage market in order to avenge herself on Fernando Seixas. On their wedding night, she says to his face,

> I am rich, very rich, I am a millionaire; I needed a husband, a trinket that every respectable woman must have. You were in the market; I bought you. You cost me one hundred thousand; it was cheap. You did not place a high enough value on yourself. I would have given twice, three times as much, my entire fortune, for this moment.[17]

Aurélia knows that her personal revenge entails Seixas's socio-economic debasement and humiliation. Seixas always considered money to be the only conquest that really matters in life, but now his humiliating position eventually makes him change his mind.

The conflict established between material ambition on the one hand and sincere feeling and clear conscience on the other is restricted to the protagonists. This situation builds a degree of disconnection between the pair Aurélia–Seixas and all the other characters in the novel. It is true that money is an impediment for Adelaide Amaral and Torquato da Costa Ribeiro's love. However, early in the narrative (Chapters 4, 8 and 9 in Part 1), this problem is quickly solved by Aurélia as part of her plan to marry Seixas. Aurélia's corrosive vengeful feelings do not undermine her true concern for poor Torquato, who stood by her when she herself was poor and an orphan. While money has central importance in the conflict lived by the protagonists, general material comfort and/or security is a matter of careful consideration for some of the secondary characters, such as Dona Firmina Mascarenhas and Mr Lemos (Aurélia's uncle and guardian). Dona Firmina lives in Aurélia's house to serve as her chaperone and does her best to please the young lady at all times. Mr Lemos constantly adjusts his plans for and his ideas about his niece so as to guarantee his position by her side and, thereby, to guarantee his personal profit. Dona Firmina and Mr Lemos understand that pleasing Aurélia and indulging her whims are the only safe means they have to maintain their comfortable economic position. The unstable economic circumstances under which these characters live (circumstances that have implications for the socio-economic connections they wish to establish or maintain) are highlighted by the narrator with a humorous tone throughout the narrative. The narrator also has a different approach to presenting Lourenço Camargo's violence against the relatives who have tried to live on his wealth. The passage in question is narrated with a humorous and matter-of-fact tone, implying that old Camargo's brutal physical reaction to his idle relatives is to be expected from a man of means.[18] The content of this particular passage in *Senhora* (physical violence lightly narrated so it feels like an ordinary event) is predominant in another important, and peculiar, nineteenth-century Brazilian novel – *Memórias de um sargento de milícias* [*Memoirs of a Militia Sergeant*] (1854–5).[19]

In *Senhora*, money (rather than old forms of wealth, such as land possession) brings a serious narrative tone and is the cause of dramatic moral conflicts intensely experienced only by Aurélia and Seixas. In contrast, the secondary characters in the novel form

> a simple and familiar milieu, which has potential for suffering and conflict, without itself being called into question, since it is legitimized by the natural and appealing ability of the characters to get by on the day-to-day level. The businessmen are rascals, little sisters are self-effacing, relatives are on the make; vices, virtues and defects are calmly acknowledged and described in such a way that the prose retains its sense of proportion. It is neither conformist, since it does not set out to justify, nor is it critical as such, since there is no desire to transform.[20]

Roberto Schwarz goes on to argue that the secondary characters are responsible for the realistic tone in *Senhora* because they represent 'the local social scene',[21] which is narrated in 'a more relaxed tone'.[22] However, this realistic content runs through the margins of the narrative as 'local color rather than as an active, structural element'.[23] Schwarz points out that this imbalance in the construction of the plot in *Senhora* expresses the lack of linear correspondence between important European social issues, which were central themes of European novels, and Brazilian social issues. It is worth noting that the central line of action and some strong characteristics of the protagonists in *Senhora* echo those in Balzac's fiction. Alencar was a reader of Balzac and is acknowledged to have taken the French writer's novels as models for his own work. In his autobiographical account of how he became a novelist, Alencar recalled the period when he was a law student in São Paulo. There he had access to the private library of a senior student and Balzac was the first writer he struggled to read in French. From Balzac, Alencar moved on to Alexandre Dumas, Alfred de Vigny, Chateaubriand and Victor Hugo.[24] Balzac's realist construction of plots and characters underpins important elements of Alencar's urban novels, notably *Senhora*. In Schwarz's words:

> the plot and its characters [Aurélia and Seixas] are in the tradition of Balzac. With much self-analysis and suffering they play out one of the great ideological themes of the period to its improbable logical conclusion ... Aurélia is fashioned in the iron-clad, unyielding mould of the avengers, the alchemists, the money-lenders, the artists, the social climbers, etc., of the *Comédie humaine*; like them, she grasps an idea – one of those that had caught the imagination of the century – and from then on, without it, her life has no meaning.[25]

Aurélia and Seixas's private battle as a married couple is sustained by strong moral principles regarding both the power that money can exert over personal conduct and the individual's right to live by their own principles. In one of their caustic dialogues, Seixas declares to Aurélia,

> I sold you a husband; you have him at your disposal, as owner and mistress that you are. However, I did not sell you my soul, my character, my individuality; because this a man cannot alienate from himself, and you, madam, knew perfectly well that you could not purchase it at the price of gold.[26]

Despite Seixas's strong defence of his individuality, his resignation and humiliation predominate throughout the story. For a nineteenth-century protagonist, Seixas embodies the unusual combination of indolence and ineffective action. As he subsequently says to Aurélia, 'If it is my whim that I should pretend to be sober, economical, industrious, I am fully within my rights; no one can forbid me this hypocrisy, nor impose upon me certain social skills and force me to behave like a glutton, an indolent, and a wastrel.'[27]

Schwarz does not give Fernando Seixas much consideration in his discussion of *Senhora*. The Brazilian critic is more interested in comparing Alencar's uneven narrative pattern with Machado de Assis's more successful handling of the narrative possibilities offered by the European realistic novel to construct protagonists that would express his critical view of the social mechanism in Brazil. Therefore, Schwarz highlights the disconnect between the particular Brazilian tone and socio-ideological preoccupations represented in the secondary characters, and the European ones represented in Aurélia Camargo. It is worth remarking that he uses the terms 'peripheral characters' versus 'central characters' in order to provide an analytical connection of socio-cultural and ideological aspects to narrative aspects.[28] Schwarz goes as far as to claim that if the secondary characters were removed from *Senhora*, then the internal dissonance between foreign narrative tone and content and the local ones would disappear.[29] However, as suggested above, the relation between point of view and the pair of protagonists expresses the type of dissonance and narrative instability discussed by Schwarz. It also poses the problem of representation of the modern individual in the novel. As we shall see, Alencar built narrative emphasis on Seixas's way of thinking rather than on Aurélia's. By doing so, he highlights Seixas's constricted circular rationale, expressing the suffocation of the self. Aurélia's mindset also has traces of archaic thinking that construct her as a 'master' rather than a modern individual. Thus, *Senhora* presents a conflicting combination of foreign and local content in more narrative layers than has previously been presumed.

Fernando Seixas: The Rationale of the Dependant

The first day of Aurélia and Seixas's married life is marked by strangeness and discomfort for both of them:

> Aurélia, weary of the comedy she had acted throughout the day, leaned against the cushion and, closing her eyes, became absorbed in her thoughts. Fernando respected this meditation; so much more since his spirit was also yielding to an irresistible concern.
>
> The evening had aroused in him an indefinable disquietude that now grew stronger as the time to retire approached. He did not know what he feared: it was something vague, shapeless, unknown, that filled him with dread.
>
> Thus, each at a corner of the sofa, separated even more by total alienation than by the space between them, she lost in thought, he agitated, they spent the first evening of their wedded life.[30]

Seixas's inner thinking and feelings are presented in more detail, whereas Aurélia's remain vague. She is absorbed in her thoughts, but we are not told what exactly she thinks. We know that Seixas is feeling a growing dread of something that is not clear even to himself. This difference in the amount of information about the protagonists' inner world is characteristic of the narrative. There are more and longer passages of indirect and free indirect speech for Seixas than for Aurélia. In consequence, the reader is made to follow Seixas's perspective more closely and more intensely even though the title and the plotline of the novel focus more on the female protagonist.

Indirect and free indirect speech are first employed in *Senhora* to build up a close affinity to Fernando Seixas's reasoning about his family's socio-economic situation. In Chapter 6 (Part 1), owing to a romantic disappointment, Seixas arrives home earlier than usual from a ball and overhears a conversation between his mother, his two sisters and their friends. The guests talk enthusiastically about an opera. At this moment, Seixas realizes that his family has never had any of the enjoyments that he has constantly lavished on himself:

> For the first time Seixas saw clearly the contrast which, incidentally, lay before his eyes every day, every minute, and of which he himself was one of the terms.
>
> While the hours were insufficient for the pleasures with which he sated himself, those three ladies spun long evenings with no amusement other than their daily chores or the echoes of the world that reached them through some rare visitor.
>
> Merely on himself he spent more than three times what the entire family needed to subsist. That very evening, just to attend a ball he had left almost as soon as he arrived, he had squandered an amount more than sufficient to afford his sisters the pleasure of an evening at the opera.
>
> These ideas took hold of his spirit. Instead of striking the match, already in his hand, to light both the lamp that would illuminate his poetic vigil and the cigar that would opiate his muse, he threw himself on the bed, buried his head in the pillow, and slept the sleep of the just.[31]

This passage illustrates the more complex type of focalization that Alencar was able to build in moments of crisis for Seixas. The first paragraph expresses the narrator's distance from and criticism of Seixas's egoistic attitude, which has prevented him from *seeing* his family's reality. The next two paragraphs narrate the protagonist's understanding of the injustice he has done to his mother and sisters. As the narrator stands closer to Seixas, the rhythm of Seixas's thinking emerges in the sentence that depicts his reflection about the abyss between his family's and his own lifestyle: 'That very evening, just to attend a ball he had left almost as soon as he arrived, he had squandered an amount more than sufficient to afford his sisters the pleasure of an evening at the opera.' In the next two sentences the narrator becomes gradually more distanced from the character. This movement grows in intensity in the last long sentence, in which the narrator is sharply ironic in recounting Seixas's indolence: '[Seixas] threw himself on the bed, buried his head in the pillow, and *slept the sleep of the just*' (emphasis added). This type of Austenean construction of focalization allows the reader to follow closely both the character's rationale and the narrator's critical view of the character's weaknesses and flaws.

Seixas decides then to give his mother and sisters a treat by taking them to the opera house to see the performance in question. Only when they are already in the opera house does he notice his family's unfashionable attire, which prompts a jest from an acquaintance of his. Seixas feels extremely embarrassed and for some days 'remained sullen and preoccupied with the incident'. The narrator informs the reader that 'this crisis led to a rationalization that appeased our journalist'. Seixas's rationalization is narrated through indirect speech in order to accentuate his ambitious and indolent character. Seixas considers how his promising connections with upper-class people will eventually bring him an 'advantageous marriage' and a political career. Raised to such a wealthy and influential position, he will share 'the material pleasures of this opulent way of life' with his family and 'arrange good marriages for his two sisters'. Seixas believes that '[i]nteraction with society would impart to them [his mother and sisters] the seal of distinction they would need to show themselves at their best'.[32] Seixas goes on to think to himself:

> If, on the contrary, Seixas burdened himself very early, at the beginning of his career, with the weight of his family, entangling himself in an obscure life from which he could never free them, not even at the sacrifice of all of his income, what could he expect but to vegetate in the shadow of mediocrity and fruitlessly expend his youth?
>
> Seixas therefore hardened his conviction that luxury meant not only the infallible struggle of a noble ambition, but also the only pledge for the happiness of his family. Thus his misgivings vanished.[33]

Once again Seixas follows a cynical line of thinking. As is usual for him, he starts by reasoning out the source of his difficulties and then wraps up his reflections with a dismissive attitude and/or comfortable excuse for himself. By contrast to the previous passage where the narrator ironically qualifies Seixas's sleep, the sentence 'Thus his misgivings vanished' points to Seixas's own conclusion about the most convenient way for him to deal with the embarrassment his family brings to his selfish ambition.

Contrary to Seixas's expectations, his marriage with Aurélia makes him feel deeply humiliated for being relegated to the position of dependent husband, which he compares to that of a 'white slave':

> 'No, madam, you were not wrong,' he said finally in the same cold and inflexible tone. 'I sold myself; I belong to you. You had the bad taste to purchase a debased husband; here he is just as you wanted him. You could have molded his character, perhaps warped by his upbringing, into that of a man of integrity, ennobled by your affection; instead you chose a white slave. You were within your rights; you paid for him with your own money, and generously. That slave is here before you; he is your husband, but nothing more than your husband!'[34]

Seixas sarcastically (but subtly) exposes his subservient position on more than one occasion on the very first day of their marriage. For instance, when the couple are in the sitting room after breakfast and Seixas wishes to smoke a cigar, he asks Aurélia if the smoke would disturb her. When she affirms, 'I must adjust to my husband's habits,' he replies, 'No, not for that reason. As your husband I have no habits, only obligations.'[35] Later, alone in his dressing room, Seixas feels the burden of his position:

> For his part, Fernando … breathed like a man resting after arduous and tiring labor. He wished he could leave this dwelling, rid his sight of this house, go far away from this place to enjoy those moments of solitude and *recover his freedom for an hour*. …
>
> This consideration [of Aurélia's orders to the servants that Seixas should be well provided for] which in other circumstances would have deeply pleased him, *in his current position humiliated him. He felt the influence of tutelage weighing upon him and reducing him to the condition of a nuptial ward, if not worse. But he was resigned to the ordeal to which his error had subjected him.*[36]

José de Alencar thus constructed an unusual dependent position for the male protagonist in a novel centred on the popular European theme of the marriage market. More importantly, the author explores Seixas's resentment by privileging the narration of his thinking:

> There [in the houses of acquaintances visited by Aurélia and Seixas that day], as on the street, all attentions were for Aurélia … In some

> houses, in the zeal to welcome his wife he was left behind, as *unnoticed as a servant.*
>
> In different circumstances, this *annihilation of his individuality* might not have bothered him. …
>
> But the circumstances in which he found himself must completely alter the disposition of his spirit. The higher his wife was elevated – *this wife to whom he was bound* not by love but merely *by a monetary obligation – the more debased he felt.* He exaggerated his position; he even compared himself to one of the *lady's accessories or adornments.*
>
> Had Aurélia not said on that cruel evening that a husband was a trinket every woman must have and that she had bought him for that purpose? She was right. There, in that car, or in the drawing rooms they entered, it seemed that his position and his importance were like unto, if not less than, the fan, fur, jewelry, and car in the dress and the luxury that were Aurélia's.
>
> When he offered his hand to his wife to help her alight, or carried her cashmere shawl on his arm, *he compared himself to the coachman who drove the car and the doorman who opened the step.* …
>
> Never, *after finding himself enslaved by this woman* or before the *ill fortune subjected him to her whims*, had Seixas so needed the resignation he had draped about himself to avoid succumbing to the *shame of such degradation.*[37]

Seixas's circular way of thinking does not allow him to reflect more deeply on his own situation and to take effective measures to change it. He goes over and over the idea of his debasement and economic subjugation to Aurélia, which implies moral degradation and an 'annihilation of his individuality'. As Seixas is engulfed in bitter feeling, he goes so far as to compare himself to a coachman and a doorman, who would certainly have been black slaves in nineteenth-century Brazil. Therefore, by comparing himself to them, Seixas emphasizes his sense of humiliation and degradation in living in what he considers to be a debased condition. He clearly understands that his dependent position will prevent him from developing as an individual, for he is not free to act. This condition of a man who sees himself devoid of individual freedom is explicit in the way Seixas reacts to Aurélia's proposition of divorce. The terms of his reaction initially confuse Aurélia, but Seixas's argumentation suits the archaic clientelist–slavery–patriarchal mindset that underpinned the organization and functioning of Brazilian society. Interestingly enough, he voices Alencar's own arguments against the emancipation of slaves:

> 'So, by your understanding, after having deprived a man of his freedom, after debasing him before his own conscience, after having transformed him into an instrument, it is legitimate, under the pretext of emancipation, to abandon this creature who had been kidnapped from society? I believe the contrary.'
>
> 'But what does this have to do —?'
>
> 'Everything. You, madam, have made me your husband. I have no other mission in this world. Since you have imposed this destiny upon me and have sacrificed my future, you have no right to deny me what I have paid for so dearly. I have paid at the cost of my freedom.'[38]

Seixas's previous comparison of himself to a 'white slave' is strengthened and is highly suggestive of the limited and unstable socio-economic conditions, and the consequent dependence and moral humiliation, experienced by poor free white people in a slavery society. One could object that Seixas is not really devoid of material means because he works as a civil servant. However, working does not prevent him from feeling resentment about his position, since he does not regard work as an activity that can promote self-fulfilment and individual economic independence. The only thing Seixas does (because this is the only alternative he can think of) is to become punctual and assiduous at work and to save all the money he can from his salary. Indeed, on his wedding night, after Aurélia has confronted him with the true terms of their marriage, Seixas resolves that he will only be able to live with some dignity if he keeps intact all the luxurious objects for personal use that are given to him by Aurélia and saves money to pay the dowry back to her. Remarkably, Seixas's secret plan is not discussed or judged by the narrator. Moreover, the plot of the novel tacitly affirms that Seixas's lack of 'energy and willpower'[39] is acceptable once it can be perfectly compensated by his turning into a lucky investor who suddenly finds the means to buy his independence back. By using this plot strategy, José de Alencar was able to speed up the narrative pace towards its happy ending thanks to an expedient that was backed up by the Brazilian economic system.

Near the end of *Senhora*, Seixas finds himself in possession of 'a profit of fifteen thousand'[40] in a long-forgotten joint investment that had started under the government's protection. This situation was credible in nineteenth-century Brazil, where business and financial activities were regularly sponsored by the government if personal contacts were properly established. Even a wealthy persistent entrepreneur such as the Viscount of Mauá was aware of his dependence on government stimulus to carry out his numerous business affairs, because he knew that development in Brazil would derive not from individual initiative but rather from state aid.[41]

It is this context of very limited possibilities for individual entrepreneurial activity and of discouragement of continuous individual effort to achieve socio-economic prosperity that underpins Fernando Seixas's personal trajectory and mindset. His principal line of thought entails the reactive and self-protective measures he takes in order to cope with his position as dependent on Aurélia. In this sense, his socio-economic and emotional position corresponds to that of an *agregado*, although in a very peculiar way. As Roberto Schwarz explains, the *agregados* were

> men or women attached to a family as permanent adjuncts, who could be put to any and every task at hand. In these dislocated conditions, the typical position of the poor remained below the waterline of modern liberties. As for the wealthy, who renounced neither the colonial privileges they inherited nor the liberal image to which they felt entitled as the country's civilizing elite, they entertained, inevitably, an extravagant idea of themselves.[42]

Being an *agregado* implies moral indebtedness and humiliation, as reflected in Schwarz's remarks about characters created by Machado de Assis.[43] Schwarz speaks more emphatically about the figure of the *agregado* when he discusses the new thematic emphasis established by Machado in his first novels. Machado began developing the intricacies of the patron–client relationship, Schwarz argues, from the very beginning of his writing career, for the protagonists of his first novels are *agregados*. By doing so, Machado advanced an increased realism in Brazilian fiction ahead of his innovative use of point of view. Yet, as this discussion of *Senhora* shows, Fernando Seixas represents this important complex issue in a very interesting way. Alencar's emphasis on Seixas's way of thinking expresses a deeply rooted mindset whose logic is not essentially bourgeois because it does not (in fact cannot) promote the individual's full intellectual, emotional and material development or the expression of the individual's potential.

Aurélia Camargo: The Rationale of the Master

As we have seen, Aurélia Camargo's inner world is not explored as much as that of Seixas. Critical comments about Aurélia from the narrator are also less frequent, which suggests less authorial interest in developing this character who, nonetheless, has become one of the most famous female protagonists of the nineteenth-century Brazilian novel. At a certain point of the long flashback in Part 2, the narrator refrains from scrutinizing Aurélia's mind and feelings about the loss of Seixas's love. The narrator's reasons for not doing this are vague:

> This phenomenon must have had a psychological basis, research into which we will forgo, because the heart, especially a woman's, which is her all, represents the chaos of the moral world. No one knows what wonders, or what monsters, may emerge from those limbos.
>
> I suspect, however, that the explanation for this uniqueness has already been made manifest. Aurélia loved more her love than her lover: she was a poet before a woman, preferring the ideal to the man.[44]

Despite the narrator's professed refusal to delve into Aurélia's psychology, her idealization of Seixas is narrated in some passages through the use of indirect and free indirect speech. These passages explore Aurélia's deepest concern, namely, her feelings for Seixas, as in the quotation below, where Aurélia wonders about Seixas's reasons for having broken their engagement:

> Ribeiro's remonstrations about the betrayal of which he had been victim had cast a bitter suspicion into Aurélia's mind. Could Fernando have been attracted to Amaral's wealth rather than to Adelaide's love? …
>
> She received an anonymous letter. It said that Seixas had abandoned her for a dowry of thirty thousand. When she finished reading the words, she raised her hand to her breast to sustain her faint heart.
>
> Never had she felt such pain. With resignation and indifference, she had suffered disdain and rejection, but the debasement of the man she loved was an unending torture, divined only by those who have seen their soul's spark extinguished, leaving them only nothingness.
>
> In vain Aurélia took refuge in her first dreams of love. Seixas's degradation intruded on the ideal the girl had engendered in her imagination, stigmatizing it. She had forgiven her faithless lover everything, save his being unworthy of her love.
>
> What a poignant dilemma! Either banish from her heart this fallen love, and leave life forever barren of affection, or humiliate herself by worshiping the defiled being and linking herself to his shame.[45]

Aurélia chooses to live this dilemma to the full when she decides to make Seixas her husband on sheer material terms, although she loves him deeply. For instance, after the waltz (during which Seixas and Aurélia are physically close for the first time and she is overwhelmed by emotion), in her bedroom, she considers the idea of surrendering to her love for Seixas. When she looks in her desk drawer for the key to unlock the door that connects their bedrooms, 'her hand touched the steel, the coldness of the metal made her shiver. She cast the key aside and shut the drawer.'[46] The coldness of the metal of the key is a metaphor for the coldness of money, which Aurélia despises as much as she despises those who crave it. She then speaks to herself (in a passage written in dialogue form):

> 'No! It is too soon! He must love me enough to win me, not merely enough to allow himself to be won. I can, I no longer doubt it, *I can, at the moment that suits me, bring him here to my feet*, imploring, inebriated with love, *subject to my call. I can force him to sacrifice everything for me, his dignity, his pride, the final scruples of his conscience*. But the next day both of us would wake from that terrible nightmare, I to despise him, he to hate me.'[47]

Aurélia's language is typical of the master. She flaunts her whimsical character and her power to subjugate Seixas to her own wishes and decisions. Aurélia's expression of personal power and control of her husband is soon followed by growing tenderness as she looks at and speaks to the portrait of her idealized Seixas which she keeps in her bedroom. Her tenderness is strong enough to make her wish to reverse the position of master with Seixas:

> 'When he convinces me of his love and plucks from my heart the last root of this loathsome doubt that lacerates it; when I find you within it, my ideal, the master of my love; when you and he become one, and I cannot distinguish the two of you either in my affection or in my memories – on that day, I shall belong to him – No, I already belong to him now and always, since I fell in love with him! – On that day, he will take possession of my soul, and make it his!'[48]

The last paragraphs of the novel manifest the reversal of positions announced in this passage. As the novel ends, Aurélia kneels at Seixas's feet, declares that she 'adores [him] as the master of [her] soul',[49] and hands her fortune over to him. By doing so, Aurélia transfers to him the exclusive socio-economic control she has exerted up to that point and ties the last knot of this particular socio-economic relationship in which economic power is at the service of personal caprice.

Soon after the passage quoted above, the narrator informs the reader about the lives of Aurélia and Seixas during a different period of their married life. The intense and contradictory emotions they experienced at the night of the ball lead to longer periods of 'remission', during which Aurélia observes the changes in Seixas's character. We then encounter Aurélia's self-congratulatory thinking about her positive influence over her husband:

> Aurélia observed her husband and witnessed the transformation taking place in his character, once weak, mundane, and inconstant, now restored to his generous nature by a wholesome influence.
>
> She imagined, or rather saw, that thoughts of her filled and completely dominated her husband's life. At every moment, in the most inconsequential circumstance, this absolute possession that had taken hold of his soul became manifest. There was in Fernando something like a resonance of her. …
>
> Sometimes, Aurélia, standing apart, had heard him, while talking about others, condemn the life of enticements and gallantry in which he had consumed the early years of his youth. At any opportunity he revealed his present stern and austere way of regarding society, and of solving the practical matters of existence.
>
> Like soft wax, the man of heart and honor had been molded by the touch of Aurélia's hands.[50]

It is worth remarking that Aurélia never considers marriage as a means of social upward mobility. Moreover, she regards wealth not as an aim in itself, but as the means to obtain what she needs or wishes if things go against her expectations. Therefore, Aurélia's personal feelings are never subjugated to capital. She regards with contempt those who place money and all forms of material wealth above everyone and everything else. As the narrator shows on more than one occasion, the rich and unmarried Aurélia often humiliates her suitors in public:

> She delighted in *dragging them* [her suitors] *behind her, trailing them in the dust,* and *flogging them* with sarcasm, these associates and emulators of Fernando Seixas's, like him eager to sell themselves, albeit for a higher price.
>
> *She had therefore reduced them to merchandise or trinkets, assigning them a price as had been the custom in the past with bands of slaves.*[51]

Once more, the language used for Aurélia expresses the mindset of a master. In this case, Aurélia's attitude is overtly associated with that of the slave-owner: the narrator compares her cruel treatment of her suitors to that dispensed to slaves 'in the past'. The narrator refers to this attitude as a past custom because by 1875 the slave trade was no longer legal. The 1850 Eusébio de Queirós Law (named after the minister of justice at the time) suspended the slave trade in Brazil. Nevertheless, Aurélia's way of dealing with her suitors echoes the deeply rooted mindset of the Brazilian master of slaves.

In general, then, it is clear that Aurélia's domineering character is intrinsically associated with her upper-class socio-economic position. Together with her grandfather's wealth, she inherits the means to make her wishes and whims rule the lives of those who are below her and/or somehow materially dependent on her (this is the case for Dona Firmina, Mr Lemos and Seixas). Thus Aurélia does not fully correspond to the model of the modern individual, because the context in which she lives does not give her opportunities to try out her personal characteristics and, consequently, strengthen her individuality through conflicts with the others. For Aurélia, the others are all dependants and, as such, they have to yield to her wishes and decisions. Dona Firmina, Mr Lemos, Adelaide and the protagonist's suitors readily submit themselves to this subservient role, without suffering any apparent pain of their own. Nor does the narrator make any critical judgement of this situation. It is true that Seixas offers some resistance to Aurélia, but his attitude is basically self-defensive and inefficient. Aurélia is, indeed, a strong character and has more personal energy and initiative than any other in the narrative. She is also determined and has clear ideas about how to achieve her goals. In principle, these characteristics would qualify her as a character of modern times; that is, as like a bourgeois character. However, Aurélia does not fully represent the modern individual because the clientelist–slavery paradigm is strong in her and determinative of her mindset and the type of relationship she has with the other characters.

Brazil on the threshold of bourgeois society

Senhora is a novel of ambiguities and paradoxes, which derive from the particular way in which Alencar developed its themes and constructed its formal elements. The implications of the structural problems and instabilities in the novel therefore deserve further comment.

The central theme – the 'marriage market' – was much explored, with greater or lesser intensity, in nineteenth-century novels. The term itself is revealing of the new socio-economic and cultural conditions that became dominant through the century and entailed the monetization of people and their relationships. The marriage market is a socio-economic–cultural practice that expresses the potential and the personal traits of individuals who act and interact according to their own inclinations and purposes. Alencar employed this theme as the driving force of *Senhora*, but in a particular way. Firstly, he placed the female protagonist in the position of deciding how the game should be played, although, in the end, she transfers her masterful position and her wealth to her husband. Thus, if the title of Alencar's novel highlights a woman's ascendancy over those who are connected to her, it is male pre-eminence – typical of paternalistic Brazilian society – that is confirmed at the end. Secondly, it is significant that Aurélia and Seixas speak of their marriage as a matter of buying/selling a husband. The contractual and financial aspects of their relationship are made explicit by the protagonists in more than one moment of conflict. Consequently, despite the matter-of-fact tone with which characters (including the protagonists) talk about the business of matching young people with profitable prospects, the dynamics of the marriage market seem to be anomalous in this narrative because the protagonists do not manage their own situation as if it were part of an ordinary social practice. Aurélia and Seixas's social interaction follows a paradigm different from and not easily adaptable to the prevailing capitalist bourgeois logic. Finally, Alencar explores this theme through an uncommon emphasis on moral humiliation as an insurmountable sentiment intrinsically associated with the inescapable powerlessness of the dependant.

The sub-theme of humiliation predominates in the novel because Alencar developed it through internal focalization of the protagonists, mainly Fernando Seixas. Interestingly enough, Alencar's use of internal focalization highlights the issues raised by the amalgamation of foreign and local matters. The sophisticated narrative techniques of indirect and free indirect speech were already employed by European writers to build more consistent representations of individuals by amplifying their particular psychological traits. The character becomes more intensely particularized because their subjectivity is magnified as a worldview or an ideological standpoint that is worthy of the reader's attention and perhaps of criticism too. The intense individualization and particularization that result from this narrative process became an important literary achievement in opening up possibilities for the problematization of modern subjectivities. In an apparent paradox, Alencar used these techniques to amplify existing subjectivities that are not completely modern. As the analysis of internal focalization for Seixas and Aurélia shows us, their mindsets are archaic rather than modern. Moreover, as Seixas's thinking is privileged, the reader is made to follow the logic of the dependant more intensely. Thus, by using modern European techniques to explore archaic local content, Alencar built up a realistic effect, turning the deeply rooted Brazilian mindset into the organizing principle of the novel.

The narrative emphasis on Seixas's thinking and the organization of the plot to support his consequent modus operandi allowed Alencar to portray vividly what Brazilian critic Antonio Candido affirms was 'the hard choice of the man of sensibility at the threshold of bourgeois competition'.[52] Candido observes that 'the society in which [Alencar] lived' did not require 'the harsh struggle of Rastignac or Julien Sorel'; therefore Alencar 'almost always settled his heroes with paternal solicitude without hurting their susceptibility'.[53] Despite the narrator's negative remarks about Seixas, this character with deep archaic and superficial modern characteristics is much favoured by the author. The amalgamation of foreign and local content, which Alencar knew to be intrinsic to Brazilian culture and literature, is represented in a very productive way in *Senhora* because it allows in-depth perception of the lines of force and paradox that structured Brazil's nineteenth-century socio-cultural context.

Notes

1. Alencar 1959a.
2. Alencar 1959a, 696. All translations from Portuguese are mine unless stated otherwise.
3. Alencar 1960, 934.
4. Assis 2004.
5. De Marco 1986.
6. Alencar 1959a, 697–9.
7. *Lucíola* (1862), *Diva* (1864) and *A pata da gazela* (1870) are novels by José de Alencar. Together with *Sonhos d'ouro* and *Senhora*, they are categorized as 'novels of manners' or 'urban novels' and are set in Rio de Janeiro, the most developed urban area in Brazil. The second paragraph in this passage is also quoted by Roberto Schwarz in 'The Importing of the Novel to Brazil and Its Contradictions in the Work of Alencar' (1992). I quote Gledson's translation throughout.
8. Watt 2000.
9. Watt 2000, 60.
10. Moretti 2013, 16.
11. Alencar 1959b. All quotations from *Senhora* come from Catarina Feldmann Edinger's English translation (Alencar 1994).
12. Schwarz 1992, 46.
13. Alencar 1994, 82.
14. Alencar 1994, 23, 82.
15. Alencar 1994, 71.
16. Alencar 1994, 5.
17. Alencar 1994, 61.

18. Alencar 1994, 90.
19 Almeida 2003; Almeida 1959. This novel is the subject of Chapter 2 by Edu Teruki Otsuka in this book.
20. Schwarz 1992, 46–7.
21. Schwarz 1992, 65.
22. Schwarz 1992, 46, 57.
23. Schwarz 1992, 52.
24. Alencar 1955.
25. Schwarz 1992, 54.
26. Alencar 1994, 125.
27. Alencar 1994, 125.
28. Schwarz 1992, 48, 51.
29. Schwarz 1992, 52.
30. Alencar 1994, 115.
31. Alencar 1994, 29.
32. Alencar 1994, 30.
33. Alencar 1994, 30.
34. Alencar 1994, 97–8.
35. Alencar 1994, 108.
36. Alencar 1994, 112–13, emphasis added.
37. Alencar 1994, 132–3, emphasis added.
38. Alencar 1994, 141.
39. Alencar 1994, 25.
40. Alencar 1994, 183.
41. Faoro 2000, Vol. 2, 38–9.
42. Schwarz 2012, 44.
43. Schwarz 2012, 44.
44. Alencar 1994, 83.
45. Alencar 1994, 85.
46. Alencar 1994, 179–80.
47. Alencar 1994, 180, emphasis added.
48. Alencar 1994, 180.
49. Alencar 1994, 197.
50. Alencar 1994, 180–2.
51. Alencar 1994, 94, emphasis added.
52. Antonio Candido 1993, Vol. 2, 205.
53. Antonio Candido 1993, Vol. 2, 205.

Bibliography

Alencar, José de. *Como e porque sou romancista*. Salvador: Progresso Editora, 1955.

Alencar, José de. 'Benção paterna'. In *Obra completa: volume I. Romance urbano*, 691–702. Rio de Janeiro: Editora José Aguilar, 1959a.

Alencar, José de. *Senhora: perfil de mulher*. In *Obra completa: volume I. Romance urbano*, 949–1214. Rio de Janeiro: Editora José Aguilar, 1959b.

Alencar, José de. 'Castro Alves. Carta a Machado de Assis'. In *Obra completa: volume IV. Teatro, poesia, crônica, ensaios literários, escritos políticos e epistolário*, 931–5. Rio de Janeiro: Editora José Aguilar, 1960.

Alencar, José de. *Senhora: Profile of a Woman*, translated by Catarina Feldmann Edinger. Austin: University of Texas Press, 1994.

Almeida, Manuel Antonio de. *Memoirs of a Militia Sergeant*, translated by Linton L. Barrett. Washington, DC: Pan American Union, 1959.

Almeida, Manuel Antonio de. *Memórias de um sargento de milícias*, apresentação, edited by Mamede Mustafa Jarouche. São Paulo: Ateliê Editorial, 2003.

Antonio Candido. *Formação da literatura brasileira (momentos decisivos)*, 7th edn. Belo Horizonte: Itatiaia, 1993.

Assis, Machado de. 'Notícia da atual literatura brasileira. Instinto de Nacionalidade'. In *Obra completa: volume III. Poesia, crítica, crônica, epistolário*, edited by Afrânio Coutinho, 801–9. Rio de Janeiro: Editora José Aguilar, 2004.
De Marco, Valéria. *O império da cortesã. Lucíola: um perfil de Alencar*. São Paulo: Martins Fontes, 1986.
Faoro, Raymundo. 'A direção da economia no Segundo Reinado'. In *Os donos do poder: formação do patronato político brasileiro*, 10th edn, 1–45. São Paulo: Globo; Publifolha, 2000.
Moretti, Franco. *The Bourgeois: Between History and Literature*. London: Verso, 2013.
Schwarz, Roberto. 'The Importing of the Novel to Brazil and Its Contradictions in the Work of Alencar'. In *Misplaced Ideas: Essays on Brazilian Culture*, edited by John Gledson, 41–77. London: Verso, 1992.
Schwarz, Roberto. 'Beyond Universalism and Localism: Machado's Breakthrough'. In *Two Girls and Other Essays*, edited by Francis Mulhern, 33–53. London: Verso, 2012.
Watt, Ian. *The Rise of the Novel: Studies in Defoe, Richardson and Fielding*. London: Pimlico, 2000.

10

Maria Benedita Câmara Bormann's *Lésbia*: The Creation of the Woman Writer in Brazil

Margaret Anne Clarke

Maria Benedita Câmara Bormann's *Lésbia*: Context and Themes

The subject of this chapter is the novel *Lésbia*, which tells the fictional story of a writer-protagonist who is both Brazilian and a woman.[1] It was authored by Maria Benedita Câmara Bormann (1853–95), active as a poet, novelist and author of short stories between 1880 and the year of her death. *Lésbia* was completed in serial form in 1884, the final decade of monarchical empire in Brazil, and was published as a bound novel in 1890, one year after the downfall of Brazil's monarchy and the advent of the First Republic. The narrative, still untranslated into English, describes the literary formation and development of the eponymous heroine Lésbia, who, after a disastrous marriage and further romantic disappointments, undergoes a crisis of values and makes a conscious decision to reject her destiny as wife and mother. She reinvents herself as a writer of short stories, novels and poems and establishes an independent career as a successful author and powerful society mondaine in Rio de Janeiro. The novel concludes with a dramatic denouement when the protagonist takes her own life, an act that Bormann portrays as a rational and autonomous decision, a natural consequence of Lésbia's 'tumultuous and eventful life'.[2]

My aim here is to present a case study of *Lésbia* within the novel's most significant contexts and from three interrelated perspectives. Firstly, I will examine the novel in relation to the socio-historical, philosophical and literary transitions taking place in Brazil in the last two decades of the nineteenth century. Recent scholarship has reassessed the influence of these transitions on the Brazilian novel of this period[3] and in particular has re-evaluated the certainties, prevalent up to the 1860s, that the genre could function as an unequivocal and unmediated representation of Brazilian reality, an integral component of the 'political self-legitimation of the emerging nation-state'.[4] Highly problematic to begin with, these convictions about the role and place of the novel in national life were challenged by subsequent generations of writers emerging from more varied social backgrounds, who engaged with divergent ideas as the nineteenth century drew to its conclusion. The transition from Empire to Republic and beyond brought with it conflicting and divergent debates about the nation's ideological identity and future direction and posed special challenges for the novelists of the era, including Joaquim Maria Machado de Assis (1839–1908) and contemporaries such as Maria Benedita Câmara Bormann. The quest for an aesthetic equal to the task of representing and engaging with the issues of the age is fundamental to the theme of *Lésbia*.

Secondly, I will illustrate the ways in which *Lésbia* may be regarded as a nineteenth-century precursor of the modern *Künstlerroman* in Brazil, that is, a novel that expounds the formation and development of its principal protagonist as artist or writer, and the process of coming to maturity through the cultivation of the aesthetic self.[5] According to Sara Castro-Klarén, 'This emphasis on the acquisition of a thinking and writing craft is particularly acute in Brazilian writers'[6]; an emphasis that may be partly traced to a fundamental characteristic of the nineteenth-century novel which scholars such as Zephyr Frank have recently discussed: the protagonist's problematic *Bildung*, or development, and the crafting of an identity, in relation to Brazilian society and the national situation of the age.[7] It has also been argued that the theme of the conflicted protagonist became an ever more integral component of the novel in the last two decades of the nineteenth century, a part of the 'crisis of representation' in Brazil which came with the advent of the First Republic and beyond.[8] In Bormann's *Lésbia*, the themes of the *Bildungsroman*, or novel of development, are recast in a novel about the protagonist as artist, whose evolution takes place on a literary and discursive as well as a biographical level. Since the intention of the *Künstlerroman* is to elucidate the process of writing, to examine the novel from this perspective will provide further insight into the antecedents of the contemporary Brazilian novel.

Thirdly, I will trace the particular ways in which Bormann appropriates the genre of the *Künstlerroman* to document and discuss the vicissitudes befalling the woman author in the late nineteenth century, the choices available to her in her writing and publication, and the negotiation of ideas in society and literature which inform her identity. A related theme of the chapter is the question of how the retrieval and study of these works by nineteenth-century women authors have also served to challenge long-standing dogmas and tenets in Brazilian literary historiography, to transgress established and schematized patterns characteristic of literary history in Brazil and to revise key ideas about the development of Brazilian literature.

Maria Benedita Câmara Bormann: Life and Work

Details of Maria Benedita Câmara Bormann's own life are scanty: the author was born into a prestigious family of some social and political standing in Porto Alegre in the southern state of Rio Grande do Sul, and the family moved to Rio de Janeiro when Bormann was 10. She was married to her maternal uncle, a hero of the Paraguayan War and government minister, but remained with her parents until her death from a stomach ulcer in 1895.[9] Throughout the 15 years up to her death, Bormann published articles, serialized novels and short stories in newspapers such as *O Paiz* (1884–1934) and *A Gazeta de Notícias* (1875–1942). These publications were of Republican orientation and advocated the abolition of slavery in Brazil. Bormann was also a regular contributor to *A Família* (1888–98), edited by Bormann's contemporary Josefina Álvares (1851–1913), a journal dedicated to the advocacy of women's suffrage and right to education. Under the pen name 'Délia', Bormann also published six bound works of fiction, three of which are still extant: besides *Lésbia*, a collection of three novellas – *Uma vítima, Duas irmãs, Magdalena* (1884)[10] – and another novel, *Celeste* (1893),[11] reissued in 1988.

From the internal evidence in the extant novels, Bormann's subject matter and style owe much to the aesthetics of popular serial fiction favoured by Brazilian readers: melodramatic in tone, featuring emotionally charged themes of domestic conflict, betrayal, thwarted love and inescapable death, expressed in a 'language of tears' intended to evoke an empathetic reaction in the reader.[12] In both plot and theme *Lésbia* conforms in its essentials to the widely prevalent conventions of domestic and sentimental fiction, a genre that derived from the eighteenth-century European 'novel of sensibility' frequently authored by women. Adapted and developed by female authors in the Americas, sentimental fiction remained 'a dominant fictional type until after 1870'.[13] The narrative of sentimental fiction was frequently structured around the young female protagonist, deprived in youth of supports such as marriage and a family, and obliged to develop her inner resources to attain self-mastery and confront the world.[14] We cannot know to what extent *Lésbia* was autobiographical, or otherwise pertained to Bormann's own life, but the depiction in the novel of the formation, development and discourse of the young female protagonist as a brilliant author who must establish a separate identity enables Bormann to subvert and readapt the literary conventions she adopts in order to intervene in the national political and cultural debates of her time, reflect on the transformations in the production of literature in Brazil and introduce her own modes of intertextuality, which provide important pointers to the ways in which the nineteenth-century novel in Brazil may be assessed and revalued.

Lésbia was retrieved, edited and republished by Editora Mulheres in 1998. The work, therefore, is one of the texts rediscovered and published by Brazilian scholars dedicated to the recovery, publication and revisionary study of prose and poetic texts of female authorship written and published in Brazil from the advent of independence in 1822 and throughout the decades preceding the end of Empire in 1889 and beyond.[15] The recovery of these texts has enabled the revision of traditional perceptions of the status of women in this epoch, summed up as 'the dependent female, a prisoner in the web of patriarchal authority'.[16] As Viotti da Costa points out, this bleak portrait, created by holding married middle-class and upper-class women at the beginning of Empire to be representative of the female population, may not have been entirely accurate to begin with.

Although the profoundly patriarchal system established in the colonial era by the plantation-owning oligarchy and their political representatives had scarcely been modified by independence in 1822, changes took place over the course of the nineteenth century, beginning with the ascent of Dom Pedro II to the throne in 1831 and his majority in 1840, continuing during his reign and accelerating with the collapse of the Empire. From 1836 onwards, the most prevalent publishing outlet for prose fiction was as a serial published in instalments in a dedicated section of a periodical. This mode of publication, described by Mary L. Daniel as 'fundamental to both long and short fiction in Brazil during the first half of the nineteenth century',[17] originated from the French feuilleton (meaning 'leaf') – a section, usually at the foot of the page, dedicated to the arts, theatre, popular culture and light literature.[18] Once transplanted to Brazil, the feuilleton form was adapted to accommodate fiction of various kinds, beginning with translations of European narratives, but also adopted by Brazilian authors for whom this mode of publication ensured some form of distribution to the literate public, and payment.[19] Once the serials were collated, published and distributed in bound form by the printing press established in Brazil after independence, a national literary culture was established in the 1840s. Beginning with the adaptation of the sentimental novel of manners in local settings, a canon of Brazilian novelists – including José de Alencar (1829–77), Joaquim Manuel de Macedo (1820–82) and Joaquim Maria Machado de Assis (1839–1908) – emerged in subsequent decades. The aesthetic and themes of European serial fiction, which broadly consisted of either human drama in everyday contexts or material of historical import, were combined and adapted by Brazilian authors, gradually extending in ambition and scope to include broader contemporary social and national themes, in accordance with the quest in a recently independent nation for an autonomous identity and a national consciousness. But this emergence of the novel as a genre in Brazil also entailed the establishment of a reading public that largely consisted of women of the bourgeois and upper-class households of Rio, São Paulo and the northeastern coastal cities. This readership could not be ignored by the press, the nascent publishing industry or, indeed, by established Brazilian male authors. It was precisely to this readership that much of the work of novelists such as José de Alencar and Machado de Assis was directed.[20] The expansion of this market meant that opportunities for enterprising and literate women also expanded. These included increasing opportunities for the publication of didactic and children's literature by Brazilian publishing houses from the 1880s onwards, and the foundation of dedicated periodicals for women, which included in their pages the dissemination of new ideas advocating liberal republicanism and the abolition of slavery. There were some opportunities for literate middle-class women to participate in certain roles in these movements, and these developments at the end of Empire had important implications for the production of literature in various genres by women. They also provided an opportunity for Bormann and her contemporaries to insert their own voices and perspectives and establish a literary or polemical career:

> Women's voices began to make themselves heard, whether in the form of the *crônica*, novels, in *folhetim* form of polemical texts, although almost always in conditions of explicit censorship or the complacent gaze of the masculine world, which saw in this indulgence or writing merely a feminine whim or an affront to good taste or breeding.[21]

This body of diverse and heterogeneous texts, including novels published by Bormann, has remained in a state of obscurity, neglect or limbo, and the names of their authors exist at best as fleeting or unexplained references in established literary histories documenting the evolution of Brazil's national canon of literature. Bormann's works, for example, already rare by the end of the nineteenth century, had vanished altogether by the beginning of the twentieth; there is only one brief reference to her work in Wilson Martin's study, *História da inteligência brasileira*.[22] There are several reasons for this state of neglect. Firstly, the ephemeral nature of the mode of literary production available to women meant that much of this fiction has been lost to posterity and with it the names of its authors, even though they were known, popular or even lionized in this period. Notwithstanding the development from mid-century of an autonomous canon of Brazilian fiction with established authors, problems still existed with respect to copyright, authorial rights and publication which rendered the process of authoring books 'a thankless task for authors'.[23] Although the number of publishers in Brazil increased during the 1880s and throughout the Republican era, the rights of authors over their intellectual property were not fully guaranteed by law until 1898.[24] Until the 1870s, just one established France-based publisher, Baptist-Louis Garnier and its subsidiaries in Brazil, held a monopoly on the publication of bound works, which were otherwise the purview of typographic companies such as Typographic Central and Magalhães e Companhia, both of whom printed Bormann's extant novels. Published books were still issued in limited editions. Distribution and the securing of a readership were frequently the responsibility of the author. In *Lésbia*, Bormann describes at some length her protagonist's quest to find a publisher for her first prose novel. She eventually encounters a sympathetic newspaper editor who agrees to publish the work as a serial, and then to issue the bound novel in an edition of 1,000 copies, giving Lésbia half of these to distribute herself.[25] Furthermore, serial fiction in domestic or sentimental genres authored by women did not enjoy much prestige among Brazil's intellectual elites. Eminent scholars such as José Veríssimo, Sílvio Romero and Araripe Júnior were the founders of the central tenets underpinning Brazilian literary historiography in the nineteenth century.[26] This critical trinity, who were also founding members of the Academia Brasileira de Letras [Brazilian Academy of Letters] in 1897, worked exhaustively in their studies to assert the importance of Brazil's men of letters in the context of the development of national life and thought, but disregarded or eliminated altogether the copious production of the female authors, activists and polemicists popular with their contemporaries: Silvio Romero authored a five-volume history of Brazilian literature over a period from 1888 to 1907,[27] yet excluded any reference to the women authors who were active from the late eighteenth century onwards; José Veríssimo also omitted any work of female authorship in his seminal study *História da literatura brasileira*, published in 1916.[28]

For women writers active in this epoch, therefore, the development of their craft entailed a long and arduous process of self-definition. In addition to the vicissitudes of publication, distribution and acceptance of their work by the public, particular challenges also arose from confrontation and negotiation with mythologies of many kinds pertaining to the construction of gender in this era. But the negotiation and synthesis of these myths of recreation acquired ever-increasing complexity towards the end of the nineteenth century, when women writers such as Bormann could draw for their inspiration on successful and influential European predecessors such as George Sand and Germaine de Staël, both cited in *Lésbia*[29], and could create protagonists who constituted 'a powerful, intelligent, witty female figure'[30] quite different from depictions of the frustrated female artist as confined madwoman or monstrous figure, and in total contradistinction to the virtuous heroines of the domestic novel.

Lésbia: Plot and Theme

This is the case in *Lésbia*, which adopts the pattern of the classic *Künstlerroman*, based on an archetypal pattern of birth, death and rebirth as a writer. According to Grace Stewart, the novel takes the form of a voyage from early and innocent childhood experiences into an initiation into an underworld that threatens to blight the protagonist's talent or to alienate them from society. This is followed by a subsequent re-evaluation of the self and, finally, a definitive statement of the heroine's position vis-à-vis her art and what she intends to accomplish with it.[31] The protagonist of *Lésbia*, Arabela, or Bela to her family and friends, begins the novel as a delicately nurtured young lady of good family endowed with a precocious intellect and brilliance. She is married at an early age to a boorish and oppressive husband, from whom she finally effects a separation with the aid of her family, only to endure more emotional trauma at the hands of a faithless and superficial dandy, a stock character in this period. Bela's natural resilience asserts itself, however, and she rebels against her condition, passing through what Carolyn Heilbrun has termed the moratorium: 'the decision to place oneself outside the bounds of society's restraints and ready-made narratives'.[32] As an outcast who is now unable to fulfil society's expectations of her with respect to romantic love, marriage and children, Bela vows to sublimate her trauma through writing and establish a literary career for herself with or without public approval:

> I will learn not to pursue fruitless and vain chimeras, and work only for my own consolation. After that, would the appreciation of the public compensate for my sufferings, my despair? No! So, what would it be good for? I will write for myself alone, avoiding any public opprobrium that would disturb me, adding to my woes.[33]

Thus far, the plot of the novel conforms to the traditional pattern of the *Künstlerroman*, which may also take the form of a voyage, or quest: from innocent childhood experience comes the fall into a psychic underworld or miasma, which obstructs the writer's talent and capacity for self-expression, blighting her place in society and threatening to engulf her. From this point, the nascent writer effects a separation from her past, and her present milieu, and re-evaluates her identity, her values and her position in society. Finally, a process of liberation takes place and there is a definitive statement of independence, repeated and developed in the author's writing.

This resolution effected, Bela now undergoes a 'violent moral revolution', is transfigured, and her environment with her. Her dressing table is transformed into a study desk. The first fruits of her labour are created from 'that life which was hers, and those torments, which had convulsed her in piercing despair'.[34] Bela begins to seek, and finds, publication for her prose fiction and poetry in newspapers and subsequently as bound books. At this point Bela adopts the pen name 'Lésbia', signalling her autonomy as an author, and an independent literary expression that will inform her subsequent and copious production of novels, short stories and poems. Bormann further reinforces her protagonist's independence by having her win one of the numerous lotteries popular during the Empire, a device also used by Machado de Assis in *Dom Casmurro* (1889)[35] to improve the situation of the novel's lower-class heroine, Capitu.[36] Lésbia elevates her own situation by purchasing a townhouse, described as 'a small palace' in Rio's most fashionable quarter, the Rio Comprido. Far from being confined to an attic, the heroine writes on a rosewood desk that combines signifiers of feminine refinement with those of wealth and power. To allow herself the necessary latitude to both negotiate and reflect on Brazilian upper-class society, Lésbia appropriates and uses to her own advantage several images of women prevalent in the fin de siècle; the enigmatic sphinx, the inspirational muse whose writings have an extraordinary effect on all who read them, and the figure of the beautiful and powerful society mondaine. She is imperious in her dealings with others, invulnerable and impregnable in the heart of the nation's capital. Having established her identity and reputation beyond all question, Lésbia relaunches herself into society to ease her self-imposed exile.

Brazil: Society and Letters

The setting for Bormann's novel is the high bourgeois and aristocratic milieu of Rio de Janeiro, the capital of Empire in Brazil since the transposition of the Portuguese court and its retainers from Lisbon in 1808. Lésbia, who operates in this world, but is not of it, observes her milieu. Her engagement with society not only forms a backdrop for the novel's plot and denouement, but has a direct bearing on her philosophy vis-à-vis society and humanity, and her writing life. Thus Bormann is no less involved than other intellectuals and writers of the 1880s with questions of broader import in the national arena, and engages fully with these questions in *Lésbia*. At the time of the novel's publication in serial form in 1884, the monarchical regime was in the last decade of its existence, five years from its final overthrow in 1889 through a military coup supported by a group of Republican sympathizers from the burgeoning coffee-producing state of São Paulo. Up to this event, the decadence of a society whose oligarchs presided over an economy almost entirely dedicated to the export of plantation-led commodities continued to make itself felt. This regime was presided over by an emperor and court that readily dispensed titles of nobility such as 'baron', 'count' and 'viscount' as well entitlements to land and credit.[37] The system was further buttressed by middlemen linked to the 'patronage machine' responsible for dispensing foreign capital, imported policy prescriptions and imported goods – including bound novels.

Lésbia's self-invention enables her sardonic observation of this gallery of oligarchs, elites and hangers-on in the last decade of Empire, described by the contemporary critic Sílvio Romero as 'an aristocracy of money … the most vicious and bastard of all aristocracies'.[38] *Lésbia* portrays the petty jealousies and vindictiveness of social climbers in a society ruled by patronage and favour, and the writers for whom the composition of prose and verse in pallid neoclassical style was a means of social ascendancy. Bormann and her protagonist give no quarter when it comes to titled aristocrats with no credible roots in heredity: 'Now, speaking of Brazil, I would say that our aristocracy is merely a fiction, but in its place we have a bourgeoisie with possibly some money, more or less, corrupted by debt and entangled in defaults, with little class or tone: and that's how we recognize them.'[39]

In the novel's engagement with the prevalent literary and philosophical ideas that informed the era of Empire and beyond, Bormann and her protagonist must use and subvert the faithful adherence of Brazil's elites to inherited and imposed European tradition. For the bourgeois classes of Rio and their retainers, literacy and letters evidently held significance only insofar as they were a means of social ascendancy and admission into the nation's oligarchy. French, and to some extent Portuguese, literature, philosophy and thought continued to dominate literary production in Brazil into the last decade of the nineteenth century and beyond.[40] Bormann associates much of the predominance of poorly understood European-derived philosophy with a demeaning situation of neocolonial dependency, inextricably linked to a 'contagion of self-doubt and alienation'[41] which stifled the capacity for independent thought. She critiques this situation many times in the novel: 'The descendants of Brazil suffer from a chronic affliction: foreign parlance, which leads them to glorify other countries, diminishing their beautiful native land, and the many and varied efforts of their compatriots, not realizing that they also degrade the nation, destroying the good impulses of those who have merit.'[42]

These observations on philosophical and literary trends prevalent at the time of *Lésbia*'s publication form a starting point for understanding Bormann's stance on the political issues and ideological cross-currents of the late nineteenth century in Brazil and its complex ramifications for literary production. As Lésbia's parallel observations about 'the positivist conclusions of the nineteenth century'[43] make clear, the author-protagonist is also prepared to adapt to a certain extent the philosophies propounded by the French intellectual Auguste Comte (1798–1857), which held that the advance of scientific, empirical knowledge was the foundation and driving force of social progress.[44] At the time of the novel's first publication in 1884, positivist ideals strongly informed the debates of two groups: firstly, the emerging class of intellectuals with Republican affiliations who had emerged from regions of Brazil beyond Rio de Janeiro and, secondly, the new professional groups in Brazil's urban areas with no affiliation to traditional landowning elites.[45] The Republican movement, first formally established as a political party in Rio de Janeiro in 1870, was gaining unstoppable traction by the 1880s. Moreover, the increasing incentives to accelerate the long decline of slavery as an institution, also linked to the federalist interests of the Republicans, finally came to fruition in 1888 when the Lei Áurea [Golden Law] legally ended slavery. By the time of *Lésbia*'s publication in bound form in 1890, Comtean positivism had been formalized as the intellectual structure that would underpin the regimes of Brazil's First Republic from 1889 to 1930.

Bormann's protagonist is clearly of the expanding urban and broadly Republican class by upbringing and temperament. Bormann's choice of classical names for her own pen name, Délia, and for her protagonist, Lésbia, also reveals the novel's Republican sympathies, for it was the custom of Republican activists in this period to adopt Roman names for themselves.[46] The writer-protagonist Lésbia's espousal of the Republican ideals that were to be imperfectly implanted in Brazil at the end of the 1880s, together with the ideals of equality and justice for Brazil's slave population, is asserted in her outspoken discourse in the purportedly aristocratic society in which she operates. For example, her riposte to an absurd proposal of marriage from a titled gentleman, 'the baron of Buriti, the viscount of Pacoval',[47] is a polemic against the landed aristocracy's practice of the bogus manumission of slaves to gain kudos and an honorarium;[48] a practice that reflected the contradictory situation throughout the 17 years from the introduction of the Rio Branco Law, or Law of the Free Womb, in 1871 to the final prohibition of slavery with the Golden Law in 1888. Intended to provide liberty, with some monetary compensation, for all children born to slave mothers, together with those slaves who were the property of the state and monarchy, the poorly enforced Law of the Free Womb had little effect on the institution of slavery at the time of *Lésbia*'s publication.[49]

Lésbia also critiques the reception of her work by her readership, and the reputation she has acquired as a dissolute maverick. She complains of the misapprehension of her work and the intentions behind it in the following terms:

> They said that she was a realist writer who was more dissolute even than Zola himself; however, none of these fools knew how to distinguish one school from another. … they were all mistaken, since Lésbia adopted an eclectic style, harvesting from here and there what was best, disregarding effeminate and timid sentiments and inconvenient vulgarities, adapting with fine judgement the exigencies of the positivist conclusions of the nineteenth century with all the contemporary evolutions of psychology and physiology.[50]

Bormann is referring in the quotation above to the naturalist currents in literature extended and adapted by the French author Émile Zola

(1840–1902), based on contemporary scientific ideas, including theories of evolution and medicine. In Europe, these ideas underpinned the themes of novels whose protagonists' characters and destinies were influenced in great measure by their biological inheritance and their environment. By the 1880s, the adaptation of the broad tenets of naturalism to the trajectories of conflicted protagonists within contemporary Brazil was increasingly evident in novels authored by Bormann's contemporaries. This emerging body of works included the novels *O mulato* (1881) [*The Mulatto*],[51] *Casa de pensão* (1884) [*Rooming House*][52] and *O cortiço* (1890) [*The Slum*][53] by Aluísio Azevedo (1857–1913). Works such as *A carne* [*The Flesh*] by Júlio Ribeiro (1888)[54] and *O Ateneu* (1888) [*The Athenaeum*] by Raul Pompeia[55] confirm this emerging orientation in Brazilian letters. Scholars such as Eva Paulino Bueno and Elizabeth A. Marchant[56] have argued that these novels and their successors in the Republican era represent the first attempts by a group of Brazilian writers born or located outside established oligarchical or intellectual elites to 'turn a de-centred or ex-centric gaze at the totality of Brazilian society of their time'.[57] In so doing, these writers established both a critique and a new aesthetic derived from representations of different voices in conflict with the society into which they were born. In this, Bormann's work may reflect the concerns of her peers, since *Lésbia* too reflects the discourses of a heterogeneous society that could not entirely conform to any one European-derived school, representing instead a gradual move towards a style capable of engaging with the highly contested ideological and political concerns of the age. But, as Schaffer points out, 'Naturalism was coded as an exclusively masculine form, for the naturalist writer described aspects of life that only men were supposed to recognize.'[58] Bormann's engagement with socio-political issues, the conflict of the individual protagonist with society, and the implications for the Brazilian novel of the late nineteenth century is therefore of a different order from that of male contemporaries such as Azevedo and his successors, and for several reasons.

Firstly, the experiences of Bormann's protagonist do not extend beyond those which a Brazilian upper-class woman, albeit one financially independent, might realistically have had in this era: writing and journalism, participation in society events, and a sojourn in continental Europe. As a self-defined aesthetic writer, Lésbia regards herself as a scrupulous scientific recorder of psychological types and their motivations and actions. What Bormann's protagonist does not acknowledge, however, are positivist doctrines that maintain that the individual holds no great significance in the movement towards a society based on the twin pillars of order and progress, or the idea that facts of any kind are free from values or can be integrated into one 'science'.[59]

Influences and Affiliations

Lésbia's relationship to her literary forebears and the European literary inheritance constitutes what Gilbert and Gubar define as female 'affiliation' rather than 'influence', a term that connotes 'an influx or pouring in of essential power'.[60] The concept of affiliation carries with it the possibilities of both choice and continuity, in that one may consciously or not choose with whom to affiliate, and so exercise full autonomy as a writer. Since Lésbia is operating from a marginal if privileged position, and somewhat apart from her social milieu, she is engaged in constant assessment of herself and her situation vis-à-vis both her craft and the human condition, to reflect upon and learn from experience. Thus a substantial part of the novel consists of the author-protagonist's multifaceted odyssey through her many and varied literary influences, philosophers and mentors, who aid her in her frequent withdrawals to reflect and meditate on her literary and personal development and her observations of the motivations, idiosyncrasies and idioms of those around her. It is to Lésbia's advantage that she retains her freedom from the 'anxiety of influence'[61] exacerbated and complicated in much Brazilian writing by male authors of this epoch. She takes advantage of both a 'matrilineal and patrilineal inheritance' and oscillates between the two within an arduous process of self-definition.

Lésbia's abandonment of her former name and patronymic, and the adoption of a pen name, is a sign of rebirth and newly assumed 'authority and power to name her environment around her'. This was a not uncommon practice of women writers in the nineteenth century; it was 'the mark of a christening into a second self, a rebirth into a linguistic primacy'.[62] Bormann's adoption of a classical pen name for herself and a classical pseudonym for her protagonist has further connotations in the context of the literary milieu in which both had to operate, and in the context of the gradual collapse of the Empire and the diffusion of Republican ideals at the time of the novel's writing. Bormann and her protagonist affiliate themselves with figures and literary modes deriving from Graeco-Roman civilization, held by the aesthetic writers of Brazil's belle époque as the authentic foundation of Western literary tradition. The foundations of Bormann's protagonist's thought on Platonic and aesthetic ideals are made abundantly clear in Bormann's preface to the first edition of *Lésbia* in 1890: 'Regarding the book, also a work of art, it is likewise … since the subject is the fantasy of the author, it can be happy or mournful, grandiose or even banal; what is important is that the form is correct, the idea well developed and the deduction logical.'[63]

In *Lésbia,* this tradition is reclaimed and redefined as a new form of literary matrilineage. The names of Délia and Lésbia, together with other female literary forebears of French provenance liberally cited in the novel, affirm the affiliation of the writer-protagonist to a specifically women's literary genealogy and imagination. The self-signification of Bormann's protagonist Lésbia connotes an autonomous and mature woman who is lauded at the height of an empire. This figure is also associated with Sappho, whose feminine brand of lyricism was inherited by George Sand and Germaine de Staël, inspirations for other woman writers of the epoch and the creators of the myth of the female artist which was to become the counterpoint of 'Romanticism's Prometheus/Icarus myth of artistic manhood'.[64] These two authors are also cited by Lésbia, who has occasion throughout her odyssey to remind herself that these writers too suffered at the hands of an uncomprehending public and envious literary competitors.

Bormann acknowledges two works by different authors as her guiding texts, both of which have no apparent connection in terms of genre or period, but do inform much of the action and reflection in the novel. The first of these texts is the *Enchiridion*, the manual of maxims attributed to the Stoic philosopher Epictectus, active as a teacher in Rome and Greece in the first and second centuries AD.[65] Precepts from this work precipitate Lésbia's liberation from her existential crisis and subsequent moratorium and provide a coherent thread that underpins Lésbia's beliefs and actions.[66] According to classical Stoic philosophy, care, respect and attention to oneself through the practice of reading, writing and reflection play their part in a system of reciprocal obligations and, in consequence, they also constitute a social practice upon which authentic communion with others may be based. The identity and development of the writer thus entail the education and cultivation of the self.

The same principle of the emergence of the individual both as a citizen who engages with society and as an author is evident in Lésbia's other principal literary association, the epistolary novel *The Sorrows of Young Werther* (1774) by Johann Wolfgang von Goethe.[67] This novel, and Goethe's oeuvre in general, is linked to Lésbia's Stoic philosophy inasmuch as the German author maintained that no action is free of consequences and that the vicissitudes of life are in a state of balance and counterbalance and require constant evaluation and re-evaluation.[68] These philosophical premises adopted by Lésbia also lead her to reject essentialism or determinism of any kind, especially when it comes to matters of gender and woman's position in society. Women, as well as men, are responsible for their own improvement and their own destiny:

> It is not just the Brazilian spirit which is still contaminated by prejudice; men in their majority don't look well on the emancipation of women, through study and through the cultivation of independent opinion.
>
> These lions without claws are at least partly right; if all women were to explode, lifting themselves up through instruction, moved by ambition, copying men's defects and virtues, men would indeed spend a miserable quarter of an hour.[69]

Notwithstanding such frequent and pithy observations about the male sex, Bormann rejects the premise of male mastery and dominance by diffusing a wide range of temperaments among the plethora of male characters who people her book, including her enlightened and progressive physician and a string of absurd suitors. Bormann also has her protagonist acquire a sympathetic companion in her odyssey, a gentle poet renamed Catulo, who, as Lésbia's counterpart and platonic soulmate, is indispensable to her creative process. Lésbia's trajectory through the social milieu of Rio society is interspersed with moments of contemplation and reading in which she engages in platonic dialogue with Catulo concerning the significance of all that has happened to her.

We see, therefore, that Lésbia's literary praxis as an aesthetic writer consists of writing, rewriting and constantly reassessing the ever-fascinating story of her own life; her main plot, or story, is the 'terra incognita' of her own self.[70] As the above quotation illustrates, the author-protagonist's incessant efforts to effect a synthesis between mutually exclusive concepts and forms associated with fixed gender positions have great repercussions for the language used in the work. A novel produced by Lésbia entitled *Blandina*, which finally establishes her as a popular writer with the reading public, is described thus:

> That work displayed a vigorous spirit, which lay in the concept and development of the plot; at the same time the gentle flexibility of the style, unfolding with a refined feminine touch, revealed those tender depths which a man could scarcely guess at and which only a woman is accustomed to possess and express.[71]

But, as we have seen, Lésbia devours what she terms 'foreign parlance', and combines it with thoughts, reflections and insights drawn from her own experience, not refusing the conflict and tension that may arise in the process. The paragraphs are short, to the point of becoming aphorisms, and Bormann provides her protagonist with an epigrammatic language that becomes itself an instrument against dependency and the objectification of the author-protagonist, 'a refusal of mastery, an opting for openness and possibility which can itself make women's writing a challenge to the literary structures it must necessarily inhabit'.[72] The novel's stylistic mutability, its shifts from one register to another, from lovingly detailed descriptions of clothes and domestic artefacts as typical of the domestic and sentimental novel, to reflections on the writing of Rousseau, Spinoza and Goethe, make for a bricolage effect throughout the work. This is what Norma Telles, the editor of the current edition of *Lésbia*, terms a 'mestiça aesthetic'.[73] Lésbia's multiple readings and integration of texts from a wide range of sources imply an eclecticism with an almost proto-modernist quality. The nascent modernism of fin-de-siècle women's writing has been noted by other critics; tactical revisions of contemporary thought, abrupt shifts in register and psychological introspection were used by female authors of the fin de siècle to bring together and reconcile mutually exclusive definitions of femininity.[74]

The Return of the Quest: Denouement and Suicide

The novel reaches a dramatic conclusion when the author-protagonist, after a sketchily described eight-year sojourn in Europe, returns to Brazil and subsequently takes her own life, an act graphically described by Bormann. The sequence of events that leads to the suicide occur after Lésbia, now 40 years old, undergoes another existential crisis, resulting from the onset of old age and the diminishing of her artfully constructed persona. On her return to Brazil, she experiences once more the original schism that provoked her separation from society and the accepted and traditional destiny of woman. This crisis is precipitated by an encounter with an ardent young admirer 20 years her junior, who awakens in Lésbia a long-suppressed passion, and resultant anguish. Lésbia finds her physical stamina and physical beauty declining with age; none of her carefully constructed defences or her long and arduous process of self-creation can, in the end, stave bodily suffering: 'Yes, that ugly and degrading flowering of old age, bitter, biting, ashamed of itself, is what I feel! ... Forty years! A cruel age, in which the remnants of girlhood evaporate, giving way to the sad diminishing of beauty and freshness!'[75]

The true cost of Lésbia's self-creation is made clear at this point. The conversion of Lésbia into writer, muse and mondaine has entailed the renunciation of her body and physical impulses as a precondition for 'the symbolic interchange with language', which endows the author-protagonist with the necessary objectivity to enunciate and define herself through textual creation, binding her created and creating self into the world of external symbols: 'Negation of the body and of the impulses which go with it engenders the peace which allows for thought and reflection, abstraction and generalization of the external world, making it possible to master "that which is absent".'[76] We have seen the ways in which Bormann and her protagonist consciously affiliate themselves to the aesthetic literary tradition; yet, following this literary praxis, Lésbia can only exercise her reason and craft in the absence or petrification of the flesh. Nor have the heterogeneity and synthesis of her writing practice enabled Lésbia to overcome fully the boundaries that society has set on her role and conduct as a woman. At various points in the book, Lésbia stresses the fundamental schism between her femininity and her intellect; her transgression has produced both a monstrous nature and the petrifaction of her body. In a lengthy monologue expounding her philosophy of writing and art to her companion Catulo, she states,

> One is a writer, the other a woman: in me those two entities are almost always in opposition. … As a writer, in practical life, I profess a little of Spinoza, finding within my own spirit a very strong point of support, which helps me attain the perfection of my being. As a woman, however, I still let myself be moved by the impulses of an enigmatic heart made almost monstrous by the excess of its aspirations.[77]

Female melancholia and psychic disintegration are familiar themes in the work of Brazilian nineteenth-century novelists; Bormann's contemporaries Aluísio Azevedo and Júlio Ribeiro documented in some detail their female protagonists' nervous or hysterical attacks caused by unrequited passion or doomed love.[78] Gilbert and Gubar assert that the trope of female crucifixion or sacrifice, 'sexual or social, literal or figurative', haunts texts by fin-de-siècle women writers.[79] There are also echoes of Goethe's Werther, who, caught in an untenable situation between a grand passion and loyalty to his friends, commits suicide for the sake of the latter.[80] Similarly in *Lésbia*, the protagonist takes her fateful decision after a visit from Alberto's despairing fiancée, Heloisa, who pleads with Lésbia to take into account her lover's betrothal. Like Werther, Lésbia takes the decision to sacrifice herself for the sake of others: 'Lésbia voluntarily renounced the last happiness of her life, for the benefit of that innocent girl who had the courage to be humble and simple.'[81]

There is a marked contrast between the motives behind Lésbia's decision to end her own life and the motives of Goethe's Werther or behind the suicides of many female protagonists in nineteenth-century novels. According to Mary DeGuire, young Werther's demise is a result of the failure to achieve the balance needed between romantic ideals and practical application of them in the wider society.[82] The decision of the mature Lésbia, on the other hand, is only taken after much reflection and, in fact, is a logical outcome of the Stoic philosophy that transformed the author-protagonist's destiny and now brings it to an end. The human subject benefits their friends and community through the exercise of control over their own will and perceptions, even to the point of bringing about their own death, if they have fulfilled the destiny marked out for them or have contributed what they are meant to.[83] The point is reinforced when the conclusion of the book reveals that Lésbia has distributed the remainder of her fortune to the founding of an educational establishment for abandoned and destitute female orphans and the creation of a secondary school for girls.[84] This conclusion is another example of Bormann's subversion of the prevailing themes and motifs in the literary frames of reference of the era in which she wrote. The rationale for Lésbia's self-sacrifice enables at least a partial resolution of the contradictions inherent in the position of her protagonist, and enables a final outcome that points towards the future. It suggests a basis for the literacy and redemption of future generations of Brazilian women and further demonstrates the status of *Lésbia* as a landmark in the difficult construction of an autonomous tradition of women's writing in Brazil: 'the pathway of the Brazilian woman towards her cultural emancipation'.[85]

Conclusion

In this chapter, I have set the most relevant contexts in which Maria Benedita Câmara Bormann's novel was written, its key themes and stylistic features. What, then, is the contribution of *Lésbia* to our understanding of the nineteenth-century Brazilian novel and the place of the work within contemporary readings of literature? Bormann's singular work was published at two specific junctures: firstly, when opportunities for women authors to present their own thematic and linguistic perspectives through published works opened out in late nineteenth-century Brazil. These opportunities arose parallel to changes in the nation's public life that were also reflected in diversified ideological and philosophical frames of reference for writers to adapt. Secondly, these changes brought with them the further evolution of the novel from the first adaptations of the genre as a representation of national identity after Independence in 1822. We have seen how divergent and conflicted voices emerged in the subsequent decades before and after the advent of the First Republic in 1889, including those of Machado de Assis and the Naturalist trend in the novel. If, as the scholars cited in this study suggest, the *Bildungsroman* with its conflicted protagonist reflects the nascent signs of emerging capitalist modernity in the late nineteenth century, then it was also at this point of transition that Brazil's first *Künstlerroman* appeared, a form which enabled a woman writer with a female protagonist to emerge 'on the border between two epochs'[86] and engage on multiple levels with the national issues of her time, on a socio-historical, ideological and literary level. As a close reading of the novel illustrates, the conscious intertextuality, reflexivity and strategic revisions in *Lésbia* read as a notable example of the evolving orientation in the late nineteenth century towards the formation of 'new patterns of interrelationship, cross-fertilisation and elective affinity that emerged within and around the "virtual cosmopolis" of the colonial city'.[87] From then on, these trends gathered momentum throughout the era of the First Republic, finally reaching their full expression in the radical iconoclasms of the Semana de Arte Moderna [Modern Art Week of 1922] and beyond. Viewed in this way, the historiography which informs readings of the contemporary Brazilian novel may be recast as the dynamic process of ideological, philosophical and textual revisions, rather than as chronological sequences divided into discrete periods and determined by one or more specific literary movements. Further, and following recent currents in contemporary scholarship, more nuanced attention to these texts may enable a revision of the novel as a genre and canon formed by Anglo-American and European authors, towards a process of two-way and mutually reciprocal exchange of aesthetic, epistemological and linguistic concepts within the novel itself, and as embodied in emergent protagonists such as Bormann's Lésbia.

Notes

1. Bormann 1998.
2. Telles 1988, 13.
3. Bueno 1992; Bueno 1995.
4. Schmidt 2015, 122.
5. Pooler 2015, 30–1.
6. Castro-Klarén et al. 1991, 16.
7. Frank 2016, 3.
8. Bueno 1992, 367.
9. Telles 1988, 6.
10. Bormann 1884. The edited manuscripts of all three novellas in the volume are available at: Norma Telles, 'Coleção Rosas de Leitura', http://www.normatelles.com.br/colecao_rosas_de_leitura.html
11. Bormann 1893; reissued as Bormann 1988.
12. Vasconcelos 2014, 78.
13. Campbell 2018.
14. Baym 1993, 19.
15. The task of recovering the works of nineteenth-century women authors from obscurity gained momentum from 1985 onwards, beginning with the creation of a federal group of academic networks, the Organização Institucional Sobre a Mulher na Literatura, and a series of conferences and seminars, Encontros Nacionais Sobre a Mulher na Literatura. These initiatives provided the base for subsequent academic research and collaboration, including the foundation in 1996 of a publishing house, Editora Mulheres, dedicated to the editing and republication of works by women authors of the era, including *Lésbia*.

    The two most comprehensive anthologies of works by women authors and accounts of their contexts are Muzart (2004) and Coelho (2002a). For a comprehensive overview of the literary historiography, bibliographies and anthologies published since the beginning of the twentieth century, see Pinheiro (2006). For a contextualized overview of these nineteenth-century authors in English, see Schmidt (2015).
16. Viotti da Costa 2000, 1.
17. Daniel 1996, 128.
18. Nadaf 2009, 120.
19. Lajolo and Zilberman 2017, 65–7.
20. Zilberman 1989, 138.
21. Coelho 2002b, 96.
22. Martins 2010.
23. Lajolo and Zilberman 2014, 182.
24. Lajolo and Zilberman 2014, 195.
25. Bormann 1998, 101–2.
26. Guimarães 2004, 269–70.
27. Romero 1980.
28. Veríssimo 1977; Veríssimo 2016.
29. Bormann 1998, 108.
30. Schaffer 2000, 43.
31. Stewart 1981, 102.
32. Heilbrun 1988, 50
33. Bormann 1998, 75.
34. Bormann 1998, 74.
35. Assis 1998; Assis 2009.
36. Gledson 1984, 52.
37. Levine and Crocitti 1999, 61.
38. Viotti da Costa 2000, XV.
39. Bormann 1998, 134.
40. Veríssimo 1977.
41. Dean 1986, 77.
42. Bormann 1998, 99.
43. Bormann 1998, 107.

44. Nekrašas 2015, 105.
45. Sharpe 1999, 144.
46. Telles 1988, 8.
47. Bormann 1998, 131.
48. Mattoso 1997, 117–38.
49. Mattoso 1997, 118.
50. Bormann 1998, 107.
51. Azevedo 2012b (translated by Murray Graeme MacNicholl [Azevedo 1994]).
52. Azevedo 2015.
53. Azevedo 2012a (translated by David H. Rosenthal [Azevedo 2000]).
54. Ribeiro 2015.
55. Pompeia 2018 (translated by Renata R. M. Wasserman [Pompeia 2015]).
56. Bueno 1997; Bueno 1995; Marchant 2000.
57. Bueno 1997, 363.
58. Schaffer 2000, 43.
59. Hazareesingh 2001, 11.
60. Gilbert and Gubar 1988, 11.
61. Bloom 1997, 4.
62. Gilbert and Gubar 1988, 241.
63. Bormann 1998, 33.
64. Lewis 2003, 17.
65. Epitectus 1991.
66. Heilbrun 1988, 50.
67. Goethe 2012.
68. Tantillo 2010, 17.
69. Bormann 1998, 87.
70. Ledger 1997, 187.
71. Bormann 1998, 103.
72. Jacobus 1979, 16.
73. Telles 1988, 13.
74. Ledger 1997, 193.
75. Bormann 1998, 182.
76. Bronfen 1992, 27.
77. Bormann 1998, 129–30.
78. Verona 2008.
79. Gilbert and Gubar, 82.
80. Goethe 2012, 103.
81. Bormann 1998, 221–2.
82. DeGuire 2011, 30.
83. Epitectus 1995, 4–14.
84. Bormann 1998, 255.
85. Gotlib 2003, 107.
86. Bakhtin 1986, 23.
87. Boehmer and Matthews 2011, 285.

Bibliography

Assis, Machado de. *Dom Casmurro*, translated by John Gledson. Oxford: Oxford University Press, 1998.

Assis, Machado de. *Dom Casmurro*. São Paulo: Editora Saraiva, 2009.

Azevedo, Aluísio. *The Mulatto*, translated by Murray Graeme MacNicholl, edited by Daphne Patei. Plainsboro, NJ: Associated University Presses, 1994.

Azevedo, Aluísio. *The Slum*, translated by David H. Rosenthal. Oxford: Oxford University Press, 2000.

Azevedo, Aluísio. *O cortiço*. São Paulo: Martin Claret, 2012a.

Azevedo, Aluísio. *O mulato*. São Paulo: Martin Claret, 2012b.

Azevedo, Aluísio. *Casa de Pensão*. São Paulo: Martin Claret, 2015.
Bakhtin, Mikhail. *Speech Genres and Other Late Essays*, edited by Caryl Emerson and Michael Holquist, translated by Vern W. McGee. Palo Alto, CA: Stanford University Press, 1986.
Baym, Nina. *Women's Fiction: A Guide to Novels by and about Women in America, 1820–1870*. Champaign: University of Illinois Press, 1993.
Bloom, Harold. *The Anxiety of Influence*. Cambridge: Cambridge University Press, 1997.
Boehmer, Elise, and Steven Matthews. 'Modernism and Colonialism'. In *The Cambridge Companion to Modernism*, edited by Michael Levinson, 284–300. Cambridge: Cambridge University Press, 2011.
Bormann, Maria Benedita (Délia). *Uma vítima, Duas irmãs, Magdalena*. Rio de Janeiro: Typografia Central, 1884.
Bormann, Maria Benedita (Délia). *Celeste*. Rio de Janeiro: Editora Magalhães e Companhia, 1893.
Bormann, Maria Bormann (Délia). *Celeste*, edited by Nanci Egert. Rio de Janeiro: Presença Edições, 1988.
Bormann, Maria Benedita (Délia). *Lésbia*, edited by Norma Telles. Florianópolis, Santa Catarina: Editora Mulheres, 1998.
Bronfen, Elisabeth. *Over Her Dead Body: Death, Femininity and the Aesthetic*. Manchester: Manchester University Press, 1992.
Bueno, Eva Paulino. 'Brazilian Naturalism and the Politics of Origin', *MLN* 107, no. 2 (1992): 363–95.
Bueno, Eva Paulino. *Resisting Boundaries: The Subject of Naturalism in Brazil*. New York: Routledge, 1995.
Campbell, Donna M. 'Domestic or Sentimental Fiction, 1820–1865'. *Donna M. Campbell*. Last modified 15 December 2018. https://public.wsu.edu/~campbelld/amlit/domestic.htm
Castro-Klarén, Sara, Sylvia Molloy and Beatriz Sarlo. *Women's Writing in Latin America: An Anthology*. Boulder, CO: Westview Press, 1991.
Coelho, Nelly Novaes (ed.). *Dicionário crítico de escritoras brasileiras*. São Paulo: Escrituras Editora, 2002a.
Coelho, Nelly Novães, 'A literatura feminina no Brasil'. In *Gênero e representação na literatura brasileira: ensaios*, edited by Constancia Lima Duarte, Kátia da Costa Bezerra and Constancia Duarte, Vol. 1, 89–107. Belo Horizonte: Estudos Literários/UFMG, 2002b.
Daniel, Mary L. 'Brazilian Fiction from 1855'. In *The Cambridge History of Latin American Literature, Vol. 3: From Independence to c. 1870*, edited by Roberto González Echevarria, 127–36. Cambridge: Cambridge University Press, 1996.
Dean, Warren. 'The Brazilian Economy, 1870–1930'. In *The Cambridge History of Latin America, Volume 5: c.1870–1930*, edited by Leslie Bethell, 725–76. Cambridge: Cambridge University Press, 1986.
DeGuire, Mary A. 'Intertexuality in Goethe's *Werther*'. PhD thesis, University of Illinois at Urbana–Champaign, 2011. https://www.ideals.illinois.edu/bitstream/handle/2142/24503/DeGuire_Mary.pdf
Epitectus. *Enchiridion*, translated by George Long. New York: Prometheus Books, 1991.
Epitectus. *The Discourses of Epitectus*, translated by Robin Hard. London: Everyman, 1995.
Frank, Zephyr. *Reading Rio de Janeiro: Literature and Society in the Nineteenth Century*. Palo Alto, CA: Stanford University Press, 2016.
Gilbert, Sandra M., and Susan Gubar. *No Man's Land. The Place of the Woman Writer in the Twentieth Century. Volume 1: The War of the Words*. New Haven, CT: Yale University Press, 1988.
Gledson, John. *The Deceptive Realism of Machado de Assis*. Liverpool: Francis Cairns, 1984.
Goethe, Johann Wolfgang von. *The Sorrows of Young Werther*, translated by David Constantine. Oxford: Oxford University Press, 2012.
Gotlib, Nádia Battella. 'A literatura feita por mulheres no Brasil'. In *Refazendo nós: ensaios sobre mulher e literatura*, edited by Izabel Brandão and Zahidé Muzart, 20–65. Florianópolis: Editora Mulheres, 2003.
Guimarães, Hélio de Seixas. 'Romero, Araripe, Veríssimo e a recepção crítica do romance machadiano', *Estudos Avançados* 18, no. 51 (2004): 269–98.
Hazareesingh, Sudhir. *Intellectual Founders of the Republic: Five Studies in Nineteenth-Century French Political Thought*. Oxford: Oxford University Press, 2001.
Heilbrun, Carolyn G. *Writing a Woman's Life*. London: Women's Press, 1988.
Jacobus, Mary. 'The Difference of View'. In *Women Writing and Writing about Women*, edited by Mary Jacobus, 10–21. New York: Barnes & Noble, 1979.
Lajolo, Marisa, and Regina Zilberman. 'How to be a Professional Writer in Nineteenth Century Brazil'. In *Books and Periodicals in Brazil 1768–1930: A Transatlantic* Perspective, edited by Ana Cláudia Suriani da Silva and Sandra Guardini Vasconcelos, 176–98. London: Legenda, 2014.

Lajolo, Marisa, and Regina Zilberman. *Literatura infantil brasileira: uma nova outra história*. Curitiba: PUCPress, 2017.
Ledger, Sally. *The New Woman: Fiction and Feminism at the Fin-de-Siècle*. Manchester: Manchester University Press, 1997.
Levine, Robert M., and John J. Crocitti. *The Brazil Reader: History, Culture, Politics*. Durham, NC: Duke University Press, 1999.
Lewis, Linda. *Germaine de Stael, George Sand, and the Victorian Woman Artist*. Columbia: University of Missouri Press, 2003.
Marchant, Elizabeth A. 'Naturalism, Race and Nationalism in Aluísio Azevedo's *O mulato*', *Hispania* 83, no. 3 (2000): 445–53.
Martins, Wilson. *História de inteligência brasileira, Vol. 5 (1897–1914)*. Ponta Grossa: Editora UEPG, 2010.
Mattoso, Katia de Queirós. 'The Manumission of Slaves in Brazil in the Eighteenth and Nineteenth Centuries'. *Diogenes* 45, no. 179 (1997): 117–38.
Muzart, Zahidé L. (ed.). *Escritoras brasileiras do século XIX: antologia*. Florianópolis: Editora Mulheres; Santa Cruz do Sul: EDUNISC, 2004.
Nadaf, Yasmin Jamil. 'O romance-folhetim francês no Brasil'. *Letras, Santa Maria* 19, no. 2 (2009): 119–38.
Nekrašas, Evaldas. *The Positive Mind: Its Development and Impact on Modernity and Postmodernity*. Budapest: Central European University Press, 2015.
Pinheiro, Maria de Conceição. 'Lilithes, do século XX, abrem a Caixa de Pandora das Sherazades do século XIX', *Letras de Hoje* 4 (2006). http://revistaseletronicas.pucrs.br/revistapsico/ojs/index.php/fale/article/view/637
Pompeia, Raul. *The Athenaeum*, translated by Renata R. M. Wasserman. Evanston, IL: Northwestern University Press, 2015.
Pompeia, Raul. *O Ateneu*. São Paulo: Ciranda Cultural, 2018.
Pooler, Mhairi. *Writing Life: Early Twentieth-Century Autobiographies of the Artist-Hero*. Liverpool: Liverpool University Press, 2015.
Ribeiro, Júlio. *A carne*. São Paulo: Martin Claret, 2015.
Romero, Sílvio. *História da literatura brasileira*, 7th edn, edited by Nelson Romero. Rio de Janeiro: José Olympio, 1980.
Schaffer, Talia. *The Forgotten Female Aesthetes: Literary Culture in Late-Victorian England*. Charlottesville: University Press of Virginia, 2000.
Schmidt, Rita Terezinha. 'Nineteenth Century Brazilian Women Writers and Nation Building: Invisibilities, Affiliations, Resistances'. In *The Cambridge History of Latin American Women's Literature*, edited by Ileana Rodríguez and Mónica Szurmuk, 117–32. Cambridge: Cambridge University Press, 2015.
Sharpe, Peggy. 'Book Review of Eva Paulino Bueno, *Resisting Boundaries: The Subject of Naturalism in Brazil*', *Luso-Brazilian Review* 36, no. 1 (1999): 144–7.
Stewart, Grace. *A New Mythos: The Novel of the Artist as Heroine 1877–1977*. Montréal: Eden Press Women's Publications, 1981.
Tantillo, Astrida Orle. *Goethe's Modernisms*. New York: Continuum, 2010.
Telles, Norma. 'Introdução'. In Maria Benedita Bormann (Délia), *Lésbia*, 5–22. Florianópolis, Santa Catarina: Editora Mulheres, 1988.
Vasconcelos, Sandra Guardini. 'Migratory Literary Forms: British Novels in Nineteenth-Century Brazil'. In *Books and Periodicals in Brazil 1768–1930: A Transatlantic Perspective*, edited by Ana Cláudia Suriani da Silva and Sandra Guardini Vasconcelos, 68–86. London: Legenda, 2014.
Veríssimo, José. *Estudos de literatura brasileira*. São Paulo: Editora Itatiaia, 1977.
Veríssimo, José. *História da Literatura Brasileira: de Bento Teixeira (1601) a Machado (1908)*. Brasília: UnB, 2016.
Verona, Elisa Maria. 'O romance, a mulher e o histerismo no século XIX brasileiro', *Histórica – Revista Eletrônica* 32 (2008). http://www.historica.arquivoestado.sp.gov.br/materias/anteriores/edicao32/materia06/texto06.pdf
Viotti da Costa, Emília. *The Brazilian Empire: Myths and Histories*. Chapel Hill: University of North Carolina Press, 2000.
Zilberman, Regina. *Estética de recepção e história da literatura*. São Paulo: Ática, 2008.

11

O Ateneu: A Singular Masterpiece about the Nineteenth-Century Civilizational Crisis

André Luiz Barros da Silva

O Ateneu [*The Athenaeum*], the only novel written by Raul Pompeia (1863–95),[1] draws together and integrates at the aesthetic level several elements of the powerful transformations that made the latter decades of the nineteenth century a period at once riddled with conflict and very rich in both Brazil and the wider world. The outbreak of the First World War in 1914 may be taken as a political result of these transformative contradictions, just as the placidly prosperous European belle époque was an earlier moment during which only certain groups experienced and bore witness to those intense contradictions. One such group included writers, among them Raul Pompeia, who demonstrated both his political combativeness and his restlessness in the aesthetic field. As well as pursuing for his only novel a high-flown and eloquent prose at odds with the naturalistic vogue of the time, he wrote some prose poems after the manner introduced by Aloysius Bertrand,[2] a leading light in the aestheticization of the cultural crises of the nineteenth century.

One way of broadly encapsulating the transformations that affected the European literary field over the years 1856–7, which saw the publication of *Les fleurs du mal* [*The Flowers of Evil*] and *Madame Bovary*,[3] would be to highlight the exhaustion of the promise of both the Enlightenment and romanticism. In the Brazilian context, such general cultural frameworks had been at the basis of the formation of nationalism, positivism, republicanism, abolitionism and much else. Such were the various currents of thought that made up the fabric of polemics with which writers, politicians and intellectuals had to deal, especially from the 1870s, as movements in favour of the Republic and the abolition of slavery overlapped. Moreover, they found themselves in a milieu where scientism and the technologization of daily life were bringing about large-scale aesthetic reactions (for example, art nouveau and impressionism), which emerged as ways of integrating the visual arts – architecture, interior design, clothing and so on – to take advantage of a new and crucial opportunity as capitalist industrial activity gathered momentum. In the case of impressionism, for instance, there is an implied response to the invention of photography.

It is in this larger context, Brazil being on the cultural periphery of capitalism, that various facets of *O Ateneu* should be understood. It is a novel that for many decades was seen critically as close to realism or even naturalism, which shows the centrality Brazilian critics accorded such limited concepts when evaluating diverse and unconventional literary works of the nineteenth century. In 1941, the leader of the Brazilian modernist movement, Mário de Andrade (1893–45), recognized the hyperbolic ('work in which traits are voluntarily exaggerated') and highly rhetorical style of the novel ('there is in the book less of poetry … than of the ardent eloquence of sonorous verbalism, images and dazzling rarities'). For Andrade, these styles do work, despite their excesses: 'But he got what he wanted: an artist's writing, artificial, original, personal.'[4] He concludes the essay with a contestable critical position, holding up the novel as the high point of naturalism.

In the same year that *O Ateneu* appeared, the critic Araripe Júnior (1848–1911) became fascinated by what he called the transposition of the decadent movement in Europe to Brazil, and similarly of parnassianism (in poetry) into symbolism – all this, of course, in open aesthetic opposition to naturalism. In a show of enthusiasm to embrace the new theoretical and poetic waves emanating from Europe, Araripe sees in the novel an amalgam of René Ghil's thesis (the fusing of music with language), the experiments of Arthur Rimbaud, Stéphane Mallarmé and Francis Viellé-Griffin and the aesthetic of Edmond and Jules de Goncourt (*écriture artiste*), by way of the 'morbid realism' of Charles Baudelaire's hero, Edgar Allan Poe. He also refers to German Wagnerism and English pre-raphaelitism.[5] There is here a somewhat chaotic effort to characterize a singular prose. And yet this evidence of the poor assimilation of the novel's impact (but with anti-naturalism as a common denominator) is in tune with assessments by later critics, from Eugênio Gomes (1897–1972) to José Paulo Paes (1926–98). The former, in 1958, saw in *O Ateneu* Parnassianism tempered by literary impressionism. The latter, in 1985, brought it closer to art nouveau in the visual and decorative arts.[6]

In 1959, Antonio Candido (1918–2017) echoed the synaesthetic concerns voiced by Araripe. Commenting on an excerpt from the novel, he writes, 'Sounds are *described* here by how they affect sensibility ... The movement of the sentence is due to the impressionistic characterization of rhythm ... The resulting sensorial density leads him to move from the description to the effect of sounds.'[7] The mixture of aestheticization and a subjectivism that imploded realism's objectivist agenda is obvious. In 1965, Roberto Schwarz would highlight a 'superseding of Realism by the narrator's emotional presence', that is to say, the new subjectivism alone would distance the novel from realism and explain the 'hyperbolic and metaphorical tone. ... Language loses, in part, its function of indicating the processes of the real; it is dramatized to the point of being a pure expression of the rise and fall of emotion.'[8]

Two years later, Silviano Santiago would use this subjectivism represented by the split between Sérgio the character and Sérgio the narrator (Sérgio, already old, is narrating his childhood schooldays).[9] Furthermore, he would call attention to two facts. Firstly, the possibility of subjectivism turning into allegorization of the political context (the Athenaeum as a microcosm of Brazil). Secondly, he would highlight the two lectures by Dr Claudio, the only teacher, or the only man (besides his father, who is absent) whom Sérgio respects ethically and intellectually. They are lectures on aesthetics and ethics, with an implied political dimension. They are pseudo-theoretical or pseudo-philosophical interventions in the course of the novel's action; they highlight that the aestheticization of the environment and the self is the sole positivity in the face of the predatory and agonistic negativity of the action of men against men, inside and outside institutions. We can hear echoes of the pessimism of Schopenhauer and Nietzsche. The former was an author known to Raul Pompeia and his contemporaries; the latter would only become known a few years later, through readers attentive to international currents, such as Araripe Júnior.

In 1979, Sonia Brayner approached *O Ateneu* from two standpoints: the satirical aspect (a characteristic that pervaded the output of the first writers in Brazil, from Joaquim Manuel de Macedo and Manuel Antônio de Almeida to Machado de Assis) and that of the political allegory, reaffirming the label of 'impressionist novel'.[10] Heightened sensation, vision as the prime sense of a 'sensationalistic vitalism', satire, irony – the critic links all these elements to modern thinkers from Schopenhauer to Bergson and Freud. There is no reference to satire (from the Latin *satura*) as a genre that originated in Roman antiquity, or to rhetoric as premodern knowledge, although it still dominated the curricula of Brazilian schools during the nineteenth century.[11]

In 1988, in line with an approximation made between Raul Pompeia and Isidore Ducasse,[12] the author of the anti-civilizational *Les chants de Maldoror* [*The Songs of Maldoror*], Alfredo Bosi highlighted the traumatic aspect of Sérgio's socialization at school, the institution that is the entryway to literate civilization. He refers to an 'internalization of the work of writing' that would serve to 'replace, in a tentative, experimental, but intense way, the certainties of the neoclassical poetics still scholastically alive throughout the nineteenth century'.[13] In 1995, Roberto de Oliveira Brandão, pointing to this neoclassical and rhetorical backdrop, noted Pompeia's ironizing of this traditional framework: 'this genuine libel on rhetoric is situated at the very core of its innermost redoubt – the school'.[14] The critic consigns this (self-)criticism based on his own presuppositions (rhetoric against rhetoric) to an anti-institutional and hypercritical view of discursive and action frameworks that seem moribund in the eyes of the boy as he suffers under the yoke of these social and institutional structures; literal destruction ensues when the school is consumed by fire at the end of the novel.

A Negative *Bildung*: Against the Institution

In *O Ateneu* it is Sérgio in adulthood who narrates the memories of Sérgio as a child. This temporal distance implies a doubling-up of memory to include emotional and resentful (or vengeful) remarks about the injustices suffered. The very first paragraph shows that this looking back tends to unveil the idealizations that ought to support the positivity of the cultural and emotional (subjective) grounding that civilization offers the boy. The father says that he will 'enter the real world', and that he ought to 'be brave' because it will be 'a struggle'. In the present, the narrator says that this warning 'stripped me, with one swift gesture, of the illusions I carried as a child nurtured, like an exotic plant, in the loving hothouse of domestic affection. … Let us remember, then, with hypocritical nostalgia, those happy school years.' The indignation even reaches as far as the mother and the ingrained cultural way of pampering the child with affection without preparing it for (or at least warning it about) 'disappointments that still offend us'.[15]

From the beginning of the novel, the Athenaeum (the school) shows itself to be an unhealthy environment, where the principal, Aristarco, exhibits two facets: that of the self-eulogizing speaker lacking in character and ideas (symbolic of the speakers and politicians of a country pervaded by overblown and hollow oratory) and that of the businessman whose love for the Athenaeum and for teaching appears to be a disguise for his taste for profit. 'The chair swiveled back … and the paternal figure of the great educator dissolved into the simplified, dry, attentive slyness of the manager … The speculator and the miser inhabited him in an intimate camaraderie, arm in arm.'[16] Aristarco[17] will come to symbolize the corruption and degradation of the very foundation of the institution's (male) authority. The entire description of him holds an ambiguous tone of hostility towards his empty artificiality. 'That expansiveness overcame us; he irradiated himself over students, spectators, over the magnetism of battle pennants. … A consummate actor, he embodied, almost literally, the diaphanous, subtle, metaphysical role of spirit of the feast and soul of his institute.'[18]

The other male authority figure, Sérgio's father, absent for most of the novel, does at last resurface in a letter. At this point, Sérgio is languishing in the college infirmary, under the care of Aristarco's wife, Ema; this, his last emotional relationship (and his only one with a female), is obviously Oedipal and vindictive in relation to Aristarco. From Paris, the father, also unwell, advises his son to 'save the present', in line with the Latin maxim *carpe diem* ('seize the day' in order to enjoy the present moment), for 'the future is corrupting and the past is a solvent'.[19]

From the outset of the novel, among the classmates the climate is one of extreme violence and cruelty, both of which are often endorsed by the institution itself, indicating the political backdrop of this bitter satire (broad and objective, all-encompassing, Lukács would say). It is no coincidence that the boy who serves as the laughing stock of the class, wizened and sickly, is called Franco. 'It's Franco. … On his knees like a penitent expiating the guilty of an entire race. The headmaster calls him a dog … The father … sent him here with a letter that describes him as incorrigible,' says Rebelo, the teacher's best disciple and Sérgio's first trusted friend.[20] As we have already seen, the character's rectitude and stoicism in his studies are represented in a style that some critics have called impressionistic and others sensorialist, somewhat lost in the translation:

> The curved lenses of his spectacles hid his eyes completely, concentrating his attention fully on the teacher's desk. As if that were not enough, the zealous student covered his temples with his cupped hands to impede any stray glance escaping from behind his glasses.[21]

Some lines further on, Rebelo himself becomes a scathing satirist when describing his classmates. As in the case of Aristarco, the narrator describes a self that transmutes on the phenomenal level: 'I then saw, sprouting from within the patriarchal mildness of Rebelo, a kind of unexpected Thersites, uttering insults and curses.'[22] In the students' recreational bathing, Sérgio experiences both eroticism and cruelty. Eroticism when, seeing and playing with the boys from afar, Angela, the beautiful Spanish girl who works in the school – and will be the cause, as an object of disputed desire, of the gardener's assassination of one of Aristarco's servants – is shown 'opening like a flower through her white teeth'.[23] Cruelty when Sérgio is pulled by the ankles and almost drowns. In that ambiguous and dangerous moment, his saviour, whom he now considers to have been the tormentor himself, becomes his first great companion. Consequently, the description of three of these friendships mixes the precariousness typical of childish relations with insinuations of homosexuality.

The novel can be read as a *Bildungsroman*, where the *Bildung* is a rather traumatic and negative formative experience in contrast not only to the family 'hothouse of domestic affection'[24] (a level of Freudian analysis limited to Oedipal relations) but also to pre-institutional precepts. The work is thus a radical critique of the oppressive powers of the institution (scholastic, but political too) which is based on an idea of justice linked to a pre-civilizing vitalism: the bodily free, and pre-moral, boy who must fit in as an obedient student in the face of authorities that do not convince him (or do not convince his body, not just in biological terms but as a physical, spiritual, emotional and phenomenal whole with a pre-logical and even a pre-linguistic existence). The language and codes of the school as the first human institution (after that of the family) are irreconcilable with the child's vitality and its emotional, pre-rational and pre-linguistic being.

Throughout the novel, a variety of figures represent the openly decadent public culture (institutional and political in that microcosm that allegorically represents other human institutions). As we have seen, there is a repeated focus on the deterioration in the public rhetorical language of several characters, not just that of Aristarco. This refers to the immediate draining away of the legitimacy of any position of power in the eyes of the protagonist. According to the subjectivist doubling of Sérgio as narrator versus Sérgio as character, if in adulthood he recognizes and defends as righteous that pre-institutional vitality of the boy who suffered the trauma of entry into civilization, in his boyhood Sérgio only felt oppressed, sick and scared at the degree of hypocritical artificiality that his own culture presented to him at school.

The gap is always painfully clear between, on the one hand, violence, eroticism and the cruelty of the clash of young bodies full of vitality (a line of thought linked to Schopenhauer and Nietzsche) and, on the other, the postures and speeches the establishment lays down to try to conceal and, ultimately, to destroy that original vitality, which may be cruel but at least it is intense and does not suffer from the degradations that civilization wants to impose.

Two comic examples may illustrate this point. One day, model student Nearco da Fonseca appears in the school to positively offset – from the institution's standpoint – the murderous crime of passion that has just occurred in the schoolyard.[25] He is the son of a famous politician from the Northeast, a less economically developed region of Brazil renowned for its nepotism and political oligarchism known as *coronelismo*.[26] For a start, he is a champion of acrobatic gymnastics, a regimented and institutionalized way of dealing with (and neutralizing) original bodily vitality.[27] The end of his presentation is striking: 'Nearco stretched as much as he could his lamentable lack of musculature and gave us … a *siren*! The siren is the most elementary, the most contemptible, the most stupidly ostentatious of all the apparatuses. … we looked at each other stupefied, stupefied, in the dispirited posture of those who had been conned.'[28] The hollow spectacle of power always results in a slump in morale for the onlookers.

Nearco is also a champion orator. Aristarco, with an eye to the money and prestige of the boy's father, makes a point of presenting the newcomer to the other students as an example, and one who is not necessarily inspiring and is certainly oppressive to the students. Rhetoric, moreover, is the ornamental gymnastics of discourse: 'In the first session after the triumph of the trapeze, I had occasion to appreciate him in verbal gymnastics.'[29] Nearco is soon made a member of the Grêmio Literário Amor ao Saber [Love-of-Learning Literary Guild], dedicated to rhetorical activities apparently originating from a single source:

> Eloquence was represented in the Guild by a number of categories. Cicero tragedy – cavernous voice, gesturing with dagger, which seems to cry from within the tomb … Ciceronian modesty … Ciceronian circumspection … Ciceronian storm (verborrheic … fluency precipitating him down the stairs … a sweaty, breathless, disheveled, deafening eloquence punctuated by jabs as in a boxing bout); Ciceronian candor … Ciceronian priesthood, – priestly, solemn … lifting his forehead like a miter, requesting a cathedral for each statement, on his feet two rostrums instead of shoes … Nearco introduced another type, not then represented: Ciceronian penetration.[30]

It can be seen that the singular rhetoric integrated into Pompeia's poetics, full of archaisms, refined tropes and erudite references, taken from the very oratory he wants to criticize, aims, even when this is not immediately obvious, to vituperate against the vices of the community, whether serious or comical; this makes the very laborious and seemingly (sometimes comically) hermetic verbal constructions pleasing to the reader. The attack on the degradation of institutional verbalism comes to a head in the final homage to Aristarco. During the encomium, Aristarco will be transformed. It is worth quoting at some length:

> The orator patiently gathered all the glorifying epithets, from the rare metal of sincerity to the vibrating, ductile copper of adulation. He fused the mixture in a fire of warm emphases ... Aristarco forgot himself in the delight of a metamorphosis. Venancio was his sculptor. The statue was no longer an aspiration: it was forged right there. He felt his flesh turning into metal as Venancio spoke. ... an iron coldness was freezing his limbs; on his skin, his hands, his face, he saw or guessed unknown glimmers of polish. The folds in his clothing were as if welded into a fixed mold. Inside, he felt strangely massive, as if he had drunk plaster.[31]

In the end, Aristarco will be jealous of the bust that the students reveal as a surprise tribute, since all the homage was directed at the bronze and not at him or his ego. The comic situation raises the (serious) issue of the splitting of the self, which is fundamental to the novel: the division between Sérgio as adult narrator and Sérgio as child character is central to the work. This is the subjectification of narrative that will mark fictional prose in the twentieth century. Like Machado de Assis, born 24 years earlier, and several writers in Brazil from the 1860s onwards, Raul Pompeia had read of Schopenhauer's philosophy of will, one of the foundations of the novel's psychologism. Each writer mixed the influence of Schopenhauer with the new vision of the individual subjective domain. Let us take a particular passage that sheds light on this. After showing how, as a boy, he assumed a haughty air at school, the narrator reflects,

> And that was the character I settled on, after all those oscillations. For it seems that it is only tentatively that we arrive at the outlines of character, like a sculptor molding the flesh of his own face in accordance with some ideal; or perhaps it is because, before moral individuality can manifest itself, it will try on different costumes, available

> in the psychological wardrobe of possible manifestations. ... The middle [environment], let us say, is a reversed hedgehog: instead of the centrifugal explosion of darts, we have a convergence of spines toward the center. Caught in the stinging mass of spines, it is necessary either to find a duct toward the exit or accept the unequal contest between the skin and the quills. Generally, one chooses the duct. The maxims, the headmaster, the inspections by the beadles, for instance, were three such quills ... Youth transgressed them as best it could, under the circumstances.[32]

The moment of synthesis indicates that the choice, or conflicted decision-making of hyper-individualized will, in the context, can be very dangerous, because nothing guarantees its victory. Nor is advancing by the 'duct' (*meato*, an archaic Portuguese word signifying a narrow channel) guaranteed, a reference to the urgency of the present and to the potential abyss of misfortune in upbringing that Freud (the famous disciple of Schopenhauer) would call 'structural masochism' some years later: the morbid taste for the 'prickles' that spike the skin. This danger hangs over young Sérgio from the beginning; his classmate Franco, 'always doing penance' and the target of every punishment, is his first living example. The same happens in the field of sexuality, where nothing guarantees the so-called normal course of events amid a supposed threat of deviation from the normality of the time, namely homosexuality, in an entrenched society.

Vitalism and Sexuality: Against the Degradation of Bodily Energy

High-flown language and hyper-rhetoric establish an expressive contrast to the content they must represent – the low, violent world of bodily strife and seduction, disputes, imminent ridicule, or vexation, the unstable sexuality of an environment that Freud would soon expose by putting forward the intrinsically scandalous theme of 'Infantile Sexuality', a famous chapter in his *Three Essays on the Theory of Sexuality* (1905).[33] Note the fundamental paradox: hyper-rhetoric is serving purposes that are not just political and ideological by highlighting the emptiness of the master orators, but also philosophical and psychoanalytic amid the thinking (yet to be called 'drive theory') on *will* (Schopenhauer), *will to power* (Nietzsche) or *drive* (Freud), namely the vital and spiritual will anchored in the body.[34]

On the other hand, the hyperbolic lists (very common, from the description of the classmates[35] through to the parading of Aristarco's manias) often serve to show the prodigality and exuberance of that (agonistic) life of the lower body (Bakhtin).[36] In *O Ateneu*, a Rabelaisian cornucopia may appear at a picnic lunch in the open air or at a party full of school pomp – of course, it will always be threatened by artificialism and institutional interests. In listing the apparently harmless stamps from various countries, which stoked price disputes among students in a veritable black market, the narrator concludes, 'all the colors … with which states [countries] set the rate for sentimental or mercantile correspondence, indiscriminately exploiting a minimal discount on gigantic speculations and the blood tax on the homesickness of the émigrés of hunger'.[37] We see that the prodigality of the children's activity here and in other cases is an image that grows to represent not only wide-ranging economic and geopolitical activities but also the suffering behind those activities, which the institutions treat as having no human or emotional dimension.

In a few episodes, such as the picnic outing, the cornucopia of bodily vitality opens up small gaps in the control that the institution must maintain. Faced with the ebullient joy of the students, Aristarco 'roughly' asks 'if we wanted life to now become a perpetual picnic of degeneracy. Tacitly we deny it and normal tranquility has fallen into place.'[38] Pages later, faced with a revolt about the endless repetition of the same desserts at meals, Aristarco says, 'But why, my friends, did you not convene a delegation? A delegation is a mutiny in its orderly and paper-based form!'[39] The headmaster is relieved to learn that the insurrection had a concrete motive that could be refuted by his discursive ability and authoritative performance: dislike of banana compote. Could this relief denote fear of a widespread insurrection that could marshal all the motives of oppression and revolt and would be much more difficult to neutralize? Raul Pompeia was connected with a movement branded as radical and Jacobin in the politics of the day, along with abolitionists like his friend Luiz Gama (1830–82), an ex-slave who succeeded in becoming a lawyer and achieved the release of more than 500 black men and women from slavery. Among other things, in writing *O Ateneu,* Pompeia created one of the most important novels of nineteenth-century Brazil: a political and psychological novel where the school is portrayed as an allegory of human institutions. Hence this work is a powerful critique of a civilization that girds the body of the child with language and sacrosanct rules of conduct in order to control and direct its original vitality.

Notes

1. Ateneu is the name of the school in the novel. It is a literary representation of Abílio, a school founded in 1871 in Rio de Janeiro, whose students were the children of the city's elite. At that time, Rio was the capital of Brazil. Brasília, constructed on the central plateau, became the capital in 1960. Pompeia 1995; Pompeia 2015.
2. Aloysius Bertrand (1807–41) is known as the poet who introduced prose poetry into French literature.
3. Baudelaire 1857; Baudelaire 2008; Flaubert 1857; Flaubert 2003.
4. Andrade 1974, 183.
5. Araripe Júnior 1978, 145–64.
6. Gomes 1958, 224–47; Paes 2008, 75–95. The concept of literary impressionism is quite vague, as is art nouveau in literature. In my view, these concepts demonstrate the difficulty of classifying the multiple literary styles of a transition period, after the triumph and crisis of romanticism and realism and before the true modernist experiments: the transgressions of the avant-garde mix with a new subjectivism to explore the radicalization of the narrative focus of the solipsist self.
7. Antonio Candido 1992, 149.
8. Schwarz 1981, 26.
9. Santiago 2000.
10. Brayner 1979, 121–45.
11. Acízelo 1999.
12. Perrone-Moisés 1988.
13. Bosi 2003, 81.
14. Brandão 1995.
15. Pompeia 2015, 3.
16. Pompeia 2015, 20–1.
17. Referring to Aristarchus of Samos, the astronomer and mathematician who first proposed that the Earth revolves around the Sun. Throughout the novel, characters' names are never gratuitous.
18. Pompeia 2015, 14.
19. Pompeia 2015, 213.
20. Pompeia 2015, 29.
21. Pompeia 2015, 24.
22. Pompeia 2015, 28.
23. Pompeia 2015, 37.
24. Pompeia 2015, 3. As a genre that focuses on the emotional and intellectual (and thus scholarly) formation of the protagonist, the *Bildungsroman* in eighteenth-century Germany flaunted the same type of figuration of the tensions between the desires of the young protagonist and the demands of the institution as representative of the adult world. Since *Wilhelm Meister's Apprenticeship* (Goethe 2007), the clash between the young individual and the collective, formalized rules of established institutions has been a common narrative path to structure the inner formation of the young character. Marcus V. Mazzari (2010, 159–96) includes *The Athenaeum* in his study of the *Bildungsroman* and novels that have the school as a central setting in the German tradition. He compares Raul Pompeia's novel with *The Confusions of Young Törless* by Robert Musil (2001).
25. In ancient Greece, Nearco of Elea was the tyrant who tortured the philosopher Zeno, accused of participating in a conspiracy against him, and had him executed.
26. *Coronelismo* [colonelism] is a socio-political practice that flourished in rural areas and small towns in the interior of Brazil during the First Republic (1889–1930) and operates as a form of top-down local autocracy, in which the elite, embodied by the rural landowner, despotically controls the means of production, concentrating and wielding local economic, social and political power.
27. Bergson 1998; Deleuze and Guattari 2009. Although this bodily vitality can be approximated to what I call here the 'vitalism' of Henri Bergson's concept, I prefer to treat it as a way of designating pre-institutionalized body intensity, i.e., before it gets captured in the controlling and sense-making networks of public or private institutions. It can be seen as following on from

the conceptual framework Deleuze and Guattari proposed in *Anti-Œdipus* (2009). Another path of interpretation of this vitalism, linked with the cultural moment in which the novel was published, is proposed in the very interesting essay 'Darwinism, Max Nordau, Raul Pompeia and the Struggle for Existence' by César Braga-Pinto (2015).

28. Pompeia 2015, 95.
29. Pompeia 2015, 98.
30. Pompeia 2015, 98–9.
31. Pompeia 2015, 203.
32. Pompeia 2015, 82–3. The word *meio* has been translated as 'middle'. The meaning here is 'environment'.
33. Freud 2017.
34. Nietzsche 2017.
35. Theophrastus 1998. There is an article that links the descriptions of the students in *O Ateneu* to the tradition of Theophrastus, author of *The Characters* (Teixeira 2010, 72–3).
36. Bakhtin 2009.
37. Pompeia 2015, 124.
38. Pompeia 2015, 152.
39. Pompeia 2015, 161.

Bibliography

Acízelo, Roberto. *O império da eloquência. Retórica e poética no Brasil oitocentista*. Rio de Janeiro: EdUERJ/EdUFF, 1999.

Andrade, Mário de. '*O Ateneu*'. In *Aspectos da literatura brasileira*, 173–84. São Paulo: Livraria Martins Editora, 1974.

Antonio Candido. 'Música e música'. In *Brigada ligeira e outros escritos*, 145–50. São Paulo: Ed. UNESP, 1992.

Araripe Júnior, Tristão de Alencar. *Teoria, crítica e história literária*. São Paulo: LTC/Edusp, 1978.

Bakhtin, Mikhail. *Rabelais and His World*, translated by Hélène Swolski. Bloomington: Indiana University Press, 2009.

Baudelaire, Charles. *Les fleurs du mal*. Paris: Poulet-Malassis et De Broise, 1857.

Baudelaire, Charles. *The Flowers of Evil*, translated by James N. McGowan. Oxford: Oxford University Press, 2008.

Bergson, Henri. *Creative Evolution*, translated by Arthur Mitchell. New York: Dover, 1998.

Bosi, Alfredo. '*O Ateneu*, opacidade e destruição'. In *Céu, inferno*, 51–86. São Paulo: Editora 34 and Livraria Duas Cidades, 2003.

Braga-Pinto, César. 'Darwinism, Max Nordau, Raul Pompeia and the Struggle for Existence'. In Raul Pompeia, *The Athenaeum*, vii–xxvii. Evanston, IL: Northwestern University Press, 2015.

Brandão, Roberto de Oliveira. '*O Ateneu* e a retórica', *Remate de males* 15 (1995): 47–60.

Brayner, Sonia. *Labirinto do espaço romanesco*. Rio de Janeiro: Ed. Civilização Brasileira, 1979.

Deleuze, Gilles, and Félix Guattari. *The Anti-Œdipus*, translated by Robert Hurley. London: Penguin Books, 2009.

Flaubert, Gustave. *Madame Bovary*. Paris: Michel Lévy Frères, 1857.

Flaubert, Gustave. *Madame Bovary*, translated by Lydia Davis. London: Penguin, 2003.

Freud, Sigmund. *Three Essays on the Theory of Sexuality*, translated by Ulrike Kristner. London: Verso, 2017.

Goethe, Johann W. *Wilhelm Meister's Apprenticeship*, translated by Anna Swanwick. Los Angeles: Aegypan, 2007.

Gomes, Eugênio. *Visões e revisões*. Rio de Janeiro: MEC/INL, 1958.

Mazzari, Marcus V. *Labirintos da aprendizagem. Pacto fáustico, romance de formação e outros temas de literatura comparada*. São Paulo: Editora 34, 2010.

Musil, Robert. *The Confusions of Young Törless*, translated by Shaun Whiteside. London: Penguin Books, 2001.

Nietzsche, Friedrich. *The Will to Power: An Attempted Transvaluation of All Values*, translated by Anthony M. Ludovici. Seattle, WA: Createspace, 2017.

Paes, José Paulo. 'O *art nouveau* na literatura brasileira'. In *Armazém literário. Ensaios*, 75–95. São Paulo: Companhia das Letras, 2008.

Perrone-Moisés, Leyla. *O Ateneu. Retórica e paixão*. São Paulo: Brasiliense, 1988.

Pompeia, Raul. *O Ateneu*. São Paulo: Editora Scipione, 1995.

Pompeia, Raul. *The Athenaeum*, translated by Renata R. M. Wasserman. Evanston, IL: Northwestern University Press, 2015.

Santiago, Silviano. '*O Ateneu*: contradições e perquirições'. In *Uma literatura nos trópicos*, 66–102. Rio de Janeiro: Rocco, 2000.

Schwarz, Roberto. '*O Atheneu*'. In *A sereia e o desconfiado*, 25–30. São Paulo: Paz e Terra, 1981.

Teixeira, Ivan. 'Machado de Assis e o figurino retórico dos caracteres', *Revista do Instituto de Estudos Brasileiros* 50 (2010): 69–98.

Theophrastus. *The Characters of Theophrastus*, edited and translated by R. G. Ussher. Bristol: Bristol Classic Press, 1998.

12

O aborto and the Rise of Erotic Popular Print in Late Nineteenth-Century Brazil

Leonardo Mendes

In the last two decades of the nineteenth century, there was an unprecedented growth in publishing and reading in Brazil which has been overlooked by traditional historiography. This is so because scholarly discourse typically takes as the pulse of literary life the activity of authors like Machado de Assis (1839–1908) – Brazil's greatest writer then and now – and of booksellers like Baptiste-Louis Garnier (1823–93), who allegedly only published consecrated writers. It disregards other publishers and the circulation of erotic popular fiction because it falls outside canonical definitions of literature. What has gone unnoticed is a dynamic late nineteenth-century book market, with an abundance of titles, formats, genres and good prices, implying thousands of readers eager for material, despite the notorious illiteracy rates of 50 per cent in the city of Rio de Janeiro and around 80 per cent in the rest of the country.[1] Apparently these two facts – low literacy rates and high sales of popular fiction – could coexist.

This vibrant picture contradicts the bleak scenario that elite writers of the period tend to project, habitually complaining about poor sales and the lack of qualified readers, and hence the need to educate the public to appreciate the literature they deemed authentic, that is, their own.[2] Taking the self-image of elite writers as a mirror of reality, Brazilian historiography tends to confirm there was little interest in books and reading in the period.[3] However, during those same years when leading critic Valentim Magalhães (1859–1903) famously declared that some Brazilian writers could now earn enough money to buy bread but not butter,[4] publisher Pedro Quaresma (1863–1921), of Rio de Janeiro's People's Bookshop, was selling several thousand copies of *Elzira, a morta virgem* [*Elzira, the Dead Virgin*] (1883), a popular 'sensation novel' by the obscure writer Pedro Viana which remained in catalogue until the 1920s.[5] Such wide readership was culturally grounded and was as legitimate as the reading practices of the elite.[6]

Besides 'sensation novels' like *Elzira* and other late-century hits like *Maria, a desgraçada* [*Maria, the Unfortunate Girl*] (1891), by Alfredo Elisiário da Silva, also published by Pedro Quaresma, erotic fiction had a niche of its own in the new publishing market. To avoid the negativity associated with pornographic discourse, licentious works were called 'happy books', 'joyful reading' or, most commonly, 'books (or reading) for men'. The labels functioned as a description of the works on sale, marketing them as 'erotic', 'obscene' or 'pornographic'. The latter terms circulated in the press and in literary conversations of the period and worked as synonyms, broadly meaning 'immoral writing'. The present-day distinction between 'pornography' – meaning transparent sexual representation – and 'erotica' – meaning aestheticism and verbal games –[7] did not exist before modernism and therefore does not apply to nineteenth-century material. Back then these words were interchangeable and will be treated as such in this chapter. Instead of as a genre with formal characteristics, 'pornography' can be viewed as 'a way of reading'.[8] It refers to 'an interaction between reader and text, not to text or authorial intent alone'.[9]

The bookshops openly implied that the descriptor 'books for men' was a joke, postscripts in smaller print saying that women could buy and read the works if they wanted to or that people of all sexes and ages would find something to suit their taste. Even if 'books for men' was meant as a joke, it is reasonable to assume some women would be put off by the branding or view it as an interdiction. However, there is much evidence that women read erotic literature.[10] A common anecdote in the newspapers' humorous columns was the story of the woman who confessed to the priest she had read all of her husband's 'books for men'. In the manual of 'practical philosophy' *O que as noivas devem saber* [*What Brides Should Know*] (1905), the Condessa de Til – pseudonym of Portuguese writer Alfredo Gallis (1859–1910) – advised women about the convenience of intimate hygiene after reading certain 'misleading novels' capable of provoking 'abundant glandular ejaculation' in single, married or widowed women.[11] Women who dared to read these books had of course to be more discreet than men.

There were books for all budgets and in all formats, from cheap realist paperbacks to pricy hardbacks printed on better-quality paper. After the fall of the monarchy there was no legal provision against the publishing and retailing of obscene material. Article 282 in Chapter V of the 1890 Brazilian Penal Code, 'About public offenses to modesty', set a one- to six-month term of imprisonment for those who 'offend the good customs with impudent displays, obscene acts or gestures, practised in a public place or attended by the public, that outrage and scandalize society'. It made no reference to pornographic material, but that did not mean that social morality was as liberal as the law. There was a lot of dissatisfaction with the popularization of erotic publications, especially in Catholic circles, which used the periodical *O Apóstolo* [*The Apostle*], linked to the Rio de Janeiro Prelacy and the Catholic Bookshop, to fight against what they described as a 'great epidemic'.[12] By the end of the century, 'happy books' were typically read in secret, but there was now a place for erotic fiction in bookshops, in bourgeois society, in reading rooms around the country and in the chests and drawers of family homes.

Printing shops popped up everywhere.[13] In the capital city of Rio de Janeiro, Pedro Quaresma's People's Bookshop and Domingos Magalhães's Modern Bookshop operated more openly in the erotic popular book market and offered alternatives to the traditional Laemmert and Garnier Bookshops. While the latter two were located on Ouvidor Street, the most elegant in downtown Rio, the others were in streets nearby, closer to popular traders. In São Paulo, Teixeira Bookshop started to publish and sell pornography in the 1880s. In the 1890s, sensing the profitability of the new market and aiming at a more sophisticated reader, Laemmert started to publish erotic fiction too. In other cultural centres, like Porto Alegre, in the south, and Belém do Pará, Maranhão and Recife, in the north, local bookshops sold the books printed by publishers in Rio de Janeiro and São Paulo as well as erotic material imported from Europe. For a small fee, books could be sent by mail to all valid addresses in Brazil, taking advantage of navigation routes and cabotage trade along the coast and railway systems in Bahia, Rio de Janeiro, São Paulo, Curitiba and Porto Alegre.[14]

Pedro Quaresma and the Market for Erotic Popular Printed Matter

Pedro Quaresma was a major player in the new publishing market. He joined the book business in the late 1870s, at the start of the expansion of publishing. By the mid-1890s he had become one of the city's best-known booksellers. He secured his market share by exploring the vein of popular books for practical purposes, like *Folhetos Musicais* [*Musical Leaflets*], with music scores to be played at family gatherings; *Manuais do Namorado* [*Boyfriend's Manuals*], with advice on how to express feelings and write love letters; and *Orador do Povo* [*The People's Orator*], containing a collection of family speeches for parties, baptisms and weddings.[15] As he worked out what readers wanted he started to explore the emerging niches of 'sensation novels', literature for children (of which he was a pioneer publisher in Brazil) and 'books for men'. The label for erotic fiction could accommodate a large variety of titles and genres, including humanist and libertine literature from the sixteenth, seventeenth and eighteenth centuries, contemporary naturalist fiction, anti-clerical pornography, fantasies about the unruly sexual habits of the ancients, history books about prostitution and famous prostitutes, manuals of sexual advice and the new genre of original pornographic fiction written in Portuguese for the new market.

Quaresma sold all types of 'books for men'. He stands out as the most active seller of erotic printed matter in the capital, acting as local distributor of foreign imports to sellers in other states and eventually becoming famous for his wide range of 'very cheap books'.[16] Quaresma was aware of his role in the new market and used newspaper ads to mock the elitism of other bookshops. He offered an incredibly diverse and rich menu of erotic titles and unabashedly associated the books with sex and masturbation. In advertisements in Rio de Janeiro's *Gazeta de Notícias* (13 July 1885) he advised (male) readers to get 'reinforced button pants' before opening such paperbacks. He teased the public with suggestions that he had unpublishable titles for sale that could only be revealed in private at the shop. Quaresma followed the pattern adopted by other booksellers by commercializing licentious titles as light entertainment. Erotic fiction was typically associated with the satirical press and was advertised as an invigorating pastime, advisable for the shy and the gloomy. By titillating mind and body, these books provided the reader with a private moment of repose from the stressful, lonely life in the modern city. Bookshops promised that such reading would 'activate the will' and rekindle the reader's inner fire.

A typical advertisement of erotic books available at the People's Bookshop would list under the same heading Boccaccio's *Decameron* (1353), François Rabelais' *Pantagruel* and *Gargantua* (1534), Bocage's poems, libertine novels like the anonymous *Thérèse philosophe* (1748) and *Fanny Hill* (1748) by English writer John Cleland (1709–89), naturalist novels like *O crime do padre Amaro* [*The Crime of Father Amaro*] (1875) by Portuguese writer Eça de Queirós (1845–1900), and all of Émile Zola's (1840–1902) works, but especially *L'Assommoir* (1876), *La*

Terre (1887) and *Nana* (1880), his most famous book in Brazil, continually advertised as pornography.[17] These now canonical naturalist works appeared alongside anonymous low-priced paperbacks titled *Prowess of a Clitoris, How to Treat Women as They Deserve, Jumpy Tales that Send a Chill down the Spine, Electric Readings, Love and Sensuality, Screams of the Flesh, Incendiary Mussels, The Interim Lover: Gorgeous Scenes that Take Place in the Garden, in the Bedroom and Finally in the Kitchen, Julia de Milo: Portrait of a Dishonest Woman* (a subtitle that would suit Zola's *Nana*), 'and other works that help increase the appetite with some chili pepper, suitable for rust removal in cold weather'.[18]

The tantalizing anonymous paperbacks – of which so far none has been recovered – cost as little as 200 *réis*, at a time when a tram ticket cost 100 *réis*, the same price as the daily editions of mass-circulating daily newspapers like *Gazeta de Notícias* and *O Paiz*. One thousand *réis* would buy a cheap lunch in downtown Rio de Janeiro or pay for one admission fee to the Musée Parisien, a wax museum where one could admire life-size sculptures of Émile Zola and other celebrities. A new copy of the successful naturalist novel *O homem* [*The Man*] (1887), by celebrated writer Aluísio Azevedo (1857–1913), would cost 3,000 *réis*, an affordable book, the average price of a 300-page volume and equivalent more or less to the amount a skilled worker (like a blacksmith or woodworker) would receive for a day's work. If he could read (or knew someone who could), there were plenty of cheap paperbacks available, often illustrated, in a society with few other representations of sexuality and the naked body and in which printed matter was the main vehicle for the dissemination of information about sex.

Quaresma sold the period's most notorious erotic book, in the popular subgenre of anti-clerical pornography: *Os serões do convento* [*Convent Evenings*] by 'M. L.'. The first and best-known edition, in three pocket volumes, was printed at the possibly fake Typographia do Bairro Alto, in Lisbon, without address or date, but certainly published around mid-century. The book's success can be measured by the number of clandestine editions that were circulating at the end of the century, at least one published in Brazil. As early as 1862 a pirated edition had appeared in Rio de Janeiro as a single volume.[19] By the end of the century, Cruz Coutinho Bookshop, in Rio de Janeiro, had another edition in two illustrated volumes for 10,000 *réis*.[20] The original had no illustrations. The pricy illustrated edition shows that pictures could be inserted into clandestine publications of *Os serões do convento* and other licentious works, giving them more potential as pornographic books, made to be read and viewed.[21] Loyal to his popular clientele, Quaresma sold yet another, four-volume edition of the 'appetizing book' for 4,000 *réis*.[22]

At that time, the most celebrated living pornographer in the lusophone world was 'Rabelais', another pseudonym of Portuguese writer Alfredo Gallis, with significant sales in Portugal and Brazil.[23] He was so famous that booksellers advertised his works separately under the heading 'works of Rabelais'. Most readers knew this was not the author of *Gargantua*, but the association with the French writer's triumphant lasciviousness was obvious.[24] Gallis offered an alternative – today little known – to France's dominance in the nineteenth-century market of pornographic literature.[25] Without the intent of producing homogeneous work, he published several successful volumes of erotic tales under the name of 'Rabelais', such as *Afrodisíacas* [*Aphrodisiacs*], *Amorosas* [*Loving Women*], *Diabruras do Cupido* [*Cupid's Pranks*], *Lascivas* [*Lascivious Women*], *Libertinas* [*Libertine Women*], *Lúbricas* [*Sensual Women*], *Luxúrias para rir* [*Lust for Fun*], *Noites de Vênus* [*Venus Nights*], *Cocotes e conselheiros* [*Courtesans and Councillors*], *Os crimes do amor* [*Love Crimes*] and *Volúpias: 14 contos galantes* [*Voluptuousness: 14 Gallant Tales*], his first and best-known work. Rabelais and *Volúpias* were routinely cited in the press and in fiction as exemplary of the new market for erotic popular fiction.

Alfredo Gallis lived in Lisbon, but the first two editions of *Volúpias* were published in São Paulo. The first appeared as a clandestine publication in 1886 in the last years of the monarchy. It bears neither the author's nor the publisher's name on the cover. In the second edition (Rabelais 1893), published under a more liberalizing legal framework, the author Rabelais and publishers Antônio Teixeira & Irmão appeared on the front page, admitting in the preface they had made the 1886 edition. The Portuguese brothers and booksellers Antônio Maria and José Joaquim Teixeira opened the Teixeira Bookshop in São Paulo in 1878. It sold all types of printed matter: practical manuals, stationery, school books, foreign fiction, legal literature and 'books for men'.[26] By the late 1880s the brothers felt confident enough to venture into the publishing business, bringing out *Volúpias* and other contemporary hits like Olavo Bilac's (1865–1918) debut book, *Poesias* [*Poems*] (1888). Continuously available in bookshops in Brazil and Portugal until the beginning of the twentieth century, *Volúpias* cost between 2,000 and 5,000 *réis*. As proof of the book's success, a third edition appeared in 1906 from a Portuguese publisher in the city of Porto.

Besides Rabelais's book, the Teixeira brothers published other erotic bestsellers, like the naturalist novel *A carne* [*The Flesh*] (1888) by Júlio Ribeiro (1845–90), a *succès de scandale* that famously circulated as porn until the mid twentieth century, despite the author's best intentions.[27] The book's long-lived commercial success offers a counterpoint to traditional historiography, which sees the novel as a failed work.[28] *A carne* can be best understood if we see it not as an 'experimental novel' or a 'case study' of female hysteria – as traditional historiography boringly has it – but as an erotic popular book in late nineteenth-century Brazil which sold several thousand copies over the years and went into a third edition in 1903 with another publisher. Priced at 3,000 *réis*, the book was a hit among law students in São Paulo.[29] It was famous enough to appear in the 1890 Carnival parades, represented as a butcher shop.[30] The appearance of *A carne* as a Carnival subject reveals its notoriety as an erotic publication in Brazilian society.

Like *A carne*'s, the success achieved by Aluísio Azevedo's *O homem* the year before can only be explained if we consider the book as another erotic popular publication of the late nineteenth century. As he had done when he published *O mulato* [*The Mulatto*] (1881), Aluísio and his friends (including, crucially, his influential older brother Artur) set out on an ambitious advertising campaign (conferences, dinners, favourable reviews, press releases and poems) that ambiguously presented the content of the hysterical girl's dreams as erotic material. In her hallucinations, Magdá has good sex, gives birth and murders her lover. Aluísio and his friends insinuated the eroticism and simultaneously assured the public of the scientific seriousness of the work.[31] *O homem* sold an incredible 5,000 to 6,000 copies. Since the seventeenth century, hysterical women like Magdá had been popular characters in pornography.[32] They appear in *Serões do convento* and in *Volúpias*, functioning as an excuse to describe sexual activity. Some apocryphal lewd paperbacks sold by Quaresma, like *Memórias de uma mulher insaciável* [*Memoirs of an Insatiable Woman*] and *Elvira, a insaciável* [*Elvira, the Insatiable*], dealt with the same hot topic. Ironically, the success achieved by concessions to the 'popular' in *O homem* allowed Aluísio Azevedo to sign with Garnier Bookshop (a symbol of literary achievement), which then published a fourth edition of Magdá's story – the first three having been printed by the modest Tipografia de Adolfo de Castro e Silva & Cia – as well as new editions of *O mulato* and *Casa de pensão* [*Rooming House*] (1884).

O aborto [*The Abortion*] as Erotic Popular Literature

In 1893, when Pedro Quaresma decided to publish *O aborto*, he was hoping to ride the same wave of erotic popular printed matter with yet another locally produced naturalist novel. Figueiredo Pimentel, the author, allegedly intended it to be a serious scientific work, but himself evokes its licentiousness in the preface, when he recognizes that many people will judge the book 'pornographic, immoral and dissolute'.[33]

Four years earlier the work had circulated in serial form in the *Província do Rio*, a newspaper from Niterói, the town across the bay from Rio de Janeiro, where the story (supposedly based on fact) takes place. Referring to the article of the Imperial Penal Code that criminalized abortion, the story was called *O Artigo 200* [*Article 200*]. It told about the life of 17-year-old Maria Rodrigues (nicknamed Maricota), a native of Rio Bonito (80 kilometres east of Rio de Janeiro), who together with her parents moves to Niterói in the last years of the monarchy in search of a better life. It describes in direct and blunt style the consequences of an unwanted pregnancy (by cousin Mário) interrupted by an abortion that leads to the girl's bleeding to death, and includes explicit references to urine, menstruation, orgasms and condoms. The publication caused an uproar in Niterói. After the newspaper's office was flooded with complaint letters and cancelled subscriptions, Figueiredo Pimentel was forced to rewrite the end of the story and turn it into a melodrama.

For Quaresma, who republished *O Artigo 200* without cuts and with a new sensationalist title, such complaints were a promise of good sales. From January 1893, he started to publicize in city newspapers the imminent publication of Figueiredo Pimentel's 'exciting naturalist novel'. When the book hit the shops in March as an inexpensive paperback priced at 2,000 *réis*, Quaresma published a note reaffirming the author's bond with other naturalist writers like Zola and Paul Bonnetain (1858–99), whose novel about masturbation, *Charlot s'amuse* (1883), led him to be prosecuted for indecent exposure in 1885. As expected, *O aborto* became a huge success, Quaresma claiming to have sold 5,000 copies during the first month of publication alone.[34] This could be an exaggeration in order to boost sales, but one of the four existing volumes of the first edition proves that at least 5,000 copies were printed. As a rule, publishers tested the market with initial print runs of 1,000 copies, reprinting another 1,000 as demand continued. These volumes' disappearance can be partially explained by the poor-quality paper that was used so prices could be kept low. *O aborto* caused quite a stir and many people thought its appearance was a matter for the police.[35] Convinced of the book's commercial value, even the classy Livraria Garnier had it on sale.

Predictably, elite writers repudiated the novel as inferior and immoral. They repeatedly used the word 'pornography' as a way to downgrade the book. In an ambiguous review that avoided citing the novel's title out of respect for the readers (but also to incite them), Coelho Neto made the link between *O aborto* and libertine literature, writing that the novel had the 'spicy taste' of the Marquis de Sade's memoirs.[36] Valentim Magalhães reduced the novel to 'pornographic literature', unworthy of being mentioned in a newspaper column.[37] In 1895, in a review of *Um canalha* [*A Scoundrel*] (1895), Figueiredo Pimentel's second naturalist novel, Artur Azevedo recalled the outrage caused by the appearance of *O aborto* two years before and compared it to *Os serões do convento* in terms of daring.[38] Figueiredo Pimentel himself had associated the two books in his preface as a way of denying their similarities, but in the eyes of the public this only confirmed their kinship. Even Araripe Júnior (1848–1911), a rare critic supportive of naturalism, accused the work of being 'full of pornographic audacity' that would startle 'the most daring of naturalists'.[39]

O aborto contains its own list of erotic popular books, with which Figueiredo Pimentel's novel reverberates as a work of the same kind. In the novel, Mário had a trunk where he kept a small collection of erotic books, four of which were naturalist novels: *Nana* by Zola; *O homem* by Aluísio Azevedo; *A carne* by Júlio Ribeiro; *O crime do Padre Amaro* by Eça de Queirós; *Esposa e virgem* [*Wife and Virgin*], a Brazilian edition of the 'sensation novel' *Mademoiselle Giroud, ma femme* (1870) by French writer Adolphe Belot (1829–90); and, perhaps more importantly, the period's erotic favourites: *Os serões do convento* and *Volúpias: 14 contos galantes*. Both Mário and Maricota interact with the books, alone and together. The girl changes as she gets acquainted with them, 'taking notice in several episodes she did not understand well, but where she sensed great immoralities. She appreciated them as naughtiness only.'[40] *O aborto* could also be thus appreciated. Indeed, in a demolishing review by writer Carlos Magalhães de Azeredo (1872–1963), *O aborto* was comparable to Rabelais's *Volúpias* in terms of 'moral depravity'.[41]

A carne was the newest volume in Mário's trunk, fresh off the press. It appears in Chapter 5, when the student has already noticed that Maricota is attracted to him. The young man does not want to be disloyal to his uncle and aunt, who have given him shelter, food and affection, by sleeping with their daughter. At the same time, he feels he cannot resist her for long. Not knowing what to do, he decides to read to distract his mind:

> Lying down, he randomly took the first book he found – *A carne*, a naturalist novel by Júlio Ribeiro, recently put on sale, published by Teixeira & Irmão in São Paulo. … He was struck by the pages written in the most correct vernacular, but in heavy style. … *A carne*, no matter how much art it had, aroused his body, arousing sensual feelings, activating his will.[42]

In many ways, *O aborto* was bolder than *A carne* and the other books in Mário's erotic collection. The exception was perhaps Rabelais's tales of contemporary Lisbon, which also flirted with scientism and had as backdrop the modern city, where one could meet a new person every now and then and never see them again. By choosing scientific language to describe physiological processes and parts of the body, the naturalist novel was more realistic and graphic than the libertine novel. A disturbing novelty was the exploration of the sense of smell and the introduction of odours, especially those considered unpleasant and thus curtailed by good manners. Aspects of human physiology relating to the private parts of the body – urine, faeces, sperm, saliva, sweat and menstrual blood – were taken to be obscene, even if they were not directly associated with sex in the narratives.[43] They were scandalous (and appetizing) themes in themselves. By breaking the rules of decorum, they created transgressive mental spaces and brought readers closer to their own body, 'activating the will'.

Figueiredo Pimentel did not describe sexual mechanics as closely as Rabelais, but went straight to the point and named things for what they were in the everyday life of ordinary people, without euphemisms or cultured metaphors. Because of this realistic language and crudeness, the naturalist novel was occasionally perceived as more vulgar and shocking – let us say, more pornographic – than libertine literature and anti-clerical pornography. In France, Zola's foul language was one of the first focuses of the general repudiation of naturalism. However, to many readers (especially the young), such language was groundbreaking and liberating. With a shocking title that referred to illicit sex and its criminal covering up, *O aborto* raised the pornographic consumption of naturalism to levels of audacity that had not been dared in notoriously bold (and popular) previous novels, like *Nana*, *O crime do padre Amaro* and *A carne*, as well as other works absent from Mário's trunk, like Aluísio Azevedo's *O cortiço* [*The Slum*] (1890) and even the audacious *Bom-Crioulo* [*The Black Man and the Cabin Boy*] (1895), published by Adolfo Caminha (1867–97) two years after *O aborto*.

The detached description of physiological processes connected with the stomach and the kidneys was a shocking (and liberating) novelty of naturalism, linking the aesthetic to the Rabelaisian 'lower body'.[44] In Brazil, *O cortiço* was perhaps the first novel in which people go to the toilet. In the famous description of the early hours in the slum, the narrator observes from afar people entering and exiting the 'latrines'[45] before going to work. Figueiredo Pimentel is more intimate and shows Mário urinating on two occasions. Before the arrival of Maricota, on the night of their first intercourse, troubled by reading *A carne*, Mário decides to sleep: 'He first took the agate chamber pot under the bed, stretching out his arm, and lying down he began to piss hard, making noises.'[46] On another occasion, when he wakes up with a hangover after a night out drinking with friends, he drinks the water from the jug by the bed: 'With a full bladder, his kidneys ached; he urinated for a long time in jets, and held the vessel in his hands, letting the liquid out a beautiful light-coloured amber, now dripping, now running thin, in a faint squirt.'[47] In the first scene, the choice 'to piss hard' makes the description phallic and brutal, affirming the presence of an exposed penis. The second scene is equally intimate, detailing the scene in which the young man urinates and providing enough detail for the reader to recreate it in their imagination.

Mário's penis appears a third time in the novel, on the first night with Maricota: 'Mário felt ill, feverish, dazed, and at the same time dazzled by the girl's beauty. A great desire for copulation suddenly overcame him, imprisoned by unbridled power, with his penis hard, erect, pulling the blanket.'[48] With extreme audacity, Figueiredo Pimentel describes an erect male organ, using the neutral word 'penis' rather than appeasing libertine metaphors like 'Cupid's arrow'. Priapism, the ode to the penis (or phallus), is an important mark of pornography – an essentially masculine genre – but is rare in naturalism. In *O cortiço*, the narrator's boldest gesture is to tell us that, after watching the irresistible Rita Bahiana's sensual dance, Jerônimo falls ill and 'began to stir with desire'[49] on receiving a massage from his wife, Piedade. It is so discreet a reference to an erection that it goes unnoticed by many readers. Mário's erect penis, on the other hand, indiscreetly pulling the blanket – an experience many (male) readers would recognize – is an inescapable mark of erotic fiction. Such objectification of the male sexual organ was especially troublesome to patriarchal mentality and was only admissible in pornographic discourse.

Still in the domain of bodily fluids, of what enters and leaves the body, Maricota's menstruation receives similar treatment to what we see in *A carne* and other naturalist novels. In Júlio Ribeiro's book, Lenita speaks unabashedly about menstruation, treating the subject as a banal physiological process. Pardal Mallet (1864–94) does the same in the forgotten naturalist novel *Lar* [*Home*] (1888), in which Sinhá's menstrual flow is introduced without fanfare or mystery. Aluísio Azevedo develops the theme considerably in *O cortiço*, transforming Pombinha's long-awaited first menstruation into an event catalysing great shifts in the narrative. Figueiredo Pimentel treats Maricota's first menstruation coldly, in a detached account that perhaps was a rare source of information on the subject for many people. Maricota has no problem getting her period and, like Lenita and Sinhá, is not embarrassed to talk about it. In Figueiredo Pimentel's description, the experience is a source of joy ('books for men' were about making the reader feel good). The novel registers the popular expression *estou de paquete* [I'm on my period], which at the beginning of the nineteenth century associated the menstruation cycle with the monthly arrivals of ships (*paquetes*) from Europe:

> Weeks after she turned thirteen, the menstrual flow appeared for the first time.
>
> She wasn't surprised at the menstruation. She felt a strong bellyache – quick and violent cramps – which she had thought to be purely intestinal, from an indigestion due to unseasoned fruits she had eaten the day before.
>
> She rushed to the chamber pot. And as she lifted her gown and skirts, she saw a stream of purple blood trickling down her thick thighs, leaving the shirt with a broad red stain.
>
> She had expected to be 'bothered' any day, though she did not count on it coming so soon.
>
> After the first moment of natural surprise and commotion, half-blinded, slightly reddened, she left the room, running with joy. She went to the neighbour's house and told Mr Meirelles's daughters 'that she was also a young woman because the "paquete" had come to her a few minutes before' – to them who were always mocking her, scoffing her because 'Sinhá was not yet a woman', the 'trouble' had not yet come to her, that she could not give birth.[50]

Later, in Niterói, when Mário and Maricota become lovers, the subject returns:

> The pharmacist could not resist the sight of the girl's turgid breasts. A violent, beastly desire for copulation suddenly ignited his organism. He advanced to his cousin, ripped the waistband of her dress, ripped her shirt, slightly bloody from a residue of menstruation.
>
> Maricota appeared naked, completely naked, at the entrance of the room, under the almost extinct dull light of the lamp, beautiful, divine, statuesque. The cousin placed her in his arms, like a child, holding the curves of her legs, resting her head on his shoulder, and threw himself with her on the bed, bursting the buttons of his trousers.
>
> — No, Mário, no, *estou de paquete*, she moaned.
>
> Maricota, offering weak resistance, holding him with both arms around his neck, pulling him, calling him to herself, kissed him, burying her tongue into his throat, in a spasm of pleasure.[51]

Like Zola's Nana and Ribeiro's Lenita, Maricota stars in a 'prostitute story'. From early on, in Rio Bonito, she is talkative and approachable: 'Overly frivolous, a flirt, she engaged with all those who sought her, without distinction, whoever he was, from the train chiefs to porters to the public prosecutor.'[52] In Niterói, Mário quickly understands her character: 'Playful, loud, dating all the boys and having inherited from her father all his weaknesses and the same capricious temper.'[53] Comfortable in her own skin, Maricota has the same confidence as other libertine women and goes to her cousin's room for her first experience of sex, without fear or guilt. Such anti-patriarchal behaviour, the effect of a female character's free thinking, was only admissible in pornography. Maricota's autonomy, the student's erect penis and the triple orgasm of the first night were the stuff of 'books for men'.

> It was late. Everybody was asleep. He had a beautiful, appetizing woman in his room, who loved him madly enough to come looking for him. And he tried not to rise quickly, and without her being able to avoid it, to grab her, to throw her to the ground, in a brutal, savage urge, to tear her shirt apart, and to relish her in the spasms of delirious pleasure.
>
> He refrained from moving, though.
>
> Then the girl, always serene, leaning her right hand on the mattress, bent over, bouncing her rough, turgid breasts across the broad collar of her shirt, and kissed him on the forehead.
>
> He could hold no longer. A convulsive tremor shook his whole body, shivering all over him like a frisson of fever, finely licking the epidermis, in a rough and gentle caress of pain and pleasure, along the spine. He felt as if someone had come to him with iron gauntlets to give him a great blow on the skull. He heard a prolonged, subterranean noise. His ears were ringing. The eyes saw tiny sparks, sparkling red in a dark background.
>
> He didn't think. Frantic, maddened, mad, he grabbed her by the waist, threw her brutally on the bed, forced her sturdy legs, separating them, and, lying on top, kissing her, biting her, burying his tongue in her mouth almost to her throat, hugging her with frenzy in a long, narrow squeeze, he came once … twice … three times.[54]

Maricota also has opinions about Mário: 'She thought he was shy, timorous, not very bold towards women.' For a long time, she had wanted him, without him noticing: 'She had even wondered how he had dared to love her that night, not pretending to sleep.'[55] She thought the first time had not been a 'big deal', leaving her sore, but she already knew it was supposed to be so. Therefore, she longed for the next time, when 'pleasure [should] be complete'.[56] A friend told her there were 20 ways of doing it. But Mário cowered away after the first time and fled to Rio de Janeiro, only returning several days later: 'What a fool! she thought. He is still embarrassed and tries to avoid me when, if he wanted, we could be together every night. It must be so good!'[57] After they resume their meetings, Maricota is infatuated with Mário for some time and fancies that they could marry and be happy after he has graduated as a pharmacist. But she soon realizes that she does not love him: 'She had surrendered, kissed him unconsciously, desiring him only as a MAN. She knew that they couldn't marry, not only because the cousin did not love her, but also because he hoped for a rich marriage.'[58]

Indeed, Mário never loves Maricota. For a few weeks he thinks he does and even writes poetry inspired by her, but the prospect of opening a drugstore in Niterói and becoming a teacher's husband – the girl has recently joined the training school – is depressing: 'Damn what just happened! … All the dreams of ambition he hoped to accomplish were now destroyed.'[59] He consoles himself with the idea that he was seduced by her and, being a man, could not reject her: 'I would be a fool if I saw the open crotch of a pretty woman and ran away. If she thinks I'm going to marry her, she's mistaken. Damn it!'[60] He plans to marry a wealthy woman – 'my father's son would never marry a poor girl' – and start a political career in Rio de Janeiro. Or maybe return to his homeland, in Campos (270 kilometres northeast of the capital), where he would marry a girl from an important family of local landowners. Another secret ambition is to enter medical school after graduating in pharmacology and make a fortune as a physician. Anything but 'marry, have children, and live in the mud, like [the apothecary] White Bear, just making enough not to starve'.[61]

After graduating, for lack of a better alternative (in typically naturalist disillusioned fashion), Mário stays in Niterói and accepts Old Goat's offer to open a pharmacy in Largo do Marrão, a neighbourhood nearby. Old Goat is a rich libertine lawyer, married to a sick woman, who has lived near to Maricota's parents since they settled in Niterói. He is obsessed with the girl. By purchasing a house for her and finding Mário a job in the city, after her mother dies in childbirth and her father goes mad, he hopes he can turn her into his mistress. Alone in the world, aware that Mário cannot marry her, Maricota accepts the lawyer's protection, but manages to keep him at bay during the last happy months of her life in her cottage in Largo do Marrão, across the street from Mário's pharmacy. The cousins become lovers. Up to the end of the novel, despite her fantasies of becoming a famous courtesan like Nana, Mário remains the only man Maricota has ever been intimate with.

From the first night, Mário fears an unwanted pregnancy. By talking about abortive medicines and promoting the use of condoms to avoid conception, the book disseminated hard-to-find information about sex and the prevention (or discontinuation) of pregnancy:

> The difficulty will be if a child comes to spill the milk and I will have to make her drink a medicine to abort. Remember Article 200 of the criminal code, about which we so often teased each other during lectures! But I must be careful … and Venus rubbers were not made for anything else.[62]

In the end, when she becomes pregnant, Maricota cries for help and asks Mário for some medicine that will interrupt the pregnancy. Aware that he is committing a crime, Mário says there are options, but demands she tell no one about it:

> — There are many, although there aren't really abortive drugs. The only infallible thing is the puncturing of the egg, but I do not dare to do that: it is a very risky operation …
> — But some syrup, a home medicine?
> — I'll see to it … Look, it's a serious thing we're going to do. The law punishes provoked abortions in Article 200 of the criminal code. We know that well, because at school we often teased each other. It's imperative it remains a secret.
> — And there's no danger?
> — No, not at all. I will arrange everything in the best possible way. In any case, keep calm.[63]

To provoke the abortion, Mário resorts to a beverage called *cozimento de sabina*. The scientific name of the plant from which the syrup was extracted is *Juniperus sabina*, from the Cupressaceae family, a shrub species related to cypresses. Owing to its capacity to restore the menstrual flow, the plant was sought for abortion, despite containing toxic substances that poison the woman's body, causing haemorrhages that can lead to death, as is the case in Figueiredo Pimentel's novel. Not knowing what to do, Mário leaves the tragic scene. Stunned, Old Goat understands everything. He has been a fool. Mário and Maricota were lovers and have both taken advantage of him. He rushes out to call a doctor, but it is too late: 'When he arrived, Maricota, lying in a pool of blood, her shirt suspended, her legs wide open, pale, very pale, turned her muffled eyes and expired.'[64] If Mário owned a copy of *O aborto*, as many did, he would keep it safe in the trunk with other naughty erotic books.

Conclusion

Thanks to the increasing digitalization of documents and new technologies to find and process information, we now have access to an array of sources that were unthinkable for scholars who authored traditional historiography and manuals of canonical literature. With book and cultural history, new players and agents are introduced as legitimate creators of meaning, like the publisher and the common reader. Literary life is expanded to include all disseminated reading practices, such as the appropriation of naturalist fiction as erotic literature. These new sources and paradigms allow us to put into question the traditional hypothesis of the lack of interest in books and reading in late nineteenth-century Brazil. For booksellers and thousands of readers, books like *O homem*, *A carne* and *O aborto* were erotic popular works that happened to be called 'naturalist novels' by their authors. Publishers like Pedro Quaresma valued naturalism as long as it signalled the description of sexual activity or 'immoral' deeds, because that attracted buyers. While elite authors like Machado de Assis lamented the lack of readers and claimed that naturalism was a brutal, failed aesthetic doomed to disappear, booksellers celebrated what they experienced as the rise of erotic popular print, selling naturalist books for a tidy profit while gratifying thousands of readers with their spicy plots. Figueiredo Pimentel's *O aborto* was a major title in that trend.

Notes

1. El Far 2004.
2. Guimarães 2004.
3. Sodré 1964, 360.
4. Magalhães 1896, 24.
5. El Far 2010.
6. Chartier 1988.
7. Maingueneau 2010.
8. Moulton 2000, 11.
9. Thauvette 2012, 46.
10. Mendes 2016.
11. Til 1905, 96. All translations from Portuguese into English are mine.
12. *O Apóstolo*, 24 April 1896.
13. Deaecto 2011.
14. Barbosa 2010.
15. Leão 2012.
16. El Far 2004, 79.

17. Mendes 2018.
18. *Gazeta de Notícias*, 5 May 1885.
19. El Far 2004, 223.
20. *Gazeta de Notícias*, 28 June 1896.
21. Abreu 2008.
22. *Gazeta de Notícias*, 14 October 1889.
23. Duarte 2017.
24. Bakhtin 1984.
25. Santana 2004.
26. Pina 2015.
27. Bulhões 2002.
28. Mendes 2014.
29. Broca 1991.
30. *Gazeta de Notícias*, 20 February 1890.
31. Garcia-Camello 2018.
32. Peakman 2003.
33. Pimentel 2015, 21.
34. *O Paiz*, 29 April 1893.
35. Vieira 2015.
36. *O Paiz*, 26 March 1893.
37. *A Notícia*, 20 November 1895.
38. *O Paiz*, 9 August 1895.
39. *A Semana*, 8 August 1894.
40. Pimentel 2015, 72.
41. *Gazeta de Notícias*, 3 July 1893.
42. Pimental 2015, 65.
43. See Peakman 2003.
44. Bakhtin 1984, 368.
45. Azevedo 1998, 22.
46. Pimental 2015, 66.
47. Pimental 2015, 76.
48. Pimental 2015, 67.
49. Azevedo 1998, 66.
50. Pimental 2015, 30.
51. Pimental 2015, 106.
52. Pimental 2015, 30.
53. Pimental 2015, 55.
54. Pimental 2015, 67.
55. Pimental 2015, 72.
56. Pimental 2015, 73.
57. Pimental 2015, 73.
58. Pimental 2015, 99, emphasis in the original.
59. Pimental 2015, 68.
60. Pimental 2015, 79.
61. Pimental 2015, 68.
62. Pimental 2015, 79.
63. Pimental 2015, 129.
64. Pimental 2015, 132.

Bibliography

Abreu, Márcia. 'Sob o olhar de Príapo: narrativas e imagens em romances licenciosos setecentistas'. In *Imagens na história*, edited by Alcides Ramos, Rosângela Patriota and Sandra Pesavento, 344–73. São Paulo: Hucitec, 2008.

Azevedo, Aluísio. *The Slum*, translated by David H. Rosenthal. Oxford: Oxford University Press, 1998.

Bakhtin, Mikhail. *Rabelais and His World*. Bloomington: Indiana University Press, 1984.
Barbosa, Marialva. *História cultural da imprensa. Brasil: 1800–1900*. Rio de Janeiro: Mauad X, 2010.
Broca, Brito. *Naturalistas, parnasianos e decadistas. Vida literária do realismo ao pré-modernismo*. Campinas: Editora Unicamp, 1991.
Bulhões, Marcelo. 'Leituras de um livro obsceno'. In Júlio Ribeiro, *A carne*, 9–59. São Paulo: Ateliê Editorial, 2002.
Chartier, Roger. *A história cultural: entre práticas e representações*. Rio de Janeiro: Bertrand Brasil, 1988.
Deaecto, Marisa Midori. *O império dos livros: instituições e práticas de leitura na São Paulo oitocentista*. São Paulo: Edusp, 2011.
Duarte, Aline Moreira. 'Alfredo Gallis: o pornógrafo esquecido', *Graphos* 19, no. 2 (2017): 7–20.
El Far, Alessandra. *Páginas de sensação: Literatura popular e pornográfica no Rio de Janeiro (1870–1924)*. São Paulo: Cia. das Letras, 2004.
El Far, Alessandra. 'Ao gosto do povo: as edições baratíssimas de finais do século XIX'. In *Impressos no Brasil: dois séculos de livros brasileiros*, edited by Aníbal Bragança and Márcia Abreu, 89–99. São Paulo: Editora UNESP, 2010.
Garcia-Camello, Cleyciara dos Santos. 'A filha do conselheiro: cientificismo, licenciosidade e promoção publicitária em *O homem*, de Aluísio Azevedo'. MA dissertation, Universidade do Estado do Rio de Janeiro, 2018.
Guimarães, Hélio. *Os leitores de Machado de Assis: o romance machadiano e o público de literatura no século 19*. São Paulo: Edusp, 2004.
Leão, Andréa Borges. *Brasil em imaginação: livros, impressos e leituras infantis (1890–1915)*. Fortaleza: INESP, UFC, 2012.
Magalhães, Valentim. *A literatura brasileira 1870–1895: notícia crítica dos principais escriptores com escolhidos excerptos*. Lisbon: Livraria A. M. Pereira, 1896.
Maingueneau, Dominique. *O discurso pornográfico*. São Paulo: Parábola Editorial, 2010.
Mendes, Leonardo. 'Júlio Ribeiro, o naturalismo e a dessacralização da literatura', *Pensares em revista* 4 (2014): 26–42.
Mendes, Leonardo. 'Livros para homens: sucessos pornográficos no Brasil no final do século XIX', *Cadernos do IL* 53 (2016): 173–91.
Mendes, Leonardo. 'Zola as pornographic point of reference in late nineteenth-century Brazil', *Excavatio* 30 (2018). https://www.academia.edu/36829340/Zola_as_Pornographic_Point_of_Reference_in_Late_Nineteenth-Century_Brazil
M. L. *Os serões do convento*. Lisbon: Typographia do Bairro Alto, n.d..
Moulton, Ian Frederick. *Before Pornography: Erotic Writing in Early Modern England*. Oxford: Oxford University Press, 2000.
Peakman, Julie. *Mighty Lewd Books: The Development of Pornography in Eighteenth-Century England*. London: Palgrave, 2003.
Pimentel, Alberto Figueiredo. *O aborto*. Rio de Janeiro: 7Letras, 2015.
Pina, Paulo Simões de Almeida. 'Uma história de saltimbancos: os irmãos Teixeira, o comércio e a edição de livros em São Paulo, entre 1876 e 1929'. MA dissertation, Universidade de São Paulo, 2015.
Rabelais [Alfredo Gallis]. *Volúpias: 14 contos galantes*. São Paulo: Teixeira & Irmão, 1893.
Santana, Maria Helena. 'Pornografia no fim do século: os romances de Alfredo Gallis', *Portuguese Literary and Cultural Studies* 12 (2004): 235–48.
Sodré, Nelson Werneck. *História da literatura brasileira*. Rio de Janeiro: Civilização Brasileira, 1964.
Thauvette, Chantelle. 'Defining Early Pornography: the Case of Venus and Adonis', *Journal for Early Modern Cultural Studies* 12, no. 1 (2012): 26–48.
Til, Condessa de [Alfredo Gallis]. *O que as noivas devem saber. Livro de filosofia prática*. Porto: Empresa Literária e Tipográfica, 1905.
Vieira, Renata Ferreira. 'Uma penca de canalhas: Figueiredo Pimentel e o naturalismo no Brasil'. MA dissertation, Universidade do Estado do Rio de Janeiro, 2015.

13

Machado de Assis and the Novel

Sandra Guardini Vasconcelos

Beyond Boundaries

There is in the works of novelist Machado de Assis[1] 'everything for those who know how to read'.[2] The set of nine novels[3] he published between 1872 and 1908 constitute a true compendium of the genre which, having risen to prominence in the early eighteenth century in Great Britain and France, had already become the hegemonic literary form in Europe by the time Machado came to adopt it. One can thus read in Machado's works the condensed lines of force that, from the genre's beginnings in the seventeenth and eighteenth centuries, had come together through the accumulated contributions of a formidable line of novelists. His wide-ranging reading made him familiar with the many different novelistic traditions and with writers stretching from founders of the genre, like Miguel de Cervantes, Daniel Defoe, Henry Fielding, Alain-René Lesage and Bernardin de Saint-Pierre, through to his own contemporaries, such as Eça de Queirós and Émile Zola. If we add to his private library the holdings of the Portuguese Circulating Library, of which he was an honorary member from at least June 1881,[4] we can say that Machado had at his disposal most of the fictional output of two centuries, which he drew from and absorbed in his own work.[5]

It is through the double movement between this 'external influx', to use a phrase which he himself coined,[6] and his acknowledgement of his predecessors in the genre – especially Joaquim Manuel de Macedo and José de Alencar[7] – that his oeuvre came into existence. Even when Machado navigates the more secure waters of convention, as in his first four novels, he treads his own paths and challenges deep-seated canons in search of a personal voice that, without ignoring local material, transcends national borders by acknowledging and incorporating the repertoire of the European novel. On a smaller scale, this movement reproduces a process analogous to that of the genre's own history and development, for many of its features combine national and local content with transnational circulation thanks to the global dissemination of the novel, itself a phenomenon directly linked to the context of European industrialization, capitalism and imperialism. To deal with Machado, concepts such as 'romantic', 'realist' and the like, taken here to be descriptive of aesthetic movements, need to be abandoned and categories such as 'English novel' or 'French novel' renounced. Instead, the novel should be embraced as a transnational genre, especially since the contaminations, borrowings and exchanges that took place between the two shores of the English Channel make very clear that the formation of the novel involved more than one tradition. Moreover, Machado's constant references and allusions to the realm of the European novel make it impossible to consider him within a context defined strictly by national borders.

Even if the nation is Machado's subject, as scholars such as Roberto Schwarz, John Gledson and Sidney Chalhoub have brilliantly demonstrated, from the point of view of genre the Machadian novel does not respect frontiers. In order to deal with Fluminense[8] life, he mobilizes all the potential and possibilities suggested and made famous by his peers. In one of his latest essays about Machado, Roberto Schwarz explores precisely the tension and the complexity of the dialectic between the local and the universal in Machado's oeuvre.[9] One can apprehend a similar complexity in the way Machado deals with novelistic form and its conventions by submitting the genre that rose and got consolidated in the European context to local conditions and themes. Having only once left the confines of his hometown, Machado nonetheless had at his disposal a rich repertoire of techniques and procedures amassed over time and made available to him in the bookshops[10] and reading rooms he frequented in the imperial capital. His recurring references to novels that were not in his private library, like *St. Clair of the Isles*[11] in *Helena* (1876), and to novelists, like Walter Scott in *A mão e a luva* [*The Hand & the Glove*] (1874), provide evidence of his acquaintance with European novels and novelists.

Thus, each novel, from the publication of *Ressurreição* [*Resurrection*] (1872) onwards, appropriates certain novelistic traditions in order to shape what Antonio Candido has described as the 'outline of Machado de Assis'.[12] The relatively small-scale extent of Machado's 'compendium', nevertheless, contains a synthesis of the developments of the genre since its origins, with Cervantes, to its point of inflection in the late 1900s, when the first symptoms of the genre crisis that would come more visibly to the fore in the first decades of the twentieth century were anticipated by this 'master on the periphery of capitalism'.[13] In these novels an 'enigmatic and Janus-headed' Machado de Assis is discernible, 'looking to the past and to the future', as Antonio Candido suggests in an essay where he draws attention to the writer's 'heedlessness of the dominant styles and the apparent archaism of his technique'.[14] On the other hand, it makes no sense to argue, as some have, for the existence of an unbridgeable gulf between Machado's first four novels and those of his maturity. Just as Bento Santiago wonders whether 'the Capitu of Glória beach was already in the girl of Matacavalos',[15] traits of the late novels can be identified in the early ones. Even so, as a realization of a very different conception of the novel, *Memórias póstumas de Brás Cubas* [*The Posthumous Memoirs of Brás Cubas*] (1881) seems to be a watershed in that it represents a decisive change of course and a reshaping of technical issues and narrative procedures. Although in all of his books the novelist explores the 'undercurrents of the human psyche',[16] from the 1881 novel onwards a deepening of the self-reflexive dimensions of the act of writing is observable, thereby flaunting the element of construction this involves. This – breaking with realistic conventions by means of a narrator who suspends the narrative to introduce his comments and analyses – lays bare the composition of the novel and its carpentry.

Ideas on the Novel

A more well-behaved vision of the genre, which does not take advantage of all its potential, seems to be conveyed both in Machado's critical ideas on the novel, all of which he expressed between the 1850s and the 1870s, and in his early work. This enables us to read the former in the light of the latter, and vice versa. Parallels are not difficult to draw. In 1858, in a very brief reference to the 'three essential literary forms' (the novel, drama and poetry), Machado commented on the dearth of novels and studies of this 'very important form', an omission he himself undertook to remedy a few years later by examining *O culto do dever* [*The Cult of Duty*] (1865) by Joaquim Manuel de Macedo and *Iracema* (1865) by José de Alencar.[17] In his analysis of Macedo's work he criticizes the novelist's close adherence to facts and his want of imagination and spirit – that is, his deficiency in transfiguring common events with 'the magic wand of Art'.[18] Short of characters with clear contours and incapable of making readers feel anything, Macedo's book is far from being a 'literary novel, the novel that combines the analysis of human passions with the delicate and original touches of poetry',[19] a characterization that suggests an ideal that ought to be attained. *Iracema*, conversely, wins the young critic's admiration because of its 'interesting action' and 'original episodes', being described as a 'prose poem' full of 'life, interest, and truth'.[20] Machado also appreciates, from the perspective of narrative structure, the close articulation between those episodes and the main theme, laying emphasis on the action that involves characters drawn by sentiment. Thus, Alencar had achieved what was lacking in Macedo.

Years later, Machado would throw Alencar's 'fertile imagination' and magic style' into relief,[21] this time against the 'slavish and photographic reproduction of the miniscule and ignoble' which he had criticized almost a decade before in Eça de Queirós's *O primo Basílio* [*Cousin Bazilio*] (1878).[22] Leaving aside Machado's disagreement about 'Zola's realism', with which he associated the Portuguese novelist, what is prominent in these reviews is his disapproval of the composition of the characters, whom he compares to puppets and deems to be devoid of an intrinsic and necessary articulation with the episodes and the action of the novel. Machado stresses the more compositional aspects that made him object to Eça's concept, and points to the lack of a connection between the characters and the action, to improbability and to the disconnection between the events and the characters' motivations. This results in a series of structural problems which, according to Machado, justifies his critique of the novel: 'the substitution of the accessory for the principal, the shifting of the action from the nature and feelings of characters to the incidental and fortuitous'.[23] As a counter-example he chooses Shakespeare, in whose work 'drama exists because it is in the characters, in the passions, and in the moral situation of the characters'.[24] João Cezar de Castro Rocha has discussed in detail the moral principles and conservative values that informed Machado's reading, the discomfort and shock that the publication of *O primo Basílio* caused, and the implications for the true revolution that would take place in the Brazilian writer's novelistic project. Castro Rocha astutely argues that the Machado who read Eça was not yet the author of *Memórias póstumas de Brás Cubas*.[25] Rather, he was the conventional and moralistic writer of the early novels, in which he dodged the pitfalls of vulgarity and bad taste that he identified in the Portuguese writer's realism.

Having just published *Resurrection* (1872), Machado would go on in his essay 'Instinto de nacionalidade' [National Instinct] to point out 'the moral tendencies of the Brazilian novel' as positive and to praise the 'depiction of customs, and the conflict of passions, the pictures of nature, and occasionally the study of sentiments and characters'.[26] The guidelines are already provided that would later shape not only Machado's criticism, but in particular his early novelistic output. When he regrets the scarcity of 'novels of analysis', he draws attention to the prevalence of the 'domain of the imagination' and to the general disinterest in contemporary problems, and consequently the lack of interest in 'social and philosophical crises' which, in his view, could be observed in the Brazilian novel.[27] Here, it seems, was a programme that he would go on to realize in the novels that are contemporaneous with the critical essays mentioned above. When the former are read in the light of the latter, the '"philosophizing" and classic' bias that Antonio Candido notes in Machado's early novels becomes evident;[28] likewise, from the point of view of narrative construction, a kind of leitmotif can be apprehended that runs through his criticism and takes shape in the novels, namely, a relation of necessity between action and character. Thus the 1870s, during which Machado published these critical essays and his first four novels, make visible a writer concerned with the definition of points of reference that will guide his own framework and narrative method. What he identifies as missing in the work of his contemporaries is the programme he will carry out in this initial phase, as the preface to *Ressurreição* indicates. To counter the novel of manners, which according to him has hitherto been a favourite among Brazilian novelists, he asserts he has 'tried to sketch a situation and to contrast two characters',[29] which immediately suggests that his narrative will revolve around a central conflict, in the wake of one of the most fruitful traditions of the novel since its rise to popularity in the eighteenth century.

Novelistic Paradigms

Samuel Richardson springs to mind as one of the novelists who started this novelistic trend. In *Pamela, or Virtue Rewarded* (1740) and *Clarissa* (1748),[30] he centres his narrative around the clash between two characters who embody conflicting views of the world in which they live, and thereby constructs a highly dramatic plot and intricate psychological characterization. These two novels deal with inner life, exploring their protagonists' subjectivity and sensibility as they are torn between their personal inclinations and social conventions. Their inner conflicts are enacted through the discourse of a first-person narrator to which the epistolary form gives visibility and a voice. The external world as setting for the action thus moves to the background and the domestic space stands out as the privileged site for the exercise of individuality and subjectivity. Social obstacles and the weight of moral judgement on the lives of these individuals are key elements that function as propellers of the characters' destinies while lending the novel the density that results from the detailed scrutiny of their states of mind and their ambivalences of the heart.

This is the tradition with which Machado's early novels can be associated, for the omniscient narrator examines his characters, acts as the judge of their moral actions and probes their intimate motivations in order to disclose their inner truth. In these novels Machado moves with ease around themes that were dear to the eighteenth- and nineteenth-century novel, like ambition, self-interest, convenience, doubt, usurpation, deception, love and jealousy.

The narrator's attention is turned to this 'miserable human society',[31] of which he cuts out a little fragment and peoples with a small gallery of figures to enhance the dramatic nature of his plots. Scenes are structured in which two subjectivities meet, oppose and confront each other, mediated and moderated by the forceful presence of an intrusive narrator at ease in his role as demiurge and commentator – all of this organized around a central situation that connects the several episodes. The clash between two personalities, like Félix and Livia or Guiomar and Estêvão, which involves the conflict between the dilemmas of the heart on the one hand and social convention on the other, is the guideline of these novels. As the narrator of *A mão e a luva* (1874) asserts, 'the author is more concerned with painting one or two characters and exposing a few human feelings than he is with doing anything else'.[32] In the foreword of the first edition of his second novel, Machado states his main purpose to have been 'the drawing of such characters – that of Guiomar, especially', the action serving only as a canvas upon which is cast the contour of the profiles, 'incomplete' but with some luck, 'natural and true'.[33] The emphasis on probing the inner motivations of these figures, which the narrator then undertakes with the resources of omniscience in order to explore their moral and psychological impasses, lessens the role of action in the plot, although still succeeding in maintaining a close relationship between these two dimensions of the narrative structure. The early novels effect minor alterations in the circumstances of their protagonists, who are affected by some extraordinary event or crisis and returned to their initial condition without any significant change in their experience or existence.

Thus, the plot in *Ressurreição* relies less on its protagonists' intervention in the world and more on the narrator's analysis of their states of mind and on the triviality of everyday life, devoid of shock or great distress. The intentions of the narrative voice are declared at the very beginning of the novel:

> His [Félix's] character and spirit will become better known through reading these pages, and by following our hero throughout the incidents of the quite artless story I am going to tell. We are not dealing here with a constant character, nor a logical and true spirit; this is a complex man, incoherent and capricious, in whom opposing elements meet, exceptional qualities as well as irreconcilable defects.[34]

If there are no incidents worthy of note – in that they might contain something unexpected, surprising or adventurous – nevertheless, the artlessness of the action, always circumscribed and mitigated in comparison with the narrator's interest in 'character', stands out as one of the novel's most important features. Conflict, therefore, is internal and is rendered in the dialogues in which the characters' ways of being and thinking are clearly and firmly delineated. The 10-year interval the narrator interposes between the events and his account, between the past events and the narrative present, returns Félix to the reader practically unchanged; it seems that the action of time and experience have had no effect on this 'cowardly' and 'essentially unhappy' man.[35] Unhappiness and cowardice are conditions from which this character does not strive to extricate himself. That trait which is one of the defining characteristics of the eighteenth- and nineteenth-century novel – the trust in man's capacity to intervene in the world to change it or to alter his own destiny, even if this may be an undertaking bound to fail – does not arise as a distinctive feature in Machado's novels, where disenchantment is the predominant tone among narrators and protagonists.

The happy end of *A mão e a luva*, a novel in which self-interest and personal and social convenience are the driving force of the choices and decisions of both Guiomar and Luís Alves, does not represent a real departure from the narrative scheme Machado devised in his first novel. Once more, there revolves around a conflict, involving Guiomar and her three suitors, a plot that has marriage and ambition as its main themes. Each of the male characters embodies a different and contrasting profile in his relationship with the Baroness's dependant (Guiomar), so as to build up suspense and tension for the denouement. Wholly enclosed in a domestic and familial milieu, the narrative centres on the affairs of the heart and on acting according to one's interest, opening to scenes in which the characters present themselves through dialogue that is fairly elliptical, since not all their feelings and expectations can be revealed. Moreover, the selective omniscient narrator follows the comings and goings of his creatures, exposes their thoughts and begins to explore the possibilities of free indirect discourse to grant readers access to their private life. In his omniscience, the narrator does not shy away from interspersing his narrative with comments, reflections and digressions, something that is also detectable in *Ressurreição* and will become increasingly frequent and emphatic in the later novels. Likewise, the biting remarks that will later become a kind of trademark can already be observed in passages like this one, about Viana, in the same novel: 'Viana was a consummate parasite … He was born a parasite as others are born dwarves. A parasite by divine right.'[36] Or in the irony of the last paragraph of *A mão e a luva* when the narrator says of Guiomar and Luís Alves that 'the two ambitions exchanged an affectionate kiss', and concludes that 'both settled down as if that glove had been made for that hand'.[37]

Helena (1876)[38] adds a component of romance to this narrative pattern, as Machado openly acknowledges in the foreword. This translates into a melodramatic plot riddled with feuilleton moves: the suspense and mystery of Helena's birth, the reversals, the suggestion of usurpation and incest, renunciation and revelations.[39] If Machado's method is similar to that in the two previous novels, and the clash between feeling and social conventions is still at the heart of the events, the action seems to be hampered by a degree of moralism and idealism, though even now a tone of the late Machado is discernible, for instance in the presentation of Counsellor Vale, in the opening paragraphs, and in Dr Camargo's characterization. From both a formal and a thematic perspective, Machado goes on experimenting with the techniques, procedures and topics that had become the staples of the European novel in the eighteenth and nineteenth centuries. That would explain what Roberto Schwarz considers to be a more poorly structured, more precarious conception of this novel. For, according to the Brazilian critic, the novelist combines 'an ultra-romantic plot, social analysis, a deep psychology, Christian edification, and the repetition of the most unfortunate phraseology',[40] all of which form the core to which the three kisses Dr Camargo applies to his daughter Eugênia's forehead are the frame, typical of the European novel. For Schwarz, if it were handled with derision, this eclecticism would no longer be a flaw but would instead become a literary strength.

With *Iaiá Garcia* (1878), we are still in the sphere of the sentimental and domestic novel. It may seem, at first sight, that the conflict will revolve around one of the story's dramatic cores – that involving Jorge, his mother and Estela. Although it has the Paraguayan War as backdrop – the war Jorge will join in the first part of the narrative – and depicts the everyday life of the civil servant Luís Garcia and his daughter Lina, the plot is once more organized around the contrast between two characters – Estela, the haughty and proud dependant, and Iaiá, whose chess-player sagacity and patience will win her Jorge's heart.[41] In this narrowly delimited circle, in which social differences are the problem that creates the central conflict, tension does not mount considerably and arises almost exclusively at the personal level. The historical context of the war and the individual dramas are not organically articulated, resulting in a 'discontinuous and fuzzy plot'.[42] The subject matter seems quite slender and the choice to psychologically probe what each character is experiencing in their solitude divests the narrative of much dramatic tension, since neither Jorge nor Estela externalize their feelings and disagreements. Between the 'secret springs of [the characters'] action' and the 'bondage of social conventions',[43] the narrator is compelled to take upon himself the responsibility to explore their motivations. Schwarz argues that the 'three crucial moments in the story' – Estela's decision, the kiss scene and Jorge's change of heart – are 'anti-dramatic' precisely because in them there is no 'confluence of conscious intention, deep impulse, and objective circumstances, by means of which the individual seeks to affirm himself'.[44] Thus, the reader is not granted access to the characters' inner movements, the action loses its strength and the narrator takes on a more conventional role, reducing his interventions and undertaking more systematically the narration proper.

To sum up what I have tried to argue so far, the early Machado adopted a narrative paradigm that, with few exceptions, was predominant during the novel's consolidation as a hegemonic genre into the late nineteenth century, and his first four novels were a laboratory in which he experimented with techniques and procedures from the novelistic repertoire up to at least the 1870s, when he took up this form. Decorum and a moralistic and mainly conventional stance on human and social relations obtain. At the same time, features that will become prominent in the late novels can be found, still in embryonic form. Some traits herald them: the attenuation of the action in favour of reflection; irony; the intrusive and opinionated narrator given to comments, thoughts and judgements; the (as yet few) digressions.

Machado's Turnaround: New Paths

There have been several attempts to explain the major change of direction in *Memórias póstumas de Brás Cubas* (1881). I will risk a daring hypothesis here. It considers not only the explicit statement, in the prologue to the third edition of the novel, about the adoption of 'the free-form of a Sterne or of a Xavier de Maistre',[45] but also the evidence from perusing Machado's library and his allusions and references in his nine novels. From his 1881 novel onwards, it is undeniable that Machado is turning to a different tradition of the European novel which has Miguel de Cervantes, Henry Fielding, Laurence Sterne and William M. Thackeray as central figures. This tradition was less hegemonic than that of the sentimental novel throughout the eighteenth and nineteenth centuries and represented a kind of counterpoint or undercurrent that would resurge vigorously in the twentieth century by means of one of its constitutive elements – self-reflexivity and the consequent flaunting of fictionality, of the constructed nature of all literary works.

If the editions of novels that are associated with this tradition and belonged to Machado's library are examined, it can be seen that a significant number of them date from the 1880s and 1890s. The collation of these particulars with the quotations and references that are found in the later novels reveals an interesting confluence that deserves mention. The novelistic repertoire alluded to in Machado's early novels, which includes novelists like Walter Scott (in *A mão e a luva*) and novels like *Werther* (in *A mão e a luva*), *St. Clair of the Isles*, *Paul et Virginie* and *Manon Lescaut* (in *Helena*),[46] retraces a romantic trend. However, less than giving material form to set aesthetic values, this repertoire is representative of a certain conception of the novel, which I have tried to delineate in the previous section and of which the first four novels are clear examples. On the other hand, given the other tradition just referred to above, a suggestive coincidence stands out: Jonathan Swift, Henry Fielding, Tobias Smollett, Charles Dickens and William M. Thackeray are all listed in the catalogue compiled by Jean-Michel Massa and revised by Glória Vianna in editions that Machado kept in his library and date precisely to those decades in which the novelist undertook his change of path.[47] This could be sheer accident, and the data may not be worth much, for nothing can ascertain that his readings followed any rigid chronological scheme. Machado may well have been familiar with these authors and novels earlier, once they could be found in the bookshops and circulating libraries in Rio de Janeiro. The presence of these editions in his library provides, nonetheless, information about the writer's interests and the period in which they were available to him, whether at home or in a public institution. The cases of Cervantes, Rabelais and Sterne are harder to pinpoint, either because his editions of their works bear no date (as with Cervantes and Rabelais) or because they are dated 1849 (Sterne's *Tristram Shandy*) and 1861 (Sterne's *Sentimental Journey*) and therefore prior to Machado's adoption of the novel genre.[48]

What is undeniable is that the repertoire of allusions and references from *Memórias póstumas de Brás Cubas* onwards is of a different calibre and belongs to a tradition associated with wit and humour, mobilizing techniques that Antonio Candido describes as apparently more archaic when he points to 'the capricious tone of Sterne' and 'Sterne's temporal jumps'[49] and provocations to the reader. Such a move backwards to the past, whence Machado retrieves this other paradigm, is duly indicated by the narrator of *Quincas Borba*:

> Here's where I would have liked to have followed the method used in so many other books – all of them old – where the subject matter of the chapter is summed up: 'How this came about and more to that effect.' There's Bernardim Ribeiro, there are other wonderful books. Of those foreign tongues, without going back to Rabelais, we have enough with Fielding and Smollett, many of whose chapters get read only through their summaries. Pick up *Tom Jones*, Book IV, Chapter I, and read this title: *Containing five pages of paper*. It's clear, it's simple, it deceives no one. They're five sheets of paper, that's all. Anyone who doesn't want to read it doesn't, and for the one who does read it, the author concludes obsequiously: 'And now, without any further preface, I proceed to our next chapter.'[50]

Though put forward in this 1891 novel, these are suggestions that had already been taken up in *Memórias póstumas de Brás Cubas*. Even though they are conveyed by the narrator, the affiliation seems clear. The self-mockery contained in the idea that the method comes from old books does not obliterate the significance of the literary heritage referenced in the quote, which explores the metafictional nature of writing and implies that another conception of the novel is at work here. For this tradition, the critical function that the self-reflexive narrator takes upon himself is of paramount relevance. This allows him to interrupt the narrative to make comments and analytical remarks and also to muse on the very act of writing, making observations about the realm of the book and reading, and the formal structure of the novel itself. He thus resorts to a new/old array of devices, which include prologues, frequent breaks in the narrative thread in order to address the reader, the discussion of impasses in the fictional construction, remarks about material aspects of the book or about the literary tradition. All of these are procedures that expose the cogs of the narrative machinery, creating an ironic effect and intensifying our awareness of writing as an artefact. That Machado was beginning to take a path that went against the grain of the contemporary novel is evinced in Capistrano de Abreu's doubt and astonishment when he asks himself whether *Memórias póstumas de Brás Cubas* is a novel (see the prologue to the third edition).[51] The direct, unequivocal answer is yes, it is a novel. But certainly not of the kind that was predominant then.

In the early novels, Machado seemed to hesitate between which course to follow, hence a certain eclectic admixture on the level of composition – psychological analysis, interventions of the narrative voice, vestiges of the epistolary novel (in *Helena*, for example), dramatic plots, melodramatic moves, 'philosophizing', realistic scenes, a stilted style[52] – as if he were inventorying possibilities and alternatives. From *Memórias póstumas de Brás Cubas* onwards, however, he appears to have discovered a vein more congenial to his sceptical and disenchanted worldview. Local matters will find a different form, definitive and confident, in which to be configured, and romantic clichés and melodramatic scenes become the target of parody. Thus, Machado subjects his initial output to a thorough and far-reaching critique. Besides the change of tone, owing to the reiterated use of irony, derision and sarcasm, in the late novels there is also an inversion of emphasis, from the angle of narrative structure. The truly meaningful change, in this respect, lies in the fact that the action and the plot recede to the background and the figure of the narrator takes centre stage, boosting the role he generally plays in the organization of the narrative. This takes the form either of memorialist (autobiographical) discourse, wherein the voice of self looms large, or of the adoption of a narrative voice that takes precedence over the story and its events. Although in some of the novels the love intrigue still represents a kind of guideline, the action thins out and the novels give way to the essay, the philosophizing, the digressions that open cracks in the cohesive building of the narrative.

Novels in Crisis

In *Memórias póstumas de Brás Cubas*, *Dom Casmurro* (1899) and *Memorial de Aires* [*Counselor Aires' Memorial*] (1908), there is nothing to dramatize, that is, to galvanize into action, to set in motion. Cubas tells his story from the afterlife and no longer has anything to do with the sublunary world. Between the past events of his life and the narrative Bento Santiago devotes himself to writing in the present there is a gap of 40 years; he has now settled into 'a quiet, undisturbed sleep'.[53] The retired and disillusioned Counselor Aires, the author of a personal diary that contains his memories, is, in the apt description of José Paulo Paes, 'an apprentice of death'[54] and, therefore, somebody who can 'already dispense with the tough social game'.[55] It is as if they are, all three of them, out of reach of the action of time and of the vicissitudes of life. They are all 'architect[s] of ruins',[56] with no legacy to leave behind or experience to share.

The autobiography and memoirs, traditional forms of the novel since the eighteenth century, are systematically subverted, since in Machado's late novels there is less of life and more of the opinions of their 'authors' than one might expect. In *Dom Casmurro*, where Machado thematizes marriage and adultery, Bento Santiago takes 100 chapters to recount what will trigger the conflict and what would be the foremost event in a conventional sentimental novel. His marriage to Capitu, the birth of Ezequiel and the denouement, with his wife and son's departure for Europe and their deaths, take up precisely 48 out of a total of 148 chapters and appear to be less important than the construction of an argument and the presentation of a body of evidence intended to arouse suspicion and place the blame on the woman. The last chapters of the narrative retrieve the first two and the reader finally understands the reasons for the nickname 'Casmurro' ('a quiet person who keeps himself to himself')[57] and for the man's loneliness as the wheel comes full circle. The house in Engenho Novo reproduces the Matacavalos one, but the man who inhabits it now lives all by himself and seldom goes out. Lack of purpose and a prevailing sense of vacuity are not filled by the visits of his female friends, whom he describes as 'passing caprices'.[58] He is left only with his recollections and the plan to write a 'History of the Suburbs'.

The love triangles, adultery, madness and moral and financial bankruptcy – themes dear to the great nineteenth-century realistic novel – are tenuous threads that barely sustain a plot whose action can only be defined as passive. *Quincas Borba* (1891) is shaped in the manner of Honoré de Balzac and Charles Dickens, staging the rise and fall of a man from the provinces who comes to live in the capital, only to be plundered by the Palha couple. However, in place of the lost illusions of the provincial after a failed struggle for upward mobility, as in the paradigmatic cases of Lucien de Rubempré (*Illusions perdues*, 1837) and Pip (*Great Expectations*, 1861), Rubião not only sees his fantasies and dreams, like his fortune, vanish into thin air but sinks into a universe of folly, entertaining increasingly delirious illusions, fantasies and dreams until he dies, poor and alone, in Barbacena. Whereas, in the best tradition of the novel of apprenticeship, the young Lucien and Pip embody the clash between the poetry of the heart and the prose of the world[59] and thereby are reconciled with their destiny, Rubião, already a mature man and heir to a fortune, has nothing to fight for. As in Machado's other novels, the protagonist is fundamentally passive. In a dialogue between Teófilo and a deputy, to the question 'what did he [Rubião] do, or what does he do now?' the former's answer is, 'Nothing, neither now nor before. He was rich – but a spendthrift.'[60]

The rivalry between the twins – unmotivated and banal – in *Esaú e Jacó* (1904) [*Esau and Jacob*] is a meaningless conflict, resulting in a slender and fragmentary plot, which John Gledson describes as 'tedious and insipid'.[61] With apparently purposeless episodes, like that of Evaristo's inkwell (Chapter 50) or Custódio's teashop sign (Chapter 63), with imprecise character portraits, with the double point of view, Machado seems to implode, one by one, the foundations of the novel since its beginnings. In a coup de théâtre that hints at a certain feuilleton-like resolution, Flora's death puts an end to the split, the doubling, the division that at first sight seems, somehow, to inject some dramatic tension into the story of her love for Pedro and Paulo. The twins, in their turn, 'haven't changed at all; they are the same'[62] at the end of the novel, reasserting the negative action of time on these characters. All of these elements are pieces in a game of chess devised by Machado, a metaphor that describes quite precisely the composition of this novel.[63] The very complexity of point of view, which presumes an Aires as proto-narrator and an Aires as character, also involves another voice that organizes, edits or takes up the narration – and adds the note to the reader which precedes the novel and later identifies itself as M. de A. in the foreword that prefaces *Memorial de Aires* (1908). An alternative possibility is that there is an Aires who is at one and the same time narrator and character and, thus, steps in and out of the narrative, depending on whether he is playing the role of witness or participating in the events. Be that as it may, this interplay demonstrates yet another aspect of Machado's subversion of the traditional schemes of narration.

Without ever abandoning the novel of character, which he had chosen as his pathway in *Ressurreição*, Machado devised a memorable gallery of characters – Brás Cubas, Rubião, Bento Santiago, Counselor Aires, Virgília, Capitu and Sofia – and, by means of point of view, in the first or the third person, he combines his extraordinary mastery of psychological analysis with the creation of remarkable narrators. Written in the style of 'a drunkard's gait'[64] and as 'a swirl of somersaults',[65] the narrative of their lives is fragmentary and lacunary and exposes the little or almost nothing that actually happens in these novels, pervaded as they are by irony and disenchantment. In Machado's works, interpretations are unstable, carry us far from the firm ground of the canonical novel of his time and introduce a regime of radical ambiguity, for which the 'pair of spectacles' offered to the reader is mere disguise and deceit.

This thinning out reaches a climax in his last work, in which the figure of Aires takes centre stage as character and narrator, the diplomat who 'did not play an important role in this world ... pursued a diplomatic career and retired'; whose 'diary of remembrances', trimmed of 'the dead or dark pages, would only do (or still might suffice) to kill time on the launch to Petrópolis'.[66] The diary form, the foreword warns, was 'pruned of certain incidents, descriptions, and reflections' and leaves Aires' desk to roam the world, 'trimmed and spare'.[67] If the old artifice of the manuscript is a strategy used to ensure reliability – Aires has left seven notebooks 'firmly bound in cardboard' and 'penned in red ink',[68] of which the diary is the last – the first-person narrative does not reduce the ambiguity that arises with the impression of intrusion through the 'editor' – either because the reader suspects that he is responsible for including the epigraph and cutting out the excesses (a gesture implicit in the idea of 'pruning') or because he has taken decisions about 'keeping only what ties together a single theme'[69] and therefore has intervened in the selection. The composition, which juxtaposes the recording of duly dated events, looks like a puzzle whose pieces were carefully chosen and combined, but still leaves gaps and implies omissions amid scenes, summaries, and comments by the narrative voice. An oblique and sly narrator with an avowed 'skill at uncovering and covering up',[70] Aires does not live up to the expectations of the diary form, which in his case has very little of the private and confessional and would seem to be far from constituting a space for the expression of subjectivity. At one point, tired of his loneliness and thirsty for 'living people', he decides 'to see other people, to hear them, smell them, taste them, touch them, and apply all his senses to a world that could kill time, immortal time'.[71] His 'idle pen' comes, then, to record the trifles of a daily existence without disquietudes, whose background is nevertheless, no more, no less, the abolition of slavery (1888) and the proclamation of the Republic (1889). In the interstices of his observation of other people's existence and of political turning points, in the intervals, the figure of the narrator stands out and, in a low tone, leaves us the diary of an individual who relinquished action in favour of reflection and internalized the movement of life.

Aires, the man of quiet habits who abhors emphasis, puts an end to this cycle of nine novels in a minor key, in an atmosphere of melancholy and awareness of *tempus fugit*.[72] 'Desire without action',[73] old age and death prevail in this novel in which the protagonist 'is no longer of this world' and turns away 'from shore with our eyes on those who remain'.[74] In his reading of *Memorial de Aires*, John Gledson considers this novel by Machado to be 'the most implacably pessimistic and a lament for the country whose existence, as a nation, he could barely believe in'.[75] Therein, it seems, lie the historical reasons that explain why these are novels 'in crisis',[76] which in turn announce the symptoms of and anticipate the crisis of the novel genre that will deepen in the first decades of the twentieth century and produce certain developments in both the Brazilian and the European contexts. Within the theory and history of the novel, Machado's nine novels represent not only the production of a compendium but the execution of a programme that he had previously devised in his critical work. Comparing the dramatic production of Antonio José da Silva with this Portuguese playwright's models, Machado had suggested that the writer 'may go search for borrowed spice, but only in order to season it with the sauce of his own making'.[77] This is a most apt description of the novelist Machado de Assis himself.

Notes

1. 'Machado', as he is usually referred to among academics.
2. I borrow here Antonio Candido's phrase about João Guimarães Rosa's novel *Grande sertão: veredas* (see Antonio Candido 1971, 121). Unless otherwise indicated, all the translations are my own.
3. In the so-called 'first phase': *Ressurreição* [*Resurrection*] (1872); *A mão e a luva* [*The Hand & the Glove*] (1874); *Helena* [*Helena: A Novel*] (1876); *Iaiá Garcia* [*Iaiá Garcia*] (1878). In the 'second phase': *Memórias póstumas de Brás Cubas* [*The Posthumous Memoirs of Brás Cubas*] (1881); *Quincas Borba* [*Philosoher or Dog?*] (1891); *Dom Casmurro* [*Dom Casmurro: A Novel*] (1899); *Esaú e Jacó* [*Esau and Jacob*] (1904); *Memorial de Aires* [*Counselor Aires' Memorial*] (1908).
4. The writer's membership card can still be consulted in the files of the Rio de Janeiro Portuguese Circulating Library.
5. See Vianna 2001; Senna 2008.
6. Assis 1992a, 813.
7. I mention these two novelists because their work was reviewed in Machado's critical essays.
8. In the nineteenth century the demonym for the city of Rio de Janeiro was '*Fluminense*', from the Latin *flumen*', *meaning* 'river'. Nowadays, the term used is 'Carioca', from the indigenous Tupi language, meaning 'white man's house'. 'Fluminense' is more often used today as the demonym for the whole state of Rio de Janeiro.
9. Schwarz 2007.
10. Machado's *crônica* about Garnier, on the occasion of the death of the French publisher and bookseller, comments on a 20-year relationship. See Assis 1893.
11. Helme 1837.
12. Antonio Candido 1995.

13. The phrase is Roberto Schwarz's (Schwarz 2001).
14. Antonio Candido 1995, 106 and 109, respectively.
15. Assis 1998a, 244.
16. Antonio Candido, n.d., 216.
17. Macedo 1865; Alencar 1958; Alencar 2000.
18. Assis 1992c, 844
19. Assis 1992c, 847.
20. Assis 1992d, 849, 851 and 852, respectively.
21. Assis 1992e, 924; preface written in 1887 for an edition of *O guarani*, of which only the first instalments were published (English translation: Alencar 1893).
22. Assis 1992b. Eça de Queirós's novel has been translated into English by Margaret Jull Costa (Queirós 2003).
23. Assis 1992b, 910.
24 Assis 1992b, 910.
25. Rocha 2013.
26. Assis 1992f, 805–6.
27. Assis 1992f, 805.
28. Antonio Candido 1995, 107.
29. Assis 2013, 26.
30. Richardson 1740; Richardson 1748.
31. Assis 2013, 194.
32. Assis 1970, 50.
33. Assis 1970, 3.
34. Assis 2013, 28.
35. Assis 2013, 161. One should note Machado's irony in naming his protagonist Félix.
36. Assis 2013, 30.
37. Assis 1970, 117.
38. Assis 1987.
39. It is worth noting that, like Clarissa Harlowe, Helena lets herself die because of the moral abyss she is pushed into.
40. Schwarz 1977, 104.
41. 'Of the qualities necessary for playing chess Iaiá possessed the two essential ones: a quick eye and benedictine patience – qualities precious in life itself, which is also a game of chess, with its problems and games, some won, some lost, others neither' (Assis 1977, 102).
42. Schwarz 1977, 143.
43. Assis 1977, 14 and 38, respectively. Translation slightly changed because the translator's choice ('the secret explanation') is inaccurate.
44. Schwarz 1977, 146.
45. Assis 1998b, 5. I will also refer to the other translation: Assis 2008.
46. Johann Wolfgang von Goethe, *The Sorrows of Young Werther* (1787); Elizabeth Helme, *St. Clair of the Isles: or, The Outlaws of Barra. A Scottish Tradition* (1803); Bernardin de Saint-Pierre, *Paul et Virginie* (1788); Antoine-François Prévost, *Manon Lescaut* (1731).
47. See Vianna 2001.
48. There is no information, however, about when they were purchased or incorporated into the library.
49. Antonio Candido 1995, 109.
50. Assis 1998c, 159–60.
51. Assis 1998b, 3. See Abreu 1881.
52. Note this excerpt: 'Like a blessing from the stars, her tears, hitherto restrained by the presence of strangers, began to flow freely. No one saw them because the night was so dark and her retreat so enclosed, but the summer breeze, which began rustling the dry leaves, perchance heard her sobbing, perchance carried it to the bosom of God. And there came, by divine intervention, sweet consolation to her solitary tears' (Assis 2013, 116).
53. Assis 1998a, 121.
54. Paes 2008, 43. In one of his dialogues with the Baroness, Aires says, 'Now the world starts here on the docks of Glória or the Rua do Ouvidor and ends at the Cemetery of São João Batista.' See Assis 2000, 83.
55. Bosi 1999, 129.

56. A phrase with which Freitas, one of Rubião's guests, refers to himself in *Quincas Borba* (Assis 1998c, 39).
57. Assis 1998a, 4.
58. Assis 1998a, 243.
59. Hegel 2002, Vol. 4, 138. In English: 'Consequently one of the commonest, and, for romance, most appropriate, collisions is the conflict between the poetry of the heart and the opposing prose of circumstances and the accidents of external situations' (https://www.marxists.org/reference/archive/hegel/works/ae/part3-section3-chapter3.htm).
60. Assis 1998c, 220.
61. Gledson 1986, 162.
62. Assis 2000, 252.
63. See Guimarães 2012, 9–20.
64. Assis 1998b, 113. Also: 'You [reader] love direct and continuous narration, a regular and fluid style, and this book and my style are like drunkards, they stagger left and right, they walk and stop, mumble, yell, cackle, shake their fists at the sky, stumble, and fall' (Assis 1998b, 111).
65. Assis 1998b, 95.
66. 'A Note to the Reader' (Assis 2000).
67. Assis 1972, 5.
68. 'A Note to the Reader' (Assis 2000).
69. Assis 1972, 5.
70. Assis 2000, 212.
71. Assis 2000, 74.
72. At one point, Aires refers to the 'gloomy smudges of time, which consumes all things' (Assis 1972, 10).
73. Assis 1972, 43.
74. Assis 1972, 184.
75. Gledson 1986, 255.
76. Gledson 2011.
77. Assis 1992a, 731.

Bibliography

Abreu, Capistrano de. 'As Memórias Póstumas de Brás Cubas serão um romance?', *Gazeta de Notícias*, 30 January 1881, 2.

Alencar, José de. *The Guarani*, translated by James W. Hawes, *Overland Monthly and Out West Magazine* 21, no. 127 to 22 no. 131 (1893).

Alencar, José de. *Iracema, lenda do Ceará*. In *Obra completa*, Vol. 3, 233–320. Rio de Janeiro: José Aguilar, 1958.

Alencar, José de. *Iracema*, translated by Clifford E. Landers. Oxford: Oxford University Press, 2000.

Antonio Candido. 'O homem dos avessos'. In *Tese e antítese*, 119–139. São Paulo: Companhia Editora Nacional, 1971.

Antonio Candido. 'An Outline of Machado de Assis'. In *On Literature and Society*, edited and translated by Howard S. Becker, 104–18. Princeton, NJ: Princeton University Press, 1995.

Antonio Candido. *Formação da literatura brasileira (momentos decisivos)*, 4th edn. São Paulo: Livraria Martins Editora, n.d.

Assis, Joaquim Maria Machado de. 'Garnier', *Gazeta de Notícias*, 8 October 1893, 1.

Assis, Joaquim Maria Machado de. *The Hand & the Glove*, translated by Albert I. Bagby, Jr. Lexington: University Press of Kentucky, 1970.

Assis, Joaquim Maria Machado de. *Counselor Aires' Memorial*, translated by Helen Caldwell. Berkeley: University of California Press, 1972.

Assis, Joaquim Maria Machado de. *Iaiá Garcia*, translated by Albert I. Bagby, Jr. Lexington: University Press of Kentucky, 1977.

Assis, Joaquim Maria Machado de. *Helena*, translated by Helen Caldwell. Berkeley: University of California Press, 1987.

Assis, Joaquim Maria Machado de. 'Antônio José'. In *Obra completa*, Vol. 2, 726–33. Rio de Janeiro: Editora Aguilar, 1992a.

Assis, Joaquim Maria Machado de. 'Eça de Queirós: *O primo Basílio*'. In *Obra completa*, Vol. 3, 903–13. Rio de Janeiro: Editora Aguilar, 1992b.
Assis, Joaquim Maria Machado de. 'J. M. de Macedo: *O culto do dever*'. In *Obra completa*, Vol. 3, 843–47. Rio de Janeiro: Editora Aguilar, 1992c.
Assis, Joaquim Maria Machado de. 'José de Alencar: *Iracema*'. In *Obra completa*, Vol. 3, 848–52. Rio de Janeiro: Editora Aguilar, 1992d.
Assis, Joaquim Maria Machado de. 'José de Alencar: *O guarani*'. In *Obra completa*, Vol. 3, 922–6. Rio de Janeiro: Editora Aguilar, 1992e.
Assis, Joaquim Maria Machado de. 'Notícia da atual literatura brasileira: Instinto de nacionalidade'. In *Obra completa*, Vol. 3, 801–9. Rio de Janeiro: Editora Aguilar, 1992f.
Assis, Joaquim Maria Machado de. 'A nova geração'. In *Obra completa*, Vol. 3, 809–36 Rio de Janeiro: Nova Aguilar, 1992g.
Assis, Joaquim Maria Machado de. *Dom Casmurro*, translated by John Gledson. Oxford: Oxford University Press, 1998a.
Assis, Joaquim Maria Machado de. *The Posthumous Memoirs of Brás Cubas*, translated by Gregory Rabassa. Oxford: Oxford University Press, 1998b.
Assis, Joaquim Maria Machado de. *Quincas Borba*, translated by Gregory Rabassa. Oxford: Oxford University Press, 1998c.
Assis, Joaquim Maria Machado de. *Esau and Jacob*, translated by Elizabeth Lowe. Oxford: Oxford University Press, 2000.
Assis, Joaquim Maria Machado de. *Epitaph of a Small Winner*, translated by William L. Grossman. London: Bloomsbury, 2008.
Assis, Joaquim Maria Machado de. *Resurrection*, translated by Karen Sherwood Sotelino. Pittsburgh: Latin American Literary Review Press, 2013.
Barreto Filho, 'O romance brasileiro: Machado de Assis', *Machado de Assis em linha*, 5, no. 9 (2012): 1–20.
Bosi, Alfredo. 'Uma figura machadiana'. In *Machado de Assis: o enigma do olhar*, 129–48. São Paulo: Editora Ática, 1999.
Gledson, John. *Machado de Assis: ficção e história*. Rio de Janeiro: Paz e Terra, 1986.
Gledson, John. 'Quincas Borba – um romance em crise', *Machado de Assis em linha*, 4, no. 8 (2011): 29–50.
Guimarães, Hélio de Seixas. 'O impacto da obra de Machado de Assis sobre as concepções de romance', *Machado de Assis em linha* 1, no. 1 (2008): 28–39.
Guimarães, Hélio de Seixas. 'Introdução: um romance em abismo'. In Machado de Assis, *Esaú e Jacó*, 9–20. São Paulo: Companhia das Letras, 2012.
Hegel, G. W. F. *Cursos de estética*, translated by Marco Aurélio Werle and Oliver Tolle. São Paulo: Editora da Universidade de São Paulo, 2002.
Helme, Elizabeth. *St. Clair of the Isles: or, The Outlaws of Barra. A Scottish Tradition*. London: George Virtue, 1837.
Jobim, José Luís. 'Machado de Assis: o crítico como romancista', *Machado de Assis em linha* 3, no. 5 (2010): 75–94.
Kunz, Marinês Andrea, and Juracy Assmann Saraiva. 'Autorreferencialidade em *Memorial de Aires*', *Machado de Assis em linha* 4, no. 7 (2011): 76–87.
Macedo, Joaquim Manuel de. *O culto do dever: romance*. Rio de Janeiro: Em casa de Domingos José Gomes Brandão, 1865.
Matoso Câmara Júnior, Joaquim. 'Discurso indireto livre em Machado de Assis', *Machado de Assis em linha* 3, no. 6 (2010): 1–14.
Nunes, Maria Luisa. 'Machado de Assis' Theory of the Novel', *Latin American Literary Review* 4, no. 7 (1975): 57–66.
Paes, José Paulo Paes. 'Um aprendiz de morto'. In *Armazém literário. Ensaios*, edited by Vilma Arêas, 104–18. São Paulo: Companhia das Letras, 2008.
Queirós, Eça de. *Cousin Bazilio*, translated by Margaret Jull Costa. Sawtry: Dedalus, 2003.
Richardson, Samuel. *Pamela, or Virtue Rewarded*. London: Rivington & Osborn, 1740.
Richardson, Samuel. *Clarissa, or The History of a Young Lady*. London: n.p, 1748.
Rocha, João Cezar de Castro. *Machado de Assis: por uma poética da emulação*. Rio de Janeiro: Civilização Brasileira, 2013.
Santiago, Silviano. 'Retórica da verossimilhança'. In *Uma literatura nos trópicos: ensaios sobre dependência cultural*, 27–46. São Paulo: Perspectiva, 1978.

Schwarz, Roberto. *Ao vencedor as batatas: forma literária e processo social nos inícios do romance brasileiro*. São Paulo: Livraria Duas Cidades, 1977.
Schwarz, Roberto. *Misplaced Ideas: Essays on Brazilian Culture*, edited and translated by John Gledson. London: Verso, 1992.
Schwarz, Roberto. *A Master on the Periphery of Capitalism*, translated by John Gledson. Durham, NC: Duke University Press, 2001.
Schwarz, Roberto. 'Competing Readings in World Literature', *New Left Review* 48 (November–December 2007): 85–107.
Senna, Marta de. *Alusão e zombaria: citações e referências na ficção de Machado de Assis*. Rio de Janeiro: Edições Casa de Rui Barbosa, 2008.
Teles, Gilberto Mendonça. 'A teoria do romance em Machado de Assis', *Travessia* 20 (1990): 19–36.
Viana, Glória Vianna. 'Revendo a biblioteca de Machado de Assis'. In *A biblioteca de Machado de Assis*, edited by José Luís Jobim, 99–274. Rio de Janeiro: Academia Brasileira de Letras and Topbooks, 2001.

14

Capitu against the Elegiac Narrator[1]

Ana Cláudia Suriani da Silva

Dom Casmurro is Machado de Assis's most controversial novel. It was published in 1900 and in an English translation for the first time in 1953.[2] In *Dom Casmurro,* Machado de Assis perfects the hybrid quality of his works, which benefit from a combination of his deep knowledge of European literature and his experience of the political, social and gender transformation sweeping through Brazil with the end of slavery (1888), the proclamation of the Republic (1889) and the belle époque.

Machado de Assis's position between these two worlds is one facet of the originality and modernity of his works and above all of *Dom Casmurro*. In *Dom Casmurro,* he reveals his fascination with a theme that has a long history in European literature – jealousy – most notably represented in Shakespeare's *Othello,* which Bento the narrator refers to directly in the chapters 'A Touch of Iago' (62), 'A Reform in the Drama' (72) and 'Othello' (135). According to Caldwell, *Dom Casmurro* can be considered one of the best modern reincarnations of *Othello*.[3] The story is told through the eyes of Bento Santiago, the supposedly betrayed husband. Bento does not become a priest as his mother wanted, because he wants to marry, and he ends up marrying his enchanting childhood sweetheart and neighbour, Capitu. Capitu is therefore a sort of social-climbing Desdemona of suburban Rio de Janeiro, whereas Othello's incarnation in nineteenth-century-Brazil is as a decadent superstitious Catholic paterfamilias. The aged narrator represents the decadent land- and slave-owning elite in the passage from the Monarchy to the Republic; he has lost most of his wealth and has to make his living as a lawyer and from the remaining family assets.

Bento is writing a memoir for the purpose of justifying his jealousy towards his deceased wife. The evidence of the betrayal that he gathers is very flimsy and could easily be interpreted as paranoia. In fact, we can summarize a substantial part of the history of *Dom Casmurro*'s criticism as ‘fiction of a court case’,[4] which has essentially focused on the relationship between the narrator and his heroine, Capitu, and more recently, as we shall see later, on the triangular – or even quadrangular – story of friendship, love and homosocial affection between Capitu, Bento, Escobar and Sancha. This chapter will also explore this triangular relationship, by proposing a reading of Bento's accounts of his life with his wife Capitu as an elegy, or perhaps a double elegy. The self-reflexive narrator interweaves the bitter and sad lament for the death of his heroine with that of his best friend Escobar. The relationship between the narrator and Capitu is the main subject and the one that occupies the most space in the narrative, but it is not the only one. Capitu, who is the most complex character of the novel – alongside the narrator himself – is in the foreground of the narrative, but in the middle distance he lets us glimpse the relationship between himself and a hero, Escobar, shedding light on the changes in the social, sexual and gender relations at the end of the nineteenth century in Brazil. As Chalhoub and Schwarz both state, Machado de Assis's novel portrays this period of transition in Brazilian society, in which the relationship between the patriarch and his dependants – be they *agregados*, slaves, women or children – is being redefined, owing to the change of political regime, the end of slavery, industrialization and also, according to Miskolci, the new model of family and the transformation of gender relations and sexuality.[5]

I will argue more precisely that *Dom Casmurro* can be considered an elegiac romance and that Machado de Assis has chosen a woman as the heroine of his novel because of the central role that women occupied in the patriarchal urban family at the end of the nineteenth century in Brazil and by extension because of woman's role as mediator of male homosocial desire and partnership in the control of women. The elegiac romance appeared first in the early fiction of Joseph Conrad and was subsequently developed by a number of major writers influenced by Conrad, including Nabokov and Fitzgerald.[6] This chapter will present the main characteristics of the elegiac romance and compare *Dom Casmurro* to *Lord Jim* in order to highlight what makes the relationship between narrator and hero(es) in *Dom Casmurro* unique.

Lord Jim: The Double

Bruffee states that novels such as *Lord Jim*, *Heart of Darkness*, *The Great Gatsby*, *The Good Soldier*, *Doctor Faustus* and *Pale Fire* share formal and thematic characteristics that must be taken into account when defining them as works of art.[7] He coined the term 'elegiac romance' to define them: a new narrative form that allowed the tradition of the heroic quest romance to survive in the fiction of the twentieth century.

Bruffee prefers to call these works 'romance' rather than 'novel' because the hero embarks on a kind of quest similar to that found in the chivalric romances. They are elegiac because the narrators tell us the story after the death of the hero, as in a pastoral elegy.

However, as different as they may seem, novels such as *The Great Gatsby* and *Lord Jim* share the same underlying driving force: they are the outcome of the need for the narrators to overcome the feeling of loss caused by the death of their heroes. For this reason, they are heroic and elegiac at the same time. They explore the interaction between the narrator and the hero in the recent and distant past. The loss of the hero is irredeemable. As a result, the narrator begins to construct the hero, who is a product of his or her fantasy; as readers we do not have access to the hero except through the narrator, who inevitably becomes his mediating force. Even when he is given a voice, what the hero says is meticulously selected and edited by the narrator. For example, Marlow guides his listeners as follows:

> I am telling you so much about my own instinctive feelings and bemused reflections because there remains so little to be told of him. *He existed for me, and after all it is only through me that he exists for you.* I've led him out by the hand; I have paraded him before you. Were my commonplace fears unjust? I won't say – not even now. You may be able to tell better, since the proverb has it that the onlookers see most of the game.[8]

The narrative structure of the elegiac romance is a reconstruction in the narrative present of the relationship that was established between these two complementary characters in the past, blending factual reality with invention. The problem that the narrator faces is that although the hero is dead, his influence remains alive in the narrator's mind. By dying, the hero takes the past of the narrator with him. The narrator embarks on an imaginary journey as a means of exorcizing his ghosts and recovering his past, and this will result in an autobiographical account. By telling his story, the narrator manages, or at least makes an attempt, to obtain a degree of control over his underlying concern, which is the driving force behind the narrative. When the elegiac romance is compared with other narratives about heroes, the narrator of this form can be said to be much more than a mere observer: he undergoes change insofar as he gives an account of the hero and is the victim of his relationship with him or her.

The elegiac romance is thus an autobiography of the narrator disguised as the biography of the hero.

Lord Jim is a novel about the art of narrating a story, but particularly about the difficulties that Marlow faced in attempting to understand and narrate the story of Jim. Jim is a young and promising sailor, who dreams about becoming a hero of the high seas. Marlow is much older than Jim and is a ship's captain who is tired of his profession and discontented with life in general. Throughout the narrative, he has mixed feelings towards Jim, which fluctuate between admiration, curiosity and slight repulsion. Although the hero is the cause of conflicting emotions, Marlow remains loyal to his friend: he helps Jim to find a new position whenever he gives up his job in an attempt to flee from his past. He wants at all costs to understand Jim's spiritual being and find an explanation for his actions by seeking to reconstruct his story.

Marlow is not the narrator at the beginning of the novel. In the first chapters, an omniscient narrator tells the story of Jim's childhood and early years, as well as his romantic dream of becoming a hero like the protagonists of the sea adventure stories that he has read. Marlow only takes over the narrative when he arrives on the scene at the judicial inquiry about the *Patna*. From then onwards, what we read is the account given by Marlow to a group of listeners after dinner. The end of the novel is presented in yet another way: it takes the shape of a letter written by Marlow to the most attentive of his listeners.

The gist of the narrative is conveyed to the reader through Marlow, who has complete control over the story, even when he reconstructs the section on the judicial testimony and eye-witness accounts of Jim given by third parties. When the narrative is handed over to Marlow, time sequences are constantly jumbled. Past, present and future are juxtaposed in a single paragraph, which allows Marlow to manipulate the narrative flow and thus highlight certain aspects of the story. At the same time, he delays revealing (or even conceals) information from the reader concerning facts about the fate of the *Patna* and the death of Jim which are important to the plot.

The Three Elements of the Elegiac Romance

Before examining *Dom Casmurro*, account should be taken of what Bruffee regards as the three key elements of elegiac romance to emerge from *Lord Jim* (and *Heart of Darkness*), which are also present in *Dom Casmurro*, as we shall see.

The first is the ambiguity of the relationship between the narrator and the hero, which raises doubts about the credibility of Marlow. His interpretation of Jim can be tendentious because at times he arouses sympathy for Jim and at other times invites us to judge him. As Albert Guerard wrote, on the one hand, Jim 'needs a judge, witness and advocate in the solitude of his battle with himself'.[9] On the other, Marlow 'speaks of the fellowship of the craft, of being his very young brother's keeper, of loyalty to "one of us" of mere curiosity, of a moral need to explore and test a standard of conduct. But Marlow ... acknowledges a more intimate or more selfish alliance.'[10]

The second key feature is the continuous introspection of the narrator who reflects on the past and reinterprets it while telling the story. This means that emphasis on action is kept to a minimum and thus the rhythm of the narrative slows. What is most important for Marlow is to discover both the effects of the past on the life of his hero and how the past affects him, too, in the fictional present. It is all these various moments of introspection combined that lead us to conclude that the narrator is not simply seeking to explain Jim's offence, but also attempting to satisfy a personal need, as he makes clear in Chapter 5:

> Was *it for my own sake that I wished to find some shadow of an excuse for that young fellow whom I had never seen before*, but whose appearance alone added a touch of personal concern to the thoughts suggested by the knowledge of his weakness – made it a thing of mystery and terror – like a hint of a destructive fate ready for us all whose youth – in its day – had resembled his youth? *I fear that such was the secret motive of my prying.*[11]

The investigation that the narrator undertakes to discover the influence of the past on the present compels him to occupy a situation that is constantly shifting. In Bruffee's view, what he really wishes to do in the story is to exhume the past that lies buried within himself and look at it without blinking so that he can proceed with his own life.

The third key feature of the elegiac romance that Bruffee detects in *Lord Jim* is the rhetorical manipulation of the reader by the narrator. Marlow portrays a fascinating character similar to the heroes of the sea yarns in the books read by Jim (and by the readers of *Lord Jim*), which are imbued with Western cultural traditions. Bruffee thinks that the reader reacts in a conventional way to these traditions and sees Jim as in fact a hero. This is not the only 'trick' employed by the narrator to distract the attention of the reader. Bruffee states that Marlow also persuades the reader that his own interests and he himself are of no less importance for the narrative. In this way, Marlow draws the attention of the reader from himself to the figure of the hero when what he is doing the whole time, in reality, is to 'saturate his description of his hero with his own personality, his own values, and above all his own deepest emotional problems'.[12]

The presence in *Lord Jim* of the three features discussed above, or, in other words, the ambiguity of fellowship, the introspection of the narrator and the rhetorical manipulation of the reader, means that the reader of the novel remains in a state of conflict. At first, this takes place between the reader and the narrator, but it also occurs between the reader and the omniscient narrator (at the beginning of the novel) and within the reader himself or herself, in relation to his or her own values and literary imagination. All this makes for a very different experience from that of the linear reading of heroic novels and the *Bildungsroman* of the nineteenth century. As Guerard states, the novel subjects its readers to a profound experience and requires their full involvement while also encouraging them to read the book a second time. The readers go through the labyrinth of evidence without the usual guide of an omniscient narrator and find themselves alone with a manipulative narrator. The novel places us within a psycho-moral drama where there is no final solution. We read the end of the book without knowing whether Marlow has explained Jim's offence or if he has become reconciled to the past and freed himself from Jim's influence. It was probably not one of Conrad's main concerns to solve either of these mysteries. By making the pendulum swing between the narrator and the hero, the author is more concerned with establishing an interaction between the two and their respective mental outlooks. This is achieved with a degree of profundity that a modernist novel would attribute to mental processes, introspection and inner experience.

The Title: *Dom Casmurro* and not *Capitu*

'Don't look it up in dictionaries,' Dom Casmurro warns us in the first chapter of the book that he intends to write and for which he chooses as a provisional title the nickname that his neighbours have given him. The meaning of 'casmurro', he continues, 'doesn't have the meaning they give, but the one the common people give it, of a quiet person who keeps himself to himself'.[13] In the dictionaries that readers are discouraged from using, 'casmurro' means stubborn, headstrong and pig-headed. In this chapter we should, perhaps, once more question the Machadian narrator, as several critics of the novel have done, and consider it to be the first instance of what Marta de Senna calls a 'strategy of deceit' which is predominant throughout the novel: 'the device is what I call the strategy of deceit, by which I mean the narrator's ability to build, on every other page, a kind of *trompe l'oeil* that conditions the reader's eyes to see what is not there, and not to see what really is there to be seen'.[14]

Yet, if we try to see Dom Casmurro through the eyes of his neighbours, we find that he is a man who in the recent past and in the narrative present has lived 'alone, with a servant', in a house where the architecture and decor seek in an artificial way to recreate the old times of the child and teenager. Moreover, since he used to spend days and nights on end writing, he cannot be regarded by his living neighbours as anything but a man of 'quiet, reclusive habits'.[15]

This does not mean that the two definitions are mutually exclusive. They apply to the same person but at three different stages of his life. He is the narrator Dom Casmurro, Bentinho and Bento Santiago, all at once. The dictionary meaning does not bring together the features of the narrator, at least for those who see him from the outside and are still alive when the narrative begins. Moreover, it fails to define the teenager Bentinho, who we know was much more naive than his childhood playmate Capitolina and his best friend and also former seminarian Escobar. The cunning of Capitu and Escobar and the naivety of Bentinho are heightened not only by gender but also by the fact that they belong to different social classes: Capitu is a social climber and Escobar a self-made man.[16]

Out of the three facets of the same man (Bentinho, Bento and Dom Casmurro), it is Bento who is the stubborn and pig-headed one. The obsession that grips him during his adult life distances Dom Casmurro from Bentinho, and is therefore fateful for his destiny and those of Capitu and their son Ezequiel. However, it is not Bento who sits down to write the narrative. He is as much a character as Capitu and Escobar. In reality, the memoirs of Dom Casmurro are concerned with reconstructing the interaction between Bento, Capitu and Escobar at different stages of the narrator's life – according to the pattern of the elegiac romance.

Machado de Assis has been criticized for writing only histories of white men and women and this is also true of *Dom Casmurro*, the first novel he published after the change of the regime from Monarchy (1821–89) to Republic.[17] The plot explores the social destiny of free women – represented by the heroine, Capitu and Escobar's wife, Sancha – but also of free men – represented by Bento himself, Escobar and the *agregado* José Dias. It runs from the 1840s to the 1890s and provides the reader with a panorama of the period as the narrator tells us his personal story. The Second Reign particularly stands out, especially the rule of Dom Pedro II, which lasted

49 years (1840–89). With the social and economic crisis, the abolitionist movements, the Paraguayan War and the many internal conflicts, such as the Farroupilha Revolution, the ideals of the Empire began to crumble. In 1857, a key year for the plot, since it is when young Bento finds out that he is in love with Capitu, the Second Reign experienced its apogee. The image of the Emperor as a symbol of power is constantly reflected in the novel, firstly in specific scenes, such as when Bento and José Dias witness an imperial procession as they are wandering through the streets of Rio de Janeiro in 1857 (Chapter 29), and the scene in which Bento recollects Capitu's interest in historical facts, more precisely in finding out what the 'Emperor's Majority' means: that the coronation of Dom Pedro II took place in December 1840 on his fourteenth birthday.[18] Secondly, Bento embodies the symbolism of a declining but yet powerful regime and emperor through Dom Pedro's violent and failed attempt to maintain his position of control. The novel captures the figure of the patriarch in full exercise of his power, which is, nevertheless, at stake.

Only intended to be provisional, as the narrator states in the first chapter, the title *Dom Casmurro* is not referred to again in the narrative. We accept *Dom Casmurro* as the definitive title when we have finished reading Chapter 148, without asking if it was the most suitable for the book. Machado de Assis could have chosen to call the novel *Dona Capitu* or *The Gypsy Capitu* or simply *Capitu*, as in Luiz Fernando Carvalho's televised adaptation, broadcast by TV Globo in 2008. The author would thereby have given prominence to the novel's heroine, in the same way that Cervantes and Conrad highlighted the significance of their heroes by making the respective titles eponymous with them. On the one hand, *Don Quijote* and *Lord Jim* are echoed in the title chosen by Machado, owing to the neighbours' accusations that he had 'aristocratic pretensions'.[19] As Bruffee argues, the title of an elegiac romance very often draws attention to

> the ostensible hero of the narrator's tale, but at the same time qualifies that attention so as to cast doubt even before the tale begins on the ostensible hero's legitimacy both as *a* hero and as *the* hero, that is, both on his genuineness and integrity and on his role as the true central figure in the work.[20]

On the other hand, *Dom Casmurro* is set apart from *Don Quijote* and *Lord Jim* because its title already denounces what the elegiac romance initially seeks to conceal: that the interests of the narrator are of central concern. As Bosi points out, in *Dom Casmurro* 'Machado succeeded in reinstating the internal story of the narrative voice, giving it depth and tone'.[21]

Bento's Betrayal

We can understand the significance that fellowship acquires in *Dom Casmurro* if we concentrate on the three features of the elegiac romance discussed in greater detail in the section above on *Lord Jim*. These are (1) the ambiguity of fellowship, (2) the rhetorical manipulation of the reader and (3) the introspection of the narrator.

The ambiguity of fellowship must be discussed in more detail because, in the first place, the fellowship in *Dom Casmurro* is not of the same type as that in *Lord Jim*. Like *Lord Jim*, *Dom Casmurro* tells the story of the narrator's obsession with the – heroic – figure of a friend who has already died: 'the first love of my heart', as he calls Capitu in the last chapter.[22] His search is also conducted at an inner level; or, to put it another way, in attempting to recreate an interaction between the heroine and himself, he indulges in an epistemological and psychological kind of self-assertion. The narrator reveals in Chapter 2, much earlier than Marlow (who is not the narrator at the beginning of *Lord Jim*), that 'clearly my aim' in writing the book 'was to tie the two ends of life together, and bring back youth in old age', something he failed to achieve with the house that he built in Engenho Novo.[23] As the narrative progresses, the presence of Capitu and the enigma surrounding her personality become more and more imposing. However, Dom Casmurro does not cease to tell his story while at the same time conducting an appraisal of the heroine. His and Capitu's lives are as closely bound up in the narrative as the two sides of the wall that divides the houses of the two families.

In one respect Marlow and Dom Casmurro are the same: both of them reach the end of their stories without deciphering the mystery of their heroes. In the case of Jim, this is even after several accounts about him have been given by third parties whom he met on various occasions. Marlow does not manage to penetrate the mind of his hero (being only able to speculate about it) and fails to find a justification for Jim's offence. However, in Machado's novel the question is even more complex. At the beginning, Dom Casmurro is in a more advantageous situation than Marlow with regard to Jim. The reason for this is that he is married to Capitu and is thus on intimate terms with her, sharing the same house and presumably the same bedroom. Despite this, the narrator reaches the end of his account without succeeding in deciphering the mystery of Capitu's 'undertow eyes'.[24]

At the turn of the nineteenth century in both Brazil and Europe, women (and homosexuals as well) were depicted as figures of disorder who occupied a border zone between patriarchal order and sexual anarchy.[25] Femmes fatales such as Zola's Nana and Oscar Wilde's Salome were characterized as mysterious, enigmatic and a stimulant of desire in men that would cause illness or even death. An important element of seduction was their eyes, something Machado de Assis explored not only in *Dom Casmurro* but also in his short fiction, in 'A cartomante',[26] 'Miss Dollar',[27] 'Sem olhos'[28] and 'Uns braços'.[29] In *Dom Casmurro*, the narrator confesses to being unable to convey an image 'that doesn't offend against the rules of good style' to convey her eyes:

> Undertow eyes? Why not? Undertow. That's the notion that the new expression put in my head. They held some kind of mysterious, active fluid, a force that dragged one in, like the undertow of a wave retreating from the shore on stormy days.[30]

According to Bosi, Machado de Assis makes use of tautology and of the metaphor of *olhos de ressaca* [undertow eyes] to convey the narrator's inability to grasp the heroine. With regard to the use of tautology, he writes,

> It is significant that in the shaping of Capitu the narrator turns to tautology, ceasing to define his girlfriend in a narrow, rectilinear way: 'Capitu was Capitu, that is, a very particular person, more of a woman than I was a man. If I've not said it already, there you have it. And if I have, there you have it anyway. There are things which must be impressed on the reader's mind by dint of repetition.'[31] The singular in its pure state – Capitu was Capitu – marries the universal feminine (woman) and from there arises that intensifier 'very particular', which takes the refusal of classification as far as possible.[32]

As in *Lord Jim*, one of the narrative devices of the rhetorical manipulation of the reader is the characterization of the heroes of the novels through the use of male or female tropes from the literature of the time. The narrator's inability to decipher Capitu's nature goes hand in hand with her depiction as a femme fatale, playing thereby with the reader's literary imagination. This is not an innovation of *Dom Casmurro*, since Machado often employs the same prominent female tropes in his short stories and novels.[33] Reading Capitu as a femme fatale was the predominant critical reception of the novel until the mid twentieth century. Critics such as Veríssimo, Pujol and Miguel-Pereira accuse Capitu of adultery, based on Bento's assumption of Capitu's manipulative nature.[34]

The restrictions that society placed upon women meant that seduction was their only way of gaining independence.[35] The femme fragile highlights women's dependency and capacity to be manipulative, whereas the femme fatale represents strong, rational women who subvert traditional gender roles. These early critics fall prey to Machado de Assis's rhetorical manipulation and endorse the status quo: the submission of women and children to the patriarchal family structure in a society that is less and less dependent on slave labour. Indeed, these early critics are led by Bento into seeing Capitu as a threat to marriage and the hierarchical structure of the family.

However, by comparing Capitu with other female characters – Virgília of *Memórias póstumas de Brás Cubas* and Sofia of *Quincas Borba* – Bosi comes to the conclusion that the heroine of *Dom Casmurro* is far more complex and dense, remaining even today a mystery to readers: 'It is plausible that Pádua's daughter is fighting to improve her position within the paternalistic society of the time, which was focused on marriage and family wealth, but her innate character ruptures established interests, just as life will, if it can, rupture the dam of social convention.'[36]

As we read the novel we follow the progressive complication of the relationship between the heroine and the narrator, for whom being married to his heroine does not provide better insight into her character.[37] To put it more clearly, the nature of the initial ties of friendship between the narrator and the heroine changes throughout the novel to suit the particular aspects of the historical and social background depicted and the specific turns of the plot. In the beginning the heroine is the childhood friend and neighbour of the narrator. During puberty, the friendship and innocent playfulness of the two children turn into love. The ties of friendship are transfigured by the swearing of vows of love, which are sealed by the inscription on the wall shared by the two houses and are later renewed when the couple are married at a church altar.

We do not doubt that Bentinho was passionately in love with Capitu. It is her feelings that are ambiguous; at least that is how the narrator wishes us to see them. His curiosity to understand something that is indecipherable in her dates back to their childhood. Like Jim, she is the product of the imagination and discourse of the narrator, who meanwhile seeks to make up for his failings in fantasies and preparing his own absolution. At the time when they both lived in Matacavalos, Bentinho used to admire how cunning Capitolina was. Much as he may be trying to gather arguments that could be used to condemn the heroine and remove the slightest possibility that the reader will forgive her, he cannot leave unnoticed in his words the tender feelings that the memory of the heroine in her childhood and youth arouses in him. It is for this reason that, as has been noted by Roberto Schwarz, a lyrical tone prevails in the part of the narrative about the house at Matacavalos.[38]

The ties of friendship between the two families are sealed by the marriage arranged for the happiness of the two youngsters. If we employ Bruffee's terminology, which brings us back to the origins of the heroic quest romance, there is in *Dom Casmurro* a shift in the nature of the bond between the narrator and the heroine.

The historical and social background should not be overlooked, since it places the heroine in an adverse situation that is twofold: she does not have a voice in the narrative, and when she was still alive her wishes and freedom were constantly thwarted. This is because her responsibilities were confined to playing a role that was defined within a patriarchal society: looking after the household and bringing up her only child. Even a small protective gesture of Bento's towards his wife is not something genuine; I refer here to the covering of Capitu's arms by a fine veil in the dances later in the novel. It is a conservative and overprotective attitude that is prompted by jealousy of the natural endowments of the woman and the physical inferiority that Bento feels, for example, in comparison with Escobar. The exile of Capitu and Ezequiel to Switzerland, where Bento sends them after their separation, represents the final break of the fellowship between the heroine and the narrator, which I interpret here as a betrayal of Capitu by Bentinho. This reverses the line of interpretation that is usually followed and which is the most controversial area in critical essays about the novel. If the betrayal of Bentinho by Capitu can never be confirmed, we can nonetheless be sure that, in the world of the elegiac romance, no narrator has ever gone so far in his ambiguous feelings towards his heroine.

Following this line of thought, the separation of the couple, which is caused by the morbid jealousy of the husband, constitutes a break of the (conjugal) ties. We can no longer speak of 'the fellowship of the craft' or the protection 'of his very young brother', as in the case of Marlow and Jim. The nature of the bond is less changeable in *Lord Jim*. In Conrad's novel there is no break in the pact of the fellowship. The narrator remains loyal to the hero from beginning to end. He attempts to help Jim by arranging a number of consecutive jobs for him. Furthermore, he is not responsible for the conflict that finally leads to Jim's death. Marlow is hundreds of miles away and has already said his last farewell to Jim. In this respect, Marlow acts as a passive observer. This is not the case in *Dom Casmurro*: Bento sends Capitu to exile and is indirectly responsible for her lonely death, as well as that of their son. Thus, Bento betrays Capitu (and not the other way around) if we reread the novel through the lens of a heroic quest romance.

A Double Elegy?

Dom Casmurro makes plain at the beginning and end of the book that his purpose is to link the two extremes of his life and that all that is lacking is he, himself.[39] In view of this, why has criticism put so much effort into (re)reading the novel in search of clues that will confirm the infidelity of Capitu or clear her of the charge of adultery? As mentioned above, Abel Barros Baptista describes this trend in the critical history of *Dom Casmurro*, focused on the relationship between narrator and heroine, as 'fiction of a court case'. Why are we led not to see what is there before us – Bento Santiago's authoritarianism, envy, personal weakness, selfishness, scorn for religion, and indifference towards his son – and to see what is not there, that is, the adultery of Capitu?

The first study to cast doubts on the veracity of the narrator was published as early as 1900. José Veríssimo suspected that Bento's views about Capitu might be biased: 'Dom Casmurro describes her with love and hate, which may make him suspect. He tries to hide these feelings very carefully, perhaps without all-round success. At the end of his memoirs one feels a thrill that he attempts to reject.'[40]

Key critical studies throughout the twentieth century, such as those referred to on p. 286, were unanimous in their condemnation of Capitu. It was only in Helen Caldwell that the heroine finally found an advocate who defended her from the accusation of adultery. For Caldwell, Bento acts simultaneously as Othello and Iago in order to plot the condemnation of his wife. She compares the narrative to a court of law, in which Capitu is put in the dock and the narrator is Bento's own lawyer. The implied author would have left clues throughout the book, causing the reader to be wary of Bento's account. As Gledson and Schwarz argue, the reader glimpses the malfunctioning of contemporary Brazilian society through the troubled figure of Bento Santiago.

Gledson draws attention to the unreliability of the narrator of *Dom Casmurro*. In Gledson's view, Bento's whole narrative is an attempt to persuade the reader of Capitu's infidelity by reconstructing impressions of the past that are unsubstantiated and lack concrete evidence. The narrator's aim is to make his version of the facts override everything else. This means that, as the narrative progresses, the novel is revealed to be a study of Bento's pathological obsession and not of Capitu's adultery.[41]

Schwarz, on the other hand, puts the blame on the reader for having accepted Capitu's conviction for more than 60 years: the reader is sympathetic to Bento's attitude because he shares with the narrator Bento's point of view and the concerns of his social group. Capitu's conviction and the ruin of Bento's family life were undesirable but inevitable.[42]

As mentioned above, some studies have expanded the focus to examine the triangular relationship between Capitu, Bento and Escobar. Italo Mariconi, who pioneered the reading of the novel as a queer narrative, explores the sexual connotations of episodes of clear affection between Bento and Escobar. For Mariconi, some lines of the novel make explicit 'certain ambiguities and sufferings that characterize masculine homosexual desire in the paradigm of Victorian heteronormativity'.[43] For Richard Miskolci, it is a homosocial relationship to which, as Boucinhas points out, the problem of class inequality is added. Machado depicts through the ambiguity of Bento's feelings for Escobar – desire, rivalry, homosexuality and camaraderie between two seminary friends – the problematic and complex relations between men prevailing in the late nineteenth century. Based on the studies of Foucault and Ortega, for Miskolci the friendship between Bento and Escobar is socially controlled and peripheral to the relationship with woman within the nuclear monogamist family. Capitu – as well as Sancha, about whom Bentinho cherishes a small erotic fantasy in Chapter 118 – is the mediator of the relations between men who attempt to affirm their masculinity 'against the feminine ideal, embodied in women and projected by them, in sum, socially represented in that which mediates their relationship founded on a masculine homosocial desire'.[44] Miskolci employs the geometric figure of the triangle in examining the novel's social, gender and sexual hierarchies, which are crystallized in the love triangle: 'we find not only the centrality of the Bento–Escobar relationship, but above all, the fact that the apex of the triangle, which is farthest from the base, is also the most revealing'.[45]

This line of interpretation corroborates the hypothesis that the nature of the fellowship in *Dom Casmurro* is more complex because it is twofold. The narrator gives centrality to Capitu, owing to the role of women in social relationships among men, and also because Machado de Assis may have been conditioned by the literary models and female tropes in force in his time, as discussed earlier. However, the 'male knight' does not disappear from the narrative: he instead loses his role as hero to a more complex female character. His death is felt much sooner than Capitu's and is, according to Miskolci, what turns Bento Santiago's life inside out: it fills him with suspicions that are directed against Capitu and makes him question his own masculinity.[46]

One of the textual proofs that the knight loses centrality in the narrative is the way in which Machado de Assis depicts Escobar. He is not as complex as Capitu. In a few chapters, particularly Chapters 56 and 71, the narrator is able to present with precision the character's key attributes – physical and psychological features, mannerisms and habits. Escobar is seen through not only Bento's eyes but also the eyes of other characters, in a way very similar to the characterization of Dona Glória, José Dias, Prima Justina and Tio Cosme. Even his nervous twitches and flaws are described in detail in Chapter 56.

Machado de Assis does not construct ambiguity through the description of the character, as he does for Capitu. Escobar is a self-made man, as described by Boucinhas.[47] However, Machado implies the possibility of eroticizing (or even queering) male homosocial relationships in a few specific scenes, such as the one in which Bento touches the arms of Escobar – which has been extensively examined by Mariconi and Miskolci – and an earlier one during their time in the seminary. Bento is enthusiastic about Escobar's mathematical abilities and gives him a hug in public. The gesture is reprimanded as excessive and deviant from the modest normative behaviour expected of seminarists:

> I was so taken with my friend's mental agility, that I could not refrain from embracing him. It was in the courtyard; other seminarists noticed our exuberance; a priest who was with them did not approve.
>
> 'Modesty,' he said to us, 'does not permit such effusive gestures; your esteem can be expressed with moderation.'
>
> Escobar remarked that the priest and the others were speaking out of envy, and said that we should perhaps keep apart from one another. I interrupted him to say no; if it was envy, so much the worse for them.
>
> 'Let's cock a snoot at them!'
>
> 'But ...'
>
> 'Let's be even firmer friends than we have been up to now.'
>
> Escobar grasped my hand in secret, so hard that my fingers still hurt from it. An illusion, no doubt, perhaps the effect of the long hours I've been writing without a break. I'll put down the pen for a while.[48]

It would be perhaps less anachronistic and more accurate to interpret the effusive hug and the strong handshake on the sly as signals of 'friendship or male love', a pre-homosexual category of male sex and gender deviance which, according to Halperin, is revealed as much in hierarchical relations (heroic warrior–subordinate pal or sidekick; patron–client) as in relations 'between two men who occupy the same social rank, usually an elite one, and who can claim the same status in terms of age, masculinity, and social empowerment'.[49] Escobar and Bento are at first equals, since they are about the same age and are at this point both at the seminary and therefore being prepared for the same career. I would not go as far as to say that there is some hierarchy between them. It would be more precise to say that there is a small social, physical and intellectual asymmetry between the two men, much to Machado's liking, who, as Bosi describes, prioritizes in his fiction the treatment of the smallest social difference.[50] Both types of relationship are 'indissociably bound up with at least the potential for erotic signification'.[51] However, as Halperin writes further on,

> It is difficult for us moderns – with our heavily psychologistic model of the human personality, our notion of unconscious drives, our tendency to associate desire with sexuality, and our heightened sensitivity to anything that might seem to contravene the strict protocols of heterosexual masculinity – it is difficult for us to avoid reading into such passionate expressions of male love a suggestion of 'homoeroticism' at very least, if not of 'latent homosexuality,' those being the formulations that often act as a cover for own perplexity about how to interpret same-sex emotions that do not quite square with canonical conceptions of sexual subjectivity.[52]

Along these lines, I think it is more accurate to define the relationship between Bento and Escobar as male friendship that is built on their common desire to leave the seminary and reject a future life as priests, as clearly stated in Chapter 78.

It is a friendship that starts in the seminary, between two men who will later each become a paterfamilias, one representing the rising new bourgeois class, and the other the decaying elite of former land- and slave-owners. Escobar emulates the habits of the patriarch: he marries, has a daughter, buys a house for the family in the upwardly mobile neighbourhood of Flamengo and maintains extra-marital affairs, as Bento does.

Conclusion

The secret of the relationship between Escobar and Bento may still be an open question, although I believe that they were simply friends, in pre-homosexual terms. The relationship between two men remains an important element of the elegiac romance, but the female character gains centrality in the plot and therefore more complexity as a character, which is lacking in Escobar. The triangular relationship is, nevertheless, central to the development and acclimatization of the genre in this novel, which takes gender on board to fit the specificities of the plot and of Brazilian society at the end of the nineteenth century – to be precise, the change in the gender of the hero and the presence of a male friend in the middle distance.

In this simplified summary of some of the ways in which *Dom Casmurro* has been read, we can see that the rhetorical manipulation of the reader – Bruffee's second element of the elegiac romance – has already been fully discussed in critical studies of Machado. Going back to the comparison of Machado's and Conrad's novels, I believe that the rhetorical manipulation of the reader in *Dom Casmurro* is more prevalent than in *Lord Jim*. In the first place, Dom Casmurro has to shift the focus away from himself, since his aims are made clear earlier in the novel than is the case with Marlow. Secondly, there is a shift from hero to heroine as the central element of the elegy. And, third, he must persuade himself and the reader that it was necessary to break off the pact of fellowship with his heroine in order to defend his honour as a betrayed husband before he can be redeemed. He could never succeed in gaining redemption without first justifying why he has broken off the original vows. Thus his final hope lies with the readers: he wants to persuade them that Capitu has betrayed him and thus rid himself of the burden of having broken the heroic quest romance's oath of loyalty.

Before concluding, there remains the final distinctive feature of the elegiac romance – the introspection of the narrator. This has already been studied with regard to *Memórias póstumas de Brás Cubas* in the critical tradition that links it to the Shandean form. This feature of the elegiac romance roughly corresponds to the first two components of the Shandean form as outlined by Rouanet: the constant presence of the narrator and the digressive and fragmentary character of the plot.[53] The effect on the narrative of the constant introspection of the narrator is that the action slows down. Digression and introspection are employed for different reasons, however. In the elegiac romance (and this applies to *Dom Casmurro*), Bruffee argues that, insofar as the narrator grows in stature, the narrative

> tends to take on the quality of action, as the narrator talks about what he is doing, or trying to do, in telling the tale. And the narrator also manifests a growing interest in what might be called the irreducible substance of fiction. He becomes interested in the irrecoverable past and its effects on the present.[54]

Another consequence of the frequent intrusions of the narrator is that, in Bruffee's words, whenever he finds himself in conflict with himself and reveals 'his deepest emotional problems' he either contradicts or betrays himself. Hence, I believe that it is not the implicit author who adopts this role, as Caldwell argues. In Caldwell's opinion, the authorial voice is superimposed on Dom Casmurro's narrative. The implicit author signals to the reader at various points of the narrative that Dom Casmurro is only telling his own version of the story. Like the followers of Joseph Conrad, Machado tones down the effect of the frame narrator (if he does not exclude it altogether), that is, the narrative superstructure in which an omniscient narrator is superimposed on the dramatized narrator. Thus, in *Dom Casmurro*, both the heroic quest and the authorial voice are internalized. In psychoanalytical terms, the inner authorial voice is responsible for the lapses of the narrator, that is, the casual errors he commits without taking account of the repercussions of what he has written on the minds of more obtuse readers. Examples include the irony implied in the title of the book, the contradictions between the different definitions of the word 'casmurro', the effigy of Massinissa, and other allusions and quotations that can be found in the novel – all of which tell us to be wary of the narrator.

The comparison of *Dom Casmurro* with *Lord Jim* in this chapter may encourage a rereading of the Brazilian novel to distinguish its realistic aspects from its modernist aspects. Although its plot may seem to belong to the nineteenth century, the form of the elegiac romance that Machado employs, whether consciously or not, places him alongside or even ahead of Conrad.

Notes

1. This chapter is a shorter version of Silva (2018).
2. The novel was published by H. Garnier in Paris in 1899 and was on sale in Rio de Janeiro in 1900. The first translation into English was by Hellen Caldwell (Assis 1953). The translation used in this chapter is by John Gledson (Assis 1997). All other translations are mine.
3. Caldwell 1960.
4. Baptista 2003, 375. See also Franchetti 2009.
5. An *agregado* is a free poor person who lives in the shadow of a patriarchal family in a dubious and uncomfortable position, being neither a relative nor a servant (Chalhoub 2003; Schwarz 1997; Miskolci 2008).
6. Bruffee 1983.
7. Conrad 1996; Conrad 2007; Ford 2002; Fitzgerald 1991; Mann 1992; Nabokov 2012. This subheading summarizes the prologue – 'A Note on Defining Genres' – and Chapter 1: 'Elegiac Romance: A Modern Tradition' (Bruffee 1983, 15–72).
8. Conrad 1996, 136, emphasis added.
9. Guerard 1996, 404.
10. Guerard 1996, 404.

11. Conrad 1996, 35, emphasis added.
12. Bruffee 1983, 110.
13. Assis 1997, 4
14. Senna 2004–5, 407.
15. Assis 1997, 4.
16. See, for example, Meyer 1986, 222; Boucinhas 2015.
17. Costa 1985, 248–65.
18. Assis 1997, 61.
19. Assis 1997, 61.
20. Bruffee 1983, 49.
21. Bosi 1999, 41
22. Assis 1997, 244.
23. Assis 1997, 5.
24. Assis 1997, 61.
25. Showalter 1992.
26. Assis 1884.
27. Assis 1870.
28. Assis 1876–7.
29. Assis 1885.
30. Assis 1997, 63.
31. Assis 1997, 59.
32. Bosi 1999, 30.
33. Stein 1984, 112.
34. Veríssimo 1977, 28; Pujol 1934, 247–8; Miguel-Pereira 1936, 272.
35. Faoro 1974, 317.
36. Bosi 1999, 27.
37. See, for example, Merivale's article (1980) on *A Book of Common Prayer* by Joan Didion for an analysis of this work as elegiac novel in which both the narrator and the protagonist are women.
38. Schwarz 1997, 32.
39. See Chapters 2 and 144 of *Dom Casmurro*.
40. Veríssimo 1900.
41. Gledson 1984.
42. Schwarz 1990.
43. Mariconi 2008, 87.
44. Miskolci 2009, 552.
45. Miskolci 2009, 557.
46. Miskolci 2009, 556.
47. Boucinhas 2015.
48. Assis 1997, 167.
49. Halperin 2002, 118.
50. Bosi 1999, 153–4.
51. Halperin 2002, 118.
52. Halperin 2002,120.
53. Rouanet 2007.
54. Bruffee 1983, 74.

Bibliography

Assis, Machado de. 'Miss Dollar'. In *Contos fluminenses* (1870). http://machadodeassis.net/hiperTx_romances/obras/variashistorias.htm

Assis, Machado de. 'Sem olhos', *Jornal das Famílias*, December 1876 to February 1877. http://machadodeassis.net/hiperTx_romances/obras/variashistorias.htm

Assis, Machado de. 'A cartomante', *Gazeta de Notícias*, 28 November 1884. http://machadodeassis.net/hiperTx_romances/obras/variashistorias.htm

Assis, Machado de. 'Uns braços', *Gazeta de Notícias*, 5 November 1885. http://machadodeassis.net/hiperTx_romances/obras/variashistorias.htm

Assis, Machado de. *Dom Casmurro*. Paris: H. Garnier, 1899.
Assis, Machado de. *Dom Casmurro*, translated by Hellen Caldwell. London: W. H. Allen, 1953.
Assis, Machado de. *Dom Casmurro*, translated by John Gledson. Oxford: Oxford University Press, 1997.
Baptista, Abel Barros. *Autobibliografias: solicitação do livro na ficção de Machado de Assis*. Campinas: Editora da Unicamp, 2003.
Bosi, Alfredo. *O enigma do olhar*. São Paulo: Editora Ática, 1999.
Boucinhas, André Dutra. 'O segredo de Escobar', *Piauí* 105 (2015). http://piaui.folha.uol.com.br/materia/o-segredo-de-escobar/
Bruffee, Kenneth A. *Elegiac Romance: Cultural Change and Loss of the Hero in Modern Fiction*. Ithaca, NY: Cornell University Press, 1983.
Caldwell, Helen. *The Brazilian Othello of Machado de Assis: A Study of Dom Casmurro*. Berkeley: University of California Press, 1960.
Chalhoub, Sidney. *Machado de Assis, historiador*. São Paulo: Companhia das Letras, 2003.
Conrad, Joseph. *Lord Jim*. New York: W. W. Norton, 1996.
Conrad, Joseph. *Heart of Darkness*. London: Penguin, 2007.
Costa, Emília Viotti da. *Da monarquia à república: momentos decisivos*. São Paulo: Brasiliense, 1985.
Faoro, Raimundo. *Machado de Assis: a pirâmide e o trapézio*. São Paulo: Nacional, 1974.
Fitzgerald, F. Scott. *The Great Gatsby*. Cambridge: Cambridge University Press, 1991.
Ford, Ford Madox. *The Good Soldier*. London: Penguin, 2002.
Franchetti, Paulo. 'No banco dos réus: notas sobre a fortuna crítica recente de Dom Casmurro', *Estudos Avançados* 65 (2009): 289–98. http://www.scielo.br/scielo.php?script=sci_arttext&pid=S0103-40142009000100019
Gledson, John. *The Deceptive Realism of Machado de Assis: A Dissenting Interpretation of Dom Casmurro*. Manchester: Francis Cairns, 1984.
Guerard, Albert J. 'Lord Jim'. In Joseph Conrad, *Lord Jim*, edited by Thomas C. Moser, 397–423. New York: W. W. Norton, 1996.
Halperin, David. *How to Do the History of Homosexuality*. Chicago: University of Chicago Press, 2002.
Mann, Thomas. *Doctor Faustus*. London: D. Campbell, 1992.
Mariconi, Italo. 'Dom Casmurro: o claro enigma', *Matraga* 23 (2008): 74–93.
Merivale, Patricia. 'Through Greene-Land in Drag: Joan Didion's A Book of Common Prayer', *Pacific Coast Philology* 15 (1980): 45–52.
Meyer, Augusto. *Textos críticos*. São Paulo: Perspectiva, 1986.
Miguel-Pereira, Lúcia. *Machado de Assis. Estudo crítico e biográfico*. São Paulo: Companhia Editora Nacional, 1936.
Miskolci, Ricardo. 'O corte da sexualidade – a emergência do dispositivo de sexualidade no Brasil', *Anais da 26ª Reunião Brasileira de Antropologia* (2008). http://www.abant.org.br/conteudo/ANAIS/CD_Virtual_26_RBA/grupos_de_trabalho/trabalhos/GT%2028/richard%20miskolci.pdf
Miskolci, Ricardo. 'O vértice do triângulo: Dom Casmurro e as relações de gênero e sexualidade no fin-de-siècle brasileiro', *Estudos Feministas* 17 (2009): 547–67.
Nabokov, Vladimir. *Pale Fire*. London: Penguin, 2012.
Pujol, Alfredo. *Machado de Assis*. Rio de Janeiro: José Olympio, 1934.
Rouanet, Sergio Paulo. *Riso e melancolia: a forma shandiana em Sterne, Diderot, Xavier de Maistre, Almeida Garret e Machado de Assis*. São Paulo: Companhia das Letras, 2007.
Schwarz, Roberto. *Um mestre na periferia do capitalismo*. São Paulo: Duas Cidades, 1990.
Schwarz, Roberto. *Duas meninas*. São Paulo: Companhia das Letras, 1997.
Senna, Marta de. 'Strategies of Deceit: Dom Casmurro', *Portuguese Literary and Culture Studies* 13–14 (2004–5): 407–18.
Showalter, Elaine. *Sexual Anarchy: Gender and Culture at the Fin de Siècle*. London: Virago Press, 1992.
Silva, Ana Cláudia Suriani. 'The Elegy of Dom Casmurro', *Comparative Literature Studies* 55, no. 3 (2018): 541–70.
Stein, Ingrid. *Figuras femininas em Machado de Assis*. Rio de Janeiro: Paz e Terra, 1984.
Veríssimo, José. 'Novo livro do Sr. Machado de Assis', *Jornal do Commercio*, 19 March 1900, 1.
Veríssimo, José. *Estudos de literatura brasileira*. São Paulo: Edusp; Belo Horizonte: Itatiaia, 1977.

15

On Moral and Financial Bankruptcy: Adultery and Financial Speculation in *A falência* by Júlia Lopes de Almeida

Cintia Kozonoi Vezzani

Júlia Valentina da Silveira Lopes was born in Rio de Janeiro in 1862 and passed away in the same city in 1934. Throughout her life she wrote *crônicas*, plays, novels, poems and children's literature. She also received several honours from national and international institutions. Almeida was raised in Campinas and lived in Portugal, where she married the poet and journalist Filinto de Almeida (1857–1945). Together they had three children. During her lifetime, she was an active intellectual figure and prominent literary voice. A number of critics have investigated why Almeida (or 'D. Júlia', as she was known during her lifetime) was not included in the literary canon after her death, even though her work was compared to that of renowned Brazilian authors such as Machado de Assis.[1]

A commonly cited description of Almeida comes from the *cronista* Paulo Barreto (1881–1921), known by his pseudonym, João do Rio, who visited the family's house and wrote that 'Mrs. Júlia is sitting in the shade, talking about her books and her children at the same time. I believe she confuses them and thinks about her imagined characters as she kisses the sweet fruits of her life. Her voice is calm, sweet, and her gestures are maternal.'[2] In this description, published in *O momento literário* in 1905, João do Rio identifies a certain slippage or confusion in the way in which the writer talks about her children and her books. The interview captures Almeida's internal debate about how to divide her time between her domestic responsibilities and her creative work while being a mother. This tension between labour and gender is one of the topics evident in Almeida's 1901 adultery novel *A falência* [*The Bankruptcy*],[3] where she establishes a connection between economics, literature and adultery. By drawing out these links between economics and adultery in *A falência*, this essay distils a critique of both financial capitalism and the policing of female sexuality.

The novel chronicles the fall of a wealthy coffee-producing family in Rio de Janeiro in the last decade of the nineteenth century. The father of the family, Teodoro, commits suicide after losing the family fortune through stock market speculations subsequent to deciding to gamble his wealth through his broker, Inocêncio. Alongside Teodoro's calamitous financial decisions, the novel depicts the affair of his wife, Camila, with a close family friend named Dr Gervásio. After Teodoro's death, Camila is shocked to discover that she cannot marry Gervásio because, unbeknownst to her, he is still legally married to another woman whom he left after discovering she had committed adultery. Without a husband or lover, Camila goes on to live a humble life at her niece's house and commits herself to teaching her daughters how to read and write. The novel's ending manifests a social space of female companionship largely outside the patriarchal norms that Camila has transgressed. The domestic and pedagogical labour that Camila and her niece engage in stands in stark contrast to the stock market speculations that financially ruined her husband. I argue that the female-centric social arrangement and emphasis on tangible and caring labour depicted at the novel's conclusion suggest an alternative to financialization and the discounting of female labour intrinsic to many economic models. *A falência* thus belongs to and departs from the tradition of the adultery novel, a genre exemplified by Gustave Flaubert's (1821–80) *Madame Bovary* (1856).

Flaubert's novel tells the story of the character Emma Bovary. Emma marries Charles Bovary but is quickly disillusioned with her married life in a provincial town. She turns to extramarital affairs and large purchases made on credit in order to realize the life she has imagined. However, after having multiple affairs and incurring heavy debts to pay for expensive clothes and furnishings, Emma commits suicide when she cannot make the necessary payments. Both her sexual exploits and her significant loans go unnoticed by the faithful (and naive) Charles until after her suicide.

In this chapter, I compare the 1856 French novel with Almeida's *A falência* to identify how both novels manifest a crisis of credibility that extends from personal relationships to institutions, and how each novel presents different projects in its specific national context. I also demonstrate how Almeida self-consciously writes in reaction to an established genre of female adultery novels, exemplified by *Madame Bovary*, that feature female characters written by men. Not only does Almeida's text dramatize the precarity induced by unconstrained capitalism – the same forces that lead Emma Bovary to commit suicide – but she also depicts an alternative economic system predicated on feminine solidarity. Almeida's vision of a cooperative economic sphere populated by women challenges the abstract figure of 'economic man' central to modern economic theory, who is largely defined by his competitive instincts and unfettered self-interest.[4] Moreover, the economic dimensions of *Madame Bovary* and *A falência* are entwined with a preoccupation with literature insofar as Emma's habits of infidelity and consumption are attributed to the effects of the romance novels she reads whereas Camila evinces an aversion to adultery fiction which appears to be informed by a critical awareness of the limited perceptions of male writers to adequately capture female sexuality.

Emma and Camila both have affairs while married, challenging the norms of the institution of marriage and undermining their own credibility as they lie to deceive their husbands. Meanwhile, Emma's and Teodoro's bankruptcies demonstrate the role of fantasies in sustaining financial institutions. Emma's purchases and Teodoro's investments are inspired by the reading of catalogues and the comparison of external signs of wealth, respectively. Credit and stock market speculation emerge as mechanisms for Emma and Teodoro to actualize in their own lives the representations of wealth which they have encountered, but these same mechanisms introduce a fateful precarity into their lives.

To compare Emma's and Camila's affairs and Emma's and Teodoro's financial ruin and death is to articulate a link between fantasy, economics and adultery – an association hinted at by the etymology of the word 'credit'. The word 'credit' is derived from the Latin verb *credere*, meaning 'to believe', which in turn derives from the Proto-Indo-European word for 'heart'.[5] The word 'credit' names the instrument of Emma's pursuit of wealth and also gestures towards the credulity of her husband, Charles, who fails to notice her affairs. Moreover, Teodoro's decision to invest in the stock market is tied to his perception of the credibility of his acquaintance, Inocêncio, who has facilitated the acquisition of sudden wealth of other men through stock market speculation. 'Credibility' is also a key term for Camila's love life, since she tells her lover that she knows that her husband, Teodoro, lies to her by having other lovers, while she herself doesn't know that her lover is also lying to her. In both novels, misguided belief in the likelihood of future returns on investment, the indefinite deferment of debts, or the discourse of other characters in their romantic and economic relationships results in illusions that are eventually punctured by bankruptcy (whether moral or economic). The financial institutions that seduced Emma and Teodoro result in desperation – a dynamic repeated in the romantic affairs of Emma and Camila, who lie to their husbands only to be lied to in turn by their lovers.

Both novels dramatize a pattern of adultery and bankruptcy which exposes the constitutive role played by fantasies in the maintenance of social and economic institutions. Edward Said cites *Don Quixote* and *Candide* as works that satirize the 'fallacy' of assuming 'that the swarming, unpredictable, and problematic mess in which human beings live can be understood on the basis of what books – texts – say'.[6] Emma Bovary, whose visions of married life – inspired by the reading of romance novels – collide with an underwhelming reality, is a prime example of the effects of such a textual attitude. The failure of Charles Bovary to match the protagonists of these novels encourages her to seek love elsewhere.

But Emma's economic behaviour also manifests a preference for simple narratives over nuanced ones. Through the mechanism of credit, Emma is able to construct an imaginary future that has little correspondence with economic realities. As Jens Beckert writes in *Imagined Futures*:

> expectations of the future, and the actions taken based on those expectations, are the result of contingent interpretations. These interpretations take narrative form. Economic action should therefore be understood as anchored in narrative constructions, implying that no empirical inquiry of the economy can detach itself from the investigation of the hermeneutics of economic action.[7]

According to Beckert, economic action is rooted in stories told about the future. These narratives are fictional texts insofar as they make claims about futures that have not yet come to pass. If the fictional futures that underlie economic action are texts, it follows that it may be possible for those interpreting such futures to fall victim to Said's textual attitude. Not only are Emma Bovary's romantic exploits based on a failure to distinguish between literary narratives and reality, her economic life – enabled by credit – is likewise predicated on an unrealistic narrative of an infinitely deferrable future and a perpetual postponement of debt repayment.

Building on Emma's example, I contrast two manifestations of the textual attitude in *A falência*: in Teodoro's confusion of projected economic futures for financial realities and Camila's reprimand of Dr Gervásio for uncritically accepting a model of female sexuality presented in popular novels. These examples demonstrate not only the role of narratives in economics, but also the economic dimensions of adultery.

Fictions of Financial Futures

Júlia Lopes de Almeida's novel draws attention to how the introduction of the stock market initiates a process of dematerialization that separates labour from value. While Karl Marx asserted that commodities are not only material entities but also 'mystical' things 'abounding in metaphysical subtleties',[8] the financialization of the economy (the transition occurring when financial services begin to dominate an economy, replacing manufacturing as a primary source of wealth production) introduces another layer of abstraction into economic exchange. The abstraction of labour that Marx claimed 'stamps' commodities as commodities is compounded by an additional level of abstraction during the process of financialization. The abstract values stamped on commodities become themselves commodified in a kind of self-reflexive mode of speculation – an economic hall of mirrors populated by, as Fredric Jameson writes, 'spectres of value'. This stage of capitalist development, Jameson argues, is characterized by 'the increasingly feverish search, not so much for new markets (these are also saturated) as for the new kind of profits available in financial transactions themselves'.[9] As the title of Almeida's novel indicates, these financial abstractions have very real material effects on the well-being of her characters, resulting in a material and moral bankruptcy and precipitating a state of economic and emotional precarity.

One material effect of the stock market depicted early in the novel is the massive wealth it generates for certain fortunate individuals – wealth that manifests as expensive commodities. Teodoro's decision to invest in the stock market is in part inspired by the fact that his own house, 'um palacete' [a mansion], is no longer the grandest and most expensive in the neighbourhood. That distinction now belongs to Gama Torres, a younger coffee-seller who is described as a 'modern business man', since he has invested in the stock market with the support of the broker Inocêncio and been able to 'build a large house' with wealth acquired seemingly overnight.[10] The difference in the size of Teodoro's and Gama Torres's houses seems to indicate the relative wealth-generating capacities of business based on, respectively, the buying and selling of commodities and financial speculation.[11] Before the rise of the stock market, coffee exports had not only produced vast fortunes in Brazil but had played a role in configuring the global luxuries market in the nineteenth century.

Teodoro is torn throughout the novel during this transition between a traditional plantation-based economy and a financial one – a change that he interprets through a theological lens. He believes that God helps those who work for long periods, and he sees the devil's hand in Gama

Torres's sudden enrichment. Although Teodoro initially resists the promises of quick riches by criticizing Gama Torres's gambling, he eventually succumbs to the seductive possibility of tripling his wealth on the stock market over the course of a few days. Teodoro's abandonment of his more conservative business practices exemplifies an economic trend witnessed by Almeida's contemporaries. As Felisbello Freire explains in his *História constitucional da República*, this era was 'a time of gambling never before seen. True adventures where the audacity of some sacrificed the naivety of others. Fortunes that existed disappeared. Some, who the day before had come as beggars for bread from the State, at the next moment presented themselves as millionaires.'[12] Freire's remarks on the sudden acquisition and loss of fortunes speak to the economic uncertainty (and fascination) that the emergence of the stock market unleashed in the previously more economically stable lives of *A falência*'s bourgeois protagonists. In a moment of self-reflection, Teodoro laments, 'He had worked so hard to finally achieve what others had acquired with a gesture!'[13] Contrasting his own arduous and gradual enrichment with the sudden fortunes of the nouveau riche who, in a single day, obtain wealth similar to that which Teodoro took his entire life to acquire, he links the intensification of economic volatility with the decoupling of profits from productive labour.

Teodoro is eventually convinced to invest his money on the stock market by his relatively new acquaintance, the broker Inocêncio, who joins the regular meetings of his fellow coffee producers. Inocêncio's credibility stems from his role in the sudden rise of Gama Torres through stock market speculation. The narrator describes Inocêncio's discourse as designed to dissolve doubts: 'All this appeared as *irrefutably simply true*. No ornate words. Terms as *clear* as fountain water'; 'All the obscure points were *clarified*, repeated, as the difficult passages of a composition are practised until they are played flawlessly'; 'he would return to the promising thread of his proposal and extend it *seductively*'; 'During the entire exposition there was not a single calculation without foundation, ideas without arguments. Everything was a matter of knowing how to take advantage of the propitious situation, this incomparable moment for doing business, to cast your net.'[14] The clarity of the language employed by Inocêncio allays Teodoro's misgivings about the stock market. Inocêncio's speech, complemented by handwritten notes and passages from foreign newspapers, produces a vision of future economic prosperity that paradoxically mobilizes clarity of terms and arguments to conceal the fundamental opacity and uncertainty of the future. Inocêncio produces a fantasy of foreknowledge about the future in his description of an economic system that Teodoro is only beginning to understand. Despite his initial aversion to the stock market, Teodoro is enticed by Inocêncio's proposal. The narrator claims that Inocêncio 'extended the proposal seductively'.[15] There is thus a blurring of romantic and financial terms in describing Teodoro's attraction to the possibility of profits.

Teodoro's seduction by Inocêncio's account of future profits from a financial system he knows little about is a manifestation of Said's textual attitude. Said claims that one situation in which the textual attitude appears is when 'a human being confronts at close quarters something relatively unknown and threatening and previously distant'. In cases such as this, 'one has recourse not only to what in one's previous experience the novelty resembles but also to what one has read about it'.[16] Such a textual attitude is evident in *Madame Bovary*, where the romantic novels read by Emma create a simplified image of married life that fills the vacuum of her inexperience. For Teodoro, Inocêncio's discourse and the textual sources that supplement it form a representation that renders the complexities of the stock market cognizable. The clear and readily understandable explanations furnished by Inocêncio preclude the necessity for any fine-grained analysis of the complex and volatile mechanisms underlying stock prices. The simplified fantasy becomes a substitute for a sprawling and uncertain reality.

Yet, even a rigorous analysis of the functioning of the stock market would reveal the central role played by fantasy. Anna Kornbluh in *Realizing Capital* summarizes the relationship between economics and fantasy very precisely: 'something within all capital is fictitious'.[17] In financial capital, this 'something' is the set of expectations about the future which determine value. Together, these expectations produce a fictional discourse that disavows its fictionality. It is crucial that no one treats the imaginary values as imaginary.

Accordingly, finance produces an effect akin to that of the textual attitude, as when Teodoro believes his economic fantasies will materialize in the near future. When Teodoro finds out that he has lost everything, he asks the family doctor (who is also Camila's lover) to tell Camila and the children about their destitution. In the ensuing dialogue, Dr Gervásio criticizes Camila's shock and incredulity about Teodoro's bankruptcy and says, 'You, women, don't understand these things. You only know life on a superficial level, that is why you are surprised with normal facts. Today it is Teodoro's bankruptcy, tomorrow will be someone else and then another. The list will be long.'[18] Gervásio paints Teodoro as one casualty of the onward march of capital; and he claims that the conditions of Camila's gender have prevented her from seeing and understanding the risks encapsulated in the financial market upon which her husband was betting. Curiously, Gervásio does not assign Teodoro's failings to his gender, but instead describes them as part of a general economic dynamic. Likewise, whereas Camila's surprise at her husband's bankruptcy is deemed a product of the superficiality of the knowledge she has by virtue of her gender, Teodoro's surprise at going bankrupt is not attributed to any particular masculine quality.

The attribution of limited financial acumen to gendered differences in knowledge is also present in *Madame Bovary*. The narrator writes that Emma was 'troubled no more about money matters than an archduchess'.[19] Emma's frivolous attitude towards money is compared to that of a female aristocrat who, like Camila, is insulated from economic anxiety and spends without care or concern. Moreover, Emma's entrance into a system of debt obligation is undertaken without a clear understanding of the responsibilities it places on her. Just as Teodoro is seduced by Inocêncio's proposed scheme to attain instant wealth, Emma is tempted by the luxuries displayed to her by the local merchant and creditor, Monsieur Lheureux. Emma appears gripped by a perpetual propagation of new desires that, once fulfilled, are only replaced by fresh iterations.

In this respect Emma is similar to Teodoro, who is constantly pursuing wealth and social recognition of his success. The economic behaviours of Emma and Teodoro are thus not only the result of a confusion between simplified explanations and complex realities but also enabled by the distinct temporalities produced through debt spending and financial speculation. In the temporal regime of finance, Elena Esposito explains, 'the future is produced using expectations about the future, in a circularity where one loses sight of the difference between reality and illusion'.[20] In finance, value becomes tied to expectations, about future values, and money becomes a tool for adjudicating these different expectations rather than a metric of time spent in productive labour. These expectations are of course illusory, papered over a fundamental uncertainty about the future; this mixing of reality and illusion is a key element of what has been called the 'stock market novel'.[21]

In Flaubert's novel, owing to her relative lack of wealth, Emma's desires produce a slightly different temporality than that found in the stock market novel. For Emma, the promise of credit – or the deferment of payment into a projected future – serves as a means of escaping present conditions. She borrows from the future to pay for the present, whereas Teodoro gambles away his present wealth for the sake of potential future gains. These distinct modes of expenditure represent gendered dimensions of economic activity. As a female bourgeois character, Emma is not free to pursue wealth through commerce, investment or labour. Given the relatively limited wealth of her husband, Emma turns to credit. Teodoro, on the other hand, is free to gamble away his family fortune.

From Fictional Futures to Fantasies of Adultery

The preoccupation with stock market speculation in *A falêncua* is coupled with a narrative arc involving female adultery. Camila is having an affair with Gervásio, the family physician. Just as her husband is seduced by the lure of multiplying his wealth through stock market speculation, Camila is seduced by the refined manners, extensive knowledge, and passion embodied by Gervásio. While Teodoro's stock market misadventures lead to material ruin, Camila's transgressive sexual behaviour threatens the abstract ideal of the family and the broader social order.

Studying this entanglement of sex, money and fantasy in the novel, it is possible to discern from Almeida's work a critique of both capitalism and the gender norms governing turn-of-the-century Brazilian society. Reading Gervásio's claim that 'You, women, don't understand these things'[22] alongside the works of contemporary feminist economists, we can see how Gervásio's exclusion of women from economic considerations is widely replicated in mainstream economic theories. The Swedish journalist Katrine Marçal, for example, has identified how the 'primary characteristic' of 'economic man' – the rational actor central to so many economic models – 'is that he is not a woman'. She adds, 'Economists sometimes joke that if a man marries his housekeeper, the GDP of the country declines.'[23] She describes how models of economic behaviour have tended to privilege those traits deemed masculine – competition, reason and individuality – at the expense of feminine traits such as caring and cooperation. Furthermore, economics as a discipline, she argues, has discounted the unpaid domestic female labour that makes complex economic activity possible.

The literary critic Bill Overton, meanwhile, has identified in *The Novel of Female Adultery* how the genre of the adultery novel has from the outset possessed a markedly gendered emphasis. 'No classic novel,' he writes, 'let alone any fictional tradition, is based on male adultery. The widely used term "novel of adultery" is therefore a misnomer which masks a gender bias both in the novels themselves and in the critical discourses within which they have been interpreted. This is why I employ the term "novel of female adultery" instead.'[24] While women are excluded from economic theories, men are conspicuously absent from adultery novels. Overton's term 'novel of female adultery' is an attempt to make visible a widespread but little noted asymmetry in the gender of those charged with adultery.

Thus, whereas theories founded on 'economic man' exclude the contributions of women, the adultery novel excludes adultery performed by men. Despite the contrary omissions in economics and adultery fiction (one overlooking women and one overlooking men), there is a common economic dimension to novels of female adultery, which *A falência* underscores. The relationship established in the novel between moral and financial bankruptcy draws on and subverts a historical tradition of adultery fiction including *Madame Bovary*.

Indeed, Teodoro's bankruptcy and Camila's adultery share a joint literary precedent in the character of Emma. If in the French novel the three themes of adultery, illusions and debt are concentrated in the character of Emma, in Almeida's novel there is a gendered division: Camila commits adultery while it is the husband, Teodoro, who bankrupts the family. Nevertheless, in Almeida's work, both characters are subject to illusions: as we have seen, Teodoro dreams of a rapid increase in wealth while Camila is deceived in the course of her romantic adventures.

Teodoro exhibits something similar to Said's textual attitude insofar as he prefers the simple clarity of Inocêncio's explanations to a rigorous engagement with the complexities of the uncertain financial futures they occlude. Reading Almeida alongside Said thus highlights Almeida's critique of the naivety of Teodoro as a danger to social stability. In Almeida's novel, finance plays the role that literature does in conventional novels of wifely adultery, exemplified by *Madame Bovary*, in that it encourages risky behaviour that undermines the social order. Almeida portrays the seductive visions of finance as working on Teodoro in much the same way that Flaubert describes the fantasies of literature affecting Emma. As Elena Losada has pointed out, female characters exhibiting the textual attitude are a common feature of adultery fiction, in which reading is often represented as a gateway to committing adultery:

> For women, 'having literature' is always negative, it converts them into unnatural beings; in other words, monsters. ... reading is presented as the natural precursor to adultery. In novels, women found heroes, the space for an epic sense of existence that the bourgeois world had forgotten. And these heroes of another world and another time seemed to shine with perfection, highly superior to the real husbands they would meet. How could Charles Bovary compete with Ivanhoe?[25]

According to the narrator's descriptions, Charles is a simple provincial bourgeois physician, who fails to live up to Emma's image of a potential husband based on the heroic and glorious knight Ivanhoe. Emma's lovers (first Rodolphe and then Leon) similarly fail to live up to the standards of her literary models. In *A falência* the comparison is more complex, since there is no outstanding difference between Francisco Teodoro and Dr Gervásio. While Emma's lovers at least possess certain qualities that Charles lacks (such as good looks, aristocratic values, being a hunter, enjoying fashion, reading poetry, etc.), Camila's lover is not particularly different from her husband. Moreover, it is not out of boredom that Camila engages in her affair but out of what she claims to be genuine love for Gervásio.

In contrast to Emma, Camila seems relatively content with the material conditions of her bourgeois life: her mansion, jewellery and dresses seem enough for her. Whereas Emma shares Teodoro's passion for money but lacks his wealth, Emma shares Camila's transgressive sexuality. There are key differences between Camila and Emma as characters, however, which are exhibited most starkly in their different attitudes towards novels. According to Elizabeth Amann in *Importing* Madame Bovary – *The Politics of Adultery*, Emma is a 'Quixote in skirts' and, like Quixote, she mistakes tales of romance and chivalry for actual romantic life.[26] Camila, on the contrary, refuses to read a romantic story of adultery offered to her by Gervásio. In this comparison, I suggest, it may be possible to detect a critique mounted by Almeida against the tradition of adultery novels written by men which portray women as female Quixotes. Camila's resistance to the typical representations of women in adultery novels is simultaneously a resistance to the link between literature and adultery established in *Madame Bovary*. Not only is adultery presented as a uniquely feminine crime in the genre of the adultery novel, but it is also associated with a particularly feminine mode of reading which is at once uncritical and escapist.

In *Madame Bovary*, Emma is educated in a convent to become a good wife and mother. Challenging the limits of such an education, Emma also participates in the clandestine trade in romantic novels that circulate in the convent. She obtains these illicit books from an old lady who 'always carried [some novels] in the pockets of her apron'.[27] In another example of the relationship between economics and fantasy in Flaubert's novel, the old woman who gives Emma the novels that will inspire her illusory visions of romance is herself a victim of bankruptcy – prefiguring the relationship between books and bankruptcy which will characterize Emma's future. The narrator explains that she was '[p]atronized by the clergy, because she belonged to an ancient family of noblemen ruined by the Revolution'.[28] Little is known about her family's history beyond the fact that she is still respected by the clergy for her 'ancient' values; in the convent, however, the old lady is the source of love stories that will spur Emma's disappointment with married life and motivate her sexual and consumerist habits:

> Before marriage she thought herself in love; but the happiness that should have followed this love not having come, she must, she thought, have been mistaken. And Emma tried to find out what one meant exactly in life by the words felicity, passion, rapture, that had seemed to her so beautiful in books.[29]

Emma's participation at the age of 15 in this clandestine book trade, according to the narrator, has made her 'hands dirty with books from old lending libraries'.[30] Enumerating the novels that Emma reads, the critic Margaret Cohen brings attention to an overlooked point concerning Flaubert's gender bias: 'Flaubert does not name the most read novels in private lending libraries during the first decades of the Restoration. Before Walter Scott, and indeed, even contemporary with him, these novels were *sentimental novels by women writers*' (my emphasis).[31] How to understand, then, this absence of the names of female authors in *Madame Bovary*? Many of the novels that Emma reads in secret were probably written by women, but these women's names are not listed by Flaubert. Flaubert's decision to discuss Walter Scott while omitting the names of the female authors that Emma would almost certainly have also read echoes a general tendency towards the erasure of female authors from literary history, which also plagued authors in real life, including Almeida. As Rita Schmidt writes, Almeida 'participated in the inauguration of the Academia Brasileira de Letras [Brazilian Academy of Letters], for which she was nominated. But since she was a woman, her nomination was, nevertheless, refused.'[32]

Whereas Flaubert depicts a recursive dynamic wherein Emma imbibes the fantasies of romantic novels only to attempt to realize those fantasies in her own life, Almeida has Camila evince a much more critical attitude towards literature. For, in Almeida's novel, the issue of gender and authorship is explicitly raised. In the first scene where the two lovers are by themselves, Dr Gervásio gives Camila a book. When Camila asks about its content, Gervásio says that it is about 'a love similar to ours',[33] which indicates that it is a novel about adultery. Camila then rejects the book, explaining that she wouldn't read such a novel, since

> Male writers do not forgive women; they make us responsible for everything – as if we already did not pay a high price for the happiness we enjoy! In these books I am always afraid of the end; I rebel against the punishments they throw on us, and I feel desperate for not being able to shout at them: hypocrites![34]

Almeida presents Camila as being aware of the male perspective of writers of the nineteenth century, who will judge any transgressive action more harshly if the perpetrator is female. Camila even interprets these penalties in economic terms, claiming she pays a 'high price' for her happiness.[35]

Through the character of Camila, Almeida is implicitly critiquing what Edward Said calls the 'second situation of the textual attitude'.[36] Whereas, as we saw with Teodoro, the first situation occurs when humans substitute knowledge gained through texts for actual experience (believing in Inocêncio's discourse about stocks as if it accurately describes their future value), the second situation occurs when certain descriptions gain traction and are reproduced in a discourse. Said gives the example of lions: 'If one reads a book claiming that lions are fierce and then encounters a fierce lion (I simplify, of course), the chances are that one will be encouraged to read more books by that same author, and believe them.'[37] The author of these descriptions is granted the status of expert and his or her account of the nature of lions is reproduced by successive writers. The lion's fierceness predominates in subsequent representations, subsuming other qualities and emerging as its own object of study. Just as the lion in Said's example is reduced to a single quality that is simultaneously dominant yet unquestioned, fictional representations of women, Camila claims, are characterized by their misdeeds – which in the context seems to imply a tendency towards adultery. Not only is adultery the crime that Camila is guilty of, but, as we have seen, the novel of female adultery is a recognizable genre of fin-de-siècle fiction that generally presented adultery as a gendered crime that only women were capable of committing and for which they were solely to blame.

Drawing on Said, we might argue that a transgressive sexuality thus becomes the defining quality in female characters written by men, forming a genealogy of such representations that is self-reinforcing: the more such representations appear, the more accurate such representations appear to be. Indeed, the accuracy of a particular representation is judged by its conformity with previous representations. We can thus appreciate how even a genre of fiction such as realism, with its supposedly close correlation between the fictional world and reality, may yet be populated by representations of women that focus extensively on their transgressive sexuality. Following Said, we could say that the fictional worlds and the representations contained therein affect real attitudes so that reality begins to conform to fictional worlds rather than the other way around. Such a dynamic is, after all, the key claim in Said's *Orientalism* – a book about the West's 'textual attitude toward the Orient', in which fictional representations affect real perceptions of whole regions and peoples.

Unsurprisingly, as the critic João Roberto Faria explains, nearly all the most well-known descriptions of Brazilian female characters in the nineteenth century were written by male writers.[38] Against this backdrop of canonical depictions of women created mostly by men, it is possible to read Camila's critique of male writers as an example of how Almeida was also challenging conventional descriptions of women. The novel that Gervásio offers Camila appears to belong to a different genre than those read by Emma. Indeed, Gervásio presents Camila a 'novel of female adultery' – offering her precisely the same genre of novel as that in which they are appearing as characters. The double standard evinced by such literature – wherein female sexuality is a phenomenon that requires policing but male sexuality is unproblematized – appears to Camila to be yet another manifestation of the gender inequality that partially motivated her affair in the first place. Regarding her husband's affairs, Camila says,

> What woman, as ignorant or as indifferent as she is, doesn't suspect, doesn't feel the adultery of the husband on the same day that it takes place? There is always a vestige of the other, that becomes visible in a gesture, in a perfume, in a word, in an act of kindness … I found out about many things and pretended to ignore all of them! Isn't this what society wants from us?[39]

The focus of adultery novels on transgressive female sexuality is the fictional counterpart of the normative social order that requires Camila to passively accept her husband's infidelity. Almeida thus appears to self-reflexively place her novel in opposition to those novels of female adultery written by men. In a sense, Camila's dialogue amounts to a critique of the textual attitude, insofar as she refuses to accept that fictional representations of female conduct adequately or fairly capture reality.

Conclusion: Reading as Resistance (against the Textual Attitude)

In the end it is Nina, the niece of Camila, who helps with domestic chores, who saves the family after Teodoro's suicide. While the family was still wealthy, Teodoro gave Nina a birthday gift: a small house under her own name. After the bankruptcy and Teodoro's suicide, Nina invites Camila, her daughters and the domestic servant, Noca, to move into her house. Although Teodoro has lost the family fortune by gambling on the stock market, Nina is able to keep the small property because it is under her name. The contrast between what is lost and what remains indicates that, in *A falência*, there is an emphasis on the value of land and physical assets over the abstract value of stocks. In *Realizing Capital*, Kornbluh traces the history of the term 'realize', concluding that it comes from 'real estate', which was a conversion of 'money into land'.[40] Almeida's novel appears to criticize the abstract value of financial capital by depicting the relative stability and use value of real estate. The durability of the house's value as a place of shelter stands in stark contrast to the wild fluctuations of stock market values. The latter introduce precarity into the futures they conjure up through the production of fantasies of foreknowledge whereas the former (the land) adds certainty to the future by remaining useful over time.

Whereas Camila had the offer of shelter and support from her niece, Emma receives no such assistance despite appealing to her lovers for financial relief. Indeed, it is through their failure to provide monetary or emotional support that Emma realizes that her lovers were not serious about their partnership with her. What follows is a crucial event in the French novel, when Emma appears to grasp the scale of her own illusions: 'You made me *believe* you,' she says to her lover, Rodolphe; 'for two years you held me in the most magnificent, the sweetest *dream*!'[41] Emma's reaction when she realizes that her lovers have lied to her about the extent and nature of their love is similar to Camila's reaction when she finds out that her own lover is married: 'He was married! He had lied to her! So many years of lies, so many years of lies!'[42] Despite these similar moments of disillusionment, the two novels differ in the female characters' eventual destinies.

As much as Camila is depicted as critical of the hypocritical male discourse against female adultery, she fails to see that she was deluded in assuming her lover Dr Gervásio to be a bachelor. In having Camila carry out an affair with a man who she believes is single but is actually married,

Almeida once more departs from the convention of adultery novels. As Overton points out in presenting his theory on the novel of wifely adultery, '[e]ach [novel] is based on a plot in which, with minor variations, a married woman from the middle or upper classes is seduced by an unmarried man of the same class and comes to grief. They are further alike in that each is told in an impersonal narrative voice, and each was written by a man.'[43] Overton compares adultery novels by Gustave Flaubert, Leo Tolstoy, Theodor Fontane, Jens Peter Jacobsen, Eça de Queirós, Leopoldo García-Alas and Benito Pérez Galdós, identifying the features they have in common. Almeida upsets this particular narrative expectation, since Camila has an affair with a married man. Although Camila is distraught when she discovers that she cannot marry Gervásio, this departure from the conventions of the genre allows Almeida to explore a different outcome than the simple repetition of heteronormative marriage.

Besides being seduced by a single man, another convention that Almeida avoids at her novel's conclusion is the suicide of the adulteress. Discussing Emma's suicide, Bernard Paris writes that 'Literature is full of protagonists who are granted romantic deaths, who feel that they have actualized their idealized images and then die before they are subject to continued failure, despair, and self-hate.'[44] Almeida's novel, once more, strays from a narrative tradition that recurs in multiple popular examples: from Emma Bovary and Anna Karenina to Luisa in *O primo Basílio* (1878).[45] In *A falência*, it is Teodoro, and not Camila, who commits suicide.

Almeida's avoidance of these two common endings to adultery novels is a narrative strategy to develop a feminine social space in which women prove to be resilient in the face of financial crisis and emotional devastation. In *A falência*, after the dissolution of all the couples – both the married and the adulterous ones – the narrative proceeds to focus on the bonds between the female characters who find themselves left outside the bonds of romantic love or global finance. Upon realizing that her relationship with Dr Gervásio has no future, Camila directs her attention to the creation of a new future embodied by her daughters (unlike Emma, who is left penniless).[46] She invests in this future not through speculative financial transactions, but by giving her daughters through education the tools to become independent. The novel ends with her declaring her intention to teach her daughters how to read and write.[47]

After depicting the dissolution of social and financial models predicated on the policing of female sexuality and the financialization of the economy, Almeida's novel focuses on the female characters' transition from traditional models (the faithful wife, the naive daughters) to a new paradigm of woman based on female literacy and care labour. Although in constant dialogue with the tradition of wifely adultery novels, the novel presents an alternative model of female pedagogy predicated not on the relationship between male author and female reader, but on that between mother and daughter. By teaching her daughters how to read, Almeida seems to suggest, a different kind of literacy than that practised by Emma – reading novels isolated from the world in a convent – is possible. Indeed, literacy may function to critique what Said called the 'textual attitude'. Considering the critical attitude towards literature expressed by Camila in response to the book offered to her by Dr Gervásio, it seems entirely possible that such critical skills may also be transmitted to her daughters along with the skills to read and write.

In departing from narrative conventions established by Flaubert in *Madame Bovary* and widely replicated afterwards, Almeida rewrites the novel of female adultery by suggesting that perhaps women have more credibility in discussing female sexuality than do male writers and deserve credit for the caring labour they overwhelmingly perform. Despite the collapse of the financialized economic system portrayed in the novel, and the discrediting of an institution of marriage based on lies shared by husbands, wives and lovers, *A falência* provides an image of a family in which female education prevails and labour rooted in care is valued as truly transformational.

Notes

1. For more information, I recommend Wasserman 2007, 33–56; Sadlier 1992, 27–35.
2. Rio 1908, 21–7. Unless otherwise noted, all translations from Portuguese are my own.
3. *A falência* was originally published in 1901 in Rio de Janeiro by Officinas de Obras d'A Tribuna. Like all the other novels by Júlia Lopes de Almeida, it has not yet been translated into English. I translate the title as *The Bankruptcy*. Citations of the chapters and pages are drawn from the first edition issued in 1902 and digitized by Biblioteca Brasiliana Guita e José Mindlin in 2011. In 2019, three publishing houses in Brazil reprinted the book (Penguin, Martin Claret and Via Leitura). The novel has also been included on the mandatory reading list for the 2020 national university exam (vestibular) for Unicamp (University of Campinas).
4. Marçal 2014, 19.
5. 'credo: … from PIE compound **kerd-dhe-* "to believe", literally "to put one's heart"' (*Online Etymology Dictionary* 2018).
6. Said 1979, 93.
7. Beckert 2016, 274.
8. Marx 2011, 81.
9. Jameson 1998, 142.
10. Almeida 1902, 14.
11. See Palacios 2006, 249.
12. Quoted by Taunay 1939, 67.
13. Almeida 1902, 164.
14. Almeida 1902, 251–252, my emphasis.

15. Almeida 1902, 251.
16. Said 1979, 93.
17. Kornbluh 2014, 7.
18. Almeida 1902, 368.
19. Flaubert 2017, 372.
20. Esposito 2011, 93.
21. See Beckman 2013.
22. Almeida 1902, 368.
23. Marçal 2014, 60.
24. Overton 1996, vii.
25. Losada 2016, 242.
26. Amann 2006, 16.
27. Flaubert 2017, 46.
28. Flaubert 2017, 45.
29. Flaubert 2017, 43.
30. Flaubert 2017, 46.
31. Cohen 2007, 752.
32. Schmidt 2000, 91.
33. Almeida 1902, 66.
34. Almeida 1902, 66–7.
35. Almeida 1902, 67.
36. Said 1979, 93.
37. Said 1979, 93.
38. Faria 2006, 141.
39. Almeida 1902, 67.
40. Kornbluh 2014, 2.
41. Flaubert 2017, 387, emphasis added. It is this realization that she believed in Rodolphe's discourse of love and that it was not real that leads her to commit suicide.
42. Almeida 1902, 435.
43. Overton 1996, 3.
44. Paris 1997, 212.
45. Queiros 2015; Queiros 2016.
46. Flaubert 2017.
47. Almeida 1902, 439.

Bibliography

Almeida, Júlia Lopes de. *A falência*. Rio de Janeiro: A Tribuna, 1901. https://digital.bbm.usp.br/handle/bbm/2440

Amann, Elizabeth. *Importing* Madame Bovary: *The Politics of Adultery*. New York: Palgrave, 2006.

Beckert, Jens. *Imagined Futures: Fictional Expectations and Capitalist Dynamics*. Cambridge, MA: Harvard University Press, 2016.

Beckman, Ericka. *Capital Fictions: The Literature of Latin American's Export Age*. Minneapolis: University of Minnesota Press, 2013.

Cohen, Margaret. 'Flaubert Lectrice: Flaubert Lady Reader', *MLN* 122 (2007): 746–58.

Esposito, Elena. *The Future of Futures: The Time of Money in Financing and Society*. Cheltenham: Edward Elgar, 2011.

Faria, Roberto João. 'Representations of Women in Nineteenth-Century Brazilian Literature', *Brazilian Journal of Irish Studies* 8 (2006): 131–42.

Flaubert, Gustave. *Madame Bovary*, translated by Eleanor Marx-Aveling. Kindle, 2017.

Jameson, Fredric. *The Cultural Turn: Selected Writings on the Postmodern, 1983–1998*. London: Verso, 1998.

Kornbluh, Anna. *Realizing Capital: Financial and Psychic Economies in Victorian Form*. New York: Fordham University Press, 2014.

Losada, Elena. 'The Novel of Adultery in Peninsular Realist Narrative'. In *A Comparative History of Literatures in the Iberian Peninsula*, edited by Cesar Dominguez, Anxo Gonzalez and Ellen Sapega, 240–55. Philadelphia: John Benjamins, 2016.

Marçal, Katrine. *Who Cooked Adam Smith's Dinner?* New York: Pegasus, 2014.
Marx, Karl. *Capital – Volume One: A Critique of Political Economy*. New York: Dover, 2011.
Online Etymology Dictionary. 'Credo'. Last modified 25 August 2018. https://www.etymonline.com/word/credo?ref=etymonline_crossreference
Overton, Bill. *The Novel of Female Adultery: Love and Gender in Continental European Fiction, 1830–1900*. London: Macmillan, 1996.
Palacios, Marco. 'Coffee'. In *Iberia and the Americas: Culture, Politics, and History*, Vol. 1, edited by John Michael Francis, Santa Barbara, CA: ABC-CLIO, 2006.
Paris, Bernard. *Imagined Human Beings*. New York: New York University Press, 1997.
Queiros, Eça de. *O primo Basílio*. São Paulo: Penguin Companhia, 2015.
Queiros, Eça de. *Cousin Bazilio*, translated by Margaret Jull Costa. Sawtry: Dedalus, 2016.
Rio, João do. 'Um lar de artistas'. In *O momento literário*, 23–34. Rio de Janeiro: H. Garnier, 1908. https://digital.bbm.usp.br/handle/bbm/1977
Sadlier, Darnele. *One Hundred Years after Tomorrow: Brazilian Women's Fiction in the Twentieth Century*. Bloomington: Indiana University Press, 1992.
Said, Edward. *Orientalism*. New York: Vintage Books, 1979.
Schmidt, Rita Terezinha. 'Mulheres reescrevendo a nação', *Estudos Feministas* 8, no. 1, 2000: 84–97.
Taunay, Affonso. *História do café no Brasil. Vol. 9: No Brasil República (1889–1906)*. Rio de Janeiro: Departamento Nacional do Café, 1939.
Wasserman, Renata. *Central at the Margin: Five Brazilian Women Writers*. Plainsboro, NJ: Associated University Press, 2007.

Index

abolitionist
  authorial discourse 166
  campaign 85, 101, 167, 171
  lineage 94
  literature 98, 161–2, 172
  movements 284
  wave 137
  works of fiction 164
Abreu, Capistrano de 268
Academia Brasileira de Letras [Brazilian Academy of Letters] 208, 308
adultery 21, 136, 151, 269, 286, 289, 297–300, 305–13
African-American
  authors 167
  fiction 170
  narratives 104
  poetry 170
  spirituality 170
  spirituals 167
  writing 176
Afro-Brazilian 84, 92, 100–1, 104
Afro-descendant 84–5, 92, 101, 104
  woman 85, 101
  writer 18
agregado 52, 194, 278, 283, 294n5
Aijaz, Ahmad 8
Album de Señoritas 27
Alencar, José Martiniano de 17
  A pata da gazela 182
  'Bênção paterna' 180–1
  Cartas de Erasmo 111
  Como e porque sou romancista 117
  Diva 182
  Indigenist/Indianist novel 17, 107, 117
  on indigenous expression 115, 118–19
  Iracema 1, 17, 20, 107–26, 259–60
  'Letter to Dr. Jaguaribe' 118, 121
  Lucíola 182
  Mãe 176
  on the novel as a genre 114–15
  O Guarani 17, 107, 109–11, 115–16, 118, 121
  O sertanejo 144
  Senhora 19–20, 57, 180–202
  Sonhos d'ouro 3, 180, 182–3
  on Tupi language 118
Alexandre Herculano 65
Ali, Tariq 8
allegory 17, 94, 113, 153, 155, 162, 228, 235
Almeida, Júlia Lopes de
  A falência 2, 20, 297–315
Almeida, Manuel Antônio de 11
  Memórias de um sargento de milícias 18, 45–62, 70, 186
altruicide 87, 92
Álvares, Josefina 205
  A Família 205
Anderson, Benedict 36
Andrade, Francisco Berenguer 66
Andrade, Mário de 227
Andrade, Oswald de 127
Antonio *Candido* 15, 18, 48–51, 56–7, 137–9, 258–9
O Apóstolo 241
Arac, Jonathan 7
Araripe Júnior, Tristão de Alencar 208, 227–8, 247
  archery 108–9, 112
art nouveau 227
Assis, Joaquim Maria Machado de 1, 11, 20
  'A cartomante' 286
  all novels 257–72
  critical ideas, 259–61
  Dom Casmurro 20, 210, 277–94
  external influx 15, 257
  'Instinto de nacionalidade' ('National Instinct') 181, 260
  Memórias póstumas de Brás Cubas 3, 59, 93, 287
  'Miss Dollar' 286
  Quincas Borba 287
  'Sem olhos' 286
  'Uns braços' 286
Auerbach, Erich 6
Austen, Jane 11, 135
  focalization 190
autobiography 16, 18, 86, 96–7, 102–3, 162–3
  autobiographical accounts 85, 103
  autobiographical testimony 85
Aymorés 110
Azevedo, Aluísio 3
  Casa de pensão 214, 245
  O cortiço 214, 248–9
  O coruja 3
  O homem 243, 245, 254
  O mulato 176, 214, 245
Azevedo, Artur 247

Bakhtin, Mikhail 11, 235
Baldwin, James 167
Go Tell it on the Mountain 170
Balzac, Honoré de 11, 135, 138, 186–7, 269
Comédie humaine 187
Illusions perdues 269
Baptista, Abel Barros 289
Baquaqua, Mahomah Gardo 18, 85, 96–7
Bates, Henry Walter 150, 152
Baudelaire, Charles 227
Les fleurs du mal 226
Behn, Aphra
Oroonoko, or the Royal Slave 86
Belot, Adolphe
Mademoiselle Giroud, ma femme 247
Bergson, Henri-Louis 228, 236n27
Bernardin de Saint-Pierre, Jacques-Henri 18, 64, 257
Paul et Virginie 18, 150, 266
Bernheimer, Charles 3–4
Bertrand, Aloysius 226
Bilac, Olavo
Poesias 244
Bildung 204, 229, 231
blackness 87–9, 104
black feminist movement 174
black journalism 172
black reason 87–9, 92, 94, 98
Blair, Hugh 115–16, 118–20
Bocage, Manuel Maria Barbosa du 242
Boccaccio, Giovanni
Decameron 242
Bonnetain, Paul 246
Charlot s'amuse 246
book trade
clandestine 308
international 11
bookshops 13–14, 240–5, 258, 266
Borges, Jorge Luis 15
Bormann, Maria Benedita Câmara (Délia)
Celeste 205
Duas irmãs 205
Lésbia 2, 19, 203–25
Magdalena 205
Uma vítima 205
Bosi, Alfredo 229, 284, 286–7, 292
bourgeoisie 3, 48, 57, 212
Brent, Linda (Harriet Jacobs)
Incidents in the Life of a Slave Girl 18, 161–2, 167, 169, 171, 175
Bruffee, Kenneth 278–80, 284, 288, 293, 294

Calabar, Domingos Fernandes 66
Caldwell, Helen 277, 289, 294
Caminha, Adolfo
Bom-Crioulo 248
Casanova, Pascale 7
censorship 13–14, 207
centre and periphery 3–5
Cervantes, Miguel de 128, 257, 259, 266–7, 284
Don Quixote 284, 300, 307
Chalhoub, Sidney 258, 278
Chateaubriand, François-René de 15, 27, 64, 110, 120, 187
Atala 17, 110–11, 120
Child, Lydia Maria 168
Christian preaching 77
morality 81, 93
Cicero, Marcus Tullius 232
circulating libraries 11, 13–14, 266
Gabinete Português de Leitura (Portuguese Circulating Library) 257
Cleland, John
Fanny Hill 242
Coelho Neto, Henrique 246
Colégio D. Pedro II 131
colonialism 11, 116, 118, 121, 174
Comte, Auguste 212
positivism 213, 226
Conrad, Joseph 11
Heart of Darkness 278, 280
Lord Jim 20, 277–94
Cooper, James Fenimore 17, 64, 66, 110, 117, 121
The Last of the Mohicans 17, 110, 117, 121
coronelismo [coronelism] 232
Correio Mercantil 17, 46, 63, 65, 67, 70
Correio Paulistano 113
Costa, Emília Viotti da 206
Coutinho, Eduardo 13
credit 21, 299, 313
cross-dressing 40
Cunha, Euclides da
Os sertões 144

Damrosch, David 6
Daniel, Mary L. 206
debasement 185, 192, 195
decentring 4
Defoe, Daniel 11, 48, 257
Moll Flanders 48, 135
Robinson Crusoe 11–12, 182
degradation 192, 195, 230, 234
Denis, Ferdinand 65
dependant see *agregado*
derision 264, 268
Derrida, Jacques 163, 171–3
Dissemination 172
play of difference 163, 173, 174
play of textuality 163, 173–4, 176
supplement 171, 173
descent
African 104, 164–5, 175
diaspora
African 97, 100
Dickens, Charles 266, 269
Great Expectations 269
displacement 3–4, 10–12, 14, 59, 107, 127, 139
Dom João VI 129
Dom Pedro I 129
Dom Pedro II 129–30, 206, 283–4
Dom Pedro IV 129
Du Bois, W. E. B.
The Souls of Black Folk 171
Ducasse, Isidore
Les chants de Maldoror 229
Duguay-Trouin, René 68–9

elegy 278, 289, 293
pastoral 279
Epitectus
Enchiridion 216

eroticism 50, 231–2, 245
erotic literature 20, 240, 245
experience 9, 16, 18, 19
  childhood 209, 210
  erotic 249–50, 251
  female 175, 214, 215, 218
  formative 231
  historical 10, 11, 15, 45, 46, 56, 60, 113
  individual 16, 128, 129, 130, 132–3
  social 56,
exploitation 33, 87, 93
  sexual 169

Faulkner, William
  Absalom, Absalom! 163, 169
Fernández de Lizardi, José Joaquim 48
Ferrier, Susan 107
  Marriage 110
fiction
  domestic 36–7, 205–6, 208–9
  sentimental 37, 45, 57, 205–6, 208–9
  serial 2, 16, 27–8, 203, 205–8, 211, 246
Fielding, Henry 257, 266–7
  Tom Jones 267
finance 303–4, 306, 312
Fitz, Earl 2
Fitzgerald, F. Scott
  The Great Gatsby 278–9
Flaubert, Gustave 20, 304, 306, 308, 312
  Madame Bovary 21, 226, 298, 306–8, 313
Ford, Ford Madox
  The Good Soldier 278
Franco, Jean 37
Frank, Zephyr 3, 204
Freud, Sigmund 228, 234
Freyre, Gilberto 168–9
Frye, Northrop 100

Gallis, Alfredo 240, 244
  Condessa de Til (pseudonym) 240
  O que as noivas devem saber 240
  Rabelais (pseudonym) 244
Gama, Luiz 171–2, 235
Garnier
  Baptiste-Louis 208, 239
  Livraria (bookshop) 241, 245–6
Gates, Henry Louis, Jr 86
Gazeta de Notícias 205, 242–3
Ghil, René 227
Gilbert, Sandra M. 215, 219
Girardin, Madame Émile de 135–6
  Le lorgnon 135
Gledson, John 258, 270, 272
Goethe, Johann Wolfgang von 9, 64, 144, 216, 218–19
  The Sorrows of Young Werther 216, 219–20, 266
  Weltliteratur 5
Gomes, Eugênio 227
Gonçalves Dias, Antônio 65
Goncourt, Edmond and Jules 227
gothic 29, 34, 77–8, 133
Goytacaz 109, 116
O Guanabara 67
Guaycuru 113
Gubar, Susan 215, 219
Guillén, Claudio 7
Guimarães, Bernardo
  A escrava Isaura 17–18, 161–179
Guimarães Júnior, Luís
  A família Agulha 58

Halperin, David 291–2
Hegel, Georg Wilhelm Friedrich 88–9, 128
Helme, Elizabeth
  St. Clair of the Isles: or, The Outlaws of Barra 258, 266
heteroglossia 115–18
heteronormativity 290
homosexuality 231, 234, 290, 292
homosocial
  affection 278
  desire 278, 290
  partnership 112
  relationship 290–1
House of Braganza 116
Hugo, Victor-Marie 64, 181, 187
humiliation 54, 148, 184–5, 187, 192, 194
  moral 193, 199

La Illustración Argentina 26–7

imagined communities 36
impressionism 227
  literary 227, 236
individual 82–3, 128, 132, 136, 138, 180, 183, 187, 192, 194, 199
  autonomy 19, 183
  economic independence 193
  effort 194
  entrepreneurial activity 194
  freedom 192
  individualism 182–3
  individualist society 183
  individuality 187, 192, 198
  individualization 199
  initiative 194
  modern 183–4, 188, 198
Instituto Histórico e Geográfico Brasileiro [Brazilian Historical and Geographical Institute] 130
intellectual property 208
El Inválido Argentino 27
irony 42, 131–2, 135, 170, 228, 264–5 268, 271, 294

Jameson, Fredric 7–10, 301
jealousy 100, 262, 277, 288
Johnson, James Weldon
  God's Trombones 167
O Jornal das Senhoras 17, 26–7, 28, 41
Journal des Débats 28
journey 72, 75, 95, 112, 131, 142–3, 146–9, 157
Joyce, James 11

Kristeva, Julia 26, 29

landscape
  cultural 13
  literary 15
  natural 33–4, 66, 113, 130, 138, 143–4, 147, 181
  painting 144, 158n22

political 18
social 18, 47
Lavater, Kaspar 166
Leal Júnior, José da Silva Mendes 65–7
Lesage, Alain-René 48, 257
Lima, Luiz Costa 163
literary historiography 94, 205
Brazilian 17–18, 205, 208
magical realism 2
modernism 2, 4
naturalism 227–9, 254, 127–8
parnassianism 227, 247
realism 4, 45–8, 127–9, 137–9, 194, 227–8, 260, 309
romanticism 36, 100, 127, 130, 137, 150, 155, 157, 181, 216, 226
romantic literature 48, 161, 164
symbolism 227
underrepresentation of women 2
literary system 6, 14, 17, 28, 56
local colour 67, 151, 156, 181, 186
Lukács, Georg 66, 128, 230

Macedo, Joaquim Manuel de 57–8, 84, 207, 228, 257, 259–60
A carteira de meu tio 131
A luneta mágica 19, 58, 127–41
A moreninha 57, 130–1
As vítimas-algozes 137
Lições de história do Brasil 131
Memórias do sobrinho de meu tio 131
Nina 138
O culto do dever 259, 260
Macpherson, James 120
Ossian 17, 108, 115, 120–1
Magalhães, Domingos José Gonçalves de 57, 114–15
Magalhães, Valentim da Costa 239, 246
Maistre, Xavier de 266
malandro 18, 48–50
Mallarmé, Stéphane 227
Mallet, João Carlos de Medeiros Pardal
Lar 249
Mann, Thomas
Doctor Faustus 278
Manso, Juana 2, 11, 17
'Emancipação moral da mulher' 42
Guerras civiles del Río de la Plata 27
La família del Comendador y otros textos 27–8
Misterios del Plata 2, 17, 26–44
Manzoni, Alessandro Francesco Tommaso 64
marriage 16, 176–7, 287–8, 312–3
market 184–5, 190–1, 199
plot 107, 110, 269
as social mobility 209, 252
Martí, José 35
Marxism 89
Marx, Karl Heinrich 301
Massa, Jean-Michel 266
Mbembe, Achille, 87–8, 91–2
McKeon, Michael 10
melodrama 16, 35, 63, 78, 104, 164, 205, 246, 264, 268
French 78
romantic 34
Merrim, Stephanie 2
Meyer, Augusto 289
Meyer, Marlyse 14
middle class 47, 128, 130, 132, 135, 138, 206–7
Miguel-Pereira, Lúcia 286, 289
miscegenation 107, 113
Miskolci, Ricardo 278, 290–1
mixed-race progeny 175
'M.L'
Os serões do convento 243, 247
Moers, Ellen 41
monologism 17, 108, 118, 219
Montandon, Alain 12
Moraes, Friar Manuel de 66
Morais, Francisco Castro de 68–9
moral indebtedness 194
Moretti, Franco 5–7, 11–13, 183
mulatto 101, 110, 165–6, 176, 214, 245
mystery 32, 34, 74, 77–8, 80–1, 249, 264, 281
story 71

Nabokov, Vladimir
Pale Fire 278
Nabuco, Joaquim
O abolicionismo 171
narrative
abolitionist 90
African-American 104
biographical 97
of detection 76
queer 290
slave 18, 85–6, 161–3, 167–8, 172
travel 143, 148
nature 144, 155, 157
picturesque 144, 152
sublime 144
negro 98, 165, 167, 171
negresses 165–6
negros de ganho (blacks for hire) 55
Nietzsche, Friedrich Wilhelm 19, 228, 232, 234
novel
abolitionist 17, 18, 27, 85
adultery 21, 286, 297–8, 305–7, 310, 312–13
adventure 12, 14
archaeological novel 69
Bildungsroman 3, 12, 19, 82n56, 204, 221, 231, 236n24, 282
diary form 271
of education 12
epistolary 12, 216, 261, 268
ethos 32
experimental 20, 245
feuilleton 14, 86, 98, 104, 163, 176, 206, 264, 270
form and social process 128–9
genre crisis 259, 268–72
gothic 14, 16, 63, 77, 100
historical 14, 16–17, 26, 28, 37, 63–4, 66–7, 69, 108, 115
and ideologeme 29
Indigenist 17, 107, 117
as inter-national invention 13
Künstlerroman 19, 204, 209, 210, 221

of the *malandro* 49–51
of manners 45, 47, 57, 130, 137, 207, 261
as migratory form 12
national 65
and national identity 202, 204, 208–9, 211, 213, 221
and nationalist ideology 38
and nation–building 30
and naturalism 214, 221
novelistic paradigms 16, 261–5
picaresque 12, 45, 48
as political discourse 31
roman feuilleton 86, 104, 163
roman philosophique 128, 132
as symbolic act 35
as transnational genre 4, 258
sea 12
of sensibility 205
sentimental 12, 14, 207, 218, 266, 269, 308
thesis 162–3, 176
unionist 107
urban 57, 138, 183, 187, 200n7
Norberto, Joaquim 57
Northup, Solomon
Twelve Years a Slave 103

Oedipal relations 230–1
O Paiz 205, 243

Paes, José Paulo 227, 269
patriarch 231, 278, 284–5, 292
patriarchal
anti-patriarchal behaviour 251
family 38, 150, 152, 278, 287
household 103
ideology 38, 192
order 40, 91, 206, 285
paterfamilias 277, 292
power 32, 99, 100
reason 99, 249
society 288
terminology 116
transgression of 298
patriarchalism 91, 99–100, 103, 166, 169
Paula Souza, Joaquim de 113–14, 121
Payne, Judith 2
Pena, Martins 49
O inglês maquinista 58
O juiz de paz na roça 58
pícaro 18, 49
Pimentel, Alberto Figueiredo
O aborto 2, 20 245–54
Um canalha 247
Pinto, Fernão Mendes 68
Pitiguara 109, 111–12
Poe, Edgar Allan 227
Pompeia, Raul
O Ateneu 19, 214, 226–38
pornographic literature 20, 244, 246
positivism 213, 226
Pratt, Mary Louise 37
pre-raphaelitism 227
Prévost, Antoine-François
Manon Lescaut 266
providence 69, 77–9, 80
public sphere 8, 19, 32, 36, 39, 128
Pujol, Alfredo 286

Quaresma, Pedro 240–3, 245–6, 254
queer 290–1
Queirós, José Maria Eça de 257
O crime do Padre Amaro 242, 247–8
O primo Basílio 260, 312

Rabelais, François 267
Pantagruel and Gargantua 242
racism 85, 103, 107
racial prejudice 164
reading
close 5–6, 221
democratization of 11
distant 6
intensive 6
récit exemplaire 162
Reis, Maria Firmina
'A escrava' 101
Úrsula 2, 18, 84–104
religion 88, 90, 102–3, 108, 170, 289
black 175
resignation 187, 192, 195
Revista Maranhense 101
rhetoric 19, 39, 41, 115, 227, 228–34
Ribeiro, Bernardim 267
Ribeiro, Djamila 174
Ribeiro, Júlio
A carne 214, 244–5, 247, 249, 254
Richardson, Samuel
Clarissa 261
Pamela, or Virtue Rewarded 261
rights of authors 208
Rimbaud, Arthur 227
Rio, João do (Paula Barreto) 297
Rocha, João Cezar de Castro 260
Roger, Alain 143
romance 16
chivalric 279
elegiac 20, 278–81, 283–5, 288, 292–4
heroic quest 279, 288, 293
quest 279, 288, 293
romantic topoi 155–6
Romero, Sílvio 208, 211
Rosas, Juan Manuel de 26, 29, 31–5, 38
Rouanet, Sergio Paulo 293
Rousseau, Jean-Jacques 144, 218

Sá, Mem de 71
Said, Edward 88, 300, 303, 306, 309–10, 313
Saint-Hilaire, Auguste 141
Saint-Pierre, Jacques-Henri Bernardin de 64, 257
Paul et Virginie 18, 150, 266
Sand, George 154, 209, 216
Santiago, Silviano 172, 228
sarcasm 170, 197, 268
satire 228–30
Schiller, Friedrich von 64
Schopenhauer, Arthur 19, 228, 232–4
Schwarz, Roberto 3, 19, 57, 59, 129, 184, 186–8, 194, 228, 258, 264–5, 278, 288–9
Scott, Walter 17, 28, 63–4, 66–8, 108, 154, 258, 266, 308
Waverley; or 'Tis Sixty Years Since 115
Sefardy, Moysés
Da amizade ou Livro de Henoch 154

serial fiction 205–8
sermon 17, 53, 63, 71, 78, 170
Serra, Tania 137
sertanejo 141–2, 144–8, 150–1, 156–7
sertão (backlands) 8, 141–51, 156–7
sexual abuse 168
Shakespeare, William 260
  Othello 277, 289
  Romeo and Juliet 150
Silva, Alfredo Elisário da
  Maria, a desgraçada 240
Silva, Antonio de Morais 141
Silva, Antonio José da 272
Silva, João Manuel Pereira da 57, 64, 66
Siskind, Mariano 2
slave
  community 170, 174–5
  narratives 18, 85–6, 161–3, 167–8, 172
  slave-owning economy 15
  society 91, 166, 169
slavery 16, 85–7, 89–91, 93, 95, 100, 102–3, 137, 162–6, 168–76, 192–3, 198
  abolition of 86, 205, 207, 227, 271
  and Lei Áurea (the Golden Law) 213
  and Lei do Ventre Livre (the Law of the Free Womb) 213
  and pro-slavery literature 162
Smith, Adam 133–4
Smollett, Tobias 266–7
Sommer, Doris 11, 36, 124n104
Soulié, Fréderic 135–6
  Les mémoires du diable 135
Southey, Robert 141
Spinoza, Baruch 218–19
Staël, Madame de (Anne Louise Germaine de Staël-Holstein) 209, 216
standpoint theory 174–5
Sterne, Laurence 266
  Sentimental Journey 267
  Shandean form 293
  Tristram Shandy 267
stock market 298–9, 301–5, 311
stoicism 216, 220, 230
Stowe, Harriet Beecher
  Uncle Tom's Cabin 86, 164
subjectivism 228
subjectivity 16, 19, 29, 42, 199, 261–2, 271, 292
Sue, Eugene
  Les mystères de Paris 17, 28, 33
suicide 34, 68, 110, 134, 176–7, 218–20, 298–9, 311–12
Suleiman, Susan 162
Süssekind, Flora 143, 155
Swift, Jonathan 266

Tabajara 107–9, 111, 113, 118–19
Tamoyo 114
Taques, Major Melo 149
Taunay, Alfredo d'Escragnolle 11
  Inocência 1, 18, 141–160
  Memórias 149
Távora, Franklin 111
Teixeira e Sousa, Antônio Gonçalves 57
  A providência, recordação dos tempos coloniais 2, 17, 63–83
  As fatalidades de dois jovens 69, 78
  O filho do pescador 14, 63, 78
  textual attitude 174, 300, 303, 306, 309–13
Thackeray, William M. 266
Thérèse philosophe 242
Thierry, Jacques Nicolas Augustin 65
Tupi 71, 73, 109, 118

verisimilitude 95, 130, 162
Veríssimo, José 208–9, 286, 289
Viana, Pedro
  Elzira, a morta virgem 240
Vieira, João Fernandes 66
Viellé-Griffin, Francis 227
violence 145–6, 230–2, 234–5
Voltaire 135
  Candide 132, 300

Washington, George 65
Watt, Ian 18, 127–9, 133–4, 136, 138–9, 182–3
  formal realism 128–9, 136
Wellek, René 3–4
Wells, James W. 142, 150, 152–3
Wilde, Oscar
  Salome 286
Wilson, Harriet E.
  Our Nig 18, 85–7, 102–4
women
  agency 28, 30, 37, 38, 43
  authors 84–6, 204–5, 207–9, 221
  authorship 37, 101–3, 206, 209, 308
  condition of, 41
  education 27, 42, 102, 151–2, 205, 216, 220, 307, 312, 313
  femme fatale 286–7
  femme fragile 287
  motherhood 174–5
  and nation 36
  and publishing 207–9
  reading public 18–20, 207
  roles 38
  writing 17, 205, 208, 214, 216, 219

Zola, Émile 213, 246–8, 257, 260, 286
  La terre 242–3
  L'assommoir 242
  Nana 243, 247–8, 251

www.ingramcontent.com/pod-product-compliance
Lightning Source LLC
LaVergne TN
LVHW010731020926
846742LV00029B/37
* 9 7 8 1 7 8 7 3 5 4 7 2 2 *